MALCOLM SARGENT

Sir Malcolm Sargent
1964

MALCOLM
SARGENT

A BIOGRAPHY
BY
CHARLES REID

HAMISH HAMILTON
LONDON

First published in Great Britain, 1968
by Hamish Hamilton Ltd
90 Great Russell Street, London W.C.1
Copyright © 1968 by Charles Reid
241 91310 0

Printed in Great Britain
by Ebenezer Baylis and Son, Ltd
The Trinity Press, Worcester, and London

To the great amateur choirs of England in whom he delighted, as they, 'singing like blazes', delighted in him

CONTENTS

LIST OF ILLUSTRATIONS

FOREWORD
THE WHY AND THE HOW

THE FIRST time I was asked to write a biography of Sir Malcolm Sargent was in 1955. I told the publisher who made the approach that I would be willing to try.

In music there was no great affinity between Sargent and myself. It is true that his loyalty to Elgar's music and memory through years when embattled Elgarians almost succeeded in annulling both had greatly stirred me. At that time, however, there was much late-Romantic and post-Romantic music (later on there was more) which I liked and he cold-shouldered. If biographies depended upon an identity of likes and dislikes between writer and 'sitter' one of two things would certainly happen. Either none would come out, or nobody would read them if they did.

In this case there were considerations other than taste. Some professional quarters nurtured a prejudice against Sargent which, as it seemed to me, stemmed less from his circumscribed repertory and the nature of his musicianship than from his friendships with innumerable persons of 'high degree', to use the old phrase, and his open relish in such friendships; the thunderous ovations he often won from massive audiences who, or most of whom, loved Malcolm as much as whatever music (*Messiah* excepted) he happened to be conducting, from *The Planets* to the *Pathétique*; lastly his tailoring and unvarying spruceness, whose like had never been seen before for any length of time on English rostrums.

These tastes and this accomplishment of his, amiable enough in themselves, aroused envy, as might have been expected. In the train of envy came irrational resentment. In some minds Sargent could do nothing right. They damned or faintly praised his performances before he ever lifted the stick. This gave rise to a double standard of judgment which Sir Neville Cardus trenchantly assessed in an obituary essay on the morrow of Sargent's death. 'I have heard performances under Sargent's baton of Beethoven and Schubert', he wrote, 'which critics would have raved about, had some conductor from Russia been responsible for them, conducting them half as well and truthfully.'* To say that hundreds of thousands here and abroad were on Sargent's side is no hyperbole. By a minority (mostly of professionals), on the other hand, he was given what I felt to be less than a fair deal. This in itself predisposed me to champion him.

Two other considerations weighed. His origins had not been privileged. To the contrary, they were fairly humble. What latent qualities had enabled the youth from the workaday street and penny-a-week 'church school' to win companionship, even command, exercising both with suavity and briskness, in circles which, according to notions prevalent during his formative years, were hopelessly above his 'station'? The ill-disposed spoke of snobbery. It is true that he sometimes said things which perhaps lent colour to this reproach. After reading James Boswell's *London Journal* he made a remark which is well attested and curious: 'Boswell was a sycophant, although he never met any *really* important people.' That Samuel Johnson and his circle were not important came as news to his interlocutor. But in general snobs are fools. Sargent was acutely intelligent. Snobs get nowhere. Sargent sped repeatedly through five continents as 'Britain's musical ambassador' — no vain title, as later chapters of this book may show. Again, snobs aren't loved. What more in the way of love could be wished for than the thunders of ecstasy which welcomed him season after season at London's Promenade Concerts? If Sargent was fond of the 'great', it may be said that the 'great' were head over heels about Sargent. Where regard and affection are mutual, snobbery does not enter in. Such, at all events, is my reading of royal, ducal and other companionships which irked the envious.

* *The Guardian*, 4th October 1967.

Finally there were his talkings and teachings. He was one of the few laymen in public view who could speak of God without sounding sheepish or mealy-mouthed. His faith was old as the hills and fresh as dew. Without overdoing it, he asserted this faith, primarily for the ears of the young, at a time of flux and malaise, when doctrinal props were being knocked loose in all directions and nothing noticeable was being put in their place. Here a comparison. In researching and writing my biography of Thomas Beecham, I came to realize that, while in some ways a better conductor and certainly more skilled at the handling and training of orchestras than Sargent, Beecham was by comparison a philosophical 'dead-ender'. His writing, conversation, speeches, tantrums and genial hedonism denoted that, in his mind, the arts, with music in the van, and all the other joys and elegances of Western civilization, were life's purpose — and end; in the sense that a brick wall is an end: poor comfort for uncounted millions (most of mankind, indeed) who are denied these good things or can't take them in. Sargent's doctrine, which music subserved, took in the uncounted millions. He acknowledged the existence of people on the wrong side of the brick wall. This I count to his glory. Thus I saw him as a challenge; as someone important to write about. The trouble in 1955, and for years after, was that Sargent did not want anyone to write about him. That, at least, is what he told me and several others. Meeting him at a party early in 1956 I reminded him that I had had no reply to a two-month-old letter of mine in which the possibility of a 'Life' was broached. 'But', he replied, 'I don't regard *me*, my personal self, as distinct from my professional self, as of any importance at all.' His tone almost suggested shrinking self-distaste. The tone was to recur — *diminuendo*, however. In the spring of 1962, a second publisher pressed Sargent to help in the writing of a book about himself and mentioned me as the writer he had in mind. There was no one, replied Sargent, to whom he would more happily entrust the job 'if I were keen on the job being done'. But the idea did not attract him in the least, he confessed. He did not want to spend any time 'talking about me' to anybody. Significantly, however, he raised questions as to what form the book might take. *Diminuendo* had set in. He had begun to flirt with the project.

2**

Early in 1964 a third and (this time) definitive publisher came on
the scene, Hamish Hamilton, *amateur* of music and his friend
of long standing. Years earlier Sargent had promised that in the
event of his writing his 'Life' or helping somebody to write it,
Hamilton should be the publisher. In the light of this promise and
bearing in mind that he had no leisure to write much himself, he
agreed to a collaboration, and said he would rather Charles Reid
were his biographer than anyone else.

In accepting the invitation to write a book on a collaborative basis
I stressed that, apart from intimate and private matters, absolute
candour should be the aim. . . . 'Gaiety and lightheartedness, yes. . . .
There must be shadow, too, however. . . . Without shadows landscapes are dull, lives unthinkable. . . .' This point I made in a
memorandum which he found 'excellent'.

Early in 1965 we met to decide what form our collaboration
should take. He suggested that I should write the main narrative
and that he should intercalate chapters of comment and perhaps
additional biographical matter at various points. This idea I welcomed. How soon could we get to work? As a writer of 'profiles'
I had had several talks with Sargent from 1950 onwards. The outcome was a file of material, much of it hitherto unpublished. It was
important that, for the completion of the main narrative, we should
have further interview sessions. Pinning him down to these was like
trying to sprinkle salt on a bird's tail. Not that he was evasive. The
problem was how to fit me into a fantastically congested work
schedule which, as he phrased it, kept him spinning round the
world in aeroplanes for half of every year. Yet he managed to shoe-
horn me in from time to time. He talked copiously and entertain-
ingly. Between our meetings I spoke with scores of old friends, dug
deep into the B.B.C.'s sound archives and tunnelled through a
mountain of newsprint. In the end research ran to well over half
a million words. Compiling this took up a lot of time. But at
first we seemed to have all the time in the world. Even the illness
and critical operation of December 1966 seemed no great menace
to our project, for he made what looked to laymen like a good
recovery.

While holidaying in Honolulu in the summer of 1967 and after his return to England he read a considerable part of this book, three hundred pages of typescript, in draft, and confirmed that he would be contributing chapters of his own. Naturally there would have to be corrections. If he had lived long enough to read the rest there would probably have been contentions between us on various points of opinion and fact. I remember his forecasting jocosely at one of our early meetings that we should find so much to differ and dispute about that we should go on wrestling with the book and about it into old age. It was not until after his death that, through continued research, I got the true measure of English orchestral players' earlier attitudes to him (in general they had been disapproving) and traced these attitudes to their main source. As will be gathered from the chapter entitled 'Gentleman v. Players', which reviews a strained relationship and its origins, my retrospective sympathies are with the Players. We should not have wrestled with this theme. It is likely that we should have battled over it.

The time for battles was running out, however. Illness felled him again. Even to lay minds the language of the bulletins issued after his second operation in seven months had a sinister ring. During what was optimistically called his convalescence he commended me to further old friends, Lord Mountbatten among them, for information on specific points or periods of his life. He had my three hundred typewritten pages at his bedside and worked on them from time to time with a heavy black pencil of the sort he used when marking scores. He interpolated, sometimes amusingly, queried, corrected as far as he could. Four days before his death he put the draft aside. Mrs. Anne Chapman, once his secretary and a confidante for nearly a quarter of a century, was at his bedside. He said to her: 'I can do nothing more with the book, so you will have to help Charles Reid.' This she did. Her help has been invaluable.

By this time many of us knew that he was dying. What we did not know that he had only a matter of weeks to live. We had been given to understand that he had six months. I wrote to him in affectionate terms. His dictated reply said that he would love to see me, promised a bedside meeting for the following week if he felt stronger and, as to the book, advised me to obtain, if I could, a complete set of Courtauld–Sargent concert programmes (1929–40);

he stressed how far ahead of their time and how magnificent in quality these were. On the back of the letter was a postscript in his own hand. It said that in the biography he wanted *nothing* (his italics) to be said disparagingly about anyone. He admitted with regret that he had not avoided disparagement during his life — 'but can avoid it (with your help) after my death.' I assured him in my reply that, as to 'disparagement', I had not come upon evidence of any such activity on his part. Here and there a touch of raillery, a little twitting, perhaps . . , nothing more. I added, however: 'No biographer does an honest job, of course, who ignores "warts and all" — if there are any.' The date on his letter was 2nd October, 1967. The date on mine was 3rd October. On that day he died.

One thing more. It is regretted that members of the Sargent family have not seen fit to continue Sir Malcolm's co-operation. It has been conveyed to me by an eminent musical personage, however, that it was feared I might be making too much of 'Sir Malcolm's weaker side'. What this weaker side might be was not defined. Malcolm Sargent had his limitations. He had his vanities. He made his mistakes. I trust that these have not been overstated. What concerns me far more is Malcolm Sargent's strengths. These I have stated as eloquently as I could. They were a need of his time. They are an exemplar for times to come.

CHAPTER ONE

DEATH THE PROLOGUE

THIS BOOK ends on life's last heady shout in Malcolm Sargent's ear: the shout of adoration that went up from thousands when, a dying man—though the thousands knew nothing of this—he appeared against expectation on the Royal Albert Hall platform after the last piece had been performed on the last night of the 1967 Promenade concerts.

The ovation that followed his ringing and sanguine speech roared itself out. He returned along the conductor's 'bullrun' to the artists' room backstage. There he picked up his invalid's cane and accepted supporting arms up to the stage door. Nodding wordless goodbyes to old friends and servitors, he left the scene of his most grandiose triumphs as quickly as his doomed body could move. The limousine made its usual detour of remoter blocks (an old dodge for putting doorstep autograph-seekers off the scent) to an entry just across the way. Then up in the old-fashioned lift, elegant and coffinlike, to No. 9 Albert Hall Mansions, the two-floor apartment which had been his home and professional hub for twenty years. There he lay back and wittingly or unconsciously prepared for death.

It is with the spirit and manner of his dying that this book advisedly begins, for nothing else in Sargent's life so well brought out what there was of gold in him. There is said to be at least a little gold in every man. The gold in Sargent's case was a certain childlikeness. Shrewd orchestral players who worked with him for forty years sometimes called this naïvety. They say how easy it was, if you went the right way about it, to persuade him to do things he thought he didn't want to do. But childlikeness is the truer word.

Childlikeness was the note of his religious beliefs; it was this that accounted for their simplicity and strength. He was sometimes reproached for rigid conventionality in his music making. His faith, on the other hand, was pattern-free and unimposed; it welled up inside him unbidden. Again, childlikeness may have had something to do with his stoicism. He accepted pain without the rebellion or angry introspection that maturity sometimes connotes.

With acceptance went a childlike bewilderment. At one point during that last summer there had been some hope. His doctors had allowed him out for airings on secluded paths in Kensington Gardens. Then the return of pain. It was ruthless pain. 'I was getting so much better and going for a little walk every day,' he told Anne Chapman. 'Now, suddenly, I have this terrible pain. I just can't make out what it is.'

His surprise appearance at the Proms had been on a Saturday. The following day he had the Press round at No. 9. Over pyjamas he wore a silk dressing-gown with neckcloth, all in his sprucest Noël Coward manner. The old smile was there. It gleamed with bizarre radiance in sallow, shrunken features. He had not been able to assimilate food in the normal way for weeks and was kept going on complex medication and ameliorative treatment, including regular use of the stomach pump, which in themselves would have quelled or quietened most spirits. Sargent, however, was unquellable. The old resilience kept bouncing his thoughts into the future. He was full of conducting plans that reached well into 1968. There would be America in the autumn and again in the spring. Then, after a rest, rehearsals for the 1968 Proms. To these he looked forward exuberantly.

On Monday 18th September his doctors saw him as usual. He questioned them again about the pain that puzzled him so.

Suddenly he asked: 'Is it cancer?'

The reply was 'Yes.'

It was cancer of the pancreas. His case was hopeless.

For two days he lay in a state of shock or recovering from it. By the Thursday he was inwardly himself again, perhaps more the master of his spirit, indeed, than had ever been the case before. Friends were given to understand that he had six months to live.

In truth he had only a fortnight. He used this respite to make his peace with God and take leave methodically of old friends. These he called to his bedside in considered sequence.

On the professional side there was one mercy of which he was mindful. He had been struck down while in command of his old techniques and *élan*. In Melbourne, Geelong and Illinois that spring or early summer he had conducted what turned out to be the last concerts of his life with a straight back and a sprightliness that would have been startling in any other septuagenarian. His wish had long been that his gift should be snatched rather than whittled away. Ten years earlier I had met him after an orchestral rehearsal at the Royal Academy of Music, London. In a showcase there were relics of his predecessor Sir Henry Wood, founder of the Promenade concerts and inspirer of much else: baton, medals, a score in which he had scrawled phrase-markings. Wood, as will be detailed later, had been Sargent's first mentor and was one of three musical potentates—the others being Sir Hugh Allen and Rupert D'Oyly Carte—who cosseted and launched him professionally. Picking up his bowler hat and gloves on his way out to lunch, he glanced at the relics and paused. Suddenly he said: 'I know when a conductor is not doing his best. A man declines. That is inevitable. I hope my right arm may be paralysed when that starts in my case. I would much rather have paralysis strike me than go on as Henry Wood did when no longer up to it. Wood's last five years were declining years. . . .'*

After the two days of shock and emotional readjustment, death came in prospect to wear the lineaments of a friend. He had long known intuitively and had sometimes proclaimed that this was how it would be. On his seventieth birthday he had startled listeners to the B.B.C.'s Home Service by ebulliently declaring, in reply to a question on what, strictly speaking, was a different theme, that

---

* These words were noted while fresh in the memory. It should be added that *The Last Years of Henry J. Wood*, by Jessie Wood (Gollancz, 1954), quotes a letter which Sargent wrote to Wood in 1943 on the eve of his 75th birthday. In this he hoped that at seventy-five he would be doing as good work for England as Wood was then doing and that he would be held in as much honour by the discerning. Sir Henry Wood died the following year.

death was something he looked forward to greatly. He had loved
this life so much, he explained, that he knew he would love death
still more. Then came a noble simile: 'When I go into the next
world I shall not feel a stranger. As a child taken from the left
breast cries only to find consolation in the right breast, so shall it
be when we pass from life to death, *from life to life*.' During the last
fortnight he had talks with Dr. Donald Coggan, the Archbishop of
York, who came to him both as friend and as spiritual counsellor.
Dr. Coggan has made known these deathbed words of his: 'I always
had faith. Now I have knowledge.'

He was not the only prelate who brought comfort. Cardinal John
Heenan, Archbishop of Westminster, had first met Sargent, while
Metropolitan of his Church's Northern Province, during an interval
in a *Messiah* performance at the Philharmonic Hall, Liverpool. On
that occasion they talked not so much of Handel as of Elgar and
Cardinal Newman. Sargent spoke of the intense emotion he always
felt when conducting *The Dream of Gerontius*. After this they kept
in touch, exchanging greetings or messages when either was celebrat-
ing his birthday or came into the news.

It chanced that during a London visitation in December, 1966,
the Cardinal, during his customary round of hospitals, called, not
knowing him to be there, at the one where his friend was recovering
from his penultimate operation. Sargent let it be known through the
matron that he did not want to take the Cardinal away from his
Catholic patients—'but please could he see me, too?' Heenan did so
gladly. A second request of the same kind came from Albert Hall
Mansions during his last days. The Cardinal, himself recovering
from a serious illness, was on the point of packing for Rome, where
he was to attend a Bishops' Synod through October. He wrote
promising to call at No. 9 as soon as he returned, adding that Sir
Malcolm would be remembered in his prayers.

An urgent telephone message from the secretariat conveyed that
Sargent was dying and would like to see him right away. The rest
is told in the Cardinal's words:

'I went at once and found him serene and quite unafraid of death.
He spoke of his reception at the last Promenade concert of the
season and said that two days later his doctors had told him he had

only a few days to live. He spoke of the spiritual influence of music on the young Promenaders and said how grateful he was for his happy life as a musician. We prayed together. I said the Lord's Prayer and, on an impulse, "Ave Maria" in Latin. This gave him great joy. I then blessed him and bade him goodbye. No tears. No self-pity. No regrets.'

In farewell letters – which, until the day before his death, he dictated in part and, for the rest, wrote in a clear hand, although lying on his back—he often reverted to the last things. To one of his many godchildren (he had always been in great demand at the font and never forgot the spiritual duties he undertook there), he wrote five days before the end that all men faced the high jump sooner or later—'and I can assure you that it is a great privilege and advantage to have good notice'.

Another who came to his bedside was Hamish Hamilton, to whom he declared that there was no hope for him physically. Hamilton ventured to speak of something else. One must go on believing in miracles, he suggested.

'The only miracle that will happen to me', said Sargent, 'is death.'

'Well', returned Hamilton, 'you have one comfort: your religion. That must be a great help to you now. You believe in an after life and that you will be with Pamela, don't you? (Pamela was the daughter who had died when scarcely out of girlhood after years of suffering. Her death was the great grief of his life.)

'Yes', he said, 'I have absolute faith.'

Mention has been made of one young friend. There were others to remember during those last days: among them Charles Philip Arthur George, Prince of Wales, then eighteen and devotedly musical. They had first met in Australia while Sargent was touring there and the Prince schooling at Timber Tops. Each thought highly of the other. Their friendship had a great potential. But this was not to be. Towards the end Sargent wrote the Prince an affectionate letter of valediction. Soon afterwards the Prince spoke to him by telephone. Their talk is understood to have been moving and melancholy. Unwilling to touch upon his friend's illness, the Prince said he was sure he would soon be better and able to conduct at the 1968 Proms. Sargent feared this could not be and reminded the Prince of what he had written to him: that he had only six months to live. The Prince again wished him well and talked of his own efforts at 'cello playing. He said he would call to see Sargent on the Sunday he was due to pass through London on his way to Cambridge. By that Sunday his friend was dead. One of Sargent's last thoughts had been to send him gramophone recordings of the Elgar and Dvořák 'cello concertos. With the records went a letter from 'your Royal Highness's most devoted servant and friend, Malcolm' which commended in particular the slow movement and ending of the Elgar as beyond this world. A parenthesis begged the Prince to forgive 'this awful writing'; it was difficult to write lying on one's back.

His last callers were Admiral of the Fleet the Earl Mountbatten of Burma, a friend for over thirty years, and Mountbatten's eldest grandson, the nineteen-year-old Norton Knatchbull, another junior for whom he had warm regard. This friendship had begun through Mountbatten's late wife. Lady Mountbatten met Sargent after some musical happening in the early 1930s. He used to send her tickets for his concerts. These occasions meant much to her. They extended her knowledge of music and deepened her love of it. Musical reciprocation quickly became a family friendship. Sargent was often asked down to Broadlands, the Mountbattens' place in Hampshire, where he would rest and relax for a few days after strenuous conducting bouts. Although not musically receptive in the same way as his wife—'Frankly I'm a philistine', he confesses—Lord Mountbatten took equal pleasure in Sargent's companionship. The three often went to the theatre together. This bond continued between the two men after Edwina Mountbatten's death in 1960.

Mountbatten knew that Sargent had been gravely ill early in the year. Watching him on television on the last night of the Proms and noting the ring of his voice, he concluded, like millions more, that he was on the mend. Later he learned that this was not so; that his condition was grave. He had someone telephone to Albert Hall Mansions: 'When may Lord Mountbatten see Sir Malcolm?' 'On Monday,' replied a secretarial voice, 'or not at all.' This was Monday 2nd October. He had another day to live.

Mountbatten set all other plans aside and came up post haste. He found Sargent relaxed, alert of mind, light of heart. His eyes were bright, his expression gay. The old *raconteur* sparkle was undimmed; and he was in the mood for recalling old days and good times. His visitor encouraged him in this, prompting him to reminisce. It was the dying man who did most of the talking. They talked for three quarters of an hour: and the time passed quickly. The only constraint was the unspoken thought that time was being implacably spurred and that the tomb was near. Yet there was laughter. They reminded each other of the day Malcolm telephoned and said: 'Dickie, let's go to the play'. They picked on a revival of Shaw's *Too True to be Good* at the Strand. It was agreed that they should sup afterwards at the Savoy and that one should pay for the tickets, the other for supper. They arrived at the theatre:

'You got the tickets, of course?' asked Mountbatten.

'No, didn't you get them?' asked Sargent.

'No, I booked a table at the Savoy.'

'So did I!'

This was on the second night of the run. Packed house. They were somehow crammed into a remote corner of the circle and given seats in the third row of stalls at the first interval.

The talk moved back to the Mediterranean, Coronation year (1953): strong sun, salty winds and, for the landsman, new adventures and excitements every day. At that time Mountbatten was Commander-in-Chief of the Mediterranean Fleet. It was on his initiative four years earlier that Sargent had been appointed Honorary Adviser in Music to the Royal Marines, an office which had no precedent or parallel in any of the Services. His purpose in inviting his friend out to Malta in 1953 was twofold. There were to be Coronation concerts on the island. (These and other aspects of Sargent's visits are dealt with more fully in a later chapter.) Then there was H.M.S. *Surprise*, frigate, 1,500 tons. Not only was *Surprise* the C.-in-C.'s despatch vessel. She was also a floating guest house. Perhaps after conducting the concerts Sargent would care to take a holiday with the Mediterranean Fleet? Such was the Commander-in-Chief's plan. It worked splendidly. Never did landsman have so exciting and cosy a holiday. As Malcolm recalled it his

eyes danced like a ten-year-old's. After the Fleet put to sea the Commander-in-Chief invited him aboard his flagship, H.M.S. *Glasgow*,
and arranged for him to visit also three or four other ships of the
Fleet. Sargent wondered vaguely how he would get from one ship
to the next. Perhaps some sort of barge would put alongside? No,
he was told. Barges were out. Certain of the transfers were made by
helicopter, something of a physical challenge for a man of fifty-
eight. He did not step into the helicopter for take-off as into a taxi,
nor was he 'landed'. Instead he was winched up and down. A
greater sensation by far—on his deathbed he recalled it with as
much zest as if the thing had happened only the day before—was
transhipment by high-line. This was rigged by shooting a bolt from
a Costain gun with a pilot line which enabled the high-line proper
to be hauled aboard the sister ship. When it was fixed between two
ships, say H.M.S. *Surprise* and H.M.S. *Glasgow*, as they steamed
along, Malcolm put his foot in a stirrup, held on tight, took off and
was hauled aboard the flagship by a pulley arrangement. At least
once he travelled thus between ships steaming at speed in a rough
sea; his pluck and address were admired by all beholders from the
Commander-in-Chief downwards.

'The high-line,' he told Mountbatten, 'was the most exciting
physical experience of my life.'

Mountbatten's favourite Sargent story concerned his conversation
with King George VI at the ceremonial opening of the Royal
Festival Hall, London, in May 1951. He begged Malcolm to retell
it. Malcolm did so with gusto.

It should be explained that at the inaugural concert Sargent
conducted with electrifying effect his edition of Thomas Arne's
Rule Britannia. His performers were singers drawn from seven
great London choirs and an orchestra drawn from five great
London orchestras. In the final chorus these were joined by jack-
booted State trumpeters in scarlet, gold braid and black velvet
jockey caps who ceremonially lifted their trumpets (extra long ones)
and made tonal brilliance more brilliant still. Nobody but Sargent
could have organized such a coup or carried it off with such im-
petuosity and aplomb. At the end there were three or four finale-
encores. A gale of enthusiasm swept the hall from back gallery to

royal box, where, as well as the King and Queen, most of the Royal Succession could be taken in at a glance. Everybody stood up and clapped—King, Queen and Prime Minister Attlee with the rest.

Sargent used to claim that even the militantly Left Wing Aneurin Bevan joined in. Afterwards King George sent for Sargent. As he recapitulated it for Mountbatten's delight the conversation went roughly as follows:

The King: 'You know, I am not very musical.'

Sargent: 'Sir, you are ragging!'

The King: 'No, I'm not ragging. I'm serious. I have never been moved by any music as much as your arrangement of "Rule Britannia." Do remember this—whenever I come to another of your concerts I will ask you beforehand, no, I will *command* you' (here the King laughed) 'to perform it again.'

Sargent: 'That is very kind of you, sir, but it may be difficult if we have been performing Bach's B minor Mass or the St. Matthew Passion.'

The King: 'It won't be difficult. I shan't be there!'

The moment came for what both in the sickroom knew to be their last leavetaking. Norton was called in and for two or three minutes was at the bedside with his grandfather; after his grandfather went he stayed on for another minute or two. He had never before seen a man at the point of death, nor had he ever imagined that death could be confronted with such lighthearted bravery. Lord Mountbatten was asked later what were his valedictory words. He replied that he remembered them very clearly; and that this was what he said:

'Malcolm, I am no musician and cannot offer any profound thoughts on the subject. But I must say this. Through the Proms and your broadcasts and your travelling round the world you have spread the taste for decent music, for classical music, among masses of young people who might otherwise never have known anything better than "pop" stuff. We owe you a great debt because of that. Another thing. You have been one of our great ambassadors throughout the Commonwealth and all over the world. I shall never forget your concert in Stockholm. The King and Queen of Sweden and our own Queen were there, you remember. At the end the whole audience stood up. All over the place you put Britain's name sky high.'

As coda he briefly reverted to their long friendship and how greatly he had valued it. Malcolm said how good it had been to see him, asked to be remembered with love to Mountbatten's daughters and granddaughters. Then, 'Goodbye. . . .'

*

That evening it was thought he would live for another two or three days. At eleven o'clock one of his doctors paid a second call. Not long after this the telephone sounded at Anne Chapman's home three quarters of a mile away. It was the Maestro. That is what she had habitually called him ever since she had worked for him during Hitler's war. During the last phase she had been at his bedside every other day. The Maestro's voice was clear and tranquil; he sounded happy. He said, 'I am slipping away peacefully. God bless you. Goodnight and goodbye.' Mrs. Chapman said: 'You are surrounded by love. We all give you our love.'

By midnight he was in deep coma. He died the following day soon after midday. So that all who were closest to him might know first, the news was not released until evening. By next day the telephones in the secretaries' office at No. 9 were sounding continuously and were continuously manned. The callers were of several sorts and conditions, 'little' people as well as notables. Had he not claimed, with superbly timed gestures, on the night of his seventieth birthday concert: 'I have friends in high places' (waving with his right hand to the Albert Hall balcony), 'friends in low places' (waving with his left to the arena), 'and friends in between' (with a salute to boxes and stalls)? Some of the callers were stunned and incredulous. While acknowledging death, having learned of it from television and the newspapers, they could not bring themselves to believe that death had happened. It bewildered them as much as the first strike of mortal pain had bewildered the Maestro. He had been one of those, they confusedly felt, who are meant to live on indefinitely, radiating a mysterious vitality-bonus to the rest—to the young no less than to the old and phlegmatic. On Tuesday 3rd October, 1967, not the narrow world of music alone but also an outer multitude were bereaved whose numbers and affection had never been truly plumbed before.

CHAPTER TWO

FEUDAL SUNSET

HAROLD MALCOLM WATTS SARGENT was born some weeks earlier than had been expected, on 29th April, 1895, at Bath Villas, Ashford, Kent, the home of a family friend with whom Mrs. Sargent had been staying. The friend was called Amy Watts. She is commemorated in the third of his given names.

Before marriage Mrs. Sargent was Agnes Marion Hall, sometime companion-housekeeper to the headmistress, and later matron, of Stamford High School for girls. Her husband, Henry Edward Sargent, two years younger than she, was described on the birth certificate as 'organist'. At the Church of St. John Baptist, Stamford, Lincolnshire, he played the organ and conducted the choir as a semi-professional. Music was a sideline: but a sideline into which he put most of his heart.

His main occupation was as head clerk, rising to manager, of a coal merchants' firm with offices on the far side of Red Lion Square from St. John's. On quiet days he would leave his desk and slip across the Square for half an hour's organ practice. Broad-built and stocky, yet lithe, Harry Sargent, as most people called him, was inches shorter than his wife; so short, in fact, that the rector of St. John's called him Zacheus after the little publican who climbed up into a sycamore tree to see Christ pass by. Zacheus was rich as well as small. This could not be said of Harry Sargent. It is doubtful whether he earned more than four pounds a week, or even that, in the whole of his life. What he did earn was, however, enough to marry and raise a small family on: and that contented him.

A brisk walker with a multitude of errands, he sped about the town with his trilby hat at a cheerful angle, his linen always spotless, a mixed sheaf of business papers and music under his arm. For everybody he had a smile and for many the latest funny story. Of funny stories he was a connoisseur and tireless collector. Although unquestionably a 'card', he was highly considered in the town. If you wanted a ton of Derby brights, you dealt not with Ellis and Everard but with Mr. Sargent. He personified his employers to the extent of superseding them in the popular eye. On Sundays the trilby hat gave place to a silk hat. This he would raise with a flourish on the Broad-street 'church parade' after morning service, exchanging nod or bow, now with the fifth Marquess of Exeter, now with the chimney sweep, now with the town's Soccer centre forward.

Although there had been Sargents in and around Stamford for five hundred years, little is known of Henry Sargent's antecedents except that he was brought up by his grandparents and that they were reputedly of yeoman stock. He seems to have been largely self-educated and an avid miscellaneous reader; a man of parts whose career, for want of opportunity or privilege or assertiveness, never matched his talents. On this score another man might have been bitter, but bitterness was not in Henry Sargent's nature. Music was something he had 'picked up'. To say he 'liked' music would be tepid understatement. Music was an obsessive need. As a young man he ran glee parties, sang baritone (with striking flights into falsetto as required) and could play the violin as well as keyboard instruments.

His first parish organ was that of St. Martin's across the River Welland and on the opposite side of the town from St. John's. Among funerary monuments in St. Martin's was a table-tomb with robed an armoured sleeper, wand in hand, a lion at his feet. This was the effigy of William Cecil, counsellor of Queen Elizabeth I and Lord Treasurer of England, forebear of earls and marquesses who, in a social sense, were to be the breath of Stamford's nostrils down the centuries. Not far from St. Martin's stood the High School for girls. During the 'eighties and early 'nineties it was one of Agnes Hall's duties as housekeeper-companion or matron to take the handful of girl boarders to Sunday mattins. One morning a fellow worshipper said to her, 'We've got a new organist, a dark

little man with curly hair.' This was the first she heard of Henry
Sargent. She saw him the following Sunday and was not impressed;
it never occurred to her that one day she would want to marry him.

A tall, dark-haired girl with hazel-green eyes, well spoken and
lively, she was the daughter of Benjamin Hall, a landscape gardener
of Hertfordshire origin who, having contracted to lay out private
gardens near the cathedral at Peterborough, settled in the Midlands
and for a time had a house in Stamford. When his daughter first
went to the High School to help Miss Munro, the headmistress, her
duties were light as well as pleasant, for the school's expansion had
not begun. Miss Munro was a Girton graduate. Agnes Hall frequented her drawing-room, holidayed with her and mixed in a
circle whose cultivation enhanced her own. It is said that before
meeting Henry Sargent she had been engaged to marry two or
three times. She had dreamed of a man who would be different from
all other males. The earlier suitors had turned out to resemble each
other and all other males in sight. Not so the new organist of St.
Martin's. He was introduced to her one morning after mattins.
Gradually he won her over. There were two things about him
which she had not come across in combination before: irrepressible
fun and a brimming energy which his son was to inherit in double
measure. Extrovert, droll and convivially inclined, Henry Sargent
was in some ways as unlike Agnes Hall as could be. But then, he
was unlike anybody else in Stamford. He proposed, they married,
and the marriage prospered.

*

As soon as she was able to travel, during the second half of May,
1895, Agnes Sargent brought her baby son by train from Ashford
to Stamford and took a cab from the railway station to No. 24
Wharf-road, one in a row of stone cottages, solidly built and unpretentious. This was to be Malcolm Sargent's home for the next
eighteen years. Wharf-road was a workaday sort of road. Rows of
drab, small houses were gapped or neighboured by delivery yards,
workshops and small factories. People lived in the shadow of work,
their tether a short one. Even on blazing July Sundays or on a fine,
frosty Christmas morning, Wharf-road intimated that respites, if

brief, were well enough but that toil is the basic law and Monday morning inescapable. The prevailing smell, a faint one, was of coal gas. Between the Sargents' house and the nearby River Welland stood twin gasholders. 'Tenter Meadow', as old people called the site, had housed the town's gasworks for seventy years.

Round the corner from No. 24 lay Gas-street, across the way Gas-lane. Of these Gas-lane was the more important, for it led uphill, away from workaday grubbiness, to Stamford proper, the Stamford of the wellborn and well-to-do, a place of ancient spires and towers and attendant jackdaws; of tranquil residential squares and highwalled gardens; of bowed glass windows and elegant porticos which townsfolk of gentle condition and comforting possessions had been passing through since Queen Anne and the first of the Georges.

About Stamford as he first came to know it, Sargent said two striking things. First, that for an artist it is a great, because formative, thing to be brought up in so beautiful a town. Second, that Stamford gave him, as few other towns could, a close view of feudal England on its last legs. Feudalism as it survived in and around Stamford did not preclude exchanges of courtesy between high and low. Rather it imposed them. When Henry Sargent raised his silk hat and bowed to the Marquess of Exeter on Sunday morning, the Marquess did likewise to Henry Sargent. When invited by one of his coalheavers to stand as godfather to his new-born, Henry Sargent accepted with alacrity. The coalheaver had no hat of any kind to raise, only a forelock to touch. Like Henry Sargent he knew his place in a rigidly stratified society and never dreamed that a man could break away —as young Sargent was destined to—from the stratum to which he had been born.

*

At Stamford the top stratum supported an apex: and that apex was the Exeter family. A mile and a half to the south of the town—but as central to Stamford's consciousness as if fronting on to Red Lion Square itself—stood the Exeters' seat, Burghley House. Built by William Cecil during the late 1550s, Burghley House was oriel-windowed, turreted, battlemented and, in its way, intimidating. Three great parks served the mansion. One of these had long been open to the public. Families strolled and picnicked there at weekends. On quiet evenings during the early 1900s young Sargent dreamed music under its trees. A second park had a polo ground. It was a fashionable thing on hot Saturdays to drive beneath parasols to the High Park and watch from the comfort of one's carriage while the Burghley club played a visiting team.

For the benefit of the not-so-fashionable the fourth Marquess of Exeter occasionally opened his lawns to silver prize bands who would compete for thirty pounds in prize money and a gold medal for the best trombone solo. On those same lawns during the Hungry Forties, which were reasonably well-fed on the Exeter estates, the fourth Marquess had marked his coming-of-age by broaching a barrel that held a thousand gallons of strong ale, brewed during the year of his birth. Every tenant of ten pounds a year upwards got a pint, every tenant's child of ten or over, half a pint. Mountains of prime beef and newbaked bread were given away, a pound and a half of each for all comers. In all parishes where the Exeters had property the poor lined up for shillings, florins and crown-pieces according to whether they were single or married or had more than three children.

As in the 1840s, so during Sargent's infancy and for at least two further decades, the Exeter domains had something in common with the smaller German principalities. Although he held no formal court at Burghley House, the reigning Marquess received as special and automatic a deference as any crowned head. When a Marquess married, ecstasy overspread the borough and three abutting counties. Sargent had memories from his seventh year of the fifth Marquess's homecoming with his bride. It was a summer evening in 1901. The church bells had been ringing nonstop since noon. Apart from publicans and potboys few people did any work that day. Streets, shops and houses were festooned in the Burghley colours. Crossing the borough boundary in the Burghley state coach-and-four with postilions up and liveried footman on the box, the Marquess and Marchioness were met at the Tally-Ho Inn by a hundred tenants on horseback and escorted to a red-carpeted space outside the town hall where mace, mayor, wigs, cocked hats, fur-trimmed robes and loyal speeches awaited them.

Queen Victoria herself could not have been greeted with greater awe and jubiliation. The Queen was, indeed, a person of comparatively limited consequence. Not only did the Marquess own 27,000 acres; sentence felons from the Stamford bench; rebuke the police when they prosecuted frivolously; appoint new rectors as the need arose to sixteen churches within his 'gift'; and ensure, as chairman of the poor-law 'guardians', that the workhouse fed its paupers according to just and proper scales of diet. On top of these possessions and powers was one of greater moment. He owned Stamford's water supply, its spring-sources and the town's waterworks. During the year of Sargent's birth, Stamford corporation sought to buy him out. 'Not only do we want to own and run our water supply like other towns,' said the corporation in effect. 'We also want to improve it. In drought conditions your lordship supplies not more than two-fifths of the town's daily water needs. We think we could do better.' The fourth Marquess waved the corporation aside. So did the fifth. The waterworks did not pass into public ownership until 1962.

Not that the Exeter's monopoly was absolute. In 1895 a row of houses in Melancholy Walk, to cite one exception, got their water from a single pump near a cess pit. Not surprisingly, Melancholy Walk was swept by enteric fever. The Sargents' house, typical of whole quarters, had no indoor sanitation, any more than it had a fixed bath. The 'place' was down the garden. There were other archaisms and backslidings. Street lighting could not be depended on. Some lamps lit up during the day. Others stayed unlit after dark. A wag reproached the mayor for being unable to make the moon shine on nights when the lamplighters forgot to turn out. For want of a daily paper the town crier, Mr. Boor, a neighbour of the Sargents, went round with his handbell intoning election meetings, auction sales, water-supply cuts, quoits matches and where to buy boots and second-hand bathchairs. Although the town had two railway stations, people dumped parcels at a dozen inns, as in stage-coach times, for collection by delivery waggons on specified calling days. There was even an official letter-carrier, whose bedroom ceiling fell on his head during a July night storm, impairing the town's business communications for days.

For the well-off life could be exciting, pleasant and pretty. Under a standing caption, THE CHASE, the *Rutland Lincoln and Stamford Mercury* regularly gave half a page during the winter (a full page being the size of a small tablecloth) to the doings and fixtures of nearly a score packs of foxhounds which hunted contiguous counties.* For hunt balls and like gaieties—such as quadrilles, galops and lancers beneath Chinese lanterns on summer nights to the music of the Volunteers' Band in the grounds of Major This and Colonel That—you could buy Heidsieck 1889 at seventy-two shillings the dozen and Château Croixmont at one third less from Lowe and Cobbold in the High-street.

At one or another of Stamford's ten annual street fairs you could buy prime Stilton at sixpence a pound, a fine-bred carthouse for forty pounds and a spanking Welsh pony for seven. The annual cattle fair was a noisome scandal for years. Too mean to spend money on setting up a cattle market, the corporation gave farmers and traders a tollfree run of spacious Broad-street, whose cobbles were shockingly fouled. A sensitive minority complained that the youths who rounded up and drove in the beasts used them cruelly. 'Some of us,' Sargent was to recall, 'have seen terrified cattle—tiny calves among them—being driven through the streets and beaten with stout cudgels at almost every step.'

Once a year farm servants flocked in for the 'hiring statutes'. While waiting for farmers to hire them, the men and the girls would dance to fiddle and concertina in the Corn Exchange. Not much hiring was done in 1895. Ploughboys went cheap at six pounds a year, good waggoners at fifteen. Hired labourers were 'in servitude', a phrase which their betters used as a matter of course. Those who bore their servitudes cheerfully were patted on the head by a Society for Promoting Skill and Industry among the Labouring Classes.

* The Blankney, the Belvoir, the Cottesmore, the Quorn, Mr. Fernie's, Viscount Galway's, the Rufford, the Earl of Yarborough's, the Southwold, the Duke of Rutland's, the Fitzwilliam, the Woodland Pytchley, the Oakley, the South Notts, the Warwickshire and the North Warwickshire.

So much for the able-bodied and deserving poor.

For those no longer able-bodied there were seven almshouses, the oldest dating back to Henry VII's reign, each with its small colony of men and women who hadn't done as well out of feudalism as some. For the less deserving and undeserving there was the workhouse; scene, according to grudging minds, of scandalous surfeit, where replete paupers pushed their plates aside and excess food had to be thrown to the pigs. Christmas Day in the workhouse was enjoyed by good and bad alike. There was a Mr. Nutt who fumed at the thought of lazy paupers, men who wouldn't take and keep an honest job at any price, sitting down with more conscientious ones to roast beef, roast pork, stewed rabbits, plum pudding and beer. This was all wrong, he protested. Idlers should be barred from the treat. Mr. Nutt did not have his way. But his grudging scrutiny was of a kind that used to be bred by small town life; and, as to population, Stamford, although it looked big, was smallish: 8,613 souls.

*

When Henry Sargent was a small boy the town had had a theatre, in St. Mary-street. It was now a musty club where men played billiards and chess and read the papers. On the top floor of the Stamford Institution, where learned lectures were delivered, a camera obscura offered 'a good view of the town and neighbourhood'. Between them the Corn Exchange and the Assembly Rooms could seat eleven or twelve hundred for occasional shows and edifications. At one or other of these places in 1895, Stamfordians heard their first *Gondoliers*, sung by a D'Oyly Carte touring company; their first complete performance of Mendelssohn's *Elijah*, with chorus and orchestra totalling 150; a night of humorous yarns and sketches by a Mr. Banks and a Miss Peasgood, who threw in two piano duets, *Poet and Peasant* Overture and the first movement of Beethoven's Symphony No. 1 for good measure; and Herr Willibald Richter's chamber-music party from Leicester in Beethoven's G major piano trio Op. 121a and Ten Variations on the air *I am the Tailor Kakadoo*. Somebody had founded a Stamford Choral

Society, somebody else a Stamford Orchestral Society. So far little had been heard from either.

There was a Town Silver Band, uniformed in blue with red pipings, which gave evening concerts in Red Lion Square and sent round the hat towards new instruments, of which they stood in evident need. They were famous for their hardihood in bitter weather and off-pitch playing at all seasons. Once in a while they gave a Sunday night concert, which is why selections from *The Creation* figured in their repertory. Even on Sundays they would end up with something lively, such as the *William Tell* Overture. What this amounted to, thundered Mr. Hiley, rector of St. John's, was a desecration of the Sabbath, a loosening of the ties of guidance and instruction, a menace to young people, a movement fraught with mischief. The town's zealots felt that young and old alike could get all the music that was good for them in church and chapel.

What most people had in mind when they took up music was singing or playing at home. Perhaps more than ever before in middle- and lower middle-class history, families around the turn of the century made their own music, and they continued to do so, with an enthusiasm not readily imagined by later generations, for another thirty years. Malcolm Sargent grew up in an age of private music teachers and private music lessons. In this matter Stamford was better supplied than most towns of its size, perhaps because it was relatively well-off and leisured—the sort of community that automatically attracted people bent on setting up boarding schools and finishing schools and teaching what were known as the 'accomplishments'. Among the *Mercury*'s tutorial advertisements in May, 1895, appeared Mrs. Tinkler's. Mrs. Tinkler begged to announce that 'her next term for Musical Instruction was about to begin. . . . Pupils prepared for the Royal Academy and the Royal College of Music.'

Frances Tinkler was an assiduous teacher and a remarkable woman. She will recur in this narrative.

CHAPTER THREE

'TINKIE'

THE HOUSE at Wharf Road was bigger inside than it looked from the outside. The front door opened on to seven and a half yards of gloomy corridor. One side of the corridor was a blank wall. On the other side was a narrow, steep stairway leading up to the three bedrooms and the parlour (or sitting-room) door. Traditionally used on Sundays only, the parlour had an ornamental cast-iron fireplace, a smallish window that looked on to the street and a harmonium that smelt of wax polish. The harmonium had carved volutes and scrolls majestic to the infant eye. At the far end of the corridor was the kitchen-living room, so long in relation to its width that the casual visitor might have supposed it designed not as a place to eat and live in but a place to pass through and get out of. Yet once he had reconciled himself to the geometry, the visitor found snugness. On winter nights, with comfort glowing from the massive kitchen range which, like his wife, was inches taller than himself, Henry Sargent would read in his favourite chair alongside the big mahogany bookcase, then go to the piano and play bits of Stainer's *Crucifixion* and perhaps a musical-comedy number or two.

The first Wharf-road piano was old and tinny. When Malcolm took to music, his father bought a new one straight from Germany, via the piano shop in Broad-street, and paid for it by instalments marked up on a calendar card. On the living-room walls hung landscapes painted by Henry himself. They are not remembered as showing much talent except Henry's general talent for busying himself and never being bored. The biggish garden, with its flower-beds and lawn, was another of his achievements; he was the one who had laid it out. Mother saw to the weeding and the clipping and clearing. There wasn't another back garden in Wharf-road to compare with the Sargents' for well-kept prettiness. The living-room had a single window with so broad a sill that Malcolm, joined later by his young sister Dorothy, used to sit and play and listen to music there. There were several such embrasures in the house, as well as cupboards 'scooped' out of walls as thick as a fort's.

When did Malcolm first try to *make* music, as distinct from listening to and, in his infant way, marvelling at it? 'I was playing the piano as far back as I can remember,' he used to say. A story which probably stems from his parents is more specific. When visiting Wharf-road a girl cousin some years older than he played her 'party piece' on the piano. When she had finished, Malcolm, then under three, climbed on to the piano stool and picked out sounds which bore some resemblance, or so it was fancied, to what he had been hearing. Soon after this he started schooling. His mother put him into a pinafore-smock with shoulder-bows, the accepted thing then for little boys and girls alike, and took him across Wharf-road and through an archway inscribed 'National School, Founded 1817'. A dependency of St. George's Church higher up the hill, the National School had an infants' department which was managed by a spinster who lived in a cottage in the playground. Class One was up in a murmurous gallery, separated from Class Two by a curtain. Here Malcolm was taught the elements of reading and writing and simple sums, as well as hymns, texts, Bible stories and the catechism. Towards the cost of this his parents paid a penny a week, defined as a 'voluntary contribution'. A fortnight before his sixth birthday, having won a scholarship, he moved up the hill to the Blue Coat School, an ancient foundation which had relinquished its traditional blue uniform and, in its newfangled way, taught elementary physiology among other subjects. The parents of Blue Coat boys paid sixpence a week. 'Occasionally', it is remembered, 'boys had to leave because their parents were unable to pay the fee.' In Malcolm's case the weekly sixpence was safe enough. There was never much money at home, but Agnes Sargent, a prudent and tireless housewife, made what money there was go a long way.

In his free time outside school the boy began to explore the town and watch its events, usually with his father. When six he looked out from somebody's upper window while the beflagged and crowded town cheered Stamford men newly returned from the Boer War. There were eight of them: one sergeant and seven privates, all belonging to the Lincolnshire Regiment (Volunteer Battalion). As they marched to the town hall for a speech by the mayor, silver tobacco boxes and silver mounted walking sticks of ebony, a drum and fife band played their regimental tune, *The Lincolnshire Poacher*. The Volunteers were in red coats. A troop of Lincolnshire Yeomanry were in green. The reds and the greens, the drums and fifes, the bunting and cheering and pealing of church bells remained vividly in Sargent's memory. Life was ecstatic, almost painfully so. He heard a neighbour speak of a family with a shop in the High Street whose son, a volunteer, had been killed in action just before the end of the war. 'How awful it must be for his mother and father,' said the neighbour. Malcolm burst out crying and went on crying for a long time. In childhood and boyhood his sensibility was acute. As will be seen, the beauty of music could be an agony that extorted a cry for deliverance.

His outings with his father were jolly and elating, in the main. On country walks 'Harry' Sargent, as friends called him, had a sharp eye for beasts and rare birds. At all times he was a great one for pets. He knew the coal-wharf carthorses by their names and fed them sugar. At one time he kept a Scotch collie, Trim. Trim died and was buried in the garden beneath a little wooden cross. Every year a morsel of Christmas pudding was put on the grave, because Trim had always been given a bit as a treat on Christmas Day. This ceremony, in which Malcolm played a solemn part, suggests that on both sides of the family the Sargents had, in certain situations or contexts, an emotionally vulnerable strain. On Saturday afternoons in season father and son would go down to the water meadows and fish the river. Over a freak mischance that befell Henry Sargent the family laughed helplessly. Jumping up suddenly from his camp stool, he turned his back on the river and ran away from it as fast as his short legs could carry him, rod bent and line taut, as if coping with some high-speed amphibian. He came back panting with

2

laughter. A rat had taken the wormbait while he was drawing in his line and, finding itself hooked, had given him a gallop which ended only when the gut broke.

Whenever a 'twopenny gaff' parked on the Broad-street cobbles or in some paddock on the outskirts, the Sargent males were invariably there, elbows on knees, eyes agog. The 'gaff', or nomad theatre, was a ring of caravans roofed over by tarpaulins. Low wooden benches for the audience faced a trestle stage on which actors of a sort played raucous melodramas in a smell of naphtha flares. Occasionally there were laughs. At family parties Henry Sargent used to mimic a scene at the cross-roads. Villain was supposed to shoot hero. When he raised his rifle it came apart, the barrel falling off the stock. The show had to go on, however. A loud bang came from the wings dead on cue, the hero staggered and fell, and the heroine wrung her hands over his corpse, exclaiming 'Alas! Shot through the heart!'

For a church organist and wearer of the surplice, Henry Sargent's taste for Edwardian musical-comedy was bold. Either by playing piano 'selections' at home or by taking the boy to fit-up performances by lowly touring companies, usually to piano accompaniment, at the Corn Exchange, he inducted Malcolm to an ephemeral though glittering sequence: *San Toy*, *Country Girl*, *The Geisha*, *The Belle of New York*, *Floradora*. Pirated piano scores of these and other hits were on sale. They were, as Sargent remembers, peppered with apparent misprints (actually deliberate errors) which were held to protect the pirates from copyright claims. At the Wharf-road piano he would go through the piracies under his father's eye, spotting the mistakes and correcting them. At the same time he was coming to know the Gilbert and Sullivan operas. At eight he knew many of the Sullivan tunes and many of the Gilbert words and was beginning to strum out the tunes on the piano. When local amateurs started putting on Gilbert and Sullivan productions annually at the Assembly Rooms, he became a programme boy. He earned two shillings a night—one shilling as fee, one shilling in penny tips. He always stayed on for the performance, which was thrown in free. In successive years he thus heard five consecutive performances each of *The Gondoliers*, *Iolanthe*, *The Pirates of Penzance* and *The*

Yeomen of the Guard. He heard *The Mikado*, too, not as a programme boy but either on-stage or back-stage in the walking-on part of Go-To, the Lord High Executioner's juvenile sword-bearer. With nothing to say or sing, he watched and listened to what other people were about with ardour and, now and then, a precocious critical stirring. After this he attended rehearsals [of the Stamford Amateur Operatic Society] every week during the winter, his first boyish delight in Sullivan's music so deepening that he came to demand for it the same standard of performance as Mozart is supposed to get. As much as when conducting a Mozart opera or symphony, he once wrote, 'the Gilbert and Sullivan conductor must aim at clarity, shape and beauty'.

*

Mozart and Sullivan have taken us a jump ahead in our chronology. Malcolm's stage debut in *The Mikado* happened when he was thirteen. Already he was beginning to be spoken of as the town's prodigy. He had had six years at the piano with Mrs. Tinkler. In the choir at St. John's he had been singing alto—not because he had an especially deep voice but because he found it easy to sing a part other than the melody—ever since he had been able to read words. On the organ at St. John's he had been taking lessons—his father acting as both tutor and, when his son was practising, organ-blower —ever since his legs were long enough to reach the pedals. In all these pursuits he was quick in uptake and confident beyond his years. Wearing knickerbockers and Eton collar he went to Mrs. Tinkler once a week.

By this time Frances Tinkler was widowed and lived on Broadstreet in a mellow, double-fronted house with mullion windows and walls a yard thick. From the hall, with its low ceiling and panelled walls, you either turned left into the drawing-room or went forward into the garden-room according to whether you were 'taking' piano or singing. There were three upright pianos in the house. At the one in the garden-room Mrs. Tinkler not only gave singing lessons; she also rehearsed a chamber orchestra of her own recruiting. Outside ran a veranda hung with flower baskets. The garden itself was in season a glory of clematis, jasmine, honeysuckle. The two other uprights were in the drawing-room. One of them was replaced later by a Bechstein grand on which sat a plaster bust of Beethoven. On these twin uprights foursomes of boys and girls played eight-hand transcriptions of the *Hebrides* Overture, movements from Mozart and Haydn and the like while 'Fanny' (Malcolm was the first pupil to address her thus; some of the others called her 'Tinkie' or 'Tinkle' but never to her face) strode briskly around beating time. Now and then she would halt the players and have them switch parts, musical-chairs fashion. More than once she asked Malcolm to take over the beat at these sessions. This was his first taste of conducting. He was then about twelve.

Frances Tinkler was small and elegant and had strikingly beautiful though prematurely white hair. The composer Michael Tippett had lessons from her in a later decade. He speaks of her as 'bourgeoise in the best sense of the word, with a mature, warm personality—the sort of person to whom a schoolboy could take his troubles (as I often did) and be listened to understandingly and helpfully.' She had set up as a music teacher soon after her husband's death, which happened when she was in her middle thirties. Gradually she became the town's first piano teacher, with a roll of sixty pupils or more. She continued her teaching until a few weeks before her death in 1950. Theory lessons were on Saturday mornings. In warm weather a dozen pupils would sit or sprawl in a semicircle on the lawn while Fanny discoursed on the diatonic system, key signatures, the duration of demisemiquavers in relation to breves and semibreves and so on. Some of the sessions were *viva voce* examinations. Whatever the question, 'Mal', as everybody called him, was first with the answer: and always his answer was exasperatingly right. What is more, he had 'absolute pitch'. He would hum a note to some fellow pupil (usually one of the girls, all of whom he liked to impress), and say, 'That's middle C' or 'That's F sharp. Go and play it on the piano.' He was never a hairsbreadth out. For these and other feats the others did not love him the more. When Mal came out top in theory, far ahead of everybody else, or won praise from Fanny for memorizing, say, Chaminade's *Autumn* in record time, there were hurt whispers. 'O yes,' said the whisperers, 'it's perfect when Mal does it. Mal can't do anything' wrong. Sensing this mood one Saturday morning, Fanny gave the class a dressing down and ended with a prophecy.

'You may laugh at Mal now,' she said, 'but one day he'll be a knight, he'll be a Sir, and the rest of you will still be in Stamford.'

Looking back after sixty years an old friend who went to Mrs. Tinkler during the same years says that even then Malcolm impressed her and others as two persons in one. One person was a typical schoolboy, not keen on games but amiably mischievous, given to pranks, fond of his bicycle. The other person was a genius or near-genius whose thin frame and whole being seemed to vibrate under music as if music had been a current from one of those 'galvanic' machines, popular on Edwardian piers and fairgrounds, which gave an increasing shock-thrill the more you turned its metal knobs. Music and facts about music clung to his memory like iron filings to a magnet. His eyes darted more humorously than most and, like Mrs. Tinkler, he sat bolt upright. His poker-straight back, always a matter of comment among concertgoers, was first publicly remarked upon at a concert by Mrs. Tinkler's pupils at the Assembly Rooms on a wet, cold afternoon in December 1904. The only boy among twenty or thirty girls—a sort of situation he never found disagreeable—he played No. 2 in an octet transcription for four pianos, two players at each, of two pieces, *Am Abend* and a Tarantella, by a now forgotten German, Arnold Krug. Afterwards he played in a piano duet, a rondo by Gurlitt, with Kathleen, Mrs. Tinkler's small daughter.

'What a smart little boy!' said a mother to her neighbour. 'He sits just like a soldier on parade.'

Sometimes in later years he met Kathleen out of class. One of Stamford's first moving-picture shows was in a marquee with planking seats in the twopenny gaff style. Again the pitch was Broad-street. Mal took Kathleen to a flickering magic of railway trains, trotting ponies, battleships and over-moustached villains, all in spasmodic motion. There were many girl friends. But music remained paramount.

In cold weather he would run in home from school and, without taking off his gloves, play any piece of music which happened to be on the piano. For all the thickness of the Wharf-street walls his

evening practices could be heard by the children next door. They
had their own name for him. He was The Banger. Apart from the
Wharf-street piano, the parlour harmonium and the lessons with
Mrs. Tinkler, there was the Church of St. John Baptist, third
node of his musical initiation. With its embattled tower and pin-
nacles and bells that date back to the Stuarts, St. John's stands at
the top of a street that winds steeply down to the Welland. Its
position is somewhat that of an outpost or look-out. While first
absorbing music there as an infant, his legs a-dangle in a front pew
as father rehearsed the choir, Malcolm drank in the oldness and
beauty and oddities of the place. Though not missing a note, he
would stare up at the roof where a flight of carved and painted angels,
sixteen of them, spread their wings and stared with blank, innocent
faces. Each angel carried some symbol or token: fiddle, sceptre,
crown, shield, sackbut, handbell, spear, nails, crown of thorns, a
bottle containing the Wrath of God. There were boards on the
ancient honeycoloured walls with patrons' and rectors' names
painted on them. The rectors' roll included Henry Sergaunt,
Master of Arts, inducted in 1473, to whom there is a memorial brass
near the choir chancel. Could Sargent be a corruption of Sergaunt?
The matter was often pondered. Malcolm's own belief later in life
was that his surname derived from a French one, Des Argents, and
that his forebears came over at the Conquest.

When the time came Malcolm sang in the choir as alto leader
with the confidence of one who is always on pitch and knows his
way about musical print. That he should have been admitted to the
choir only after he had learned to read words was rational enough.
By that time, however, he was musically prepared up to the hilt. He
could read a chant at sight and get it note-perfect before he could
read the Psalms. There was nothing surprising about that, he used
to say long afterwards. Since music had only seven 'letters', few
rules and no exceptions, it was natural that a child should find it
relatively easy to learn.

Then the organ. At that time the only 'three-manual' in Stamford,
the organ of St. John's was perhaps forty years old when Malcolm
first played it as his father's pupil. For want of overhaul and
replacements it tended to creak and complain. Springs were rusting.

Worm had got into the wood. The boy had to wrestle with a cum-
bersome and already obsolete tracker action. To produce a note you
depressed a key that lifted a 'sticker' that rolled a roller that deflected
an arm that moved a long, long lath a quarter of an inch wide by
one thirtieth thick that opened a pallet in the wind chest that let
through the wind that sounded the selected pipe or pipes. Young
fingers were quickly fatigued by a chain process that seemed to be
modelled on The House that Jack Built. Young legs found the
archaic swell-box control even tougher. You had to kick a stick out
of a notch and press it down with all your weight. If you didn't take
care, the swing of the swell-box shutters could lift you clean off your
seat.

Instead of putting him off, these toils and hazards stimulated the
boy. Mechanically considered the tracker action was as engrossing
as his bicycle, more so, perhaps. Those archaic trackers could
summon up a rumbling, trumpeting reverberation far grander than
could be got from any piano in the world.

Henry Sargent watched his son's progress with pride. His highest
ambition for the boy was that he should become a cathedral organist.
Before Malcolm's birth he had said, 'If it's a boy I shall make him a
musician'. Agnes Sargent had other ideas. Cathedral organs were
few, musicians in general poorly paid and often out of work. Her
notion was that Malcolm should 'go into a bank'. All they had to do
was lay the matter before Mr. Sandall. Old Tom Sandall, an eminent
member of the St. John's vestry, was an admirer of young Malcolm's
playing both in and out of church. More important, he had been in
banking for fifty years and could arrange suitable introductions. The
boy had a good head for many subjects outside music. He had in
him the makings of a first-rate mathematician or scientist. So said a
headmaster of Stamford (Grammar) School. Before returning to
music a glance, then, at the rounding off of his general education.

*

Like many of the town's institutions and ideas, Stamford Grammar
School (the 'Grammar' prefix disappeared on its achieving public
school status in 1920) was very old and, on that account among

others, hallowed. It had been going since 1532. Whoever expected
to *be* anybody in Stamford could not hope to get far unless he had
'Kissed the Old Man' (see below).

In 1907 six 'free' places were offered. Of these five were won in
competitive examination by Blue Coat boys. Malcolm was one of
the five. He went in at the age of twelve and came out at fifteen. His
fees, about ten pounds a term, were taken care of by the county
council. On his first day, like other new boys, he was mobbed and
thumped and pinched by his seniors, hoisted on to a big boy's back
and made to kiss a time-worn head carved on the keystone of the
'Old School'. During various phases of the school's history, and this
was one of them, Kissing the Old Man was an obligatory induction.
For boys of gentle manners and pursuits it could be something of an
ordeal.

The 'Old School', once a church, still had a churchy look and
smell. The place could be very cold in winter. The boys sat on
benches and did their lessons at tables which at one time were
partitioned off from each other in the manner of pews or old-
fashioned eating houses. At one end hung a bell and a large, loud
clock.* Of the sixty to eighty boys in Malcolm's time up to a third
were boarders. It was the boarders who suffered the full impact of
Mr. Lovegrove's spartan regime. The day boys did not wholly
escape, however. Taking over the headmastership from the benign
Dr. Barnard a few months before Malcolm's enrolment, Edwin
William Lovegrove, a mathematics scholar and impassioned amateur
carpenter, decreed cold baths daily (the bathrooms were without hot
water anyway), four-mile runs when work finished on whole days,
ten-mile runs on half-holidays, cross-country walks on Sunday
mornings to selected churches so far away that the boarders never
sat down to dinner before half-past two, and further trudges to
outlying churches for evensong. The runs were held in all weathers.
Malcolm would appear at Wharf-road in his running things caked
with mud from head to foot. His mother would shoo him into the
kitchen and run a portable bath from the kitchen-range boiler. With
Lovegrove's arrival, games of all kinds took up more time and became
more of a test. It was common talk among teachers in the Midlands

* The 'Old School' was reconsecrated in 1930 and became the School chapel.

that many a Stamford Grammar School boy was saved from being 'ploughed' in exams by doing well at the Easter term sports.

A brisk innovator, Lovegrove scrapped the old school song, which Dr. Barnard had written and composed, in favour of *Dolce domum* and changed the school over from Soccer to Rugby football. It was in a Rugby scrum that Malcolm suffered a shoulder dislocation and injury that were to delay his call-up during the Kaiser's war. For years, it seems, he was able by rotating the injured shoulder to put it out of joint and in again repeatedly, with a bizarre clicking noise. As any master could see with half an eye, he had more of the dreamer in him than the average boy. It was conveyed to Lovegrove that Malcolm's dreams were about music and that he had rare musical talent. Although without any ear for music himself, Lovegrove after a while let the boy off games altogether. During games periods 'Mal' practised on the school piano. On speech days he officially accompanied the school choir and was always at the piano when *Dulce domum* was called for. In a community that observed uncommonly rigid discipline he had a niche to himself; he was acknowledged to be rather apart, the sort of personality for whom special rules are made as a matter of course. We shall see how he contrived discreet privileges for himself as a private soldier in the Army.

Under Lovegrove there was no time in the curriculum for music. Nor could it be said that under Lovegrove's predecessor Stamford had been a distinctively musical school. For twenty years, however, there had been an avid musical ear and practitioner at the top. Although he had retired from the headmastership at about the time Malcolm was sitting for his scholarship from the Blue Coat School, Dr. Barnard did much to develop the boy's musical insights and experience, not as a teacher (though for an amateur his musical scholarship was impressive) but as a lover and maker of chamber music.

CHAPTER FOUR

TRACKER ACTION

IF DR. BARNARD had not been bland and kindly by nature his love of learning might have taken a grotesque turn. On speech days he would give his address in English and his jokes in Latin. The boys didn't understand the jokes but laughed in the right places because he always gave an anticipatory chuckle; they knew when a joke was coming. To the end of his days, after retirement as well as before, he wore the garb of his calling. The white mutton-chop whiskers were as much a part of this as the frock coat, dog collar and tall hat. Meeting some musical crony in the street, he would fish up from his tail pocket a pasteboard oblong and invite the crony to have a look at his 'latest'. On these oblongs he wrote tunes of his own composition which read the same back to front and were identical when seen through a looking glass and when looked at plain. He had read in Stainer and Barnett's dictionary of musical terms that productions of the cancrizans or retrograde class were 'utterly valueless' as works of art. But that wasn't the point. For him they were a source of innocent fun: and that was vindication enough.

He and his son and two daughters lived in one of the 'well-off' houses up Tinwell-road. Just as all Stamfordians were expected to pass through Stamford Grammar School if they wanted to get anywhere, so a house in Tinwell-road was an accepted sign that its owner had arrived at substance and esteem. The Barnards' house stood in a high walled garden. It had a library lined to the ceiling with books. In the library stood a piano. On this piano for several years before and during the Kaiser's War, Malcolm played almost weekly in classical trios, Dr. Barnard and his grown-up daughter Dora playing fiddle and 'cello respectively on opposite sides of the fireplace. Their favourite trios were those of Beethoven and Mendelssohn. As soon as they had got through both sets they would start all over again. Papa's violin playing was atrocious. He was usually out of tune and always slowed down in quick passages; semiquavers made him snuffle with anxiety.

It was Miss Dora's habit while playing one string to touch the others accidentally. Occasionally Malcolm would refer light-heartedly to novel double-stopping effects. But hints had no effect. Dora never seemed to realize what she had been doing. The Barnards had either a special gift for not hearing what they didn't want to hear or an equally remarkable one for pretending they hadn't. On his thirteenth birthday Malcolm was given a repeater-watch. Half way through a Mendelssohn slow movement the alarm went off in his waistcoat pocket. It went on for half a minute. Inhibited by embarrassment, he didn't say or do a thing except go on playing. The others did likewise. This was a sort of situation they hadn't heard of or imagined. Therefore it didn't exist. On this night as on so many others, Malcolm had dinner with the Barnards after the music and the instruments had been put away. In a modest way it was a hospitable house. Old Barnard was as proud of his collection of teacups and saucers as of his cancrizans inventions. He had a hundred or two pairs, each pattern distinct from the next, on a bristle of hooks and wire claws in the butler's pantry. The collection was numbered, and the pairs were used in rotation. It took a long time for the first cup and saucer to come round again. The same rule was applied to them as to the string trios. You got to the end and you started again. Most townspeople looked on the Barnards as amiable eccentrics who kept themselves to themselves and lived, mainly for music, in a world of their own. Yet they were very much of their town and their time; it is hard to imagine their teacups and trios in any other milieu. The very imperfection of their playing, that of the old man especially, helped to season Malcolm as a practical musician, one whose concern it would be during the next dozen years or so to help many relatively impractical musicians over technical stiles.

*

Beyond the stiles lay a country of gods and tremors and convulsions. Among the gods Beethoven was greatest. The years when he was first going through the trios with the Barnards were the years of his first exploring the sonatas. His original set of BEETHOVEN: SONATEN is a Peters volume with title gilt-tooled on cocoa-brown over a *neues Kunst* harp design in shiny black. He inked his name in boyish hand on the front cover and on the flyleaf with date: October 1910.

The phrase 'tremors and convulsions' was no empty metaphor in his case. For his case, as an adolescent, was rare. Making his way through the Peters edition at the Wharf-road piano he found himself confronted one spring evening by the slow movement (*largo e mesto*) of Op. 10 No. 3 in D major. The crux of the confrontation was the return of the main subject with added chordal weight. At the third bar of the recapitulation a re-shaped bass line upheaves a dissonant F octave against the G of a diminished triad. It was this 'upheaved' octave, incomparably more mordant than anything hinted at in the exposition, that savaged the boy.

He played the crucial bar a second time. Then he jumped up from the piano and, leaving the house, walked blindly uphill through the dusk. His heart pounded. His head was in tumult. From the tumult one plain thought emerged. Music was a terrible power; a power not to be endured. Sitting down at the roadside somewhere on the grassy outskirts of the town, he wept and prayed to God that he should *not* be musical any more. Music was a burning, possessing force, a thing to fear and run away from. It was a torment. He prayed God to deliver him from it lest he should be driven mad. Telling of this long afterwards he reflected: 'I didn't go mad. One adapts oneself to shattering experiences. One is shattered by one's first kiss, but one goes on kissing.'

The little Sargent boy, it used to be said, was 'always' fainting in church while with the choir; some adult would carry him into the open and his mother would rub his hands to bring him to. What looked like bilious attacks were brought on by the emotional pressure of the service music. The simplest harmonic sequences could upset his circulation startlingly. As a youthful organist at Melton Mowbray not many years later he felt his arms and legs go numb and prickly, as though 'asleep', one Easter Sunday morning while he was accompanying a Psalm. Looking into the console mirror he saw that his eyes were bloodshot. Afterwards he mentioned this to a doctor friend, who explained that even simple music when coupled with religious feeling was enough to impart an emotional shock. This would drive the blood to his head and suffuse his sclerotics.

Along with emotional vulnerability went uncommon brightness, alertness and hardheadedness in matters of musical practice and theory. There is a surviving reminder of this on the very sonata page which unleashed the emotional storm in him. Pencilled over the *largo e mesto* movement of the D major Op. 10 is his own metronome marking: 60 quavers to the minute. Many of the other sonatas have pencillings that break down this movement and that into first and second subjects, links, recapitulation, rondo 'episodes', coda, key relationships and other constituents. He zestfully spots a scherzo in square time (that of Op. 31 No. 3), the first such movement ever to be written in other than three-four time, he claims. Of Op. 26, the one with the famous *marcia funebra*, he writes: 'In this Sonata there are no movements in sonata form.' Here and there he pencilled in *crescendo* and *decrescendo* signs which had not occurred to the Peters editor. On the index page all thirty-two sonatas are numbered with red ink in what he conceived to be their cumulative order of difficulty, No. 20 Op. 39 No. 2 (easiest) coming first, No. 29 Op. 106 (the 'Hammerklavier') last.

By this time his formal general education was over (he left Stamford Grammar School in the summer of 1910 after three years there); he had resumed his lessons with Frances Tinkler and was taking others (organ and harmony) with P. J. Murrell, organist and choirmaster at All Saints Church. How his career would shape he could not yet surmise. But certainly it was going to be a musical one. 'Going into a bank' had somehow become unthinkable. He knew he would have to work hard and pass 'exams'. To this end he did something long dreamed of. One weekday morning he went into the front parlour, hitherto used on Sundays only, and put his inkwell and pens on the parlour table; also a pair of bookrests with an algebra and a Latin grammar between them, nucleus of a library that grew to twenty volumes in a matter of weeks. Without asking anybody if he might do so, 'Mal' had annexed the parlour, which from then on, except for Sundays, was his study, a place where he could work undisturbed. There had been career discussions with his father. Henry Sargent took the view that music wasn't quite so precarious a vocation as his mother had made out. Admittedly there were 50,000 music teachers in England and Wales, but there was always room for one teacher more, provided he were clever enough, just as there was always room for a good church organist.

'But,' added Henry Sargent, 'I must lay down one thing. You are fifteen. You'll have to start earning your living by eighteen or drop music altogether and earn it some other way. At eighteen you'll be under your own steam.' (Sargent's comment in retrospect: 'My father was wise. It's a great adventure to have no money. Poverty compels you to use whatever talent you have. A young man with empty pockets doesn't hide his light under a bushel or let it go out.')

On the parlour harmonium he did transposition exercises. He had started these in a serious way when fourteen; during one school holiday he had transposed the entire hymn-book, starting each hymn in C and squealing his way through the key cycle. He could now play a multitude of things from memory in any key at a moment's notice. One result of this self-training was that he knew all there is to know about transposing instruments – horns, trumpets, clarinets and the like which (bewilderingly to the layman) are written for in one key and sound in another—long before he first mounted an orchestral rostrum or composed a degree cantata. He knew, incidentally, that he would have to pass transposition tests (and many others) when he sat for his organ examination in London.

*

He did this in January 1912. There had been preliminary guineas to pay. One guinea accompanied a nomination form signed by Murrell and another Stamford organist which secured him formal enrolment as a member of the Royal College of Organists. Two guineas more were paid as advance examination fee. A week before examination day he went up to London and for half a crown had an hour's practice on the 'official' organ at the R.C.O.'s headquarters in Kensington Gore, a building fronted in terracotta and cream stucco, with such elaborate allegorical friezes and panels that it looks remarkably like an organ itself. The organ room was sparsely hung with gloomy enlarged photographs of great English cathedrals. Its windows looked on to the vast drum of the Royal Albert Hall.

Built eight years earlier, the organ had three manuals, a radiating pedal board and an impressive specification. The really prodigious things, however, were its action ('tubular pneumatic') and its balancer swell-pedal. The candidates had ten 'set' pieces to choose from, as usual. That year the list ran from Bach (three numbers) and Buxtehude through Mendelssohn and Henry Smart to Rheinberger's Sonata in B minor (Fantasie and Finale only). Malcolm had chosen the Rheinberger.

Having toiled for so long with a reluctant tracker action and stubborn swell-box shutters, his fingers and feet suddenly took on wings: he had never imagined such amenable keys and pedals, so light a touch, so swift a response. (Other times, other tastes. According to Sir William McKie, sometime honorary secretary of the R.C.O. and formerly Master of Music at Westminster Abbey, the R.C.O. organ, improved and extended in 1931, was regarded by typical students of the mid-1960s as 'terrible old junk' because not of the 'baroque' type.) The boy felt like a conqueror and wore a conqueror's grin. He would have liked to play for a further hour. This, he was told, was out of the question. Other candidates were awaiting their turns. During the six weeks preceding the examinations practice time was rationed to one hour per candidate.

Before catching his return train to Stamford that afternoon, he browsed along booksellers' bargain boxes in the Charing Cross-road and picked up two vocal scores in fairly good condition, *Messiah* and Bach's B minor Mass, for threepence.

*

On the appointed date he was back at Kensington Gore by cheap 'day return'. He was no longer a name but a number. All candidates were to be anonymous. And, as far as possible, they were to be unseen. He had been given a precise time for his organ playing tests and was asked to be on the spot a quarter of an hour in advance. The candidates awaited call in chronological batches of three in the library. There was a cheerful coal fire. Malcolm warmed his hands at it, read the spines of organ classics which crammed the big mahogany bookcase. He was noticeably spruce. Already clothes meant much to him. He exchanged a civil word with the two others who had been bracketed to wait with him. One appeared to be in his late twenties, the other a few years older. That year there were 222 candidates for Associateship. At sixteen he was the youngest of all but didn't learn this until later.

The signal from the organ room was by buzzer. When Malcolm's buzz sounded he walked up two flights of chill stairs and was received in the organ room by a functionary who accepted the slip bearing his number and disappeared with it behind a green curtain, obviously a temporary rig, which mysteriously cut off the organ half of the hall from the other half. On the far side of this curtain, in the manner of Beckmessers, three eminences sat at a big table with the selected score of the moment open before them.* Other scores were piled on chairs near at hand. The three examiners in 1912, all Fellows of the College as well as doctors of music, occupied or were on their way to distinguished organ benches. They were: Alcock of the Chapel Royal, Sweeting of Winchester College, and Bairstow, soon to be in charge of music at York Minster. Having handed over Malcolm's number slip and assured the examiners that morning tea was on the way, the functionary returned and sat alongside the candidate to transmit signals and turn over the pages when necessary.

As instructions came from behind the curtain, Malcolm successively transposed some hymn tune from A natural to E flat, using pedals; played from a vocal score in four parts (in later life he could not remember what it was), three parts being in the G clef, one in the F clef; and accompanied in Anglican style two men and a boy who sprang up from nowhere to sing a canticle of the examiners' choice. None of these tests gave him much trouble. Such exercises had become second nature to him on parish organs at home. Then the examiners invited him to the Rheinberger movements. Again his feet and fingers were winged. There was no doubt in his mind

* The green curtain was abolished in the early 1950s because the 'impersonality' of it worried some of the candidates.

that he had made an impression. At the finish Walter Alcock appeared from behind the curtain. He was smiling from ear to ear.

'As soon as I saw that smile,' Malcolm said to his father afterwards, 'I knew I had passed.'

The day was not over, however.

With a score or two others he sat down to written work in the examination hall on the top floor. Each candidate had a schoolroom desk with metal slot for his number slip. Again he could see the Albert Hall through a glazed door which gave access to the fire escape. 'If the questions are too stiff,' he jested, nodding towards the fire escape, 'there's always *that*.' The fellow candidate thus addressed gave an anxious start. He was not humorously inclined. Working against the clock under the invigilator's eye, Malcolm wrote counterpoint exercises ('simple' variety in up to four parts, combined species in not more than three); an 'answer' to a specific fugue subject and an appropriate counter-subject; and a two-hundred-word essay on the structure of the symphony orchestra *circa* 1840. He was questioned on how to train a church choir, how organs were built and how they worked; how passacaglias are put together and how analysts take classical sonata form apart.

Then the ear tests. An examiner went to the piano. First he played a figured bass, then an unaccompanied melody which he had composed himself. He repeated both twice. The candidates had to write them down by ear and harmonize them. Finally the examiner played three chords that weren't closely related or didn't seem to be. The candidates were asked to write a harmonic sequence which would embody the three chords and make sense of them. . . .

So ended what must have been a gruelling day for most of the candidates. For some of the examiners the sessions were even worse. Indeed, the three behind the curtain in the organ room felt almost victimized. There were three consecutive days when, working from ten in the morning until half past six at night, they passed only six candidates. In their report they wrung their hands over ' . . . lamentable musicianship . . . rests commonly neglected . . . inaccurate note values . . . want of freedom and fluency . . . wrong pedal notes held for several bars. . . . No one could have sung to many of the hymn tunes as performed.' Out of the year's entry 172 candidates were ploughed. The remaining fifty were awarded diplomas. A man of forty came out on top. Malcolm got the second highest number of marks. He won a prize of five pounds and spent it on a musical dictionary, *Beethoven and his Nine Symphonies* (Grove) and *Studies of the Great Composers* (Sir Hubert Parry). Thus, at sixteen, he became H. Malcolm Sargent A.R.C.O. A congratulatory item appeared in the *Mercury*. Henry Sargent went bustling and beaming all over the town with the news.

Yet was there not something faintly anomalous about the occasion? Everybody in Stamford revered church organs or paid lip service to them. But weren't they rather an *elderly* instrument? Did they not make one think rather of frock-coated gentlemen nearing fifty than of fresh-cheeked adolescents? Three or four years later, as will be seen, Malcolm was to confer upon one church organ in particular a quasi-social vogue that reflected alike his personality and his talent. Meantime, organs in general were, to some ears and minds, on the frumpish side. There were musical pundits here and there who admitted as much or put up a lame, jocular defence. In a speech at the diploma-giving ceremony that year, Sir Walter Parratt, who had the St. George's Chapel organ at Windsor, conceded that 'most people who are musicians and not organists'—which was not quite what he meant to say—looked down on the instrument. However, he went on, the organist wasn't *such* a dull fellow nowadays. 'When he gets away from the organ he's often quite skittish!'

At another College function Sir Hubert Parry, on the other hand, named dullness, daughter of respectability ('horrid word!') as the organist's besetting danger. This was a dig at the 'anti-transcriptionists'. Broadcast music hadn't been heard of. The gramophone had hardly reached the threshold of symphonic music. What more natural, in the provinces especially, than that the enterprising organist with an adequate instrument should entertain himself and his congregation with transcriptions of orchestral classics? 'The organist who can play the Prelude and Liebestod from *Tristan and Isolde*,' said Parry, 'is a better musician then one who contents himself with an easy Bach organ fugue.' And Sargent was to declare that nobody had really lived if he had not played *The Ride of the Valkyries* on a cathedral organ, coupling pedals to Tuba for Brünnhilde's

warcry. Parratt and his school would have none of this. 'The organ,'
he lamented, 'has given up its proper métier, that of being an organ,
in attempting quite unsuccessfully to be an imitation orchestra.'

To this Malcolm would probably have replied that even in
transcriptions the organ remained itself and couldn't pretend to be
other. As technical and 'colour' media, organ and orchestra were
different worlds. He could speak from personal knowledge of both.
He was a crack player of the one and, in a tentative way, had begun
to conduct the other.

CHAPTER FIVE

FIRST BATON

H E FIRST conducted an orchestra when fourteen; and this is how it came about. He made a point, as has been said, of attending the rehearsals of the amateur operatic society each winter. Many of these were 'band' rehearsals; most of the players non-professionals. Such professionals or semi-professionals as were brought in, usually to 'stiffen' the wind section, rather intimidated the gently-bred amateurs; they had dinner jacket suits shiny at the knees, exchanged arcane jokes behind their hands and drew fiercely on their cigarettes. The one professional who inspired deference, because she was 'part of the town', was Mrs. Tinkler, who, although the Sullivan scores do not call for anything of the sort, 'filled out' on the piano, as was customary in amateur pits. Malcolm 'turned over' for her. Once he was seconded to the kettle-drums and was allowed to play them at one public performance.

The Stamford society's choice for 1910 was *The Yeomen of the Guard*. There were to be three evening performances and one matinée in the Corn Exchange at the beginning of February. The orchestral rehearsals went on for months. One rehearsal night, late in 1909, was so foggy that the trains stopped running. The society's conductor, Amos Ebenezer Armstrong,* telephoned that he could not get over from Peterborough. What followed was all over the town next day and became a legend that varied with the teller.

* Conductor of several musical bodies in the Midlands, including Peterborough Choral Society and local orchestra; organist; father of Sir Thomas Armstrong, who in 1955 became Principal of the Royal Academy of Music.

What seems to have happened was that Mrs. Tinkler turned to Malcolm, who as usual was seated alongside her, and said:

'*You*'d better conduct.'

'Oh no!' he objected, 'I couldn't possibly do that, Tinkie.' (Few instances are on record of his declining to conduct anything. One of them occurred in 1955, when he turned down Aaron Copland's Symphony No. 3, which he was asked to do at Edinburgh Festival. While very clever, it had 'nothing here', he complained, touching his chest.)

'Of course you can do it', insisted Mrs. Tinkler. After a word with some of the principals she came back with the stick. Handing it to him, she nodded towards the rostrum and said, 'Now you get up there. They're waiting.'

Malcolm's line later was that Mrs. Tinkler and the rest were being playful and that he took their joke seriously. From the piano at home and from previous rehearsals he knew every bar of *The Yeomen*. He conducted with a briskness and fluency that fell on him from nowhere, like a mantle. When he had to pull the players up he rapped the desk and told people three times his age to tighten their rhythm and shape their phrases. For two hours he was their leader, ageless in his authority. Laying down his stick at the finish he suddenly looked fourteen again. There were a lot of clapping and bravoing and shouts of 'Well done!' No doubt about it: Harry Sargent's boy was a marvel. He was chaired downstairs and into the street.

*

This was the beginning. As he began, so he went on.

'It was they who asked me to conduct', he told me forty or fifty years later. 'I have never sought a conducting job in my life. I have always taken the work that comes my way. When work stops coming my way I'll stop conducting.' Another claim was more notable still. 'That night in Stamford,' he went on, 'I found myself using a natural stick technique. I have been using the same technique ever since. When I say "natural" I mean something I was born with. My conducting gestures were entirely unconscious, as they are to this day. No gesture for gesture's sake. The purpose of all stick and left-arm movements is to give your players the rhythm and feeling of a piece. My rostrum technique is entirely functional. I discovered it that foggy night.'

In the years that immediately followed, music theory and organ and piano practice were what occupied him most. Bent on getting music degrees extra-murally and on becoming a fashionable concert pianist, he studied and practised with a sort of happy fury. Conducting chances were few. But Stamford was beginning to adapt itself to the century. At Claypoles in Red Lion Square you could buy gramophones as well as pianos from ten shillings a month up. And the gramophones played discs, not cylinders. A second gramophone shop, newly opened in Maiden-lane, called itself Riley's Talkeries. On weekday nights and Saturday afternoons the Oddfellows' Hall became The Electric Picturedrome, with seats as cheap as a penny. The 'fleapit', as it was called, could not afford a band. Instead it employed a pianist, in due course one Harold Rudd, who was to take organ lessons from Malcolm at All Saints. By this time the Sargents had left Wharf-road (Marion Sargent had come to dislike the locality) and were settled in a sober but handsomer looking house up the hill at All Saints-street, with a sitting-room-cum-dining-room room (big improvement on the old living-room-kitchen) and an equally big garden where later on Henry Sargent built a minute house with a door which his pet tortoise was trained to enter and leave by. The Electric Picturedrome was just over the way from No. 11. Sometimes on Saturday afternoons, when the hall was crammed and rowdy with children, Malcolm would slip across, sit by Harold Rudd at the piano and help 'fit' the films with music which they extemporized in part. Already Malcolm's personality was beginning to obsess people. Rudd quoted him often. 'Malcolm says,' he would report, 'that one day he is going to conduct a big symphony orchestra.' At the time with which we are dealing this ambition had not occurred to him. He knew a lot about big symphony orchestras from books but hadn't yet heard one. Meantime there were other orchestras, the little local ones. Malcolm quickly took the measure of these, their personalities and their potentials.

The town's orchestral organizer or 'fixer', to borrow professional slang for an amateur context, was Herbert T. Parrish, a flourishing tradesman; he and other Parrishes did well and were to do better out of the family business: a group of outfitters' shops (school uniforms were an important line) in Stamford and Peterborough. Considered by many as aloof and perhaps a bit odd, Bertie Parrish had a pointed nose in a round face and could be seen six days of the week behind his counter in the High-street. His spare time and thoughts were on music and nothing else. He had sung in St. John's Church choir for Henry Sargent and owned three clarinets, a C, a B flat and an A. All three were splendid instruments. Their pitch, unfortunately, was handicappingly high. The poor man always played sharp—'an awkward anomaly'. Sargent used to recall. There was nothing off the note about his 'fixing' operations, however. He knew what the town's amateur players and professional fringe were up to from one end of the season to the other and shook string bands, piano quintets, Haydn-sized orchestras and the like out of his sleeve with unfailing certainty as to time, place and programme.

One thing he could not guarantee was a high degree of proficiency on the part of all players. Sargent's memories of comic shortcoming are too many. A student from a crammer's though he could play first horn. Owing to the shortage of horn players he was encouraged for a while in this illusion. Taking his place on the Assembly Rooms platform one night he found he had left his mouthpiece at home. 'A providential thing', commented Sargent. ('But,' he added in a marginal note to my typescript, 'I've always half thought that Parrish had hidden it!') There was also the case of the irrepressible percussion player. Sargent was making his first attempt at Mozart's G minor Symphony. In this score there are no percussion parts. Yet five minutes before the rehearsal a man he had never seen before trundled on a full kit: bass drum, sidedrum, cymbals, triangle, tambourine, everything. In some confusion the concert secretary whispered: 'Oh, this is Mr. X. He has come five miles with his instruments. He's gone to a lot of trouble. He pushed them all the way by trolley.'

'But,' objected Sargent, 'there's nothing for him to play.'

'Does that matter? You really *must* use him. He can make up anything.'

Sargent was adamant and began the rehearsal under the impression that Mr. X had agreed to keep quiet. During the first movement, however, Mr. X began to improvise a brilliant sidedrum part. Sargent rapped the music to a standstill.

'This won't do at all,' he whispered to the secretary.

'But,' objected the secretary, 'we can't just tell him to stop and send him away. Some other time we shall really need him.'

Sargent got out of the dilemma by giving Mr. X a horn part and telling him to play it softly on the bass drum, first laying his instrument on its side. 'Of course', commented Sargent afterwards, 'he couldn't play pitched notes. Admittedly it was a mischievous thing to do. But we silenced him on the night. *And* we kept a player who otherwise might have walked out on us.'

Among the town's more aristocratic fiddles was Mrs. Hesketh Fleetwood's. This was a Stradivarius. Lesser fiddlers spoke of it in hushed tones. There was no doubting Mrs. Fleetwood's musical fervour or that of her family. Did not the Fleetwoods have an organ in their house? But her regard for her 'Strad' was such that, on reaching the end of a page, she would lay the precious thing down on her knees, sometimes the bow as well, before turning over. Then there was a bank manager who played the flute, a beautiful silver one. It took him so long to get his embouchure, that is, to arrange his lips and tongue correctly about the mouth-hole, that the performance had usually moved on four bars before Malcolm got a sound out of him. Mrs. Fleetwood's turn-overs, on the other hand, took six to eight bars.

The liveliest and unlikeliest character of all was Richard Watts, second bassoon, unique among his kind in that he played his bassoon parts on the euphonium and nothing else. If anybody asked him why he didn't play bassoon parts on the bassoon he answered, 'Because I can't.' It was acknowledged by all, Malcolm included, that he played the euphonium uncommonly well. And in those days bassoons were as hard to come by as horns. Small and spry, with gingerish hair, 'Dickie' Watts combined under one hat the functions of secretary, director, draughtsman and designer with Blackstones, the agricultural implement makers. The haymaking and kindred machines which he designed or adapted sold in thousands at home and abroad, making a lot of money for the firm. He drove the second motor-car ever seen in Stamford (the first, with a goggled fifth Marquess of Exeter at the wheel, had caused a great stir) and invented a new internal combustion engine (he called it the synchro-balance type) which didn't come to anything. He is said to have reversed the Vicar of Wakefield's famous mistake. Instead of commissioning a family portrait too big to get into the house, he built a motor-car indoors which was too big to get out; a kitchen wall had to be taken down before it could reach the road. Still told with chuckles among elderly Stamfordians, this story, unlikely on the face of it, is discounted by contemporaries who remember his scientific method and temper. But the man was a born wag or, to use the language of the day, spoofer. It may be that one of his victims set the story going as a return compliment. His inventive itch extended to music. He experimented with a dual-speaker gramophone half a century before stereo reproduction; and rather than master the bassoon's key system lived in the hope of grafting euphonium valves on to that instrument. To this dubious end he produced sheaves of beautiful diagrams, took out French and Belgian patents and applied for patent rights at home and in Commonwealth countries. His dream didn't get further than the drawing-board, however. On amateur-operatic nights his euphonium continued to masquerade mooingly at the Assembly Rooms for a generation.

*

Bertie Parrish lined up his first orchestra for Malcolm, and Malcolm made his first public appearances as a conductor, on 24th and 25th July, 1912. The occasion was a two-day historical pageant in blazing weather; the theme of the pageant a state visit by Queen Elizabeth to the Burghleys at their White Friary estate, Stamford, in 1565. The site of the Friary was now occupied by the public infirmary in aid of whose funds the pageant was held in its grounds. As public appearances go, Malcolm's double début was secluded. Since he and his players wore everyday clothes which would have clashed with the swarm of hired Elizabethan costumes, they were hidden in a sort of tent behind the shrubbery. His strings included a lone viola sandwiched between eight violins, on the one hand, and two 'cellos (one of them Dora Barnard) and two double-basses on the other hand.

Parrish played second clarinet; and there were a French horn, drums and, at the piano, Mrs. Tinkler, who for some reason figured on the programme as Mistress of Musick. Malcolm not only conducted the music; he had chosen, arranged, rehearsed and dress-rehearsed it as well. Edward German was among the composers he had plundered; as the Queen (mounted) and cavalcade entered by the west gate, maidens scattered petals and children with ropes of flowers danced before her to airs from his *Henry VIII* suite. Queen Elizabeth was played by the Honourable Mrs. Pelham in primrose brocade, with large pearl drop on her forehead; Lord Burghley by a rector of aristocratic lineage; Lady Burghley by Mrs. de Courcy Daniell; and the Burghleys' daughter Jane by Lady Falkiner. Pride of rank did not go unchecked, however. Having presented his wife and family to the Queen and ensured places of honour for them, Burghley was about to do the same for another noble family when a class-conscious alderman intervened on behalf of Stamford's townsfolk and sought precedence for the 'civic supporters'. The Queen smilingly conceded his claim. The courtiers having thus been put in their place and burgher sentiment placated, Malcolm's band struck up with appropriate pages from *The Yeomen of the Guard* while beefeaters, laying aside their halberds, carried smoking roasts to the banqueting tables and a jester did a *pas seul* with thwacking bladder and jingling bells.

On the surface all was well again with Merrie England. But the radical note had made a certain impression. Some thought it rather daring on Thomas Sandall's part as author of the scenario. 'Tom' Sandall has been mentioned in a previous chapter as a Stamford bank manager—he was the town's leading one, indeed—for fifty years. So had his father been before him. His daughter, Charlotte Sophia ('Sophie'), now in her thirties, had lived in Germany and studied the language. She came back with heightened musical tastes. A girl of independent and, for her day, original tastes, she resolved to take up the organ and went to Henry Sargent for lessons at St. John's. In return she gave lessons in German to Malcolm who, newly captured and convulsed by *Der Erlkönig*, was intent on understanding the original texts of this and other great Lieder. According to season or weather, he took his German lessons in the garden or sitting-room at Rusholme Lodge, the Sandalls' home. He quickly mastered German pronunciation by ear. Syntax and vocabulary, or what he needed of them, he got by reading from German fairy tales and pausing between sentences for Sophie's running translations.

Occasionally Tom Sandall would stop by and listen benignly, stroking his beard. This Sargent boy, with his bright dark eyes, his lively, courteous talk and his dancing intelligence, was a rare one and likely to go far. What was this he had heard about his wanting to be articled to Dr. Keeton at Peterborough Cathedral? Professional articles cost money, and Henry Sargent, a likeable man, hadn't much of it. Mr. Sandall decided to see what could be done. Not long afterwards he made the following entry in his journal:

'Young Malcolm Sargent having distinguished himself in an Examination of the Royal College of Organists, and knowing of his desire to have a course of lessons from Dr. Keeton . . . which was an expensive matter, I mentioned a proposal to Canon Williams of raising a fund of £24 which would give him, Malcolm Sargent, a season ticket to Peterborough during three years. I easily collected this myself from 33 subscribers, including the Marquess of Exeter and the Mayor . . . and, having banked the amount, the cost of the Railway ticket quarterly is provided for.'

CHAPTER SIX

ORGAN LOFT

FIVE MORNINGS a week for over two years, starting in the
autumn of 1912, Malcolm caught an early train from the
Great Northern station. He reached Peterborough, twelve and
a half crawling miles away, in good time for the opening of Dr.
Haydn Keeton's 'musical workshop' at nine o'clock. Often he was
late out of the house and had to sprint. There were familiar faces on
the train. These were not the ones that interested him. He had
wagered with friends in the amateur operatic society to kiss a fresh
girl on the outward or inward journey every day. (A fellow conductor whom he told of this at a summer school in Oxford a decade
later twirled his military moustache non-committally. 'Don't you
like kissing girls?' Sargent challenged. 'Well, no,' replied the colleague. 'I was brought up to believe one doesn't do that sort of
thing.')

As he crossed the precincts of the Cathedral Church of St. Peter,
St. Paul and St. Andrew, he would note the play of light, a little
different each day, on the finials and flutings of the towering west
front. He had explored and re-explored the cathedral to the last
cranny and loved every stone of it. He had climbed corkscrew stairs,
roamed triforium and clerestory; knew the roof as well as he knew
the garden at home. From up there he would look down upon snug
prebendal houses and medieval boundary walls with roses spilling
over them; and upon monastic traces, some of them grotesque or
squalid. Surviving gothic arches had been domesticated; they
framed the bright doorknobs and window casements of a later age
and hierarchy. Here and there lancet windows blocked with boards
or brick or chickenwire looked blindly out on to vestigial stumps of

cloister. All this and much more he had drunk in. Now it was part of him. It would not be true, however, to say that he was ever part of it.

Dr. Keeton's 'workshop', or one section of it, was the choir practice room, later turned to other uses. Under the ancient vaulted roof rows of singing desks faced each other alongside a small two-manual organ. At the singing desks choristers (as distinct from the choirmen, who had a different routine) were exercised every morning in the service music they were to sing at mattins and evensong. It was Malcolm's routine task, or some other articled pupil's, to accompany the boys at the little organ, which he used at other times for practice on his own account. Before the boys began he would hand over to Keeton the counterpoint and harmony exercises he had been set the day before. The two other articled pupils, or apprentices, did likewise. These two were Philip Taylor, later organist of Magdalen College, Oxford, about the same age as himself; and Thomas Armstrong, who was three years younger. Before becoming articled to Keeton (as his father, Amos Ebenezer Armstrong, had been before him), Tom had been a 'child' of the Chapel Royal, St. James's. In London he had learned and heard much. A year or two before their first meeting at the cathedral, Malcolm had glimpsed him on a railway station platform. Tom was getting out of the London train. Home for the holidays, he was in his Chapel Royal uniform, blue with red pipings like the Stamford bandsmen's but of different cut. In the practice room on their first morning together, Malcolm said, 'When I saw you in your red and blue I said to myself, "The lucky beggar!"' 'Why?' inquired Tom modestly. 'Because of all that London music,' exclaimed Malcolm—'and you in the thick of it!'

London seemed a longer way off than ever. Keeton's gruff ways, bulky moustache and white mane, the sheer weight and tension of his presence, turned London into an improbable, unattainable place. He drove everything out of boys' heads but the daily stints of theory he set them and how they would acquit themselves at the console when called in rotation to play the cathedral's great four-manual organ at mattins. When Malcolm came to him Keeton was in his seventies, strong as an oak and good looking in the heavy manner of W. S. Gilbert. He had been cathedral organist at Peterborough for over forty years and was the twenty-first of his line since the first appointment recorded, that of Richard Storey, in 1540. His teaching system and tradition, so far as the apprentices were concerned, dated back to Storey's day if not beyond in some respects. That system was lapsing and disintegrating; another twelve years or so would see the end of it. From the middle 1920s onward, all advanced musical teaching of an official sort would be channelled through the central music schools and colleges and the music departments of the universities.

In 1912 Peterborough Cathedral was one of two or three remaining establishments of its kind where, as had been happening for centuries, the master-of-music would enter into legally binding compacts with parents to take complete charge of their boys' musical education. The parents or sponsors paid fees, of course. In return they had the satisfaction of knowing that their boys would learn how to train and handle choirs and how to accompany them at the organ in a vast literature of service and ancillary music. They knew that on top of this they would be trained as pianists and sightreaders as well as in those mysteries and jargons of key, clef, chord and polyphony which were essential to the practical musician in any branch of the art—even if he should join the backstage musical staff at, say, the Royal Opera. What most parents had in mind for their sons was not the Royal Opera, however, but a nice berth as organist and choirmaster in some well endowed parish, with teaching connections (piano and singing lessons mainly) on the side, to supplement a small though steady salary.

Some of Keeton's apprentices came to him, as Malcolm and Tom Armstrong did, with preliminary training and evident talent. No matter. Clever and callow alike faced martinet treatment. The first sessions in the practice room must have been scaring even for the self-possessed. Occasionally he would smack a boy's head for a wrong note at the practice organ, not violently but hard enough to make the links rattle in his starched cuff. Three canes were propped against the wall just inside the doorway so that the newcomer should not fail to see them. One of them had a label tied to it which read: DR. KEETON'S CHORISTER'S SINGING METHOD. This was a sardonic quotation. Keeton had brought out a manual with the same title a year or two earlier. The canes, said Sargent, had two purposes. Beating time was *one* of them. Armstrong remembers three purposes. When some anthem-part went awry, Keeton would thwack his desk or **a** choirboy's behind according to the seriousness of the fault. His bottom thwackings were no more violent than his cuffings. He is recalled, without any sentimentality, as one of those outward ogres who are all kindness inside. He worked hard and conscientiously; thought nothing of detaining the whole choir after service for an extra hour's rehearsal if they had sung a faulty 'Amen'; had vast musical learning of a specialized sort; and knew precisely what he was about in his teaching tactics. Everything composed after Mendelssohn he lumped together as 'modern' and disliked, or at least 'distrusted', the lot, heard or unheard.

The paper work he set was ingenious and wide-ranging. He thought of everything and did a lot of humming. He would hum a *cantus firmus* to which Malcolm, having noted it down, would be required to add two or more parts within the strait-jacket of 'strict counterpoint'. The exercises became tougher week by week. Soon he was doing strict counterpoint in eight parts. All the rules had to be observed. Some notes could sound together. Others couldn't. For the dull boy it was a torment. Keeton had a quick eye for forbidden fruits. On spotting consecutive fifths he would exclaim with the glee of one exposing a fraud or felony, 'There they are, plump as partridges!' If anybody had told him that since Debussy consecutive fifths were all the rage, he would have retorted that, though the world at large might be wrong in the head, he didn't mean to go off his. He never set an exercise which he couldn't do himself. Many, indeed, he had done already. When a pupil came to him with a melody which he had been told to score and harmonize for string choir or use as a theme, adding two variations, the whole to be fully harmonized, he would turn up one of his manuscript books which contained scores of exercises in 'model' form as composed by himself decades earlier. Running his finger along the staves, he would show his pupil where he had departed from the model and where he had conformed with it.

Usually he corrected and marked paper work up in the organ loft at mattins, choosing times (prayers and reading of lessons) when no

music was being sung or played. If an exercise was good, the pupil
was rewarded with a grunt and set a more difficult one for the following day. If an exercise was bad he screwed it up and threw it into a
wastepaper basket alongside the console. The counterpoint and
harmony he taught were of the classical Viennese school and derived
basically from Albrechtsberger, a senior contemporary and sometime teacher of Beethoven. No foundation could have been better
even for those who hankered after new harmonies and 'incorrect'
part-writing.

*

So much for theory. Without practical work all the theory in the
world would have been pointless. After the practice-room session
the apprentices would gather with the choir in a corner outside the
vestry at the west end of an interminable nave. Keeton would come
up to them. There was a tendency on the apprentices' part to dodge
his eye. He would tap one of them on the shoulder and say 'Play 'em
in.' With that he would hum a tune of five or six notes which the
chosen pupil had to memorize at one go, for Keeton was not in the
habit of humming anything twice. On this tune the apprentice was
expected to extemporize a three-minute voluntary while the choir
were filing into their stalls and settling down. The apprentice might
be told also to stand by after the voluntary and accompany the Te
Deum or the day's Psalm. Alternatively he might be told to accompany the whole service, sink or swim. This was often required of
Malcolm, presumably because he was known to be a good swimmer.
   Much of the service music was in heavy, leather-bound scores
dating from the 18th century, with voice parts in the old soprano,
tenor and bass clefs. Instead of having fully notated harmonies in
front of him, the player had to work everything out from 'figured
bass', in which numbers stand for notes. When accompanying
Psalms, figured bass was his sole guide, for none of the voice parts
were printed. Thus, Sargent used to explain, the pupil did not discover the tune for the first time until the choir sang the first verse,
and no more than two verses were ever allowed the same realization".' In other words, he had to vary his realizations harmonically
out of his head and think up new 'ornaments' verse by verse as he

went along. His knack of transcription was put to new tests. He remembered having to play a five-part service in F from an open score with four different clefs, at the same time transposing it up to G.

While the chosen apprentice was at his chore, Keeton would stand behind, ready to pounce. The moment the player fumbled and seemed likely to lose his head, he would take over the console himself. He had two ways of doing this. In an urgent case he would insinuate himself on to the bench and slide the fumbler off it with a skilful elbow lunge. This he did so quickly and cleverly that his hands were on the keys and feet on the pedals without a beat missed or any worshipper the wiser. In a lesser emergency he would take his place at the treble end of the bench and, as Sargent used to tell, gradually push his pupil (still playing) to the opposite end. Then, having left the boy with nothing to sit on, he would play himself.

*

Twice a week after mattins Malcolm rode on a borrowed bicycle to Keeton's house a mile or so from the cathedral for piano lessons. The big music room was at the front of the house. You glimpsed the upright piano and shelf upon shelf of scores and books as you came up the garden from Forth-road. Keeton's mood at home was a degree milder than in the organ loft. At home he was free to smoke and did so heavily. Perhaps that accounted for the difference. He favoured uncommonly long cherrywood pipes that left rich hazes all over the house. When the 'moderns' cropped up, however, the touch of benignity went; his vetoes were as implacable as ever. While at the Chapel Royal, Tom Armstrong had gone for piano lessons to the Matthay school. There he had learned the Debussy pieces known collectively as *The Children's Corner*, then still a novelty. He thought much of them. Hopefully he brought the album with him for his first lesson at Forth-road. The old man leafed through it and said: 'Don't play that any more—or anything like it. We will start with Clementi's first sonatina.' The boy went away with a lump in his throat. He had been put back on 'baby music'. Or so it seemed at the time. Later he saw what the old man was driving at: the inculcation of classical lucidity and precision.

3

Keeton's playing was beautifully fluent, by all accounts. Fanciers of the English keyboard school said that must have been exactly how William Sterndale Bennett played at Philharmonic Society concerts in the 'fifties. Extolling finger technique to the exclusion of Lisztian wrist-play, brandished forearm and similar vain shows, as he considered them, the old man used to put pennies on the back of boys' hands before they began their scales. If the penny fell off their style was shown to be 'impure'. Malcolm prepared much Mendelssohn and Schumann with him, including a Mendelssohn concerto (solo part), which he is remembered to have played stylishly. It was one of his ambitions, as we have seen, to become a virtuoso pianist. At eighteen already he had the makings of one in his fingers and re-creative imagination.

Keeton's limited repertory satisfied him no more than it satisfied Tom Armstrong. He asked one day whether he might not prepare some of the Bach keyboard suites. This was long before the vogue, now forty years old, of the Bach recital. The old man stroked his moustache for a moment, then consented with the reckless joviality of someone giving a pound away on the spur of the moment. Bach's clavier music was so wide of 'Keeton country' that when the news reached his pupils (he had many non-articled ones) the more knowing among them exclaimed enviously over the young man's push and power of persuasion.

The young man's willpower and temperament, his capacity to please people and stay in their mind's eye, was developing at the same pace as his professional facility and confidence. He talked incessantly on all manner of subjects, often while at the piano. His monologues sometimes told 'the story' of such music as he happened to be playing. Sometimes they dealt with extraneous matters: the comicalities of this player or that in the town's silver prize band, say; or the wit and charm of his latest girl friend. In the jargon of the day he was a 'masher', exacting and precise about his trouser-creases, the tilt of his hat, what tie to wear with which socks. The immediate point of these niceties, as of certain dazzling smiles and railleries that he cultivated, was to impress young women. At the same time he had a dawning, half-realized purpose of longer range: to impress the public. Musicians in general were a dowdy race. To be dowdy was to be unfashionable. To be unfashionable meant not being noticed. And those who weren't noticed didn't get anywhere. Only one detail was wanting from the complete 1913 'masher' image. That was a nonchalant way with cigarettes. But cigarettes made him cough and splutter. He decided to do without. Already he was noticed. Already he was 'somebody'. A shrewd witness of his late 'teens and early twenties says: 'Whenever he entered a room, no matter how many or what kind of people were there, he became the *centre*.'

His hair, not yet sleeked back, stood up like a brush. He would run his fingers through it exasperatedly while arguing politics with his father. At home he was given to arguing hotly on anything under the sun: hobble skirts to Home Rule, biplanes to the wholetone scale. The compulsive emotional surges became more marked. It didn't take a great deal to bring them on. One day he rushed into the house at All Saints-street and bade his father give him half-a-crown immediately. No time to explain! He rushed out and gave the half-crown to a woman passing by.

'Why did you do that?' asked Henry Sargent.

'Didn't you see she's going to have a baby?' said Malcolm. 'I wanted to help her.'

His passion for animals had something of the same impetuousness. This had begun when he was a small boy. A travelling circus came to Broad-street. He spent hours in front of the wild-beast cages. When teatime came he had to be coaxed and pulled away. For weeks he pestered his father to buy him a puma. If not a puma, a baby elephant, then? When told that neither was practicable he went into tantrums and had to be talked out of them. Another trait was impishness. He calculated his improprieties with skill. When business took Keeton out of Peterborough, he would hand over a service or sequence of services to his apprentices. On one such occasion the choir sang the Creed to harmonies which though solemn and pleasing enough, nobody had ever heard in this context before. Malcolm was at the organ. Afterwards he leaned against a pillar, weak with laughter. The harmonies and descant which he had fitted to 'I believe in one God, the Father Almighty, creator of heaven and earth and of all things visible and invisible', were a direct transfer, at slow tempo, of the fairies' opening number (for 'Celia and 1st sops., Leila and 2nd sops.') from *Iolanthe*—'Tripping hither, tripping thither, nobody knows why or whither.' Half a century later, laughing uproariously, he would demonstrate the trick on his music-room piano at Albert Hall Mansions.

'You see how everything fits?' he would triumph. 'The modulations and tune go perfectly with every section of the Creed. I don't suppose the dear old Dean would have minded if he'd known. There was no blasphemous intention, of course. If there were no room for an occasional bit of esoteric fun in religion, religion would be in a poor way.'

By this time the apprentice was master in all but name. In his case Keeton no longer hummed themes for 'playing 'em in'. Malcolm would take a tune from whatever piece he happened to be keen on at the moment and extemporize on that. One day he would embroider a quotation from *Hiawatha's Wedding Feast*; another day from Mendelssohn's *Reformation* Symphony or the *Enigma* Variations. For outgoing voluntaries he played every note of the organ works of Bach, Mendelssohn, Rheinberger, Widor and Guilmant. This was the period when he first made Peterborough's enormous nave and its wooden ceiling panels, all painted with saints, bishops, kings and monsters, reverberate grandly to the *Ride of the Valkyries* in Edwin Lemare's transcription and to the *Meistersinger* Overture as converted by the same hand. He admired the transcriber's astuteness and imagination alike. Lemare was billed for a recital in Nottingham. This was not to be missed. Malcolm came back from it in full effervescence. 'That man,' he said, plucking Tom Armstrong by the sleeve, 'did something I wouldn't have believed possible. He made the organ *dance*.' Taking Armstrong up into the loft, he played from memory the Lemare piece which had given him this singular impression, a *Madrigal* in D flat. Heard today Lemare's trifle, elegant enough in its way, doesn't get much above the ground. But, as Armstrong recollected much later: 'We were conscious of a vast world of music outside the choir stalls. We explored that world as best we could. And we weren't musical snobs.' Of Malcolm's performances from the classical repertory there is one especially that stands out in his friend's memory. To the A minor Prelude and

Fugue of Bach Malcolm brought brilliance and bravura qualities whose like Peterborough had never heard before.

Nor did he neglect his father's organ in Stamford, though its precarious state was becoming more evident month by month. A repair fund having been given a send-off by the Marchioness of Exeter ('I love the organ better than any other instrument,' she claimed), it was arranged that, when the worn-out parts had been replaced and the overhaul completed, Malcolm should give a celebratory recital at St. John's. Turning up on the morning of the appointed day for practice, he found half the organ pipes still stacked in the pews. The overhaul men apologized for being behind schedule but said everything would be all right that evening. At the beginning of the recital they were still inside the organ case, finishing off the job. There they stayed until the end, audibly moving about to make adjustments when a note stuck. Fiasco was narrowly avoided. In other churches he gave recitals of a less nerve-racking kind. In and among his Peterborough commutings he contrived to take organ and piano pupils and so began to earn his keep, as his father had stipulated.

At the same time he was grubbing intensively for his degree of Bachelor of Music. As at Wharf-road, so at All Saints-road, he annexed the sitting-room and made a study of it. Often he did not get to bed until two or three in the morning. Doing without enough sleep somehow made him spryer. That year (1913–14) the music-examination regulations of the University of Durham required of entrants that, in addition to the usual harmony, counterpoint and figured-bass exercises, they should compose a four-part fugue on a specified subject, including a canon that was to continue for a given number of bars, the manuscript to be annotated analytically. The *viva voce* involved full scores whose titles were to be disclosed to the entrants beforehand. After his groundings with Fanny Tinkler and Murrell and Keeton's arduous drillings, the Durham papers gave him little trouble.

In October 1914 three important things happened to him. The Kaiser's war was two months old. He had tried to enlist more than once. The Royal Flying Corps was his fancy; he dreamed of becoming a pilot. Because of his shoulder injury on the school

'Rugby' field he was rejected as unfit. The *Mercury* announced that he had passed his third and final examination of Durham University's musical department and was now Bachelor of Music, one of the youngest ever to achieve the distinction. (At nineteen he was certainly the youngest on the Durham roll.) His bachelor's hood, bright violet silk with brocaded silk border, was bought by the choir members and others at St. John's. It was handed to him on their behalf in the vestry one Sunday morning before mattins by old Mr. Sandall. A fortnight later it became known that he had been appointed organist at the parish church of St. Mary, Melton Mowbray, Leicestershire, twenty miles to the north-west. Months earlier Keeton had tipped him off about the vacancy by telegram. There were a hundred and fifty-one candidates for the post, Malcolm being the youngest—naturally. The pay was thirty shillings a week, enough in 1914 for a young man to live on in an English market town.

His mother and his young sister Dorothy went with him on the roundabout train journey from Stamford and saw him settled in pleasant humdrum lodgings which are remembered for the red Turkey carpets on all floors and for little else. The Manor House, as the place was called, was gaslit. On his first night there Malcolm sat in growing darkness, the house being otherwise empty, until someone came along and taught him how to light up. At home there had always been electricity. Gas lighting was a mystery to him. His landlady was charmed. How could a musician with his head in the clouds be expected to know about domestic practicalities? He hired an upright piano for his room, which opened from the ground-floor lobby. Most of his free time from St. Mary's would be spent in giving music lessons. If pupils couldn't come to the Manor House he would go to their homes. To this end he hired a bicycle.

He kept up his Peterborough ties for a while and gave organ recitals in the Cathedral, patriotically sandwiching the Belgian, French and Russian national anthems among Bach, Widor, Rheinberger, Karg Elert, Buxtehude and *Lohengrin* excerpts. Parties of friends, relations and other admirers used to come over from Stamford to hear him. From the beginning Sargent had a highly mobile following in the Midlands. Wherever he appeared on rostrum or organ bench—whether in Stamford or Melton, Peterborough or Uppingham, Bourne or Kettering—the same 'faithfuls' were to be seen in the audience.

At Peterborough young Armstrong stayed on for a year or so as sub organist under Keeton. He, too, had wider ambitions. Before call-up and two years' military service in France, he emerged from examination grinds, and was offered an organ scholarship at Keble College, Oxford, where, twenty years later, he became Choragus and lecturer in music to the University. Before making up his mind whether to accept the scholarship, he consulted Sargent. His friend tried to dissuade him, vainly as it turned out. The world of music, Sargent counselled, was one thing. Oxford University—a wonderful place, admittedly—was another thing. For someone bent on getting into music as best he could an organ scholarship would be a waste of time. *Ars longa, vita brevis*, he quoted.

CHAPTER SEVEN

AT MELTON

IF OXFORD was something less than the world of music or, in essence, a different sort of world, what of Melton Mowbray? The note here, as in Stamford but perhaps more so, was feudal, an assertion of unchangeable boundaries between highborn, low-born and a brisk middle area of shopkeepers and small traders. Like the sister arts, music was a flourish, an incidental, something for which you negligently paid half guineas and guineas to people of no great consequence. As in Stamford there were many almshouses and charities, most of them more ancient. It was well known that man did not live by bread alone. Yet he mustn't, if it could be helped, go hungry. The town's banks secreted little hoards, rents from houses and paddocks, or interest from three per cent Consols left in pious trust as far back as Charles I's reign. From these funds free bread was to be dished out to the poor of Melton in perpetuity—twelve loaves a week here, a shilling's worth there, six-pennorth at some other point. At the other end of the social gamut came fox hunting.

On the outskirts of the town stood eight or more hunting lodges, rambling villas with gables, mullions and quaint chimney stacks in late-Victorian brick. Most of them stabled twenty or thirty hunters. They were owned by people with a lot of money and, in some cases, great names. The war had not greatly curtailed matters. From the winter of 1914–15 to that of 1918–19, *The Melton Mowbray Times and Vale of Belvoir Gazette* carried anything up to two spacious columns a week about the chases, digs, kills and other doings of the Quorn, Belvoir, Cottesmore and Fernie's packs. Fox hunting had been the region's pleasure and one of its staple purposes for nearly two hundred years. That it should be seriously impaired by anything as ephemeral as a world war was unthinkable.

Nobody could have called the Melton ambiance, either then or during the early 1920s, conducive to the ardours of young musical genius. Any other beginner would have been smothered and assimilated for ever by the town. Sargent certainly gave Melton of his best. But he got the best in return. He made Melton serve his purpose.

Peterborough Cathedral had been engulfing. St. John's, Stamford, although picturesque, had a certain grey hardness of line; and, though glad of his son's unpaid assistance, Henry Sargent was indubitably boss there. The parish church of Melton was in brown stone as well as grey. On sunny days its nave took on the hue of honey, the unnamed alabaster lady who slept with folded hands on the 14th-century altar tomb turned almost translucent, and new dimples showed on the white marble gentleman with full bottomed wig, niched nearby, and on the cherubs who tended him. St. Mary's did something more than provide the young man with a first-rate workshop and professional base. It served also as a handsome frame to his keen good looks and bright energy. The choir took to him at once. He made them, as he was to make a hundred other choirs and choruses, *believe* in what they were singing—and in themselves. Practice nights suddenly became an adventure. Mattins and evensong often ended with beams of triumph on the singers' faces. Never had a harvest-thanksgiving congregation in Melton or for a hundred miles around heard Stamford's B flat *Te Deum* or Barnby's *Magnificat* and *Nunc dimittis* in E or *The Heavens are Telling* sung with the fervour and fine shading that Sargent got out of his men and women and boys in October 1916. The county weeklies became increasingly aware of him. He had long been aware of the county weeklies. A little obsequiously, they named him Mr. Malcolm Sargent, Mus. Bac., sometimes adding A.R.C.O. But what kept and magnified him in the public eye was not so much the splendid singing at St. Mary's as his organ playing. He liked to have people stand on fitting occasions. They stood on Easter Day, when he played Handel's *Hallelujah* Chorus, and at commemorations of the

3*

town's war dead for his Dead March in *Saul*. These performances brought tears to his eyes and to the eyes of many others. At weekday recitals he made forays into the secular repertory. 'You should hear young Sargent play the *Tannhäuser* Overture and *Finlandia*!' Thus ran travellers' tales as far away as Bedford and Leicester. As well as doing the Guilmant and Mendelssohn organ sonatas, he made much of Edward Elgar's in G. Already he was assertive about the merits of native music. As time went on his Sunday night 'special voluntaries' expanded into recitals. To hear these, people came in at the end of evensong from other churches and other denominations, even from other towns. A bigger crowd was drawn by the music than heard the parson's sermon. Even a musically inclined parson must have found this invidious.

He lost no time in bridging the gap between himself and other organists of the region. Most were old enough to have been his father or grandfather. Inviting thirty of them over from Leicester for a Saturday outing, he met them at the station, shepherded them to St. Mary's and subjected them to a six-piece programme. Its backbone was Bach's Prelude and Fugue in G minor, a movement from Widor's fifth Organ Symphony and the Introduction and Fugue from Reubke's Sonata after the 94th Psalm. At the finish the visitors were effusive and a little quelled; such *brio* and self-confidence in a boy, for he seemed little more, was something new and, as new things often are, disturbing. Then, with the sun still high, he took them to Mowbray Lodge for croquet, tea and polite conversation.

A roomy villa with a parvenu look, Mowbray Lodge was the home of Canon Blakeney, who held the living of St. Mary's for over thirty years, and, as importantly, of his wife. 'Nothing so common as an ordinary vicarage for Mrs. Blakeney!' murmured those who knew the Lodge and its mistress intimately. Richard Blakeney was bald, with white tufts over the ears, and had a nose like Mr. Punch's. Until his last years, in the middle 1920s, he was never seen abroad except in frock coat and silk hat. He typified the Tory parson of an earlier age to the point of caricature. His tirades against Bolshevism were reinforced by thumpings of the pulpit cushion. In his lowlier parishioners he took a kindly, Pickwickian interest. Sometimes his

sociological quizzings drew surprising answers. 'I suppose,' he
ventured, halting a brewer's drayman in the High-street, 'I suppose
you drink quite a lot of beer on your job?' 'Well, sir,' said the drayman, 'some days I get ten or twelve pints; then other days I get
quite a lot.'

In music he took little interest. Mrs. Blakeney's interest in music
was more than enough for two. She was of stately presence, moneyed
in her own right and busy in good causes. At her bidding and cajol-
ing, those within her circle and many beyond it periodically
brought eggs and fruit to church. After these had been blessed, she
drove round the town's humbler quarters and distributed them
among the needy and the sick. Many conceded her the rôle of
Melton's first lady. After Sargent she was, although an amateur,
certainly the town's most active musician. Not the sort of person
who is readily dazzled or captivated, she now experienced both
states. Her husband's new organist was obviously a prodigy. Being
something of a prodigy herself, she conceived it her plain duty to
advance his career. She appointed herself his counsellor, advocate
and second mother. When, some years later, he became Doctor
of Music, it was Mrs. Blakeney who paid for his doctoral
gown, a garment of supreme silk and tailoring which was to last
a lifetime. Was she inclined to be possessive, perhaps? Did
she dictate rather than suggest? Was she given to 'either', 'or else'
and 'unless'? There were rumours of differences, even of tiffs. To
this day it is reported in Melton that once at least Sargent had to
take a firm stand. 'I am prepared to accept your kindnesses and
am grateful for them,' he said. 'But I'm not prepared to lose my
independence.'

*

The drawing-room at Mowbray Lodge, scene of Mrs. Blakeney's
musical evenings, where the right people spoke the right accent and
wore the right clothes, was a place of chintz and deep, comfortable
chairs. One side of the room was dominated by a rather too splendid
William and Mary display cabinet, belly-fronted, richly inlaid and
crammed with rare china, the other side by a grand piano. On Mrs.
Blakeney's piano, Sargent accompanied the likelier sopranos,

contraltos, tenors and violinists of Melton and its neighbourhood in Schubert, Schumann, Cyril Scott, Frank Bridge, Hebri-
dean folk songs and movements from the sonatas of Brahms and
Mozart. Among people who met at Mrs. Blakeney's were teachers
from the County Grammar School of King Edward VII. These
were Sargent's colleagues. From early 1915 he was a teacher
there himself, doubling a music-mastership at five guineas (later
eight) a term with his equivalent appointment at the Stamford
school.

When he first set foot in the King Edward VII School it was five
years old, having named itself after the monarch without his authority
shortly before Edward's death in 1910. For a while it looked as if the
self-conferred title would have to be renounced. After some flurry
in Whitehall and at the Palace, the new King, George V, by one of
those special precedents which nobody is expected to follow at any
price, allowed the title to stand; and the governors breathed again.
During the early years, including those of Sargent's work there, it
was not one of the happiest schools. The first headmaster had been
a psychological misfit, his sceptre three draper's yards tied in a
bundle. With this instrument he gave thirty-six strokes to a boy who
had played some practical joke on his wife, then said: 'Next time I
shall *thrash* you.' His successor, the man under whom Sargent
served, used the cane with equal rigour for trivial offences. A boy
who took his hands from behind his back when supposed to be
'standing at ease' got a beating which form mates remembered with
awe forty years later.

Even the members of the staff were treated like naughty children.
Forbidden to smoke in their staff room, they would slip down into
the central-heating stokehold for a cigarette between lessons. This
was the place where, in wet weather, children's clothes were hung
to dry. Six days a week, for Saturday morning school was the rule,
boys and girls came in from villages up to fifteen miles away, some
of them on foot via the nearest railway station, others by pony-cart
or bicycle, and at least two on cobs which they stabled in the King's
Head yard. Among a hundred or two pupils the boys outnumbered
the girls by three to two. Most were farmers' and tradesmen's
children. A few were children of professional men or of artisans and

stablehands. A quarter had free places. The remainder were fee-
payers at two-pounds-four-and-six a term.

*

To this raw, rather uneasy world, underventilated at all times and so
ill-lit that school ended at 3.30 p.m. in winter, Sargent entered as a
visiting master, giving two lessons a week. 'He was young, dapper
and popular, especially with the girls,' it was noted. 'With most of
the staff his relations were not quite so close, for it soon became clear
that . . . Sargent, although an excellent teacher, was not wedded to
the profession and aimed at higher things.'*

While all the bigger boys and most of the masters were converting
themselves into a cadet corps—they drilled against the Boche with
wooden rifles from the woodwork department and, if they could
afford, paid half the cost (30s.) of their uniforms—Sargent revivified
the choral class and got some strikingly proficient Mendelssohn and
Handel from the school choir at his first school concert. At speech
days he conducted the new School Song with a gusto that was
readily explained; he had composed the music himself. Written by
another newcomer, Miss Nesbit, senior mistress, the words saluted
the newly-introduced house system and the hunts after which the
houses had been named: 'Give a rouse to your House/Loud as any
huntsman's horn,/Wake the hill with a will—/Belvoir, Cottesmore,
Belvoir, Quorn!' But these were the wider verities. Britain was at
bay. Even child minds had to be canalized. At the school Christmas
concert in December 1917, the choir sang like angels in folk-song
arrangements, carols old and new and numbers by Handel, Haydn
and Mendelssohn. The programme was halted halfway through for
Form IIB who, equally angelical, did an exulting and macabre mass
recitation, *Ten Little Zeppelins*. It was not a time to be fastidious.
Emergencies and unforeseen calls were met blithely. The new
music master acted as accompanist at a Red Cross concert organized
by Lady Hanson, of Eye Kettleby Hall, at which conspicuous turns

* *The School on the Hill*, an Informal History of King Edward VII Grammar
School, Melton Mowbray, compiled by T. H. Corfe, W. Thornley and Son,
Leicester.

were a comedian in khaki and a one-string fiddle. When the conductor of Stamford's silver prize band, glimpsed already in this narrative, got his call-up papers, the players begged Sargent to take over: which he promptly did.

Founded in the 1880s, the Town Band were jovially regarded by their betters as lovable yokels. No garden fête or municipal bandstand was complete without their cacophonies, which prompted many a wince and indulgent smile. All the players were 'characters', the ripest of them being Sam Brittain, trombonist. Whenever anything untoward happened such as band parts lost or the solo cornet getting a valve stuck or the entire band taking the wrong train, Sam was invariably the one deputed to apologize and put things right. Having explained the latest mishap or fiasco, he would triumphantly add, as if the occasion were one for congratulations all round, 'So there y'are, yer see!' Although well versed in brass technique, Sargent had never conducted the town band or any other brass band before. He decided to start with a *Mikado* selection. At the first rehearsal he asked for the fanfare marking the entry of the Lord High Executioner. The band gave him 'the most awful sound I had ever heard in my life. The whole thing was terribly out of tune. I asked, "Have you tuned up? Have you taken the B flat so that you can play this?" They replied, "Well, sir, we haven't actually *tuned*. When we bought these instruments from Boosey and Hawkes five years ago a man came down and tuned 'em for us, and we haven't touched 'em since." ' Laughing about musical rustics is one thing. Laughing at their preferred medium, or patronizing or barely tolerating it, is another. Ever since that first encounter in Stamford, Sargent treated what is known as the brass band 'movement' seriously. He produced several transcriptions of classics for playing at the great competitive festivals. At one such event shortly after the war in the Royal Albert Hall, massed brass bands numbering 250 players did his transcription of Mozart's superb Fantasia in F minor (K. 608), originally (and absurdly) intended for a mechanical organ concealed inside a clock: a startling and exalting experience. In the same hall in 1954, the organ being temporarily out of action, he transferred the organ accompaniments of eleven *Messiah* choruses to a quartet of flugelhorns, two euphoniums and a tuba.

Nobody dropped dead. One veteran supporter of the Royal Choral Society was heard to say how well the organ sounded.*

*

The story of the Stamford yokels and their untuned instruments went down well at Mowbray Lodge. But, reflected Mrs. Blakeney, war or no war, the public must be given an early chance of seeing Malcolm conduct worthier forces. Melton had a Choral Society. Inevitably, Mrs. Blakeney was its president. Call-up had cut the society's singing strength from well over a hundred to less than seventy, and not more than fifty of these could be relied on to attend the practices. In the hope of attracting replacements the committee cut the membership fee to half-a-crown at a time when everything else was going up. Even this did not serve. Tenors and basses went on being outnumbered and outsung by the ladies. Nobody felt really happy about *The Revenge* (Stanford) and *Blest Pair of Sirens* (Parry) as sung by the society in the winter of 1915–16. Mrs. Blakeney busied herself with the problem. The society had two conductors: Mr. Warner and Mr. Smyth. At the beginning of the 1916–17 season it was announced that Sargent had accepted joint conductorship with Warner. Mr. Smyth seems to have stepped down. At the beginning of the following season it was announced that the society had been fortunate enough to secure the services of Mr. Sargent as 'conductor', jointure being no longer mentioned. After this nothing more was heard of Mr. Warner. Sargent made his effective concert début as a choral conductor on 4th April, 1918, at the Drill Hall, Melton, in a miscellaneous programme, with Edward Elgar's *The Banner of St. George*, ballad for chorus and orchestra, as its mainstay, the solo soprano part, as well as numbers in the other half of the

* Other of his transcriptions are the *Iolanthe* and *Yeomen of the Guard* overtures, Schubert's *Marche militaire* and the Prelude No. 15 in D flat (the 'Raindrop') and C minor Polonaise Op. 40, No. 2, of Chopin. The main subject of the Polonaise, written for left-hand octaves, is strikingly scored. It is heard to begin with on six euphoniums. For the reprise these are doubled by twelve tubas, making eighteen instruments. For the recapitulation nine trombones are added, bringing the total to 27. 'You'll never hear it like that on the piano!' said Sargent unchallengably after recording his transcription with the Men o' Brass ensemble in 1965.

programme, being sung by Elsie Suddaby, a young artist of whom more was to be heard on recital and oratorio platforms.

The orchestral accompaniments to *The Banner* exist in two versions, one for full symphony orchestra, the other for half as many players. Exigencies of time, place and available talent drove Sargent to a specification of his own. A string choir of eight included the usual lone viola. On the other hand he brought in two euphoniums. Neither of the printed versions asked for these. Another intruder was the piano. As in Gilbert and Sullivan pits, 'Fanny Tinkler' was there, 'filling out'. His leader that night was Grace Burrows, a remarkable young woman who four and a half years later was to help him mobilize the Leicester Symphony Orchestra and lead that as well. Miss Burrows' father, Ben Burrows, was a 'cellist, musical scholar and music teacher of repute. When he died, Grace inherited his forty or so pupils. Between them father and daughter trained two generations or more of string players in and around Leicester. Founding her own string quartet and string orchestra, she ran and conducted 'lecture concerts', becoming so proficient with the baton that years later, when leader of his Leicester Symphony Orchestra, she occasionally substituted for Sargent on the rostrum and conducted him at least once in Mozart's A major Piano Concerto (K. 488).

Nor was Miss Burrows the only conductor in the Drill Hall 'band'. There was George Tebbs, too. That night he played the one and only French horn. Alternatively he could have played the trombone or, if there had been a part for it, the trumpet. Tebbs had been an ironmonger. He did so well out of his shop in Leicester that he had been able to retire in his middle forties: ideal age for an amateur brass player who wished to make his mark also with the baton. The year before the war he had founded the De Montfort Hall Orchestra in Leicester's newly-opened De Montfort Hall. There he gave free Sunday night concerts once a fortnight. You were supposed to pay sixpence for your programme if you sat in the stalls and threepence if you opted for the gallery. His first concert opened with Nicolai's *Merry Wives of Windsor* Overture and ended with Sullivan's *In Memoriam* Overture. In between, with much else, came a *Pagliacci* selection, Luigini's *Ballet égyptien* and two Sibelius pieces, the *Valse triste* and the *Finlandia* Overture. A shrewd assessment. Mr. Tebbs knew exactly what the Leicester of 1913 expected of him. ('Sargent was to make them like what *he* wanted.'—Marginal note by Sargent.)

We must return, however, to *The Banner of St. George*. Latter-day Elgarians, however devoted, have nothing to say in its favour. It was composed for the Diamond Jubilee of 1897 and, they comment, sounds like it.* But the story, about rampaging dragon, maiden in distress and chivalrous knight, was an exhilarating tract for the times. In the spring of 1918 everybody knew who the Dragon was. Nor could there be any doubt as to St. George. The identification of the rescuer with bleeding, valiant Britain had given Elgar's music and Shapcot Wensley's blustering text a new vogue among choral societies which cheered the publishers and sent the price of the vocal score up from 1s. 6d. to 2s. 3d. That the part writing, harmonies and scoring of the concluding chorus might be commonplace as well as loud did not trouble the Meltonians at all. What mattered was that Elgar's music chimed splendidly with Mr. Wensley's final apostrophe to the British:

> Great race, whose empire of splendour
> Has dazzled a wondering world!
> May the flag that floats o'er thy wide domain
> Belong to all winds unfurled—
> Three crosses in concord blended,
> The banner of Britain's might!

To this sentiment the Drill Hall rose, eyes moist, spines prickling. The choir knew they had sung well. At the end they were smiling from ear to ear. Even to the uninstructed it was evident that Sargent had transformed the Melton choir. Before there had been drabness. Now there was lustre. Why? Because the society had been lucky enough to find 'a conductor possessed of a genius for interpretation

---

* '... among Elgar's works it must take the lowest place. It is merely dull. ... [When] Elgar deliberately sought to express the conventions of patriotism . . . he ran out of inspiration.'—Percy A. Young, *Elgar*, *O.M.*, Collins, 1955. 'The best of the music is undistinguished . . . melodies of the glib type . . . [Much] of the choral writing is of the most facile part-song style . . . the poverty of the music.'—Diana McVeagh, *Edward Elgar*, *His Life and Music*, Dent, 1955.

and an inspiring optimism that will move mountains of difficulties'. This compliment, ascribed to 'a correspondent', appeared in the following issue of the local weekly. At the choral society's next meeting Mrs. Blakeney handed Sargent a gold wristlet watch on behalf of the members. He had received his call-up papers and was accepted for military service in a low medical category. A fortnight later he was in khaki.

CHAPTER EIGHT

INFANTRYMAN

THE 27TH battalion Durham Light Infantry were strung out along the Thanet coast, with headquarters at Herne Bay. Private Sargent was posted here for basic training. The war, well into its fourth year, was going ill for the Allies. Since mid-March a crescendo of reverses, retreats and slaughter had given new grimness to the soldier's lot and prospects. Stoicism was beginning to take on a tinge of fatalism. Sargent must have been as alive to this as to the rest of his platoon. His ebullience was unquenchable, however. He adapted himself to the rigours and privations of Army life with suppleness.

The new intake at Herne Bay were under canvas, sleeping fifteen or sixteen to a tent. Because of scarcity, rationing and bad Army cooks, food was a gnawing preoccupation. A parcel from Stamford, packed by his sister, included a 2-lb tin of honey. The tin was opened with joy: a joy respectfully shared by Private Wilfred Aris. A reserved and earnest young man from the Midlands, a little older than Sargent, Aris had joined up two months earlier and still felt uprooted, cut off. At home he had been a Baptist lay preacher for three years, and he was to serve Baptist pulpits for forty or fifty years more. Not many under canvas at Herne Bay shared his outlook and mental temper or came near to understanding them.

Such, at any rate, was the situation before Sargent's arrival. Sargent had a knack of understanding anybody and everybody. All social and temperamental orbits seemed open to him. The thing that dazzled Aris from the first day, making him on the instant a lifelong devotee, was Sargent's illimitable confidence about life and the resources of the human will. Aris told him about his shyness and self-consciousness; how he had to steel himself against these handicaps every time he went up into the pulpit.

'Your trouble,' diagnosed Sargent, 'is that you are concerned all the time with what other people may be thinking. Whenever you say anything you wonder what *they* are thinking about what you've said. You are looking outside too much. You must look inside. As long as you're sure you've said the right thing, that's all that matters. Content yourself with that. Your self-consciousness will vanish.' Which, indeed, is what happened. As an old man Wilfred Aris spoke of his meeting with Malcolm Sargent as the most important thing that ever happened to him: 'He changed my life. He taught me the importance of internal truth as distinct from external truth.'

Meantime the friends rejoiced in the honey from Stamford. In hot spring weather the communal tent was stifling. The honey melted and expanded. The tin began to leak. Private Sargent asked Sergeant Hill whether they mightn't keep it in the stock tent, which was cooler. The company sergeant instinctively treated Private Sargent with a deference that wasn't a private soldier's due. He opened up the stock tent for Private Sargent and let him use an empty rifle box as larder. For three weeks Sargent and Aris ate honey and bread with their canteen tea, a luxury neither was to forget.

On parade Private Sargent had the straightest back of all and went through his drills as if he were an actor and this his favourite rôle. But he and Aris were waiting and watching for something better. Neither was a soldier at heart. One morning Sergeant Hill announced that a signals unit was forming. Those who wished to enrol as trainees were invited to put up hands. Sargent and Aris put up theirs. A few days later they and a handful more, kitbags on shoulder, said goodbye to the bell tents and entrained for Broadstairs, where a signals school had been set up in an evacuated preparatory school, St. Peter's Court. Among the jumble in Sargent's kitbag were books on musical theory. He usually carried one of these in a tunic pocket when he went on exercises and tests. On the school sports ground he and Aris were always paired. Anything from two hundred yards to a mile away, instructors or fellow trainees would send out messages by flag or heliograph mirror or winking lamp or flapper disc. Turn and turn about, Aris and Sargent would 'read' out the messages, dictating them letter by letter, while the other wrote them down.

What worried Aris was that Sargent, when on writing duty, always had a book on harmony or counterpoint open alongside his signals pad. Obviously the book interested him more than the signals. Already he was studying for his Durham doctorate. When he had to write anything down he unglued his eyes from his book reluctantly. Or so it seemed to Aris. Whether or not he passed the tests depended in part on Sargent's co-operation. Surely his partner couldn't be 'taking down' accurately if his head was full of close canon, basso continuo and the chord of the seventh as defined by Rameau? What Aris didn't allow for was that his friend's mind could work efficiently on two planes at the same time. As things turned out, Sargent never made a mistake. Aris felt awed and slightly penitent.

It was the same in the classroom. While listening to lectures about Morse buzzers or Begbie lamps and taking everything in with one half of his mind, Sargent would devote the other half to a particular piece of music and imagine himself playing or conducting it. Once he openly hummed an obsessing rhythm: *rum, ta-ta, ta-rum-ta-ta-ta-tee, ta-ta*. The lecturing officer turned round from the blackboard with a scowl and asked who was humming. Sargent grinned disarmingly. The lecturer picked up his chalk and returned to the circuit diagram he had been drawing. There was no reprimand. Sargent became a crack Morse reader and transmitter, passing his tests with ease, and did so well on the range at Birchington that the instructor advised him sardonically to miss a few bulls, 'or they'll whip you off to France as a sniper, and then you'll be a goner.' In his case the social or class wall between officers and men mysteriously crumbled. It is remembered that during the marksmanship course at Birchington the captain in charge spent most of his free time at Sargent's elbow. Private Sargent told him of the wonder that was music; how when the war was over he meant to start a symphony orchestra of his own. He was going to be a concert pianist, too. He would play in chamber music and concertos and accompany singers—if he could find singers of the right sort. The right sort of singer must have the right sort of teacher—and the right sort of lungs and larynx. He intended to do some teaching himself. He wouldn't want to teach singing to any girl who hadn't passed a chest and throat examination.

The captain knew little or nothing about music. He listened like a neophyte.

Minor disciplines were casually evaded or avoided. For being 'improperly dressed' a soldier could be sent to the guard room. Private Sargent went about with what looked vaguely like an officer's belt over his Tommy's tunic and sometimes wore civilian clothes when off duty—another impropriety. From the colonel down nobody seemed to mind. In the colonel's case there was a special relationship which probably had no precedent in the British Army and is not likely to have happened since. The fact is that Private Sargent walked out the colonel's daughter and took her to the cinema more than once. He saw to it that his exploit came to the ears of the company sergeant, who was suitably dumbfounded. One thing which irked him at Broadstairs and elsewhere had been the privates' 'ablutions'—the cramped, clamorous quarters where other ranks washed and shaved. Sergeants' 'ablutions' were roomier and quieter. He put it to the company sergeant that he might be allowed to use them. The company sergeant winked permission. Private Sargent thus became a sergeant *ex-officio* without stripes.

Sleeping quarters at Broadstairs were in the school dormitories. Central alleyways ran between rows of one-man cubicles. In his dormitory Sargent occupied the first cubicle on the left as you entered. Aris occupied the facing one. Each man was supposed to scrub once a week an area three floorboards wide alongside his bed. This task was little to Sargent's taste. It was agreed between them that Aris should take over Sargent's scrubbing, as well as doing his own, and that in return Sargent should clean both cubicle windows. Often before lights out they discussed a miscellany of chance subjects: poetry, zoology, women, coarse-fishing, Bolshevism. Sometimes they were joined by a cubicle neighbour, Private G——, who often turned their discursive talk into hammer-and-tongs debate. A university undergraduate from the North of England, G—— was tenaciously individualistic, something of a misogynist and so addicted to physical fitness that Army drill wasn't enough; every evening in the dormitory he did press-ups, knee-bends and gopacks for half an hour. His opinions were progressive and bristly. He had little use for religion, a subject broached more than once in these dormitory talks. In contesting Christian orthodoxy, as voiced with different nuances by his two friends, he sardonically cited hell-fire sermons of a kind which had only recently begun to go out of fashion in quarters that once nurtured them. What justice, what compassion, what commonsense was there, he asked, in a religion which taught, as Christianity did, that one man, after a life of roaring self-indulgence, could go to heaven on the strength of a deathbed repentance, while another, after a life of pious self-sacrifice, could be sent to hell for some fault committed within days, perhaps hours, of his death? 'A rotten time here is rewarded by a rotten time hereafter. Is that,' challenged G——, 'any way to run Time and Eternity?'

The others argued that eternal punishment or reward in specific cases was something the finite mind could not possibly assess and predict. It was all, they said, a matter of belief and faith. God was. And God was good. It was unthinkable that He should inflict unmerited punishment.

Throughout his eight months in khaki, Sargent never missed a church parade or, since these were supposed to be compulsory, sought to be excused one. After every church parade he would go to the Anglican chaplain's tent for communion, sometimes taking Aris with him. The chaplain asked no questions. The fact that Aris was a Baptist did not emerge. Neither he nor Sargent had qualms, however. 'It's right enough,' said Aris to himself. Sargent said then, and has often said since, that he accepted Christian teaching from his earliest remembrance: 'I was born with faith. Not that there's any personal virtue in that.'

*

Food continued to preoccupy. Potatoes were put into boilers with the dirt on them and served half raw and tepid. On a certain Monday tainted meat rissoles were dished up. The men wouldn't touch them. The same rissoles were served daily for the rest of the week. The men went on refusing. The sergeant said they were behaving mutinously. Whether he expected to be taken seriously isn't clear. In any case, his warning had no effect.

For Sargent and Aris and, perhaps, for others of the unit there were outside alleviations. The chief of these, Mrs. Creasy's café, was three minutes away from St. Peter's Court. Every day after their so-called Army dinner, the friends would walk over to Mrs. Creasy's for a special and private pudding of some sort. The pudding they liked best (they were to remember it as vividly as the honey and bread at Herne Bay) was hot jam tart and custard. It did not matter how many other customers there were. Something good was always waiting for the two trainees from the 27th Durhams. That Mrs. Creasy should have contrived such treats for them without extra rations in hungry times was explained by Private Sargent's personality. People of all sorts went out of their way to do things for him.

He became friendly with many aware and hospitable families in and around the town. Twice a week he would be invited to parties which in effect, if not nominally, were arranged in his honour. It is not often that a town like Broadstairs finds itself at a time of social doldrums with so brilliant, charming and gifted a young man on its hands or, so to say, within its social clutches. The opportunity was rare. Broadstairs made the most of it. He shone in a dozen intimate circles. He bubbled over with fun and anecdote. He had attentions and smiles in turn for everybody round the table or drawing-room. He let few topics pass without having something laughable or shrewd to say.

All these houses had pianos. Some of them were good pianos. He would play from memory or extemporize for two hours without halt. It was at Broadstairs that he developed his taste for telling the music's 'story' while playing it. His star narration stemmed from a sort of fantasia which he described later as Sibelius's *Valse triste* 'plus Malcolm Sargent'. The tale was of a young girl and of what proved to be her undoing: the dance. . . . A strange sickness assails her. Through her fever comes a throb of drums. Wraiths of melody throng and sway. Gripped by hallucination, she thinks she is on a vast stage. The music, *her* music, has begun. At all costs she must dance. This shall be the most unleashed, the wildest of all her dances. And, as she knows, her last. The beginning is languorous. Then a quickening of pulse and leap. Frenzy mounts. Her limbs are fire and steel. At the centre of her fury is a stillness. She is the world's pivot. To the world, suddenly, she gives the fury of her passion. Then renounces it with head thrown back and outspread arms. Death has waited. Death now strikes. Lids droop, arms ingather. She does not sink to the earth. It is as though a great hand has come up from earth and drawn her gently down, a new Persephone, for earth's renewal. . . .

Such was Sargent's story line. People listened absorbedly. The Dance of Death was one of the things (there were few others) that 'took their minds off' real horrors in a bodeful year. Some of Sargent's admirers heard it more than once. Aris, who went with him to most of the Broadstairs parties, must have heard it a dozen times. Partly because of Sargent's story variants he was as engrossed the last time as the first. Army lights-out was eleven o'clock. Sargent often found it hard to tear himself away from the piano. Chafing against frustration, he and Aris found a route from the dormitory which skirted the sports field and took them, ten minutes after they had turned in, along an alley between sleeping houses and into the town again. Unseen by sentries on the gate, they were able thus to resume interrupted parties and talk and joke and listen to music or sing it until two in the morning. ('M.S. stole a late-pass book and forged officers' signatures.'—Marginal note by Sargent.)

*

Training ended. Newfledged signallers slung their kitbags and went back to Herne Bay. Sargent, Aris and a third man were given charge of the battalion switchboard and communications room. Three hours each in rotation, they took messages from divisional headquarters in longhand, then, as 'runners', distributed copies in duplicate on foot or bicycle to the O.C., adjutant and subordinate officers as far off as Whitstable. Though they could not show a stripe between them, the three H.Q. telephonists were powerful in their domain and were empowered to bar entry even to commissioned officers. There were recurring hours and half days when they had little work. Signaller Sargent, never at a loss, found something agreeable for everybody to do. He taught or tried to teach the others how to dance—quick and slow waltzes and new things such as fox-trot, tango, two-step. His pupils didn't get far but did their best and were never bored; nobody was bored with Sargent about.

The war had taken a turn for the better. But now a second killer was walking the world, 'Spanish' influenza. Sargent was among those of the D.L.I. who went down with it. Quarantined with twenty other patients in a single room in a requisitioned dwelling house, some of the others having what he called 'unmentionable' complaints. Sargent realized that his well-being, possibly his survival, depended as much on his own initiative as upon overworked Army doctors and medical orderlies. More than ever, food was the problem. On the principle that what's considered good enough for the fit should be good enough for the ailing, regulation meals were delivered at the so-called sick bay thrice a day from Army kitchens. The mere sight of them induced nausea. Although the sick bay and precincts had been declared out of bounds, the faithful Aris ventured on a visit. Tapping on a window he called his friend's name as loudly as he dared. Sargent appeared at the window and shouted something repeatedly. His voice did not carry. Aris strained his ears and at last understood. 'Oranges and lemons!' his friend was saying. 'Get oranges and lemons!' Aris nodded a promise and made off glumly, sure that owing to scarcity he wouldn't be able to redeem it. He was wrong. Through some caprice in supply the greengrocers' shops of Herne Bay were bursting with fruit.

*

No sooner had he returned to duty than the Armistice of November 1918 hit Herne Bay as towns by the hundred thousand were hit all over the world. The sudden lifting of a nightmare to which it had seemed there would be no end sent everybody amiably mad. At battalion headquarters discipline momentarily dissolved. There was a great outpouring towards beerhouses and saloon bars. Later that day an officer who had officiously kept his head or regained it required the company to fall in and dress by the right. Forty of the company were so drunk that they could hardly stand. Private Sargent laughed uncontrollably. The officer did not persist.

That night Sargent led a celebration. With Aris, Private G——
and a third signaller he went down to a Ramsgate hotel and ordered
fixed-price dinner for four. The place was an hilarious bustle. Eyes
shone. There was jovial shouting. Several officers were in the dining-
room. Officers paid their bills in the ordinary way, after eating.
Privates did not get bills at all. They were required to pay before
sitting down. The dinner cost six shillings. Sargent paid 'entry
money' for three good-humouredly enough. Afterwards they had
port wine. Private Aris had teetotal convictions. Private Sargent
put it to him that this was a great day in the history of mankind and
should be observed accordingly, irrespective of private whims.
While the other two pinioned Aris in his chair, he tried to pour wine
down the reluctant throat, but Aris clenched his teeth, and the wine
went down his tunic. He took this good-humouredly. A very young
second-lieutenant came up and asked a little plaintively, 'Don't you
know me?' Springing to his feet, Sargent dutifully saluted and
said 'No, sir!' The officer drew him aside. They talked amiably
for some minutes. 'One of my choir kids from Melton,' explained
Sargent on returning. 'One of my stars, in fact. He's just been commissioned.'

In the hotel lounge were two good-looking 'land girls'. Sargent
whispered to the others, 'It's time G—— took a girl out. He's going
to take one of those.' Somebody whispered that land girls were a
mixed lot; uniform made it hard to judge; those two mightn't be
out of G——'s 'drawer'. 'Leave it to me,' said Sargent. He went
over and introduced himself. The girls had accents straight from
finishing school. Appropriating one of them, he conferred the other
upon a reluctant G——, who decided to make the best of a disturbing situation. Under Sargent's wand the party went to the theatre,
the two couples sitting in one row, Aris and his switchboard mate
behind. Sargent talked inexhaustibly and kept things on the bubble.
But for him the situation might have been painfully staid. Private
G—— shed a misogynist layer or two and seemed almost to be
enjoying himself. After the performance he and Sargent walked the
girls along the seafront. Private G—— was so overcome by the
adventure that he fell over the edge of the sea wall. The tide was out.
The drop wasn't great. He suffered no physical harm to speak of.

But the night had been prodigious. He needed no bruises next day to remind him of that.

*

One in a relay of message-takers, Sargent sat at the switchboard taking down through headphones a document which meant more to the people of Britain than the Armistice terms themselves. How soon or late a man got out of khaki depended on where he was placed in the schedule of demobilization categories. The schedule was coming over the line. One of Sargent's 'takes' mentioned organists. He recalled with a start that he was one himself. They were in a late-release category. Glancing through later 'takes' of the schedule before taking them over to the adjutant's office, he noticed something that made his face light up. University graduates intending to go in for post-graduate degrees were in Category I and theoretically entitled to release at once. Not content with anything so impersonal as a War Office paragraph, he wrote that day, as between fellow members of the Royal College of Organists, to Sir Frederick Bridge, who had just retired from the Westminster Abbey organ, asking him to do what he could to expedite his case. 'Here I am at an infantry base,' he wrote in effect. 'I want to go in for my degree of Doctor of Music. Please get me out of the Army.'

Three days later his papers came through. He was the first out of his unit. He was promptly congratulated by a bullying, 'old-sweat' type of sergeant-major, who thought to ingratiate himself. 'Don't forget your old pal,' he said. 'I'm not likely to,' returned Sargent.

Aris watched him empty his kitbag on to the billet floorboards. He burned or gave away things not worth taking home. There were many copies of *The Tatler*, which had been posted to him regularly; amid the squalors of soldiering he had been amused to keep in touch through creamlaid photogravure with the fashionable and the eminent as they served canteen tea or attended charity matinées or beamed maritally through confetti and guard-of-honour swords outside St. Margaret's. Among letters he had accumulated were several which pestered him to set an operetta script to music. It wasn't for him, he commented, to compete with Sullivan and Offenbach. Over one letter he paused frowningly. 'What d'you think of that?' he asked, handing it to Aris. The letter offered him a cinema organ at £1,000 a year.

'Do you think I ought to accept it?'

'For heaven's sake don't,' replied Aris. 'A cinema organ is not the sort of job you're cut out for. You've got a much better future than that.'

Sargent crumpled the letter and threw it into the stove.

Aris saw him off at Herne Bay station, sad to see him go. 'For eight months we had been like brothers,' he said long afterwards.

CHAPTER NINE

'THE TWENTIES'

NEW THREADS were picked up as well as old.
His return to Melton school that winter caused a stir.
Thomas George Wilkinson, a relative newcomer to the staff, was giving a music lesson to a mixed class in the main hall. A lithe young man with dark hair and a splendidly cut suit passed through the hall on his way to the headmaster's study. He had a wide, bright smile that seemed to reach out, taking in everybody at a glance yet one at a time. The incident is not overlooked in the school's official history. 'There was,' it says, 'a flutter among the girls, who were eager to tell Wilkinson'—who had taken over the school music temporarily—'that this was their real music master.'

'Tom' Wilkinson's regular subjects were mathematics, English, geography and games. He relinquished music without demur. Until his marriage in the spring of 1919 he lodged at the Manor House in a room across the entrance hall from Sargent's. They became companions and collaborators. At parties, accompanying himself on the piano, Wilkinson would sing sentimental and romantic sheet ballads of the day (he was said to have a hundred of these off by heart) in an agreeable light baritone. A gifted mimic, he took off his friend's conducting mannerisms and caricatured them so deftly, construing his left arm as a boxer's guard and his right arm as a fencing master's, that Sargent invariably doubled up with laughter and asked for the performance twice over. Wilkinson had studied his friend's conducting mannerisms at school choir rehearsals and those of the town's choral society. With the choral society Sargent started rehearsing Part III of Samuel Coleridge Taylor's *Hiawatha* (the 'Departure') on New Year's Day, 1919. The performance was given

84

in the town's drill hall the following May. He had a chorus of seventy and a 'band' of thirty. There were the usual instrumental dodges and expedients. He should have had four French horns. He had only one. To make up for the deficiency he brought in two cornets and a euphonium, rewriting the parts accordingly. He had the cornets play softly, contrived to keep the foursome in tune and claimed later on that, in so small a hall, the effect was 'better than full brass'.

It is from the drill hall concert of 1919 that his public champion-ship of Coleridge Taylor dates. He was soon to be identified with new English music (Holst's *The Hymn of Jesus*, for instance) in more rarified idioms but had long been impatient of those who damned the composer of *Hiawatha* for not aiming at a like austerity—or for any reason at all. 'I have been told by the highbrows,' he was to say* 'that Coleridge Taylor does not rank absolutely on the top shelf. This is not my opinion. I have done his works so often that all the "weaknesses" should have hit me. But I still love doing them. He's a first-class composer, completely equipped technically, with a remarkable and individual chain of melodic invention.' 'The whole of Longfellow's poem is set in lines that don't rhyme, each consisting of four trochees—"You shall hear how Pau-Pak-Keewis,/How the handsome Yenadizze,/Danced at Hiawatha's wedding. . . ." It would seem impossible to set a work lasting in all its three parts nearly two hours always in this scansion. . . . But it is so cleverly done and so amazingly varied in its musical rhythm that one forgets the mono-tony of the poem. The tunes are always exquisitely simple and beautiful, the orchestration masterly—I know of no choral work better orchestrated.'

The beauties hymned by Sargent had a further advantage. As will be seen from the chapter on *Hiawatha* in costume at the Royal Albert Hall during the 1920s and 1930s, they had an unsuspected box office potential.

Again the parish church pealed and purred to his after-service organ recitals: Bach, Guilmant, Boëllmann, Lemare, Mendelssohn. One Sunday the offertories were set apart 'for Mr. Malcolm

* B.B.C., N. American transmission, 5th October, 1941, and 'Talking About the Proms', B.B.C. Home Service, 29th August, 1954.

Sargent in addition to his salary, in recognition of the invaluable services he has rendered to the music of the church'. He was £43 better off. As well as giving private lessons in Melton, he went over to Stamford once a week and took singing and piano pupils in the family front parlour at All Saints-street. He had more singing pupils than pianists, and there were more young women than young men on his list. The lessons lasted half an hour. Usually he gave four in the morning and four in the afternoon at half a guinea a time. A stiff fee in those days for a small town like Stamford—'but then,' as a former pupil remembers, 'Malcolm had something to give that no other teacher had.' He laid stress on disciplined breathing and prescribed special exercises for pupils afflicted with 'wobble', a thing he detested. If the exercises didn't work the wobbler would be dismissed. He is remembered as a *firm* teacher—'very sympathetic. But if you were bad he told you so frankly. If you had a bit of talent he encouraged it.'

Between lessons and into the small hours he worked for his musical doctorate. Most mornings of the week he could be seen through his ground-floor window by the casual passer-by in Burton-street hard at work on 30-stave manuscript paper, an open cut-throat razor to hand for sharpening pencils.

The Durham regulations that year required among other things of the candidate that he compose 'a three-movement piece, sacred or secular . . . containing good eight-part choral writing and a fugue in not less than five parts . . . preceded by an overture scored for full orchestra, the whole taking about forty minutes to perform.' Sargent chose Shelley's 'Ode to a Skylark' as his text. His setting included a quartet of solo voices and was divided into seven sections. Later that year he attended convocation at Durham and was confirmed at twenty-four as the youngest Doctor of Music in the history of that or any other university in these isles. He had got through what was normally a five-year course in eighteen months 'by going to bed at three in the morning and getting up at eight'.

His doctoral gown, a present from Mrs. Blakeney, was of the sort intended to last a lifetime; he was using it still in the 1960s. The 'Ode to a Skylark' setting wasn't quite as durable. But he lifted out one of its interludes, a Valsette in A minor for full orchestra and submitted it later to Alick Maclean, a noted conductor of spa music and ballad concerts, who was then running a 'Pop' series at the Queen's Hall. Maclean said, 'It's just the thing. Come along and conduct it.' This Sargent did. He did not think to seek permission from Durham. He often wondered whether the university authorities, if they had known, 'might not have pounced on me and taken my degree away in punishment'. Of the Valsette's merit he speaks offhandedly: 'Pure Tchaikovsky. And all the better for that.' He adds, characteristically: 'Nothing original about it, thank God. The trouble with so many modern composers is that they insist on being themselves'. However much composition attracted him, he never craved for an idiom of his own. Nor, while aspiring to Elgarian flights, did he disdain the commercial modes of the day. Tom Wilkinson, who was a poetaster among other things, brought him a newly finished lyric, 'My heart has a quiet sadness', and asked him whether there might not be a Chappell ballad in it. Chappells were the music publishing firm who, as lessors of the Queen's Hall, financially bolstered the Henry Wood Promenade concerts by printing and promoting sheet ballads. Meant to be sung among potted palms by young women in ball dresses and young men in white ties and white gloves, the sheet ballad flourished from about 1890 until superseded in the early 1920s by the wireless. Eric Blom defined it waspishly as, ' a . . . light and sentimental song, generally about love, a garden or moonshine, or preferably love in a moonlit garden, the words of which are by a hack writer, set to music by a composer of no merit but that of easy melodic invention and introduced by famous singers who thus advertised them not because they believed in them but because they received handsome fees'.* From the heart's quiet sadness, Wilkinson's three stanzas modulated to a soul throbbing with madness and love waiting in the vale. Sargent ran through the words, suggested one or two variants, sat down at the piano and composed the music in two hours. The piece is fluent of its sort; its composer might have been supposed to have done little but turn out Chappell ballads since the vogue began. Chappells published it at two shillings; it was first sung at the Queen's Hall by one of the most cultivated English tenors of the time, John Coates,

* Everyman's Dictionary of Music, successive editions from 1946.

4

and encored. 'It brought me in quite a lot of money,' Sargent used to say, his tone suggesting that this was the best thing about it. For the sake of a nostalgic smile he was capable at seventy of singing a line or two of the ballad himself, *a capella* if no piano was to hand. He was no John Coates, however. This he was the first to assert.

*

As people began to forget the Kaiser's War or turn their minds from it, so did the social round at Melton accelerate. Isolated voices were not wanting to sound the Cassandra note. Thus Canon Blakeney. His burden at the town's memorial service to its war dead was Bolshevism, ' . . . a spectacle of horror beyond imagining. What is Bolshevism's great objective? The destruction of everything and everyone! . . . Misery, starvation, poverty, confusion, disease and death! . . . Bolshevism's crafty agitators, with their plausible words and wily proposals, will bring this country to ruin.'

'There's much in what old Blakeney says,' allowed the well-to-do, 'but, pending ruin and misery, let us enjoy ourselves in the old way. Who are we having in our party to the Hunt Ball?' For Melton's annual Hunt Ball the inside of the Corn Exchange was draped in white and crimson muslins and smothered in winter roses. House parties came in from lodges and halls, manors and granges fifty miles around. Punctuated by champagne corks, string bands played valetas, and the valetas were danced by jewelled women and men in hunting pink. One big question during the days preceding the Ball was whether the Prince of Wales or one of his brothers would be there. Usually they weren't. But the future Edward VIII had taken to hunting with the Quorn, and hostesses were fevered and hopeful. Meets now drew 'galleries' unheard of before 1914. Crowds came in hundreds of motor-cars to clutter lanes and hillsides. Often they marred the day's sport. This did not concern them greatly. They were there not for the chase but on the offchance of seeing the Prince or, failing the Prince, another of the nation's darlings, Lonsdale, the improvident Yellow Earl.

During Lonsdale's mastership of the Cottesmore, the Prince occasionally stayed at Barley Thorpe, the Earl's seat, a few miles outside Melton. Sargent was another Barley Thorpe guest. On Sunday mornings Lonsdale would gallop to Melton parish church with outriders, as if time had stood still for centuries. After playing the outgoing voluntary, Sargent would drive with other guests for a turn of stable duty at Barley Thorpe. Lonsdale usually had fifteen horses in training. He would show the party round, all smile, carnation and cigar. By each stall stood a young groom in livery with basket of scrubbed, sliced carrots. The guests were privileged to feed these to the horses. In his middle sixties, Lonsdale looked as blandly unassailable as the Royal Mint. There was a canker nonetheless. Within a few years Barley Thorpe had been sold and two castles he owned in the North shut up wholly or in part to raise funds and retrench.

It was a time when the decline of ancient fortunes intersected the rise of new ones. At the table of the Huntingdons, who lived near Loughborough, Sargent was asked by the Countess about Mr. C—— the biscuit millionaire, who had lavishly set up house in the district. Her inquiry had a cautious ring. Being 'in trade', on however grand a scale, Mr. C—— couldn't be regarded as a gentleman. At the same time, he was a neighbour. And one had to be neighbourly. What *sort* of people were the C——s? pursued the Countess.

'Oh, charming!' said Sargent.

'Do you hear that, Hastings?' The question was called down the table by the Countess to her husband, Warner Francis John Plantagenet Hastings, fourteenth Earl.

'Do I hear what?'

'About the C——s. Mr. Sargent says they're quite nice. We must have them to tea.'

A demarcation line had been drawn. In pronouncing the C——s eligible for tea, the Countess had conveyed that they didn't rate a dinner invitation.

In odd enclaves here and there the fevered 'Twenties arrived almost on time and made people stare. The gay, erratic Mrs. Astley Cooper had a house on a hilltop at Hambleton, three miles from the Lonsdales. Sargent went to his first party at Mrs. Cooper's for tennis and was asked to stay on for dinner. He said he wanted to so much. But what about *clothes*? Mrs. Cooper rather thought her butler could help; and so the butler did. The dinner suit he produced ('We like to look after our visitors,' he said) might have been made for Sargent, although finding a collar that approximately fitted was a hilarious business. Given to lying on a mattress in front of the fire and shooting off witticisms in a sort of 'petulant wail', as we learn from Noël Coward's *Future Indefinite*, Mrs. Cooper did not allow her eccentricities to interfere with the comfort of others. Fires in all bedrooms every night. Brass cans of hot water. Dinner clothes neatly laid out on the bed. Deep majestic baths set in polished wood. Guests went to meets and followed the hunt by dogcart. Sargent relished this milieu as much as Coward and adapted himself to it as spontaneously as to Barley Thorpe, or the company of the Huntingdons, or Mrs. Blakeney's musical evenings, or, somewhat later, the grandness of Burghley House itself.

Among more intimate friends and hobnobbers were Jean and Harold Furness, a couple who believed in enjoying life and did so with taste.

Then in his middle thirties, Furness, a physician and surgeon of note throughout the region, was a cordial and imposing figure who went in for rock-climbing, played golf boisterously and with passion and loved music more than anything else. In his drawing-room stood a splendid Bechstein grand which had been given to him on his eleventh birthday. He played it worthily. Later he blossomed as an amateur conductor. Sargent was constantly in and out of the Furnesses' house. He played in charades and led burlesque ballets in the garden on summer evenings. Some of the most hilarious charade nights involved Sargent as foil, or vice versa, to an émigré Russian concert pianist, Prince George Chavchavadze, another of the Furness circle. Between them Sargent and Chavchavadze 'took off' half the notables of Melton. With the Furnesses he went on motoring holidays to Scotland and the Lakes. Yellowing snapshots survive of picnics among the heather and boating parties on tarns. He always dressed attentively. His plus-four suits, flannel bags, snap-brims and tweed caps were irreproachable. Under Furness's tutelage he tried his hand at golf, not with much success, he owns: 'When eventually I *did* hit the ball, it either went a long way in the wrong direction or five yards into a bed of nettles.'

Their great common interest was the Bechstein. Sargent had the run of it any day of the week. A year or two later, when he was regularly going up to London for lessons with Benno Moiseiwitsch and still had the alternative career of concert pianist at the back of his mind, he practised Rachmaninov's second and Tchaikovsky's first concerto on Harold Furness's piano for public performances in Leicester. He played with such brilliance that small crowds used to gather and listen on the Park-road pavement outside the drawing-room window.

Since little in the way of professional entertainment came to Melton, the Meltonians did what they could to entertain themselves. Sargent was roped in, nothing reluctant, for amateur dramatics at the Corn Exchange. He played juvenile lead in a number of farces. In *My Lord in Livery* he did the nobleman who, with amorous designs, gets himself up first as a footman, then as a burglar. In *The Bathroom Door* he frivoled in a dressing-gown and ogled with abandon. Early that year the D'Oyly Carte company put on a Gilbert and Sullivan season at the Opera House, Leicester. Sargent, Tom Wilkinson and his wife, the Furnesses and other friends drove over from Melton for an afternoon performance of *The Gondoliers*. At the interval Sargent said to the others, 'Let's form a Gilbert and Sullivan society in Melton. You'll play the Henry Lytton parts, Tom. You, Harold, shall be pianist and assistant conductor. So-and-so shall do the tenor parts, So-and-So the heavies. . . .' The thing was agreed on the spot. Everybody was infected by Sargent's zest. Plans were laid on the homeward journey.

As a result the Melton Amateur Operatic Society, dedicated mainly to Gilbert and Sullivan, came into being during the summer of 1919, with Sargent as musical director and producer. At the same time he took on the conductorship of the newly-revived Stamford A.O.S., which had been in abeyance since their *Princess Ida* production in the spring of 1914. Rehearsals began in both towns that autumn. Melton was to put on *Patience*, Stamford *The Mikado*. Tom Wilkinson had sung Henry Lytton parts before. He seems to have been a fetching Bunthorne. In both towns the principals generally were wholly or almost untried. For want of a professional coach Sargent took his Melton singers singly or in groups at the piano, regularly jumping up from the keyboard to dictate a gesture, an amble or a stare. How had he come by this instinct for the stage? Solely by assimilating and applying what he had seen in Midlands theatres, where he missed nothing of moment, and on occasional visits to West End shows. Chorus work was no problem at all. To get thirty or so dependable singers from the choral societies and church choirs of either town entailed little more than a week of audition nights. It is true that once on the stage the chorus men and women tended to clot into phalanxes. The two pit orchestras, each twenty to twenty-five strong, overlapped in membership. As usual the horn quartet consisted of a horn and a euphonium. For both societies scenery was built and painted in the Lincolnshire village of Bourne. Costumes came from a theatrical wardrobe in Covent Garden. So did the make-up man who used to arrive early on the afternoon of first nights with a long black box, put on a smock and daub away for hours, turning excited young people into contadine, *Mikado* maidens, dragoons, yeomen and such.

The Melton society was launched with a patrons' list that read like the Court Circular on a good day. It was led by the Duke and Duchess of Rutland and the Marquess and Marchioness of Exeter and took in three earls, three countesses and a swarm of barons, baronets, honourables, brigadiers and colonels of horse. At Melton *Patience* played three nights and a matinée at the beginning of March 1920. Stamford followed with four nights and a matinée of *The Mikado* at the beginning of April. This order of going continued throughout Sargent's tenure of the two societies, which continued without break for about ten years, notwithstanding the national reputation he was acquiring and the complex conducting schedules to which he had committed himself in and out of London. Each year the Melton performances coincided with the final rehearsals at Stamford. (From 1923 onwards, as will be seen, he rehearsed and conducted a third amateur society over a hundred miles away, that of Winchester, who put on a Savoy opera, five nights and a matinée, every May.)

The Melton company's home was the Corn Exchange, a chill, drab auditorium when not garnished and warmed up for Hunt Balls. It was town's property, vested in twelve feoffees and managed by two wardens who were elected by their fellow citizens at five pounds a year. Tip-up seats had to be hired or begged from theatre or cinema circuits. Every performance that first March was crammed, all standing room taken, many turned away at the doors. At Melton and Stamford alike last nights were orgies of goodwill and facetiousness. For some years Sargent ceded traditionally and generously to the clamour for encores. A Stamford *Merrie England*, his first departure from the Savoy repertory, was performed nearly twice over on the last night, one of the choruses, 'Hey with a ho', being repeated thrice. What may have been a record was put up the following year, when he allowed *five* repeats of Dame Hannah's and Sir Roderick's duet (*Ruddigore*). It was his job, after the last curtain had fallen and risen again, to hand up presents. For the male principals there were always bouquets of bananas and leeks, beribboned bottles of beer, toy scooters, toy rifles and monster 'dumteats'. Such tokens struck many in the audience as funny. It usually took Sargent quite half an hour to pass everything up. He toiled with gleaming good humour. On the last night at Melton in 1920 he was called on to the stage, cheered, given a silver rose bowl and, to the strains of 'For he's a jolly good fellow', chaired by Bunthorne and Grosvenor. His smile, brightness, tails and white waistcoat went to all hearts. Supper followed on the stage, there was dancing, a few people got mildly drunk, and Sargent guyingly conducted numbers from *Patience*, with the men singing the women's rôles and the other way about. A month later Stamford's *Mikado* at the Assembly Rooms ended with like revels, though hardly with the same abandon, Stamford being a soberer town than flighty Melton. Stamford's last-night present to him was a baton in ivory and silver. He made use of it right away to conduct a blithe 'God Save the King' from centre footlights, everybody joining in.

Although they differed as communities, Melton and Stamford responded to their 'young genius' (the phrase had already crept into print and was in many mouths) with similar delight. To say he directed the two companies did not, in popular estimation, go far enough. In a sense he *was* the Melton amateurs, he *was* the Stamford amateurs. He turned nobodies into somebodies, small talents into sizeable ones. When he arrived for rehearsals he made everybody feel enormously glad to be alive simply because he looked enormously glad to be alive himself. This was the famous Sargent vitalism. It was to seal his success and sway, especially with great choirs at home and abroad, down half a century.

During those early years he made himself responsible—wholly at Melton, partly at Stamford—for every detail of acting, dancing and grouping. Sometimes there were crises. None defeated him. There was the night when Rose Maybud (*Ruddigore*) found herself unable to produce more than a squeak half an hour before curtain-up. One of her friends came panting with the news to Sargent. Near the Assembly Rooms was a public house. 'Get some port wine,' he instructed, 'and tell Helen,' for that was Rose's real name, 'to gargle with it. She'd better not swallow any, of course!' The trouble had been nervous constriction of the throat. She soon got rid of it. People put this down to the port wine gargle and said how clever Malcolm was. They did not know that, after the gargle, he had told her he had a good substitute ready in Leicester. Next to Sargent the main prop of the Stamford company was Patrick Johnson, a bank manager, who sang bass in the chorus and, as stage manager, helped at preliminary rehearsals, which were held in his house, part of the bank. For *Utopia Limited* he was promoted to a small part, that of Phantis, one of the judges of the Utopia Court. In the opening scene, while doing Phantis's song and dance on a dais ('Observe this dance/ Which I employ/When I by chance,/Go mad with joy.') he fell over the edge and broke an ankle bone. Sargent hunted for a substitute. He found one in the English master at Stamford Grammar School, a keen musical amateur, who was to have left for holiday in Corsica next day. Sargent sat up most of the night coaching him at the piano. After nine hours the new man had words, music and action pat. The show was saved. On a later night a disturbing experience befell the Lady Sophy who, on making her first entry with lecturer's wand and grave mien, walked into utter blankness. She couldn't think of her opening words or opening notes, didn't know why she was there, or even who she was. Sargent was busying himself with the orchestral prelude. Suddenly he glanced up. Divining her plight, he smiled assuringly and mouthed the first of her lines— 'This morning we propose to illustrate/A course of maiden courtship . . .' Instantly Lady Sophy's black-out lifted. From the opening 'recit' to the end her performance was complete and confident.

*

The Melton productions had a decisive social advantage over the Stamford ones because of princes of the blood. On the opening night of *The Yeomen of the Guard* the Prince of Wales came on from Craven Lodge, where at that time he kept a large stud. He reached the Corn Exchange an hour late and was ushered to a roped-off section of the seven-and-sixpenny balcony. That night the hall was draughtier than usual and bitterly cold. Yet the Prince seemed to enjoy himself. He said cordial things to Sargent after curtain-fall. The following two years his brothers were there. The Duke of York heard *Trial by Jury* and *H.M.S. Pinafore*, the Duke of Gloucester *Princess Ida*. Both went backstage. Sargent charmed and amused them. From these meetings stemmed his multiple and continuing friendships with the reigning family. It was not always easy to reconcile the claims of comic opera and those of sport. Out hunting one day the Prince of Wales met Lady Ravensdale, who had by this time taken the Melton Society under her wing, and said he would take twenty tickets for his staff that night. The tickets were promptly sent round to Craven Lodge. The twenty seats remained empty. Next day the Prince admitted that, exhausted not so much by a day's hunting as by his recent labours in entertaining the King of Afghanistan ('a boring business', he explained), he had fallen asleep and didn't waken up until after the show. . . . Would Lady Ravensdale convey his regrets to Sargent?

Another notable, although as yet only a budding one, was a handsome boy of eighteen, M. K. Tippett, as the programme called him, Sir Michael Tippett, as he is today. How did young Michael come to play the King's Fool, a non-singing part, in Stamford's *Merrie England* of 1923? How did he come to be in Stamford at all?

The answer tells us something about the divagations and persistence of high musical gifts and how one gifted man may react upon another. Michael Tippett's parents were much out of the country. This created a problem. The solution was boarding school. Michael

4*

went on a scholarship to a college in the North. There he suffered 'sadism, cruelty, bullying, everything'. He ran away. Another school had to be found. His parents were not rich; big fees were out of the question. They heard of Stamford Grammar School. Room for sixty boarders; fees low. They got Michael a place there. After Scotland the Stamford school was paradise. It didn't take him long, it is true, to quarrel with the headmaster. At fifteen or sixteen he knew nothing about music but, suddenly beginning to crave for it, was put to Mrs. Tinkler—'a very warm and mature personality. I was having my troubles and trials. Troubles with my headmaster because I let it be known I didn't believe in God. All my troubles I took to Mrs. Tinkler. She helped. This on top of teaching me piano. She was a Mother Figure in the Freudian sense. But never sentimental.'

Meantime he had heard about The Young Doctor. That was the school name for Sargent, who was still looking after music there as well as teaching at the Melton school. With another boy and one of Mrs. Tinkler's orchestras, Michael rehearsed a Bach double piano concerto for a school concert. Sargent came to the rehearsal. He stood now behind one soloist, now behind the other. Michael had not seen him before. 'I remember this slim, well-dressed figure,' he says. 'I was terribly frightened. Yet fascinated. He was so "un-school".' At the rehearsal and after the concert Sargent made a comment or two about the pair's piano playing. His accurate ear and memory impressed Michael.

Not long after this Michael, one of a boys' motor coach party, went over to Leicester and heard not only his first orchestral concert but also his first piece of music outside the classics. The orchestra was the Leicester Symphony, which Sargent had newly formed. The non-classic was Ravel's *Mother Goose* Suite. Already he had thought of making music his career. The Leicester concert turned an inclination into a resolve. It showed him, furthermore, what shape his career should take. He was going to be a composer.

At the same time his quarrels with the headmaster sharpened. He flaunted his atheism, refused to join the cadet corps and neglected his lessons for a whole year. Finally he walked out of school and took lodgings in the town. 'My digs were declared out of bounds to my old schoolfellows because I was regarded as a most sinister character. Nobody knew what to do with me. Even Mrs. Tinkler was at a loss.' At his prompting his parents wrote to Sargent, whom they had not met, saying they wished to put Michael to music. Sargent's reply was adverse. He stressed how precarious a profession music was. ('This,' comments Tippett, 'was the right and sensible thing for him to say.') The letter, as Tippett remembers it, added that in case Michael thought his success at the school concerts was any indication of musical talent, one might properly say his success was due less to musical ability than to a charming personality.

A year later his parents entered him for the Royal College of Music. On arrival at Kensington Gore the future composer of *A Child of Our Time*, *The Midsummer Marriage*, *King Priam*, the two Symphonies, the Concerto for Orchestra and the Concerto for Piano and Orchestra put himself down for the conducting classes. He was startled to find that these were run by Sargent, who had reached the College a term or two ahead of him.

'Again,' says Tippett, 'I was frightened, very frightened. The score in front of me would blur and disappear. But that soon passed.'

*

We have come to a major hinge in our story. A door opened. Sargent walked through it to sudden and expanding celebrity. During the five years 1921 to 1925 his career spilled over and multiplied at a pace and on levels which cannot be readily paralleled in his profession.

During the first of these five years, between the ages of twenty-five and thirty, he made his début as a composer-conductor under Henry Wood's sponsorship at a Queen's Hall Promenade concert. In the second and third years he recruited, trained and launched the Leicester Symphony Orchestra; and mobilized and drilled a choir for performances of *The Hymn of Jesus* and *The Dream of Gerontius*, works which had rarely, perhaps never before, made such an impact in the provinces. In the fourth year he became musical director of the Robert Mayer Concerts for Children, London, remaining with them until the outbreak of Hitler's War; and was chosen by the British National Opera Company to conduct the first production, at His Majesty's Theatre, of Ralph Vaughan Williams's *Hugh the Drover*. The same year (1924) saw his début as a recording conductor; he put *Hugh the Drover* on six old-type discs for H.M.V. In the fifth year he conducted his first concerts with the Royal Choral Society (Ethel Smyth's Mass in D minor) and for the Royal Philharmonic Society (Borodin's Symphony in B minor, etc.); and, having conducted fourteen productions of ten Savoy operas in the provinces, was listed by Rupert D'Oyly Carte as a likely chief conductor for his big London season the following year.

He had, in other words, become a minor though much canvassed national figure in next to no time and was soon to be accepted as a full-sized one.

Somewhere along the career sequence he had fallen in love.

At the Furnesses' and other parties he was seen much with a slim, elegant girl, Eileen Laura Harding Horne. Miss Horne lived at Beyton, Suffolk. She was a keen rider and made many friends in Melton hunting circles. She and Malcolm married on a mellow September day at Drinkwater Church, Suffolk, where an uncle of hers, the Rev. Frank Horne, was rector. The uncle officiated and a cousin, the Rev. Richard Faithfull, rector of Chislehurst, assisted. It was a day of warm sunshine, silver lamé and old English lace, old gold satin, flowers made of velvet and an abundance of real ones. The choral music was copious. Some of it had been composed by old Dr. Keeton, Sargent's one-time master. The village street was bright with bunting. The wedding cake was surmounted by a hunter in sugar icing. An avalanche of presents was detailed by the weekly papers of three shires. The Huntingdons, Lady Tichborne, Lady Paston-Cooper, Mrs. Astley Cooper were in the list. And scores more.

For a closer look at some happenings which preceded and immediately followed the Sargents' setting up house in London (1924) we must turn back in our tracks for a chapter or so.

CHAPTER TEN

ENTER SIR HENRY

THE DAY the door swung open can be named. It was Thursday 3rd February, 1921. On that day Sir Henry Wood brought the Queen's Hall Orchestra to Leicester and gave a concert at the De Montfort Hall in aid of the blind. What was billed as *the* social event of the Leicester season drew a capacity house including standers at two shillings a head. A last-minute blocking of the entrances resulted in shoving, shouldering, a scramble for seats and a clink of programme money that continued for a minute or two after Wood had begun the *Magic Flute* Overture. As well as Mozart the programme included things by César Franck, Wagner, Järnefelt (a best-seller, the *Praeludium*), an orchestral arrangement of Bach's Air for the G String and an *Allegro impetuoso* subtitled *An Impression on a Windy Day*. The last was Sargent's own work, his Op. 9. It had been written for the occasion and accounted for some of the advance excitement.

The concert committee had commissioned it months earlier. A fortnight before the concert not a note had been written. Wood wrote sharply to the committee. It was too late now for him to prepare the commissioned piece, he said. 'Whoever this young fellow is,' he added, referring to Sargent, 'he will have to conduct it himself.' Sargent sat down and composed his *Allegro impetuoso* 'quickly and easily' and sent off his manuscript to the copyists. He had had an outline of the piece in his head for months. The 'feel' and to some extent the thematic material of it came to him while golfing with Furness and other friends at Cromer in gusty weather. ('I hit six balls into the sea in quick succession.') Wood gave him a rehearsal on the afternoon of the concert. This was his first assignment with a professional orchestra. Although there were exquisite artists among the Queen's Hall men, all were hardbitten practitioners and inclined to be sardonic about human nature. For most provincial boys, however gifted, the encounter would have been paralysing. When Sargent bounced on to the rostrum in his ebullient way the players exchanged covert smiles. Unlike Wood, who had some idea of Sargent's age, the players had known nothing except that he was a doctor of music and a parish organist. Naturally, as the first oboe told him afterwards, they had expected someone obese and bald and were amused at the way their expectations had been cheated.

Perhaps because of his inexperience, perhaps because of excitement—'I was so excited by my music that I forgot to be overawed'—that night's performance did not satisfy him. In retrospect he called it 'rather slapdash'. There was excitement in the audience, too. Many had come in from Melton and Stamford and had fixed a special late train for the journey home. Sargent was hero and darling. They loved his music before hearing a note of it. As he bowed before the general ovation he looked very handsome in hired tails that might have been cut for him. Clapping went on insatiably. There was a rule against encores for orchestral items, but the concert was being held up. When Sargent returned to the wings after a second 'curtain' call, Wood said to him; 'You'd better give them a repeat. We haven't time for the whole thing, of course. Can you shorten it?' 'Certainly,' said Sargent. 'All right, then,' said Wood, 'do the best and briefest you can.' The full score of *Windy Day* ran to seventy-one pages. Back on the rostrum Sargent said 'Letter O' and lifted his baton. Letter O was at page forty-four and started conveniently with an upward run for flute, with harp glissando. The last twenty-seven pages appeased the audience while delighting them. Sir Henry was able to get on at last with the *Meistersinger* Overture and the *Tanhäuser* March.

Later that night Sargent went round with Wood and his manager Robert Newman to their hotel. Wood said: 'You will come to the Promenade, and this piece shall be played.'

'But this is wonderful, Sir Henry' returned Sargent. 'We shall now get a performance of it that is proper.'

Wood: 'That's as may be. Anyway, you are to conduct it.'

Windy Day was scheduled for 11th October at the Proms. At the rehearsal Sargent was preceded on the rostrum by Wood, who went to work on the *Pathétique* Symphony, paying special attention to the *Allegro con grazia* (5/4) movement. When the break came Sargent went downstairs to the artists' room at the Queen's Hall convulsed with laughter. He said to a violist of his acquaintance who was coming up the stairs: 'I've been enjoying myself. Did you ever see anything so funny in your life as Henry trying to beat five in a bar?' The violist was bewildered. Wood's 5/4 beat had struck him as lucid and quite uncomical; and, anyway, who was this infant to make game of an admired practitioner with a hundred times his experience? When it came to his turn on the rostrum the infant comported himself like a battery of wound-up clocksprings. His stick vibrated so dizzily at times that it momentarily disappeared from view like the spokes of a carriage wheel. And all the time he talked through the music, scattering encouragements, warnings, exhortations. Orchestras do not greatly care for loquacious conductors, especially when they are young. Mother, father, sister, Uncle Bert and Uncle Bert's wife and daughter came up for the concert, and after the rehearsal all had luncheon at a stylish restaurant in Piccadilly with Malcolm, who talked instead of eating, as was always his way, whether before or after concerts.

He conducted with aplomb and collected civil, even cordial notices. Critics and gossips alike made play with his background. 'No mere academic exercise,' said the *Daily Telegraph* with a glance at his doctorate and parish organ, 'but as breezy as a day with the hounds at Melton Mowbray.' Some critics detected influences of Mendelssohn and Elgar in *Windy Day*. 'It is not nearly as good as either of those,' said Sargent in the middle 1950s before one of many revivals of the work at the Henry Wood Proms. 'What it *does* sound like is the young Sargent who, although the piece was extremely successful, decided to compose very little more and take up conducting.'*

* For a Hallé concert in Leicester, mentioned later in this chapter, he composed a year later a *Nocturne and Scherzo* subtitled *A Night with Pan*, which he conducted the following month in London with the Royal Albert Hall Orchestra and the following October at the Proms. Of the latter performance *The Musical*

In this resolve he was egged on, not that he needed anything of
the sort, by the Russells of Leicester, who saw in young Sargent a
talent and personality which, if boldly exploited, might boost the
concert-promotion side of their music business. W. H. ('Billy')
Russell, remembered as something of a rough diamond, owned what
he called The City Piano and Organ Saloons in the London-road.
Here in the early 1920s you could buy a secondhand Bechstein for
anything from a hundred to two hundred guineas. Older people
recalled Russell's obscure beginnings. Until well into the reign of
Edward VII he had sold secondhand pianos and harmoniums from
his house in Saxe-Coburg-street, where stock cluttered parlour and
dining-room. Both at home and later at the Saloons he was helped
by his son George Karl, to whom the business reverted on the elder
Russell's death. In appearance and temperament Karl Russell
differed sharply from Billy Russell. Small and inclined to foppish-
ness, Karl went up regularly to London to have his hair dressed,
played the piano plausibly, collected expensive editions of the
classics, and lived in a big, tastefully furnished house, with a ping-
pong room next door to the library.

In the autumn of 1921, a week before Sargent's début as composer-conductor at the Queen's Hall, the Leicester papers carried
display advertisements (the one in the *Leicester Mercury* took up a
third of a page) for a series of four Russell Subscription Concerts at
the De Montfort Hall. They were to be spread over the coming six
months. All were ambitious or unusual in one way or another. Three
of them and part of a fourth were to be conducted by Sargent. Karl
Russell's hand is evident in the blurbs. 'The Hon. Directors,' he
announced, 'have been fortunate in securing the services of Dr.
Malcolm Sargent as their Musical Director. These concerts will
give Dr. Sargent every opportunity to display his undoubted
Genius and amazing Versatility as Composer, Conductor, Pianist
and Organist.'

*

Times reported that the Scherzo 'went with a bang, not a little of its effect being
due to the tremendous energy of the young conductor, who bestrode the whirlwind in fine style'.

The series opening with an outsize Gilbert and Sullivan concert in the De Montfort Hall at the end of October 1921. Four rising professional soloists, including a baritone who is now a legend, George Baker, came down from London on an early train to gear in at the afternoon rehearsal with the combined Gilbert and Sullivan choruses of Stamford and Melton and an orchestra which, made up of professionals, 'semi professionals' and amateurs, was twice the size usually seen in comic opera pits. The programme consisted of excerpts from *The Mikado*, *The Gondoliers* and *The Yeomen of the Guard*. When he conducted *Windy Day*, Sargent had struck the Queen's Hall Orchestra as boyish. On his Gilbert and Sullivan soloists he made a different impression. 'He was twenty-six, looked thirty and had the manner and authority of thirty-five,' recalls Baker. Leicester had been assured by Karl Russell's 'ad' that, under Sargent's direction, the performances would be 'brilliant and fascinating'; and so they turned out to be on the orchestral side and as to some of the solo singing. To some ears, however, the spatchcocked choruses, seemed under-rehearsed, and there is said to have been a glaringly wrong entry in the opening chorus of *The Gondoliers*. After the concert the artists' room was overrun by women with county accents and imposing manners, either committee people or backers from Melton and further afield who had come to tell Sargent how marvellous it had been and how wonderful he was. Influential women were on his side and at his side from the start. Earlier that year the Marchioness of Exeter, Lady Cecil, Lady Martin Cecil, Lady Falkiner, Lady Alice Willoughby 'and party' had heard him partner a local girl violinist in Mozart's B flat major sonata and Brahms's A major sonata for violin and piano at a matinée in the Stamford Assembly Rooms. Some of the Brahms may have been on the learned side. But Malcolm made even development sections endurable; his charm and sprightliness transformed everything.

For the second Russell concert, in December, he and his devoted 'fixers' (in this capacity Grace Burrows was already hand in hand with Bertie Parrish) enrolled an orchestra of fifty with a bigger proportion of professionals than usual. He drilled his players ruthlessly. They were to accompany one of the newest, youngest and most talked about piano virtuosos of the day, Benno Moiseiwitsch, in

Beethoven's *Emperor* Concerto. On the night, cool and fluent, he prefaced this work and the remaining items (they included the *Bartered Bride* Overture, Moussorgsky's *Gopak* and the *Children's Overture* of Quilter) with brief analytical talks of the sort to which he had inured the boys and girls at Melton school. Hearing Sargent amuse himself at the piano the following morning, Moiseiwitsch cocked an ironical eyebrow and said something to this effect: 'If I don't watch out you'll be playing me off the platform. You've got quite a lot in those fingers. Would you like me to give you lessons?' Sargent jumped at the idea. Arrangements were made on the spot. Sargent went up to London for several sessions at Moiseiwitsch's home. During one of the early lessons Moiseiwitsch walked about the room, stared out of the window, fiddled with a book. Sargent broke off touchily and asked, 'Are you listening? Are you interested? If you aren't there's no point in going on. It would be a waste of time.' Moiseiwitsch said mildly that he often fidgeted while listening to other people; it was just a way of his. After this master and pupil got on amicably. At most lessons they sat side by side, playing the same music on two pianos. This was Moiseiwitsch's way of teaching by example. The teacher rarely spoke, thus imposing silence without asking for it. Sargent once ventured to ask how he practised a certain exacting rhythmic passage in Schumann. 'I bite my lips until they bleed,' was the reply. Moiseiwitsch declined to take any fee. The lessons had taught *him* quite a lot, he said whimsically.

At the third Russell concert—for which Hamilton Harty and his Hallé Orchestra came over from Manchester—Sargent conducted his *Night with Pan* in the second half and played solo in Tchaikovsky's B flat minor Piano Concerto before the interval. This was the piece which had drawn pavement audiences when he practised it in the Furnesses' drawing-room. His performance was praised by everybody, Harty included.

'Yes,' Harty used to say, 'Sargent played splendidly. But I had the devil of a job to stop him from conducting the orchestra as well as playing the piano.'

Less than a year later Sargent played in Rachmaninov's C minor Concerto. The conductor this time was another rising talent, thirty-three-year-old Adrian Boult. Forty years later Sir Adrian

spoke of Sargent's performance as 'brilliant'. Henry Wood heard
about the brilliance and rather demurred. After all, he had launched
the young man as a conductor, and a conductor he must be. Sometime in 1923 he advised Sargent to give up the piano. Sargent had
already decided that, so far as public appearances were concerned,
the piano should henceforth be an occasional indulgence or sideline.

*

The most important of the Russells' 'pilot' concerts was the fourth
and last. On 6th April, 1922, after arduous and widely flung choral
rehearsals, he conducted *The Dream of Gerontius*. His choir was a
fusion of the Leicester Oriana Choral Society, the Leicester Choral
Union and the Melton Mowbray Choral Society. His orchestra was
the usual mixture of amateurs and professionals (whole or 'semi').
He brought Charles Woodhouse, one of the noted 'concertmasters'
of the day, from London to lead it. John Coates was his Gerontius
and Soul, Phyllis Lett his Angel, Horace Stevens his Priest and
Angel of the Agony. Elgar's oratorio had had an ill-starred and
near-chaotic first performance at Birmingham twenty-one years
earlier. Amateur choirs were a little scared of it. Not so Sargent's
forces. They sang the Demons' Chorus with a bite and bravura
which, as was commented at the time, would have astonished the
average provincial choir of ten or fifteen years earlier. In effect this
1922 *Gerontius* was Sargent's true beginning. It signalled his
realization of a great purpose. That purpose was to affirm the
greatness of Edward Elgar during decades when Elgar's essential
'smallness' and 'out-of-dateness' were a received opinion. For contemporary accounts of the performance one has to go to the two
Leicester newspapers, the *Mail* and the *Mercury*, both served by
critics of note, one of whom wrote the comment about the Demons'
Chorus cited above. After nearly five decades it is impossible to
read the fading newsprint without catching something of the performance's strength and flame. These came straight from young
Sargent. *Gerontius* was a work for which he was preordained, a
work which sent roots deeper down in him than superficial judges
thought there was depth for roots to go. It is material, therefore,
to know how he first came upon *Gerontius* and how this led him

to its composer. The story goes back to his early Peterborough days.

Keeton had been giving him an eight-part counterpoint lesson. As he was leaving the Presence the old man threw a Novello score at his head, saying, 'Here, young Sargent, this may interest you. I can't make head or tail of it.' He caught the copy in mid-air. It was *The Dream of Gerontius*. He heard it performed for the first time a year or two later. It was sung in Peterborough Cathedral, and Amos Ebenezer Armstrong, conductor for a time of the Stamford Gilbert and Sullivan shows, was on the rostrum.*

Sargent had a seat behind a pillar and couldn't see anything or anybody. He was exalted and bowled over. Afterwards there was a party at the Armstrongs. Somebody asked Sargent about his career. He was sitting in the dining-room window seat, legs crossed, hands in pockets. 'I'm going to be a composer,' he said. 'I'm going to be a second Elgar.' This was said burningly.

At the 1922 performance and general rehearsal, John Coates and Charles Woodhouse, seasoned judges, were struck by three things: the young man's fervour for the music, his transmitting of this fervour to every singer on the platform and his supple technical control of the choir. It seems that without consulting each other Coates and Woodhouse wrote to Elgar about the prodigy they had discovered in Leicestershire. Elgar got in touch with Sargent and invited him to call when next in London.

At their first meeting, prelude to others and to a friendship which lasted until Elgar's death twelve years later, the composer put the *Gerontius* score on his piano desk and, as Sargent played, commented discursively. As became clear during their later meetings, disappointments and hurts lay deep in the old man. He often shunned his own music. When Toscanini and his New York orchestra on their maiden visit to the Queen's Hall (June 1930) did the *Enigma*

---

* When Armstrong lay on his deathbed in 1946 Sargent sent him his newly issued recording of *Gerontius* with a heartfelt note which, recalling the Peterborough performance said that what he knew about *The Dream* he learned from Armstrong at Peterborough. Sir Thomas Armstrong comments: 'That message, although not strictly true—for Sargent learned much about *The Dream* from its composer—made a lot of difference to my father's last days.'

Variations a great shout went up at the end for the composer. Sargent was among the shouters. But Elgar was not there.

'The performance left me in such a ferment,' Sargent was to say, 'that I walked by the Thames until three in the morning, absent-mindedly cutting a party at the Courtaulds [Mr. and Mrs. Samuel Courtauld, his associates in the Courtauld-Sargent concerts], who were furious because left with a table of thirteen.' At his next meeting he told Elgar of the *Enigma* furore. Elgar gave one of his wry smiles and said:

'It's rather late in the day, is it not? Toscanini was touring the *Enigma* as his *pièce de résistance* nearly thirty years ago; and Rimsky-Korsakov wrote that the *Enigma* Variations were the greatest ones since Beethoven.'

Sargent singled out 'Nimrod' and said he had not come upon any crescendo in orchestral music more perfectly managed than the one in this variation.

'It is interesting you should say that,' Elgar rejoined. 'Richter once put the "Nimrod" crescendo side by side with Wagner's crescendo in the *Meistersinger* Overture and, comparing them, showed that mine was the better of the two. But let's talk about something else. What do you know of John Philip Sousa?'*

*

We must return for a while to the cradle of Sargent's career.

In the early 1920s, Leicester seemed the unlikeliest of cradles for any conductor's musical fame. It was a handsome, bustling city of a quarter million souls, with as much cultivation as could be found in most communities of its size, perhaps a little more. Cultivation did not extend conspicuously to music, however. The De Montfort Hall was a stately, stucco-fronted auditorium which seated 2,500. How to fill the place oftener than once in a while was a recurring problem for impresarios, especially those who dealt in 'international celebrities'. Within three months, Wilhelm Backaus, the pianist, then approaching the height of his fame, had played to a half-empty house; Sir Thomas Beecham and the London Symphony Orchestra

* 1854–1932, American bandmaster, composer of military marches, operettas, etc. Elgar greatly admired him.

to rows of empty seats in the dearer parts. Beecham had conducted a rousing Beecham programme: a Mozart symphony, the *Prince Igor* dances, a Wagner overture and an overture by Berlioz. On being told of the box office 'take' he concluded: 'The people here don't want music. Those who came did so only because somebody had told them it was the proper thing to do.' In the autumn of 1921 Karl Russell estimated that for every successful concert in Leicester during the preceding season there had been four unsuccessful ones. Things might, he added, take a turn for the better if the town had fewer choral societies. Two or three of these ought to merge. Nine choral concerts in one season were too much for the town to swallow: 'English choral music would be better off if *Messiah* and *Elijah* had never been composed. Choral Societies mark time year after year over the graves of Handel and Mendelssohn.' Himself a loquacious Rotarian, Russell made these points at a Rotary Club luncheon in the Bell Hotel. Having demonstrated that in the way of music Leicester had too much of too many things, he went off and saddled the town with one thing more: a permanent orchestra.

What looked like a charming inconsequence was shrewd calculation. In promoting Sargent and backing Leicester's new Symphony Orchestra, Karl Russell and his father were aiming a competitive blow at a rival music shop, that of Sir Herbert Marshall, long supreme in Leicester. First steps were taken towards the founding of the orchestra immediately after the 'pilot' concerts of 1919–20. With the help of Grace Burrows, who was to be his leader and assistant conductor, Sargent enrolled a hard core of players from theatre and cinema pits and supplemented them by amateurs or semi-professionals many of whom played with George Tebbs's De Montfort Hall Orchestra and a more desultory body, the Leicester Orchestral Union. (Tebbs's orchestra survived both the drain on its talent and, in 1923, its founder's death.* The Orchestral Union, long conducted by a retired major who played second bassoon in other amateur bands, wound itself up within twelve months.) Auditions for string players were held on a hot Sunday afternoon in

---

* At the first rehearsal of the orchestra after Tebbs's death the players stood while Sargent spoke from the rostrum in praise of his work. 'In all Christian reverence,' he concluded, 'we trust our loss will be His gain.'

the summer of 1922. Sargent accompanied aspirants on the piano in sight reading tests (the violinists had to play tricky pages from Falla's *Love the Magician*), and they subjected him to their prepared pieces. A boy from an insurance broker's office wrestled unhopefully with something from a Mozart sonata. Sargent cut in mercifully with: 'Oh well, that will do. A bit of practice and you'll be all right.' As this player remarked forty years later, it wasn't practice that made him into an orchestral player but 'Sargent's hypnotic power. I couldn't play really. The first rehearsal was the greatest thing that happened to me. Suddenly I found myself *playing*. What had been impossible became possible. What was possible became almost easy.' For first clarinet, two horns, second trumpet and one contra-bass fiddle he went to the Leicester gasworks band, a devoted and conscientious woodwind pool. The amateur strings, especially the more nicely nurtured young ladies among them, tended to look down on 'those rather common people from the gasworks'.

Since neither minutes nor other paper records have survived from the early years or even from interim ones, it is not easy to determine how many professionals there were or what they were paid. The impression is that a handful of players got a guinea-and-a-half a concert. A privileged few were paid an extra five or ten shilings for the final rehearsal. This was always held on the last Sunday afternoon before the concert, which usually fell on a Thursday. Having finished morning service at Melton and played the congregation out, Sargent would swallow a quick meal, then motor to Leicester with Phyllis New, a solicitor's daughter, who was one of his 'cellists. At the end of an intensive, shirtsleeved afternoon, he would be driven back to Melton for the evening service at 6.30. There are veterans who remember a brief period when Sargent drove in to Leicester at a steering wheel of his own. His motor-car was a battered Chevrolet tourer with wheel wobble, its wings and lamps tied up by string. He once reached De Montfort Hall fifteen minutes late with oil-blackened hands, mildly swearing, having had trouble on the way.

For each concert there were four preliminary rehearsals, some of them taken by Miss Burrows. During the first season the playing strength went up from seventy to seventy-five and from seventy-five

to eighty at successive concerts. Women preponderated among
the violins. Sometimes the firsts and seconds included thirty women
to ten youths and men. 'Women,' Sargent used to say, 'bring
qualities of string tone to an orchestra which you never get from
all-male sections.'

In the act of training his players he was schooling himself. Every
concert during his first Leicester seasons was a probation towards
metropolitan platforms and triumphs. Some account follows of his
first nine concerts (1922–24), with comments and incidents that
relate Sargent's talents and newly acquired authority to basic
musical currents and tastes as well as to the repertory of the time.

*

The inaugural concert was on 24th October, 1922, at eight. He
conducted Mozart's G minor Symphony (K. 550), Daisy Kennedy
(then Mrs. Benno Moiseiwitsch) in the Beethoven violin concerto
and, daringly, a tone-poem, *Byron*, inspired by that poet's *Ode to
Victory* and including an ad lib part for chorus, by a much canvassed
English composer, Josef Holbrooke (1892–1957). For the tone-poem
Sargent had what Russell described as 'A Festival Choir of 300
Voices', actually an ad hoc merger of the Leicester Choral Union
and his Melton Mowbray choir. There was a solo soprano, too, the
well-known Flora Woodman. At the final rehearsal Miss Woodman
had asked that the conductor's rostrum should be moved to one
side so that she could sing her numbers from the centre of the
platform. 'Exercising much tact and firmness, Sargent persuaded
her that such a move wasn't necessary,' reported Karl Russell long
afterwards. In his relations with soloists, however popular, he
began as he meant to go on. He did, however, tolerate Miss Woodman's encore. *Swanee River* accompanied on the piano by Dvořák's
Humoresque. Later that season Adrian Boult took the rostrum, so
that Sargent could play the solo parts in Rachmaninov's C minor
Piano Concerto and Walford Davies' *Solemn Melody* for Organ.

How did Boult come into the picture?

The first he heard of Sargent had been through a friend's
sister who (characteristically) hunted in Leicestershire and was full
of this extraordinary young man who did Gilbert and Sullivan all

over the place and was going to conduct a piece of his own at the
Proms. Boult had been at the rehearsal as well as at the Queen's
Hall première of *Windy Day*. 'The work and the performance
impressed me tremendously,' he recalls. 'I got to know Sargent at
once. We saw a lot of each other.' One day at Keble College,
Oxford, where Sargent was booked for lectures at a summer
school run by Boult, Sargent said over coffee: 'The Leicestershire
people are always pressing me to play the piano as well as conduct.'

'Why not oblige them?' said Boult. 'I'll come and conduct you in
a concerto.'

Delighted that his hint had been taken, Sargent proposed the
Rachmaninov. This and the date were quickly agreed.

On the day of the concert they had what Boult remembers as a
'jolly rehearsal'. After the orchestra had dispersed, Mr. L. V.
Wykes, an honorary co-director of the orchestra and a man of
practised musical taste, went up to Boult and said, 'I think I should
tell you, Mr. Boult, that I heard very little of the piano.' Boult was
horrified. 'My God!' he exclaimed. Then: 'I realize what happened.
I was conducting on the wrong side of the piano—between the
piano and the auditorium. From under the piano lid I heard only
the piano, not the trombones. I didn't realize how loud the trombones were. Thank you for telling me.'

That night he said to Sargent: 'Your Mr. Wykes has taught me a
lesson I'll never forget. I'm going to conduct you tonight from the
orchestra's side of the piano. I'll see to it you aren't smothered a
second time.' And so things turned out. Sargent was given a 'fore-
ground' performance. Boult has never since conducted a piano
concerto except on the orchestra's side of the piano. He has maintained that England is the only country where the general practice
[that of Sargent himself among others] is to conduct concertos from
the 'outside'.

On the last night in 1922–23, before a full house, instead of the
half-empty one which had been feared, he conducted 'A Modern
English Composers' Concert', which brought Henry Wood from
London to preside, as it were, in a central balcony seat, and sent up
the standing price from sixpence to a shilling. Programme: Holst's

Hymn of Jesus (with Leicester and Melton choralists), the *Mars* and *Jupiter* movements from the same composer's *Planets* suite, the Bach–Elgar Fantasia and Fugue in C minor and Sargent's own *Night Time with Pan*.

While rehearsing the movements from *The Planets* the trumpets and trombones had come a cropper. There were titters from the strings. Those common chaps from the gasworks again! Sargent ran a severe eye over the titterers.

'I say, you down there,' he said, 'you are pleased to be amused. I'm afraid you don't appreciate what some of the poor brass people up above have to contend with. Do you realize that because their trumpets are F trumpets they're having to transpose up a fourth? I wonder what I'd get if I asked you strings to transpose *God Save the King* by as much as a tone?'

The titterers were subdued. From that day on the brass section enjoyed undisturbed prestige.

People came away from *The Hymn of Jesus* in a mood of relief, almost of jubilation. 'After all,' they seemed to be saying, 'we've survived. We've been brave and up-to-date. Holst's not half as bad as we feared.' *Jupiter* they positively acclaimed. Sargent turned round and, holding up his hand for silence, said: 'I enjoyed *Jupiter* so much and the orchestra played it so well that I propose treating myself to an encore.' The audience approved with a shout.

The success of the first season delighted the Russells. The new orchestra had started off with four concerts. They decided that in the second season there should be five. The peaks were to be an all-Wagner programme, Schubert's 'Great' C major Symphony and the first performance in Leicester—or by Sargent anywhere—of Beethoven's 'Choral' Symphony. Again there was a bow to English music. The 'Great' C major night—which was also a Haydn night, with the queenly Guilhermina Suggia playing in the 'Cello Concerto —introduced Herbert Howells' orchestral piece *Procession*. Professor Howells, as he became, had been a pupil and passionate admirer of Stamford at the Royal College of Music and returned to teach composition three years before Sargent arrived there. Like Boult, he had been introduced to Sargent, after the 'Prom' rehearsal of *A Windy Day*, by Henry Wood, who had said much the same to him as to several others, although with a different nuance: 'Here's a young man who may not be one of our next composers, but he is definitely one of our next conductors.' At a time when immersed in Dostoievsky, Turgeniev and other Slav authors, Howells dreamt one night that he was in some Russian city and that a great procession was advancing menacingly upon him with music. He wakened up with the music intact in his head, wrote it down in full score, which took a week, and had it accepted for the Proms, where it was encored. 'We must do *Procession* in Leicester,' said Sargent next morning, 'and you must come down to hear us.' Booking his ticket for Leicester on the day of the concert, Howells ran into Suggia, and both of them fell in with a small, stocky man with a pipe who was buying a ticket in broken English. He, too, had a 'cello. 'Casals!' exclaimed Suggia joyously, recognizing her former teacher. Casals was bound for Manchester by the same train. The three shared a compartment, ex-pupil and immortal master sitting side by side in contentment though saying little. Arrived at Leicester, Suggia said a farewell word to Casals through the carriage window. She was radiant. In the taxicab on the way to the De Montfort Hall she said: 'Tonight I shall play like a goddess.' She was as good as her word and looked like a goddess into the bargain. It was a long time before Leicester forgot her geranium-red gown; or the imperious profile that Augustus John had recently put on canvas; or how Malcolm held his own, not to be outshone.

Then Beethoven's 'Choral', March 1924. This rounded off the season. As has been said there had been no previous performance of it in Leicester. No city is much of a city until it has had its first 'Choral' Symphony. That night Leicester finished growing up. The same may be said of Sargent. He was twenty-eight, young for such a venture. Looking back, he said to me in 1964:

'My chorus was good. My orchestra *wasn't* good. I rehearsed them hard. And, d'you know? I don't think there was any material difference between my reading then and my reading today. So long as one approaches Beethoven with humility. So long as one is at the same time uplifted. . . . At the end I went off the platform in a highly emotional state and locked myself in the loo. I didn't want to speak to anybody. I couldn't be sure of controlling my feelings.

They surmised where I was hiding and knocked on the door and persuaded me to take my call. Or rather my calls. There were many. The applause went on and on.' Forty years later these memories brought tears to his eyes. What moved him was not the thought of himself on the De Montfort Hall rostrum as a masterful twenty-eight-year-old but wonder at Beethoven's music, the unbroken power and presence of it in his life and the lives of millions more.

Getting up a 'Choral' Symphony from scratch a hundred or two miles from London in 1923 was a harder—and in some ways simpler—job than it would be today. Simpler, because the conductor had fewer models and examples at call. Three months earlier the orchestra had clubbed up and bought him as a wedding present a handsome cabinet gramophone. Sargent had said he needed a gramophone to help him in 'the study of orchestral method'. In this he was thinking ahead rather than topically. Symphonic recording in the serious sense had only recently begun. There was no 'Choral' Symphony on disc. (The first two recordings of it were released the following summer—a version on H.M.V. label conducted by Albert Coates; and Parlophone's, conducted by Dr. Weissmann.) Nor had he heard it in the concert hall or over the air, for public broadcasting was still in its infancy. Ten years earlier at Peterborough he had played a four-hand piano transcription with Keeton. That was all. 'I had to learn most of my repertory from the score, from the printed page. I never heard any of the Beethoven symphonies, except for the *Pastoral*, or any of Mozart's, until I conducted them myself. In this I was fortunate. I cannot imagine better training.'

*

During the next twenty years his commitments, prestige and comings and goings multiplied prodigiously. No matter. He found time for concerts with the Leicester Symphony Orchestra season after season. Stories piled up about his dodges at rehearsal—and of his assertiveness on the orchestra's behalf if outsiders didn't show it proper respect.

At the end of a Sunday rehearsal he asked his players to take up their instruments again so that a group photograph could be taken for publicity purposes. A 'guest' oboist from afar ignored the request and went on dismantling his instrument. Sargent called him to order: 'What's this? Are you ashamed to be seen playing with the Leicester Symphony Orchestra?' The player shrugged compliantly and put his oboe together again.

There were droll phrases which passed from mouth to mouth. When playing their quick bits in the march from *The Golden Cockerel* the trombones were 'doing their knitting'. When a harpist had difficulty in setting his pedals he was warned not to go into reverse. Nervous young players were handled circumspectly and with imagination. A young printing trainee who had taken up the cor anglais was listed for Berlioz's *Fantastic* Symphony. Rehearsals left him nervous about his exposed solos at the beginning and end of the *Scène aux champs* movement. Sensing this, Sargent instructed him on the night to stay off the platform during the two preceding movements and practise in the bandroom, keeping his instrument warm (therefore in tune) and his reed blowing freely. The solos went satisfactorily. It is not this fact, however, or the technical prudence implied but Sargent's human concern that the player remembers after all the years.

A bizarre happening marked preparations for the beginning of the third season in October 1924. Karl Russell had said to Sargent: 'I want you to conduct a piano concerto with the solo part played by a roll on one of these new "reproducer" pianos. All you have to do is give the orchestra their beat and cue in the piano by an electric switch held in your left hand.' The concerto Russell had in mind was Grieg's. The solo part, first movement only, had been recorded for demonstration purposes on reproducer roll by Myra Hess, who had played the concerto complete on the same platform, winning much admiration, nine months earlier. Sargent suggested that, as the demonstration was in the nature of an advertisement, Russell should acknowledge the players' co-operation by paying a hundred pounds into the orchestral fund. To this Russell agreed.

At the rehearsal the reproducer piano was trundled on and placed to the left of the rostrum. There were two electric leads: one to a socket behind the platform, the other to Sargent's desk. First rehearsal business was Schubert's *Unfinished* Symphony. The orchestra was nicely launched upon the Andante when a clattering descant of A minor chords obliterated all else. The piano had started playing of its own accord. No matter how hard Sargent worked the switch button the piano went on. There was a page and a half of pause, as prescribed by the score. Then it implacably started again without any cueing in, keys moving as if under invisible fingers. Players nearest the 'rogue' put their instruments down and groped vainly for control mechanism. The trouble stopped as surprisingly as it had begun. It came out later that an electrician backstage had thrown a wrong switch. The reason why Sargent had been unable to halt the performance was that his 'cue' switch had not been connected. At the concert the roll was cued in without mishap. The demonstration left people wonderstruck. They would have preferred to see somebody at the keyboard nonetheless. When it was over Sargent stepped down, went over to the piano and beamingly went through the motion of shaking hands with the absentee virtuoso. Sargent 'regulars' were delighted. This was Malcolm 'all over': funny, charming, debonair.

His concerts at the De Montfort Hall drew devoted parties from Melton, Stamford and other little towns or big villages. From Stamford thirty or forty members of the amateur opera society used to travel by a special saloon coach hitched to a late afternoon train. They took sandwiches, coffee flasks, bottled beer or perhaps something stronger in the case of Henry Sargent who, alike on outward and homeward journeys, kept everybody on the simmer with his stories and mimicries. When Stamford got its first motor coach, known as The Shara, short for char-à-bancs, the saloon coach was superseded. The driver, nervous because of his heavy load, used to make a longish detour to avoid Wardley Hill, accounted a dangerous gradient, although it was taken cheerfully enough by others in jammed motor-cars, with extra passengers sitting on knees, and by motor-cycle combinations that carried up to three Sargent fans as well as the driver.

Such was Malcolm Sargent's first gallery of faithfuls. Their love of music meshed inextricably with their joy in his personality.

Unwittingly they set the psychological pattern for generations of Promgoers, choir-fanciers, *Hiawatha* adherents, Elgar lovers and Courtauld–Sargent subscribers at the Queen's Hall, the Royal Albert Hall and many other places.

CHAPTER ELEVEN

'SARGENT IS A CAD'

B Y THE end of 1923 Sargent was coming up to London once a week to take a conducting class at the Royal College of Music. He had been enrolled as a junior professor. He wasn't allowed expenses and hadn't much money. Talking his way round the manager of the Gore Hotel, four minutes' walk from the College, he was conceded overnight bed and breakfast at half price, his bed being made up, after other guests had gone to theirs, on planks over the bath in one of the remoter bathrooms. He made it a rule never to spend more than half a crown on lunch.

He continued intermittently hard up for some years. When money started coming in he was apt to spend it so freely, as much on others as himself, that there were times when he thought twice about taking a taxicab. As late as the winter of 1930–31, coming away from the City Chamberlain's Court, Guildhall, where he had received the parchment necessary for his introduction to full membership of the Worshipful Company of Musicians, he put the document under his arm and dropped it while running for a bus. The parchment was found in the gutter, and taken back to Guildhall. When somebody there telephoned him he felt acutely embarrassed and made matters worse by pretending for a while not to know what the man was talking about.

His appointment to the Royal College—where he presently became a full member of the professional board, with responsibility for the Opera Orchestra among other matters—was the outcome of cordial things which the director, Sir Hugh Allen, had heard from Adrian Boult, who had been on the staff since 1919, and from the pluralist Henry C. Colles, who was Allen's professor of musical

(a) In precinct of Royal Albert Hall, London, mid-1920's. (b) With
Merrie England principals, Stamford, 1923. Seated right: Master (now Sir)
Michael Tippett

(c) With friends at Cromer, Norfolk, 1921, year
of *Windy Day* and Proms début

With Mrs Tinkler, his first piano teacher, Stamford, 1948, after being
made Honorary Freeman of the borough

history, editor of the forthcoming third edition of Grove's Dictionary and chief music-critic of *The Times*. On the strength of their praises Allen went to Leicester for one of Sargent's concerts and was sufficiently impressed to take the prodigy under his wing.

*

Then in his middle fifties, Hugh Piercy Allen was bald and bulky, a man of 'drive'. When he looked over the top of his spectacles his air was that of a country solicitor who doesn't mean to be fooled. In his youth, it was said, choirs had quailed before his abrupt bluntness of speech. 'Sing like hell!' was one of his pet adjurations. He was noted at all times for his short, effective way of dealing with knotty administrative problems. Extending from the College to other wings of the Musical Establishment—among them the Royal Choral Society, the Royal Philharmonic Society and Sir John Reith's newly hatched B.B.C.—his authority and sway during the 1920s and later were such as to make him the acknowledged though unofficial head of the musical profession in this country. Bach, Beethoven and Brahms were his idols. About other people's idols, if they weren't the same ones, he could be scathing. One of his sports as an organ scholar at Cambridge had been to play a parody of Liszt's *Tasso*, 'among the most degraded pieces of false sentimentalism ever put on paper', with grotesque registrations on the organ of Christ's Chapel.

For all the weight of his presence and tongue, Allen had sentimentalisms of his own. They did him credit. Having himself been trained in a cathedral organ loft (Chichester) where, as a youth, he had to transpose at sight from full scores and extemporize accompaniments from figured bass and voice parts in every sort of clef, he diagnosed in young Sargent a musician of his own kind (the only *genuine* kind, he would insist) and, into the bargain, a quicksilver intelligence beyond compare. From the start he treated Sargent as a son, pushed him with the Royal Choral and Royal Philharmonic societies and found him useful stand-in jobs, including some with the Oxford Bach Choir, which had been a fief of his own. At the College Sargent helped incidentally with another of Allen's pets, the choral class.

5

'Here,' said Allen, introducing him to the choral students, 'is a young man from Melton Mowbray. You'll be hearing more of him. He's going to be an outstanding choral conductor.'

In 1924 the Sargents moved from Oakham, near Melton, and settled in London. Except for an interlude at Sevenoaks, they usually lived within handy radius of the College and its near neighbour, the Royal Albert Hall. Brompton Road, St. Petersburgh Place, Wetherby Place, Chesham Place and Brompton Square were successive addresses. Allen watched over his protégé's exploding career—ballet seasons for Diaghilev, joint billings with Igor Stravinsky and Sir Thomas Beecham, opera seasons for Rupert D'Oyly Carte and miscellaneous choral and orchestral concerts up and down the country—with pride, solicitude and fatherly grumbles. A thing that disturbed him was Sargent's fondness for fashionable parties at his own or other people's houses after a night's conducting. 'He stays up all hours, dancing and making himself agreeable,' he would complain, 'knowing perfectly well he has a rehearsal at ten or earlier. It's bound to affect his work.' Parties were not the only distraction. Having, during the 1927–28 season, conducted some massive choral programme, he turned up to take 'second orchestra' at College at half-past nine the following morning. A pupil asked whether it wasn't rather a fag having to take an early rehearsal after so heavy a night.

'Not at all,' he boasted. 'I was out on the Thames with the river police all night looking for corpses. Got to bed at four. Had two hours' sleep. Then got on my horse and rode in the Park for an hour before breakfast.'

Many at the College thought he was overdoing it. Others viewed the case differently. They sensed that conducting left Sargent in a state of euphoric tension which put normal sleeping out of the question. Parties and jaunts into the small hours or, failing these, long, lonely walks by the river were essential for unwinding or, as was said then, letting off surplus steam. Before he was rich enough to afford sleeping berths, he would travel back from remote provincial concerts by night train in an ordinary compartment, alternately dozing and score-reading in a corner seat if lucky enough to get one. Often these journeys were on a Friday night, followed by a 9 a.m.

rehearsal-call for a Robert Mayer children's concert at the Central
Hall. He would appear on the rostrum as the clock struck, radiant
and springy, feeding his zest to everybody on the platform and off
it. After the concert he usually lunched with Sir Robert and Lady
Mayer at the Arts Theatre Club. There he would expatiate on music
he had been conducting, music he was going to conduct, and music
in general, the elusiveness of its nature and the recurring terror of
its beauty. Food would go cold on his plate. Dorothy Mayer would
bully him into eating an absentminded mouthful or two. Soon she
and her husband stopped puzzling over how a man could be so
bright on so little sleep. They came to understand that undersleep
and wide-awakeness were complementary in Sargent's case. He was
governed by a special law.

To the Robert Mayer concerts for children we shall return. A
glance in the meantime at his early conducting classes.

*

Down the years his methods varied. In the early days he would
assemble his dozen or so students in a big practice room at the
Royal College and give them an hour's coaching with piano before
they went off to play under some student's baton in the student
orchestra.

His practice was to take the vocal score of, say, a Handel oratorio
and work through the recitatives which join aria to chorus and
chorus to aria. This student or that was deputed to sing the recitatives. Sargent accompanied at the piano. Another student gave the
beat. The recitatives being in 'free' style, it was the student-
conductor's business not to impose his beat but give the singer his
head, while Sargent at the piano followed the conductor exactly, no
matter where the singer was. It happened more often than not that
voice and accompaniment drifted hopelessly apart. Sargent is
remembered as exclaiming more than once: 'You are a pretty poor
lot. None of you can sing recitatives properly at sight. If only you'd
had the sort of training I had at Peterborough. . . . There is no better
test of professionalism than conducting a Handel oratorio with an
amateur orchestra. The curse of English conducting is amateurish-
ness. That's where so much English conducting begins—and

ends. . . . Now we'll try again. This time I'll sing the recitatives and somebody else will accompany.'

From oratorio he would pass to concertos. He spent no time on aesthetics and never attempted to teach how the classics should be 'interpreted'. His points were severely technical and practical. How, for example, to put things right, if the soloist went astray. You held the orchestra with one finger on the first suitable chord while beating two or more bars with the right hand to bring the laggard into line. Sometimes he had his students stand in front of a long looking-glass and watch their beats as he dictated them, from two to twelve in a bar, with sudden switches to fives, sevens and nines. 'It will do you a world of good,' he would say, 'or save the world a lot of trouble, if you realize in good time just how you look to the people who are paid to watch you.' Once the 'second orchestra', which rarely had more than two' cellos at the best of times, was reduced to one 'cello by influenza. Sargent had his five conducting pupils sit turn and turn about in the vacant seat and *sing* the 'cello line—'so that you'll get some idea what these poor chaps, orchestral players, have to put up with from the likes of us.'

But what did music *mean* to his students? On the answers to this depended what, if anything, his students were going to mean to music. There were mornings of ruthless probing. He wanted to know what they all did with their free time; at what o'clock they got up in the morning; how many hours they spent on meals, aimless strolling and pointless reading. 'In the evening I read a book, sir.' 'What book?' 'Oh, a book.' The acid question was: 'What are you doing for *music*?' Boys who could give no better account of their day than that they had come to the College and sat in front of their teacher for an hour were told they could never be conductors—or even musicians. A student who had been to the Queen's Hall and had heard Beethoven's Fifth conducted by Henry Wood was asked what he made of it. 'I didn't think much of the conducting,' he owned. Had he heard the Fifth before? Only when playing it in a four-hand arrangement; never by an orchestra.

'Yet,' commented Sargent, 'all you can talk about is the conducting! Anybody's first experience of Beethoven's Fifth, if he's worthy the name of musician, should be absolutely shattering, whatever the orchestra, however it's conducted. The first time I heard the Fifth played by an orchestra was when I conducted it myself. I was in a dream for three days. You're a born critic. Conducting will never be your line.'

Of one student batch Sargent reported to Allen that seven out of the twelve were no good at all. Of the remaining five three were 'possibles' and two were 'triers'. The seven duds should be dismissed out of hand. They were a waste of time and money.

Allen saw the point. It was a point which had occurred to him independently years before. Through scholarships or fee-paying the College was committed, however; the seven would have to be retained, he said, much as he would like to turn them off. Sargent persisted. Surely there was some constitutional way of sacking inept students. 'No,' said Allen, this time with some anger, 'we have taken their money and we've got to give them the goods.' On 'intake' systems generally Sargent's attitude remained unchanged: 'The trouble,' he said, 'is that the music colleges have twice too many students. Quite half of them just don't have the root of the matter in them. As Holst used to say, any aspirant should regard the Royal College of Music—or, for that matter, the Royal Academy of Music—as on top of a nearly unclimbable mountain.'

All three 'possibles' mentioned by Sargent to Allen graduated from his conducting class to English concert hall or studio rostrums. They modelled themselves so closely on their teacher, not only in baton technique but also in such extraneous matters as length of baton (little more than twelve inches) and of dresscoat tails that, as one of them says, 'we could all have been taken for him from behind.'

*

'When I came as a youngster to London,' he remembered in 1960, 'I was always excited about my work, never frightened. At rehearsals and, before rehearsal, going through the score at the piano, I prepared everything very thoroughly. When I was asked to conduct any choir or orchestra for the first time I said to myself: "The best you can do is the best you can do. If it's no good you won't be asked again. But there's no point in worrying about that now." '

Demands began to rain upon him. Some were marginal and freakish. For a while he worked with the backstage musical staff of the British National Opera Company, that unsubsidized, gallant and shortlived attempt to pick up grand opera in English and carry on from the point where money difficulties had obliged Sir Thomas Beecham to drop it. At Covent Garden and in the larger provincial cities their cycles of Wagner's *Ring of the Nibelungs*, conducted by Albert Coates, won deserved praise. In *Siegfried* it was Sargent's job during the fight scene, Act II, to give cues to the machinists on what beat, approximately, to make Fafner the Dragon show his teeth, snap his jaws, snort steam, lash out with his tail and glare at Siegfried with red electric eyes. In *Rhinegold* during the first and second transformation scenes (from river bank to the depths of Nibelheim and back again) he played the famous anvils which sound the Nibelungs' tinker-rhythm from a darkened stage. He set out the anvil bars, as tradition prescribed, on a green baize table in the wings and practised assiduously with the beaters to make sure that the most hair-raising percussion pages in Wagner should lose none of their effect. Everything went well at rehearsal. Coates was pleased. On the first night, however, somebody on the production staff noticed that the desk light over the anvil bars was reflecting on to the stage and, without realizing what he was about, switched it off. Anvil bars are dodgy things. They slide about on the baize and have to be re-positioned by hand. Impossible to play them by touch in the dark, like a piano. Yet that is what Sargent was so misguided as to attempt. The sounds he produced were a painful fiasco. After taking his curtain calls Coates came storming round. Affecting to turn up his coat collar, Sargent muttered resignedly as the storm broke: 'I know, I know! Go on! Get it off your chest! Then I'll explain just what happened.'

With the B.N.O.C. he undertook at least one provincial tour. He was required to conduct *The Mastersingers*. Two of the performances were scheduled for Scotland. A noted English operatic bass travelled north with him. From the moment the train pulled out of King's Cross he had his nose buried in the score. At Carlisle he closed the score with a triumphant slap and said: 'There now, I know *The Mastersingers*!' 'Indeed?' inquired his companion indulgently.

As a 'quick study', to use an old theatrical phrase, Sargent was unrivalled. It was said, with some exaggeration, that he could get up a new piece in as many hours as other men took days. The question was, however, whether streamlined score-study always produced the best aesthetic results. Of two performances of *The Mastersingers* which he conducted on this tour one is remembered as being relatively quick, the other relatively slow. At rehearsals there were minor discontents and one slight brush. During a passage in the second act he persistently sang in unison with the first clarinet. At last the first clarinet threatened: 'If you are going to sing it, I'll stop playing it.' Sargent promptly went *tacet* and stayed so for the rest of the rehearsal. There was a certain division of opinion as to his capabilities. A young horn player said to his section leader, the influential Henri van der Meerschen: 'I don't know how it is but this Sargent chap seems to get between the music and me.' Van der Meerschen, portly and florid, smiled from behind his blue-tinted spectacle lenses. 'You are still young in music,' he replied. 'You'll have to play with this man for another thirty years. You may as well get used to the fact here and now. Young conductors always irritate young players. I have come to realize that no conductor finds his feet until he's in his fifties.'

It cannot be said that his début year (1925) with the Royal Philharmonic Society worked out altogether as wished or planned. His first programme, in April, an exacting 'contemporary English' survey, bracketed Vaughan Williams (the *Pastoral* Symphony), Bax (*The Garden of Fand*), John Ireland (*Mai Dun*), Lord Berners (*Fantaisie Espagnole*) and Herbert Howells (first Piano Concerto). A week before the concert Howells took his recently completed score to Sargent. They sat down to it in a room without piano, Sargent hearing the music in his mind's ear as he turned the pages. Using three pencils, blue, red and black, for woodwind, brass and strings, he arrow-marked passages which he judged to be of special significance. Howells agreed with his analyses all the way and was impressed by his speed and acuteness. He said to someone later: 'His arrows pointed to the *truth* of the music.'

On the night a noted pianist, Harold Samuel, played the solo part. When he and Sargent had finished and were acknowledging the applause, a man stood up in the circle. 'What *I* say is, Thank God it's over!' he shouted. Two others in the audience got to their feet— a lady in the stalls who yelled 'Take that man out—he's drunk!'; and Ralph Vaughan Williams who, from a seat in the circle immedi- ately over the orchestra, clapped demonstratively, leading what grew into an ovation when Howell appeared on the platform. Word went round later that the brawler had been the militant advocate of another English composer, E. J. Moeran, whom he and certain others considered to be unjustly neglected by the world at large and the Royal Philharmonic Society in particular.

His second concert with the R.P.S. that year was early in Decem- ber. Queen Alexandra, widow of Edward VII, had just died. It was arranged that the funeral march from Elgar's *Grania and Diarmid* music should be played in *memorium* as the first item of a programme which included Gluck's *Iphigenia in Aulis* Overture, the suite from Falla's *Love the Musician*, Borodin's Symphony No. 2 and Saint- Saëns' *Havanaise*, in which the celebrated Jacques Thibaud was to play the solo violin part. That night Sargent gave himself three quarters of an hour to get to the Queen's Hall from his hotel in Kensington. While he was dressing in a leisurely way a paralysing fog settled on the town. He succeeded in getting a taxicab, but the driver lost his way and dumped him at an unfamiliar Underground station. He reached the hall half an hour late, heart in boots, to find that the *Grania and Diarmid* march had been conducted by W. H. Reed, the leader of the orchestra who, after a decent wait, had stepped to the rostrum from the first desk of violins. In the artists' room the R.P.S. officials were very charming and understanding; but he felt horrible and didn't wholly recover his spirits for twenty- four hours. One of the senior critics, Richard Capell (*Daily Mail*) found that, perhaps through flurry, he had overconducted and spoke of 'choppy and violent' readings.

The R.P.S. was not his first 'Royal'. Through Allen's introduction he was engaged by the Royal Choral Society as one of their guest conductors and in the autumn of 1924 began rehearsing the choir for his début concert. This was to be on a Saturday afternoon in January 1925. He was to conduct Dame Ethel Smyth's Mass in D (1893) and two Elgar pieces, the *Enigma* Variations and *The Spirit of England* for soprano, chorus and orchestra to poems by Binyon about the burdens and challenges of war. His age was twenty-nine. At the first rehearsal Allen brought him on to the platform and said, 'You are going to be in the hands of this *boy*.' The average age of the singers tiered up in front of him was at least forty, an age that was to be reduced by auditions and weedings out in the years ahead. Some of the older singers did not 'take' to him on sight, simply because they weren't 'used' to anybody young. This situation, too, was to change for the better. On this first night he made no attempt to charm the choir; he was concerned solely to make it clear, modestly but firmly, that he knew his business. As soon as Allen left the platform he began a run-through of the Ethel Smyth Mass.

This was the problem piece of the occasion. Not because it was especially hard to understand, conduct or sing but because of its composer's authoritarian and combative personality. Dame Ethel was now in the middle sixties, noted for her tweedy stride, cigar-smoking and other mannish ways and for a residual Suffragism which, once the vote had been extended, expressed itself witheringly at the expense of the male sex (masters of the musical profession as of all others) for neglecting her music and doing it down. They did this, she insisted, not because of her music's demerits but simply because they were men and she was a woman. That the Royal Choral Society was reviving her thirty-year-old Mass as devotedly as Beecham had, decades before, produced her *Wreckers* and *Boatswain's Mate* (operas) did little to take the edge off her militant feminism. Allen and others inside the R.P.S. who had seen something of Dame Ethel at close quarters warned Sargent in good time that, supposing him to be raw as well as young, she would try to relieve him of the rehearsals and perhaps of the concert itself. He was therefore prepared for what ultimately happened.

Turning up at all rehearsals, she sat facing him on the platform with her feet up on a second chair. While the rehearsal was on she would try to put the young man right about louds and softs, slows and fasts, phrasing and balance. Most of her suggestions he declined good humouredly, avoiding open altercation in a supple way. After rehearsal she would write him with new *tempi* and expression

5*

directions. One day a passage would be *rallentando*. Next day it would
be *accelerando*. He got into the way of saying to her over the telephone
on Monday morning, 'Well, Miss Smyth, where's the *accelerando*
going to be this week?' His irony rankled. She wrote in her diary*
that Sargent would be a fine conductor some day. 'He began by
being more cheeky to me than words can say. And I had met him
only once and had been specially nice to him. It's the old tradition
started by Beecham: "Show E.S. *I* won't stand any nonsense."
But M.S. ended by being my thrall and couldn't believe I was the
person he had "heard about". Well! Well!' Before the concert,
then, some sort of truce happened or was tacitly arranged. It was
not to last. Meantime Miss Smyth gave a striking exhibition of her
'pull' in high places. Although she had little more than a year to
live Queen Alexandra was sprightly still and got about a good deal.
One day after rehearsal Miss Smyth said: 'We'll get her to the
performance. What's the telephone number of the Palace? I'll
invite her.'

'But,' it was objected, 'you can't get the Palace on the telephone
and invite her just like that.'

'Stuff!'

Picking up the receiver she instructed a reluctant switchboard,
who got the Palace number (it was in the telephone directory anyway) and connected Miss Smyth not with Queen Alexandra, it was
true, but with some high Court functionary whom she addressed
by his Christian name. The invitation was provisionally accepted
within an hour and formally two days later. Queen Alexandra duly
attended the concert. And everybody, Sargent not least, felt a little
awed. Ethel Smyth had had exalted friends for a long time. It was
by talking in the 'network' vein to a friend at the Palace a few days
before the first night that she got King Edward to a hastily rigged
gala performance of *The Wreckers* at His Majesty's in 1909.

A repeat performance of the Mass in D was mounted by the Royal
Choral Society in November 1928. This was when the truce seems
to have broken. Conflict became open. As usual Miss Smyth was at
all rehearsals. Halfway through them she genially remarked: 'Well,

* Quoted in *Dame Ethel Smyth*, *A Biography*. Christopher St. John (Longmans Green), 1959.

Dr. Sargent, I have decided to conduct the performance my-self.'

'But, Miss Smyth,' he demurred, 'I'm afraid that cannot be.'

'Oh? Why?'

'Because this is a matter for the Council of the Royal Choral Society to decide, and they have decided that I should conduct.'

'But I, as the composer. . . .'

'I fear it isn't a matter of composing. It's a matter of conducting. If you think I'm an incompetent conductor and that somebody else, say Sir Henry Wood, could do better, you are at liberty to raise the matter with the Council. If they decide to drop me I would with-draw graciously. In the meantime I propose to do their bidding.'

'We'll see!' said Dame Ethel in jovial menace.

A meeting of the Council had been convened for the following day. A messenger came with a letter from Dame Ethel. It was addressed to the Earl of Shaftesbury, who was in the chair, but intended for the general ear. Unreflectingly, perhaps, the chairman started to read it aloud. The opening sentence ran: 'Dear Shaftes-bury, Sargent is a cad.' The rest he read in silence, then screwed the letter up and threw it into the waste-paper basket. She was claiming the right, it seems, to replace Sargent and conduct her Mass in person. The claim was ignored.

She did not love Sargent any more for this.

*

Theatre assignments ran parallel or dovetailed with those in the concert hall. Ballet rehearsals jogged Elgar nights and were apt to be followed by mornings with *Madame Butterfly* or *Carmen*. For Diaghilev he helped to prepare Stravinsky's *Les Noces* for the controversial revival at His Majesty's Theatre. Even today this score is quellingly complex, with its rhythmic and harmonic inter-gearings for chorus, solo singers, four grand pianos and an excep-tional array of percussion. Forty years ago few musicians had yet got the hang of it aesthetically, which made it tougher still in the rehearsal room. 'Very tricky, very clever,' commented Sargent. 'Igor has been thinking hard all the time.' To the end of his days, like Beecham, he considered *Firebird* Stravinsky's best work. He was once heard to say, 'When you come down to things like *Les Noces. . . .*' The unfinished sentence had its own eloquence.

His first public appearances on a Diaghilev rostrum, in the summer of 1927, were as a stop-gap. One morning he was asked urgently to see Diaghilev at the Princes Theatre. Eugene Goossens, due to conduct *Firebird* and Poulenc's *Les Biches* that same night, had fallen ill. Could Dr. Sargent deputize for him? At that time Sargent knew neither score in the professional sense. Nor did he know much about the conventions and niceties of ballet *tempi*, which, as between theatre and concert hall, are apt to differ for the same work. When he reached the theatre a perturbed Diaghilev stopped pacing the stage, flung his arms round Sargent and exclaimed: 'You are my saviour.' 'But,' said Sargent, 'I don't know the scores. The thing's impossible.' 'In that case there will be no ballet tonight,' said Diaghilev in the manner of one announcing the end of the world. Sargent hastened to Goossens's bedside with the two scores and had a coaching session that went on for six hours. Propped up in bed Goossens, one of Europe's young *avant-garde* batons, hummed salient themes and conducted with one finger while Sargent, following from score, made notes about *tempo* changes and technical pitfalls. There was no time for any sort of rehearsal.

That night, before going down into the pit, Sargent stood with his back to the curtain, talking to the stage manager. Already lined up on the stage or in the wings, the dancers suddenly realized that a new and presumably malleable conductor was taking over. Most of the principals made an unconcerted rush at him, each concerned to stress the importance of the *tempi* for his or her particular numbers. While demonstrating their steps they explained and cajoled in pidgin English, bad French or good Russian. He backed away from the babel.

Until Goossens recovered, he took home the scores of next day's ballet each night after the performance and tried to master them in time for a run-through next morning on a rehearsal piano with dancers or producer. When the season ended Diaghilev said he would never forget what Sargent had done for him. Of his feats of conducting virtually at sight, he said, 'C'est une spécialité anglaise,' then sighed, as if sorry he couldn't say as much for other countries.

During the 1927 Diaghilev season and at His Majesty's the following year, Sargent was in the pit for fourteen ballets, including apart from the two already mentioned such classics as Stravinsky's *Pulcinella*, *La Boutique fantasque*, *Aurora's Wedding*, *The Three Cornered Hat*, *l'Après-midi d'un faune*, *Cimarosiana* and the *Prince Igor* Dances. When, in 1927, King Fuad of Egypt and his suite, all wearing the fez with evening dress, came with a security squad to a flower-smothered Princes Theatre for a gala night, it was expected by most in the audience that Beecham would share the rostrum with Sargent and Goossens. The three names had been billed together in graded glory. Beecham withdrew overnight through illness, however. Goossens conducted the three chosen ballets (*Carnival*, *The Triumph of Neptune* and *Aurora's Wedding*), while Sargent attended to the 'symphonic interludes', conducting Bizet's *Jeux d'enfants* and Chabrier's *Fête Polonaise* with the curtain down. In 1928, conducting *Cimarosiana*, he shared the rostrum on the opening night with Stravinsky, who directed the first English performance of his *Apollon musagètes*. These two were to see more of each other during the early phase of the Courtauld–Sargent concerts.

*

Those were times when English opera, as distinct from opera in English, was trying hard to break out of its shell and get off the ground. Among standard operas and what were considered to be advanced or especially demanding ones (e.g., *Pelleas and Melisande*, *The Golden Cockerel* and *Parsifal*) the B.N.O.C. would conscientiously slip in a new native piece from time to time. On *Savitri*, *The Perfect Fool* and *The Boar's Head*, all by Holst, Rutland Boughton's *Alkestis* and Ralph Vaughan Williams's *Hugh the Drover*, the company spent in the ordinary way as much talent, money and trouble as upon *La Bohème*, *Aida*, *Faust* or any other of their best sellers. For *Hugh the Drover* and *The Boar's Head* (as well as for a number of *Butterflys*, *Carmens* and *Gianni Schicchis* on tour) they brought in Sargent, whose reputation in English music of post-Elgarian schools had run ahead of him from Leicester and his *Hymn of Jesus* production.

Of the five English operas listed above, *Hugh the Drover* is the only one which, on the evidence of its revivals (e.g. Sadler's Wells 1937, 1939, 1951 and 1953), made much impression on the opera-going public. For years Vaughan Williams had wanted to write an opera about a prize fight. Harold Child, a leader writer on *The Times*, gave him more or less (less rather than more) the sort of libretto he was after. Cotswold village during the French Wars. Fairground with side-shows, ballad sellers, winkle sellers. Stocks into which the tenor hero is stupidly clapped as a spy. Prize ring where he humbles the baritone villain in a bare-fist match before walking off with the villain's sweetheart. All this to hearty and richly atmospheric music with an abundance of folk tunes and folk-type tunes. First there were private performances by students in the Royal College theatre. Sargent had nothing to do directly with these. He had charge of the first professional performances (these were at His Majesty's during a memorable B.N.O.C. season in the summer of 1924) and other performances on tour during the succeeding twelve months.

The first prize fight seen on a London stage since a dimly remembered dramatization of Conan Doyle's *Rodney Stone* at the Adelphi Theatre took the fancy of popular paragraphists; the critics were respectful, even cordial; and Sargent came in for many compliments. Few in the audience on the first night knew of the harassments there had been. *Hugh* came on towards the end of a taxing seven weeks season that took in such heavyweights or nerve-teasers as *Parsifal*, *The Mastersingers*, *Tannhäuser*, *The Valkyrie*, *Pelleas* and *Aida*. Untypically for the B.N.O.C., the opera was 'terrifyingly under-rehearsed and the singers all tired.' Vaughan Williams said after-wards that Sargent had saved the first night from disaster every few bars and pulled the chestnuts out of the fire in a miraculous way.*
It is chilling to speculate what might have happened if the B.N.O.C. chorus had not been augmented—and helped out—by the chorus from the Royal College, who had had time to get the music into their bones. For once in a way professionals were stiffened by non-

* *R.V.W., a Biography of Ralph Vaughan Williams* by Ursula Vaughan Williams (Oxford University Press), 1964.

professionals or, at any rate, sub-professionals. Holst's *Boar's Head*, with its Falstaffian theme and Shakespearean provenance, equally might have suffered at its first performances (Manchester and Golders Green, April 1925) but for Sargent's precision and control. A devastatingly clever work, remembers the composer's daughter. But the cleverness was all on paper; the only way of enjoying it was by reading it in an armchair. 'On the stage there could be no hope of sweeping gestures or generous abandon when the soloists were struggling with ensembles as exacting as any of those in *Figaro*. Malcolm Sargent conducted and, with consummate skill . . . steered the singers through the intricacies of the score.'*

Hugh, on the other hand, was promptly taken up by a recording company or, as it was regarded by most Englishmen then, *the* recording company: H.M.V. During the summer of 1924 most of the original principals, with a skeleton chorus and orchestra, travelled early one morning on a suburban stopping train from Paddington to a rudimentary record factory at Hayes, Middlesex. There they were crowded into an oblong room with walls and ceiling in varnished deal. This was the company's original acoustical studio, the place where most or many of its records were made before electrical recording came in. Highly sensitive to sound, it picked up the remotest whisper. At either end horns protruded from holes in the wall. Down these horns the sounds went straight to the recording needle which engraved them on wax discs driven by weight and pulley, grandfather-clock fashion.

The wax discs were stocked in heated cabinets to take off the brittleness and make them workable. As a result the studio became a hothouse. First jackets were cast, then waistcoats. Sargent conducted from a shelf, strapped to the wall lest he fall off. Taking their places in turn at one recording horn or another, the singers had to squeeze and insinuate themselves past fiddlers who were trying to keep their elbows out of reed players' ribs and trombonists who found it hard to extend their slides without hitting somebody in the neck. For one of his entries the baritone had to crawl between fiddle desks, surface in front of the horn, then bob down and crawl back. Not only did Sargent give the beat and cues from memory,

* *Gustav Holst* by Imogen Holst (Oxford University Press), 1938.

watch everybody at once and pay attention when the recording manager popped his head through a hatchway to say what had gone right or wrong with the latest run. He had the additional job of positioning the singers, according to acoustical rules. For example, while conducting with his right hand, he would keep his left hand for long stretches on the leading soprano's head, pushing her now towards the horn on low notes so that these should register well, now drawing her back from it on high ones to avoid 'blast', in those days a vocational nightmare.

How many days, sessions and 'reject' waxes were expended on *Hugh* nobody now remembers, and there are no surviving studio sheets to consult. When it was all over there was a hilarious last train ride back to Paddington. In 1924 opera recording was still a fabulous adventure. The set came out in November: five twelve-inch discs (D.922–26) at six and six each. 'Orchestra conducted by Malcolm Sargent', said the blurbs, as if he had had nothing to do with the singers, whose names were listed separately. Yet the recording was accounted a feather in his cap. It opened a connection with H.M.V. which in forty years and more filled seven feet of shelving in Sargent's personal disc library.

CHAPTER TWELVE

WITH D'OYLY CARTE

'I'LL NEVER be content,' Sargent had said to 'amateur' friends of his in Melton after *Patience* in 1920, 'until I've conducted Gilbert and Sullivan with the D'Oyly Carte company in London.' Six years later, without any string pulling on his part, the thing happened.

For his forthcoming London season (September to December 1926), Rupert D'Oyly Carte had booked the Princes Theatre, Shaftesbury Avenue, and was looking around for a conductor to replace Geoffrey Toye, his previous London baton, who was no longer free. To Sir Landon Ronald, always dependable for a bird's eye view of the musical scene, he said: 'I want somebody good. Whom do you recommend?' Ronald mentioned Sargent. The two of them went to Winchester for a double bill—*Trial by Jury* and *H.M.S. Pinafore*—at the Guildhall. A minor point that impressed them was audience discipline. Two minutes before Sargent appeared in the pit the doors were closed, and there was respectful silence for the overture, traditionally an occasion for toe-treading by latecomers and smalltalk by everybody else. Clearly, Sargent had Winchester well in hand.

By the spring of 1926 Sargent had rehearsed, conducted and, in some cases, stage-directed eighteen productions of eleven Savoy operas in Winchester, Stamford and Melton. There had been few probations to compare with his. After his Winchester visit, Carte asked Sargent round to his office at the Savoy Hotel. They had an agreeable talk. In confirmation of what had been orally agreed, he wrote next day appointing Sargent principal conductor of the forthcoming Princes Theatre season. The understanding was that

he should 'vet' the orchestra, take all necessary rehearsals and conduct not less than four performances each week, including all first
nights of new shows, the repertory to be: *The Mikado* (in a new
production designed by the fashionable Charles Ricketts), *Patience*,
Trial by Jury and *The Pirates of Penzance*, *Iolanthe*, *The Gondoliers*,
Cox and Box and *H.M.S. Pinafore* (double bill), *Ruddigore*, *Princess
Ida* and *The Yeomen of the Guard*. Taking into account a week of
preliminary rehearsals in the theatre, the engagement would last
fourteen weeks. His pay was to be fifty pounds a week, something
like £200 a week in today's money.

New fads and upheavals in the theatre had in no way tarnished
the appeal of the Savoy operas. Advance bookings at the Princes
ran to £1,200 a day. Full houses were the rule. For the opening
night the theatre could have been sold out twenty times over. It
drew a typical mid-'twenties audience. Running an eye over the
stalls before the curtain rise observers found it hard to tell mothers
from daughters. All were slim; all wore 'shingles' and the same type
of full, short skirt. The place tingled with euphoria and expectation,
the latter accounted for in part by Ricketts' breakaway designs. It
had got about that the Gentlemen of Japan were to wear blue
'Oxford bags'. What next? Days before the curtain went up ironical
readers wrote to the papers suggesting that Ricketts should round
off a tasteless job by giving Yum-Yum an Eton crop and Nanki-Poo,
as the wandering minstrel, a saxophone to carry. The chorus women
had their own adverse slant on the Ricketts arrangements. Backstage they were wrestling with his curiously weighted wig-head-
dresses; their bias gave the girls a feeling their heads were being
pulled off.

For some days B.B.C. engineers, a new and awesome race, had
been tinkering and experimenting at rehearsals. They settled for
two microphones on a ledge just in front of the footlights. After
years of resistance, Carte and the Gilbert and Sullivan copyright
holders had conceded relays of two half-hour excerpts. Previous
attempts at 'live' transmission from theatres did not promise much.
As things turned out the *Mikado* transmissions were an unqualified
success. At that time there were about two million licensed receiving
sets in this country. It is probable that most of them were tuned in

to the *Mikado* opening, which thus reached an audience of anything up to eight million, an unheard of thing.*

From 2LO, as the B.B.C.'s original London transmitter called itself, somebody announced that Dr. Sargent was about to take the rostrum. A moment later a roar of cheering and clapping came over the air. The listening millions concluded that this Dr. Sargent must be an extraordinarily popular young man. What they didn't know, there being no running commentary, was that part of the ovation was for the Prime Minister, Mr. Stanley Baldwin, who entered the auditorium on his way to an inconspicuous stall at the moment Sargent made his bow from the orchestra pit. He aimed his first bow specifically at Mr. Baldwin, and Mr. Baldwin bowed back.

About the performance most of the critics wrote cordially. Ernest Newman stressed the 'new life put into the score'. Eric Blom said that Sargent's vitality and firm grasp 'are bound to have a most salutary effect on these productions before long'. Two other critics qualified their praise with a gaffe that benefited Sargent on the rebound. Both Capell and *The Times* alleged that Sargent had permitted himself orchestral 'gags' or interpolations, presumably of his own invention. They were especially troubled by a bassoon obbligato in the 'Three little maids' trio which they allowed to be pretty in its own right but said it had no right to be there. Both took their stand on the vocal score as printed, holding that Sargent had made audacious additions to it. *The Times* glumly hoped that Sullivan was not destined to be buried, like Handel, under 'additional accompaniments'.

Neither writer knew that throughout the rehearsals Sargent, while conducting from a cued-in vocal score, as was the standard D'Oyly Carte practice, had Sullivan's autograph full score to hand and that either this or authoritative band parts carried several additions, mostly for woodwind instruments, of which the printed scores in general circulation gave no hint. Sargent prepared all the operas that season, indeed, from the Sullivan autographs, most of them

* 'Probably the number of people who heard the first half-hour [8.15 to 8.45 p.m.] was the largest audience that has ever heard anything at one time in the history of the world.'—*Evening Standard*, 21st Sept, 1926.

having been placed at his disposal by Herbert Sullivan, the composer's nephew. He took some of them home for study, handling them and showing them to close friends with as much reverence as if they had been Mozart manuscripts. Some of his friends responded tepidly. Many musicians of those and later days were pleased to look down their noses at Sullivan's theatre music.

Capell and *The Times* were promptly routed. The bassoon ornament in 'Three little maids' was certified by a veteran on the D'Oyly Carte musical staff to have been introduced by Sullivan himself at a band rehearsal for the *Mikado* revival of 1895. While writing the ornament in on the band part, which had been handed up to him from the pit, Sullivan remarked with a smile: 'I have waited ten years for an opportunity to add this. It's been in my mind all this time.' Such, it seemed, had been Sullivan's general habit. Several of the operas had retouches which he made long after the original run and which had therefore eluded the official piano reduction. In any case, these did not purport (piano reductions rarely do) to reflect every orchestral detail.

Carte himself clinched the matter with a letter to the newspapers, written the day after the opening.

Dr. Malcolm Sargent, [he wrote] has most carefully studied the original full score and, in addition to piano rehearsals with principals and chorus, has had six hours of orchestral rehearsals with the full score before him. His main object this season is to bring out the full beauty and humour of Sullivan's orchestral colouring. It would seem that he was so successful in this respect last night and that the details of the orchestration sounded so fresh that some of the critics thought them actually new. This is not the case, however. Not one note has been added to Sullivan's score or any alteration made, with one important exception, that being the illustration of 'He whistled an air', the tune of 'The girl I left behind me' being given; this has been done for many years in place of the original, and now unknown, popular air Sullivan first used. With this exception, the opera was played last night exactly as written by Sullivan.

This put the murmurers in their place. Nothing more was to be heard of interpolations. Another grumbling campaign began, however, which lasted on and off for years. It concerned *tempi*.

*

To some ears, including certain influential ones connected with the company, Sargent was too fiery and headlong a young man by half. During the rehearsals at the Princes Theatre and in a big lower floor room regularly set aside for this purpose at the Savoy Hotel, there had been conflict and incipient mutiny. To get this hidden warfare into perspective we must look at some of the personalities who were involved in it.

When Rupert took over the running of the D'Oyly Carte companies, as the son of Richard D'Oyly Carte, their founder, in 1913, *tempi* and stage business down to the last wink and semiquaver were as tradition prescribed them and (or so it seemed for a long time) precisely as the public wanted them. The 1914 war came. The company lingered on in the provinces. After the war Rupert saw that rejuvenation was necessary. A quarter of the chorus singers had lost their bloom and had to be replaced. The newcomers, all young people, brought down the average age pretty sharply. The man who auditioned new candidates for the chorus was the remarkable John McRobbie Gordon.

At the time of Sargent's first season, Gordon was seventy-one; he had been stage-director for over twenty years and before that had sung for the company as chorus man and understudy. His first show had been the original *Princess Ida* (1883). He had retained every nuance laid down by W. S. Gilbert as to spoken inflection, gesture, lighting and other stage business not only for *Princess Ida* but also for every other piece in the repertory. White maned, gentle and fussy, he wore gold-rimmed spectacles through which he twinkled benignly on the world, or with anguish if somebody emitted the wrong sort of vowel at rehearsal. When ticking the audition lists he was for ever whipping off one pair of spectacles and putting on another. Singers spoke of him as an enormously clever old dear. His work was his life. He could rehearse all day like a tiger on nothing more in the way of food than an apple. At night he would stand under a gas-jet at the back of the stalls, spectacles well down on the bridge of his nose, his eyes now on the stage, now on a shorthand-typist's bulky notebook. In this he jotted down what went wrong on the stage or might be bettered. At the end he would post up rehearsal calls for the following morning and, before going to bed, transcribe his notes over a glass of whisky. He trod the wings as one treads a chancel. Once during a rehearsal at the Princes he accidentally brushed against a set of tubular bells backstage. At their faint jingle he whipped round and shushed them, finger on lips. This was done gravely, with no idea of drollery.

The company had long been noted for manners and accents which reflected or were copied from the finishing school and Belgravia's drawing-rooms. Gordon understood and thoroughly approved. At a run-through of *The Yeomen of the Guard* a new Phoebe was instructed at the end of the first act to throw herself into Fairfax's arms and faint. Derek Oldham was singing Fairfax. 'But,' objected the Phoebe, 'I haven't been intro*duced* to Mr. Oldham.' Stopping the rehearsal, Gordon stepped forward with his little cough: 'Ahem, Miss So-and-So, may I introduce you to Mr. Derek Old-ham? Mr. Oldham, I would like you to meet Miss So-and-So.'

It might have been evident from the start that differences of age, outlook and temperament would make for friction between him and Sargent. Perhaps Carte foresaw something of the kind and worked on the assumption that conflict and compromise would result in the sort of production he had in mind: rejuvenated enough to appease the more questing minds among postwar audiences and traditional enough, even when Ricketts' innovations were added to Sargent's iconoclastic beat, to keep older and more conservative customers in their seats.

Disputes over this *tempo* and that spilled over from sectional rehearsals to general ones, with chorus and backstage staff all ears. The autumn of 1926 was sunny and warm. Sargent used to work in his shirtsleeves, waistcoatless, the cued-in vocal score in front of him, the autograph score on a desk to his left rear, with somebody from the musical staff going through it page by page as the rehearsal progressed. Briskly good humoured, never wasting a word or a second, quick in the uptake when anything went wrong or somebody brought up a technical point, capable of the tart phrase when faced by what looked like mulishness, he pleasantly awed youngsters and newcomers and was frankly admired by all old hands who didn't seek to cross swords with him. A row or two behind in the stalls, Gordon watched and listened like a benevolent lynx, advance-miming every action for the guidance of the people on the stage. Before conflict had dispirited him a little, he would cut into a conductor's rehearsal with borderline points or matters outside his province, first apologizing to Sargent in refined, faintly Aberdonian diction. Thus during the *Gondoliers* finale:

'Ahem, Dr. Sargent, I know this is *your* rehearsal. But please may I say one word to the chorus? . . . Ladies and gentlemen of the chorus, you have just been told that Luiz is none other than the King of Barataria. In Gilbert's words, this is a *wonderful revelation*. But you aren't making it sound wondrous at all.' Here his tone became pleading, almost tearful. '*Do* make it sound like a revelation, ladies and gentlemen! Put every ounce you've got into it. Now again. Thank you, Dr. Sargent.'

When it came to spoken lines he often cited W. S. Gilbert.

'I'm afraid,' he would say, pulling up some fledgling Corcoran or Elsie Maynard, 'I'm afraid there's only one way of saying that line —Gilbert's way. You want to say it your way. People often want to say Gilbert's lines their way. They're always wrong. Now the right way is this. . . .' Having inflected the line as the author would have delivered it, he sometimes added a reminiscence. For example: 'As Sir William himself pointed out, that line was the final result of half a page of writing. You mustn't fool about with it.'

Singers new to the company and many a seasoned and celebrated one unhesitatingly obeyed his rulings. In a tentative and circumspect way he tried his placatory cough and Gilbertian citations on Sargent. He made no impression. Sargent would cheerily dismiss his intervention and go his own way. Gordon was left wringing his hands.

One of their sharper tussles was over *Princess Ida*. Staring excitedly into the wings the chorus declaim: 'From the distant panorama/Come the sons of royal Gama.' Arac, Gurion and Scynthius then clank on in full armour, with staccato string accompaniment, for their Handelian trio, 'We are warriors three.' As

Sargent took it at rehearsal their entry music was quicker than anybody remembered its having been taken before. Gordon interposed with a clucking noise.

'Tck, tck, tck! . . . Now, now, Dr. Sargent, we really can't have it like that. They're supposed to be wearing armour and marching in it.' He was up on the stage near the rehearsal piano and moved his knees up and down to make it clear what he was talking about.

Sargent was immovable. He gave the beat as before.

'But, Dr. Sargent,' persisted Gordon, 'it can't be done. Not at that speed. Not in *armour*. The way we do it is this.' Moving his knees up and down as before, he rum-tummed the traditional speed.

'And this,' retorted Sargent, tapping the rostrum rail correctively, 'is the way *I* do it. It happens to be Sullivan's way, too, Mr. Gordon. You will have noticed his direction—*Allegretto moderato*. We mustn't turn it into a funeral march, must we?'

The rehearsal continued as Sargent wanted it. There is no reason to suppose he modified his pace in public performance or that Arac, Gurion and Scynthius fell on their faces through trying to keep up with him.

Animosities continued. During Sargent's second season for D'Oyly Carte (1929–30) they reached such a pitch that, according to a veteran Savoyard who witnessed more than one rehearsal wrangle, Gordon neared nervous breakdown. At an orchestral rehearsal he plumped down in the stalls alongside this witness and said: 'You know, I can't bear it, Mr. X. I won't have it. I said to Mr. Carte the other day, "The man's impossible. I won't have it, I won't have it!"'

'And what did Mr. Carte say?' inquired the other.

'Oh,' replied the old man, 'I didn't let Mr. Carte *hear* me. I said it under my breath.'

When Gordon tried to assert himself he was speaking not only for himself but also for others in the company: especially Bertha Lewis and Henry ('Harry') Lytton. At the Princes Theatre that year Miss Lewis sang eight heavy contralto rôles, all of them demanding, grotesque and (presumably because of some emotional oddity in Gilbert) misogynistic in after-taste. She was still in her thirties, an actress of power, though not much of a voice. Sargent soon had her bristling. It got around that there had been a 'scene' at one of the preliminary rehearsals for *The Mikado*. As usual this was at the Savoy Hotel, where the company, then as now, had their business quarters. After disputing Sargent's *tempo* in one of the Katisha numbers she burst out of the rehearsal room and into Carte's office a few paces away.

'I won't go on with that little upstart!' she fumed.

'What's the matter?' asked Carte.

She gave a furious account of right speeds and wrong speeds and Sargent's obstinacy.

Carte patted her on the shoulder. 'Don't be a fool, Bertha,' he said. 'Go back now.'

She complied. Sargent had won. But he was not forgiven.

Miss Lewis's outburst reflected Lytton's attitude as much as her own. She worshipped Lytton. So, for that matter, did England at large. What Lytton said was law—and not for her alone; it was a law that had to be accepted by everybody else. 'Everybody' meant conductors conspicuously.

One of the best loved drolls and character actors of the Edwardian and Georgian reigns, Lytton was dapper and as bright as a bird in spring. He had the air of good breeding, looked youngish when over sixty and wore an eyeglass as if it had grown in place. His reminiscences came out six years before his retirement. He called them *The Secrets of a Savoyard*. Those secrets did not include the arts of *bel canto*. 'Not much of a voice,' commented the conductor who auditioned him for Richard D'Oyly Carte in 1886. Lytton reported this as though it were something to be rather proud of. He would set the table in a roar by quoting what a provincial critic had written, or appeared to have written: 'Mr. Lytton warbled his way manfully through his rôle.' What the critic really meant, he added, was not 'warbled' but 'wobbled'. Sometimes he wondered testily why people expected him to sing at all—in their fastidious acceptation of the word. He could never read music. In the 'eighties and 'nineties, when getting up something new, he would have the indulgent Arthur Sullivan, if Sullivan happened to be about, 'tra-la-la' the tunes to him. Around the time of the Princes Theatre season, if an old title was being revived after lying fallow for a long time, a repetiteur would help by going with him through his tunes on the piano. The main tune-outline he would quickly re-master. The things that troubled him were what he called the 'twiddly bits'— Sullivan's turns and other ornaments. These he found elusive. They had to be repeated time after time. In the eyes of a public who adored and laughed until happy tears rolled down their cheeks, he could do no wrong. One thing they roared at especially was the topical 'gag' which he always introduced, according to precedent, at Ko-Ko's inclusion of 'the apologetic statesman of a compromising kind' in his list of people who never would be missed. At this point he would mimic Arthur Balfour playing golf, Joe Chamberlain screwing in his eyeglass, young Winston Churchill trying on hats, and so on.

Once he miscalculated. The occasion was his *Mikado* first night with Sargent. With Mr. Baldwin watching from the stalls alongside Lord Willingdon, the newly appointed Governor General of Canada, he mimed 'Honest Stanley' striking a match on his trouser seat and puffing at his pipe, that precursor symbol of Churchill's cigar. Some were displeased by this. There was a boo from the gallery, followed by counter cheers.

*

For many seasons, not only in London but on provincial tours that covered scores of towns and cities all over Britain, Lytton, Gordon and Lewis—the first two always citing what Gilbert and Sullivan had laid down in person—determined the speeds at which the operas were taken. Lytton wielded more authority than the other two, perhaps because he was the one who brought most money into the house. Certain detached onlookers whispered: 'Tradition my foot. Harry's getting old. That's why he's slowing everything down. Bertha backs him up because she thinks he's the "bee's knees".'

Sargent's tactic at first was to strike the persuasive note. 'Couldn't we have it just a *bit* faster, Lytton?' 'Oh, all right then,' Lytton would broadly concede in the manner of one who gives a hundred pound note away and thinks nothing of it. Making a promise is one thing, keeping it another. People who were on the stage or in the wings at the time remember open clashes. Again the opera was *Princess Ida*. In this Lytton played venomous old King Gama. For his opening number he stomped down to the footlights and, standing almost with his feet in them, as near to the conductor as he could get, ostentatiously ignored Sargent's introductory *tempo* and sang the number through at his own speed, a slower one, of course, defiantly emphasizing the difference with taps of his stick. Sargent refused to be deflected. He and the orchestra finished two bars ahead. He had stopped beating time, his arms hung by his side and he was rocking with laughter. The audience laughed too. For them the whole thing was a joke, an endearing tiff which had been whimsically put on for their benefit. Another account which, however, may refer to a different occasion, has Sargent slowing down his pace to that of Lytton, who ended top dog.

Lytton's feelings were less amiable. Coming off he said: 'I'm supposed to be lame. I walk with a stick. An old crock can't walk that fast. The man's an idiot. He just *won't* learn.'

Did Lytton ever try to turn the tables on his antagonist? There is trace of a *Pirates of Penzance* night when he took Major General Stanley's patter song at a pace which made some of the words unintelligible and had Sargent and the orchestra almost scrambling in his wake. Sargent had brushes at rehearsal or public differences on *tempo* with other Savoyards, including two newcomers. A tenor who was then in the first phase of a prosperous career looks back ruefully on his début in *The Yeomen of the Guard*. He and Sargent differed irreconcilably on how Fairfax's opening number, 'Is Life a boon?' should be taken: 'We had high words with each other after three performances when he publicly "drove" me, beating half a beat ahead all the way through the song.' Martyn Green, upon whom the 'Henry Lytton rôles' were to devolve during the following decade, seems to have been the only singer who ever objected to his taking a number 'slowly'. This, again, happened at one of the 1926 rehearsals. The opera was *The Gondoliers*. Green had been given the small part of Antonio. In the opening scene Antonio does a little dance before and between different sections of his song 'For the merriest fellows are we'. Unable to fit his relatively quick dance steps to Sargent's beat, he stopped dancing and singing altogether.

When asked what was wrong, he said that in dancing, as in much else, what went up had to come down. The law of gravity had a *tempo* of its own and didn't take much notice of anyone else's. Without a sharper *tempo* the number couldn't be done.

'You know nothing about it,' Sargent is said to have retorted. 'That's my *tempo*, and that's how it's going to be.'*

Neither would budge. The final rehearsal brought further argument and some heat. But, reports Green, there was a compromise before the first night. After that the two men got on famously.

With the chorus he was on glowing terms from their first meeting. At the general rehearsal of *The Mikado* he stepped on to the rostrum as from a bandbox, flower in buttonhole, with a smile of welcome that went from ear to ear. Lined up for 'If you want to know who we are,' the Gentlemen of Japan, twenty-two in number (it was boasted that every tenor among them had a foolproof top B flat) instantly knew that somebody at last was really glad to see them. 'Ah, good morning gentlemen!' he carolled. Nor did he mean 'Gentlemen of Japan' merely. They were gentlemen in their own right. Up to then D'Oyly Carte chorus men had inclined to the view that they were nobodies or, as one of the more sardonic among them puts it, 'poor bloody plebeians'. Sargent gave them pride and a pedestal. He did the same for the women's chorus.

Under his baton the Gilbert and Sullivan choruses were sung as never before. Sometimes they stopped the show. The chorus were in high spirits, in love with Sargent from front row to back. His brisker *tempi* did not trouble them at all. They revelled in them. The supreme 'hit' of the men's chorus was the Peers' entry in *Iolanthe*. Sargent had thought much about this scene, not only as music but also as spectacle. Soon after his appointment in April he had pressed upon Carte the notion of a small stage band—four trumpeters and, possibly, a drummer, who would reinforce the pit brass in the fanfares and look picturesque. Citing the last act of *The Mastersingers* and the trumpet scene in *Aida*, he thought it would be a capital thing and good House of Lords style, to use *long* trumpets with banners. Thinking perhaps that the young man was straying out of

* *Here's a How-De-Do* by Martyn Green, London, Max Reinhardt, 1952.

his province, Carte pleaded the smallness of the Princes Theatre stage and let the matter drop.* So Sargent had to make do with the male chorus ungarnished. They proved enough. On the first *Iolanthe* night their entry chorus raised the roof. Heartened by thunders of applause and by Sargent's jubilant smile, the Peers went off and up eighty-seven steps to their dressing-room, hung up their cloaks and coronets and, having nothing more to sing until the grand finale, settled down to cards and quart bottles of draught beer. Sargent, too, climbed the steps. Throwing open the dressing-room door at the interval he said with a semicircular glance that omitted nobody, 'Gentlemen, it is a pleasure to conduct you. You were excellent. Thank you very much. It is a joy to hear you sing.'

The chorus women came in for equivalent bouquets and head pattings. In their case the note tended to be *galant*. At the Princes they were distributed over three smallish chorus rooms, seven or so in each. Before the overture call every night, Sargent would make a round of these rooms, knocking on the doors and entering before anybody had time to say 'Come in!' 'Hello, girls!' he would say. 'How pretty and splendid you all look.' Sometimes he caught one or two of the girls in semi-undress, causing flutter and confusion. Malcolm, they used to tell each other, could be rather naughty. Nobody really minded. Working to a strict timetable he allowed himself four or five minutes for these chit-chats, with possibly a little mild flirtation thrown in. In his tailcoat and white tie he looked as smart as Noël himself. The girls fussed over him delightedly. The more enterprising ones jockeyed for an individual word or smile. Again, this was not mere frivolity. He was there to wish the girls good luck for the night and give them what is now called a 'lift'. They liked to be noticed at least as much as the men. Their work was hard, the pay four pounds a week. By Saturday night many of the girls used to feel listless. Slow *tempi* did nothing to lessen this feeling. Gordon was always asking them to look bright. But who could look bright in, say, the finale of *The Gondoliers* with the gavotte becoming staider and staider season by season? Sargent's

---

* Something came of it decades later. For the 75th anniversary performances of *Iolanthe* (Savoy Theatre, 1960–61) Sargent had eight trumpeters from the Grenadier Guards band on the stage.

coming made a sharp difference. Impossible to feel listless or bored when he was about.

At the Princes in those days the conductor didn't duck up from a manhole in the orchestra pit but walked along the orchestra rail in sight of all. Here was an opportunity for showmanship. He made the most of it. Head and shoulders well back, brisk of tread, he wore a smile that did more than assure the audience they were in for a good time; it conveyed into the bargain that the world was a splendid place, life an unending marvel. Chorus singers, who were lined up on the stage in readiness for the opening number, got into the way of breaking station to watch his nightly entry. This they did through peepholes in the curtain. They noted everything. The fit of the tail coat. The white carnation. The brisk, unobsequious bow. The cheerful glance over the pit to make sure his players were on their toes. The authoritative rap on the rail. The zestful plunge into the first bar of the overture. What timing! And what self-confidence!

*

Rupert D'Oyly Carte's next London season was planned for 1929–1930. It was to run for twenty-two weeks. Redesigned productions of *The Gondoliers*, *Pirates*, *Pinafore* and *Patience* were commissioned from Ricketts in the case of the first and from George Sheringham in the case of the others. The theatre was to be the Savoy, cradle of the Gilbert and Sullivan operas and part of the D'Oyly Carte estate. The inside was to be gutted for the occasion, rebuilt and modernized. All this newness, brightness and branching out assumed a matching presence at the top. In a word, it assumed Sargent. There could not well be any other choice.

In three years much had happened to him. The Royal Choral Society had made him their conductor-in-chief. The King and Queen had attended one of his R.C.S. performances at the Albert Hall. For the Mayers he was conducting children's concerts at the Central Hall, Westminster. In 1928 the Queen attended one of these. The Courtauld–Sargent concerts, his famous series for Mrs. Samuel Courtauld, were preparing. Impresarios pursued him untiringly. In the spring of 1929 several London newspapers quoted him as having turned down an offer of £7,000 a year from an unidentified West End cinema. His duties would be to play classical music on their Wurlitzer organ for ten minutes three times a day. (Other cinema organists in the West End played up to five hours a day and were paid as little as £1,000 a year.) He refused the offer because, he said, the appointment would have got in the way of other professional commitments and was of its nature unpalatable. 'Money alone,' he concluded, 'will never tempt me from my real work.' Choral and orchestral commitments piled up for him in the provinces. From concert to concert he was shuttling over 20,000 miles a year. How to fit twenty-two weeks at the Savoy into his other obligations? At the Princes Theatre in 1926 he had averaged four Gilbert and Sullivan performances a week. He asked Rupert whether he might conduct rather fewer performances at the Savoy. In his letter of reply Rupert made it clear that he was rather alarmed and hoped Malcolm would not take on any other conducting work than was 'really essential for you to keep in with'.

That summer the Sargents holidayed at Soval Lodge, Carte's place on the Island of Lewis in the outer Hebrides, where shooting and fishing were life's main business. There was no telephone. Urgent business with London was done by telegram. With Carte he went over the Savoy schedule and finally accepted it. As before he was to conduct an average of four performances a week. He undertook also a 'repertory run' at the end of the season which brought up a different opera every night. All this was more onerous than his 1926 arrangements. Overwork threatened. Not that Carte was to be blamed for this. Before travelling back to London Sargent applied himself to the rustic and social pleasures, practical jokes included. For his men guests Carte had built an annexe just wide of the lodge. Here they slept in small single bedrooms. Sargent's corridor neighbour was a fastidious young man who dressed immaculately for dinner, although this was never a rule at Soval. One night after dinner some party or parties smuggled a sheep into the young man's bedroom. Although he never admitted as much—whenever the incident was mentioned he went off into speechless laughter—nobody doubted that Sargent was the culprit or the instigator. Getting the sheep into so small a room must have been hard work.

Getting it out was harder. The young man took off his dinner jacket and pushed. The sheep bleated querulously.

'Oh, stow it, old man,' came Sargent's voice from the corridor. 'We know you're awfully good at animal noises, but once is enough.'

*

The gutting of the Savoy Theatre and its internal rebuilding for the company's return in October 1929 took a hundred and thirty-five days and was said to have cost a quarter of a million pounds. Sargent had a week's rehearsals in the relatively roomy new orchestra pit which, with the stage, was said to function like a giant loudspeaker; his every aside was plainly heard—or imagined—on the back row of the top tier. In air washed and warmed to the semblance of perpetual spring, reporters and gatecrashers admired an azure roof flecked with painted clouds and floods of mild sunshine from thousands of yellow electric bulbs behind frosted glass. Countesses, marchionesses and other noble or rich fry crammed the stalls for Ricketts' new *Gondoliers* on the opening night. It was reckoned that fifty million pounds of invested capital occupied the row where Lord Vestey and Sir John Ellerman sat. Four months earlier Britain's second Labour government had come to power. Nobody would have surmised this from the festive and privileged look of the house. Sargent had festive observances of his own. During the repertory phase at the Savoy, with a different piece coming up every night, he got into the way of taking half a bottle of champagne and a dozen oysters in the grill room of the Savoy Hotel before curtainrise (8.15 p.m.). At twelve minutes past eight he would stroll across to the theatre. As the man on the door took his hat he would ask, 'Well, what is it tonight?' The doorkeeper would name the chosen piece and receive a nod of thanks. This looked like whimsy. It was, in fact, a protective device. He already had more music on his mind than was good for him. Realizing this, he said to himself and to others: 'I know every one of the Gilbert and Sullivan operas like the back of my hand. Why should I be told which particular one I shall be conducting tonight and tomorrow night and the night after? If I knew what was coming on I'd be *thinking* the music and worrying over it all day long. The operas would begin to go stale on me. Or

Portrait of Sir Malcolm Sargent by
Sir Gerald Kelly, P.P.R.A.

Last night of 58th season Henry Wood Promenade
Concerts, Royal Albert Hall, September 1952

I'd begin to go stale on the operas. Whereas if I keep myself in the dark until the last three minutes, I can walk into the pit, thoroughly excited whatever opera it happens to be, and put over a show that's likely to have life and vitality.'

Ovations came his way night after night. Always he had happy, effervescent houses. The newspapers, on the other hand, had become pernickety. About Sargent's *tempi* most of the critics said reproachful or sharp things which must have gratified the Lyttons, Lewises and Gordons. After *Ruddigore The Times*, leading a deprecatory chorus, referred to occasional divergences of *tempo* between the conductor and the singers. 'Dr. Sargent constitutionally likes things fast,' commented the writer, 'while the singers, either for the sake of tradition or because this "particularly rapid, unintelligible patter" is hard to sing, like them a little slower. If they reached an agreed compromise they might neither of them be satisfied, but we of the audience would probably feel more comfortable.'

As an editorial note in *The Gilbert and Sullivan Journal* put it, Sargent's *tempi* had opened 'the floodgates of criticism'. The note was written by D. Graham Davis, acting editor, who on amateur stages had specialized in 'Henry Lytton' rôles. Of these and others he had some hundreds of performances to his credit. His tone was faintly but unmistakably disapproving. Published on a spare budget and inexhaustible funds of enthusiasm, the *Journal* was written for and by Gilbert and Sullivan addicts of the kind who delight in textual and historical minutiae. It was the official organ of the Gilbert and Sullivan Society, who thought to spread the cult further by musicological lectures. These, if they did not convert the indifferent or hostile fringe, at least confirmed the faithful in their zeal.

It is at this point that Ethel Smyth re-enters our story, breathing ire and highmindedness.

The Society's *Journal* for March 1932 reports a lecture given the previous month by Dame Ethel on 'the vexed question of speeding up the opera'—Mr. Davis's introductory phrase. He headlined his report: THE MENACE OF TOO MUCH SPEED. When she came to edit her fulmination Dame Ethel entitled it DELIRIOUS TEMPI IN MUSIC. Although she seems not to have directly

6

named him, it was obvious to her hearers and to outside commentators that she had Sargent in mind. Recalling her friendship with Sullivan when a young woman, she described, with metrical rappings, how he would repeat Gilbert's words to himself until their rhythmic 'heartbeat' begot the melody almost unconsciously. Another thing which this process begot was the right *tempo*. Sullivan knew exactly at what rate the point of Gilbert's wit could be intensified and brought home.

'When words are adequately wedded to music,' she continued, 'the pace is predetermined and implicit in the structure; and if you adopt a *tempo* which renders it impossible for the singer to give full point to the text, you are murdering both words and music. . . . I must no longer conceal from you the fact that for the last year or two I have given up attending Gilbert and Sullivan performances! What with the scampering *tempi*—and, still more shameless, commercial encore traffic that pulls these perfect constructions out of gear*—I found listening to them is more a source of anger and disgust than of pleasure.' How had these 'ridiculous, idiotic and uncultured' practices come to prevail? 'One cause, even in people who ought to know better, is a sub-conscious but servile fear of not being thought smart unless they rush through certain parts of a score at full gallop. . . . Yet another cause is . . . that a second-rate musical intelligence fatally connects the idea of wit and gaiety with "snappiness". But on the whole I believe this evil is owing to a microbe that aeroplanes and racing cars scatter as they pass; a microbe that induces the infected one to believe that rapidity is the be-all and end-all of existence, and that if you don't bow down to this fetish you risk being a bore.' After further disobliging thoughts about motor-racing, aeronautics and the God of Rapidity ('his finger is in every pie!') Dame Ethel sounded a call to mutiny: 'If anyone here agrees with me—and, I may add, with every cultured person I ever came across—that the bad modern practices I refer to degrade a particularly delicate art, I invite you to take action about it! Write

* Critics had occasionally complained that Sargent conceded too many encores at the Princes and the Savoy. A typescript interpolation by Sargent conveys that encores were, in fact, agreed with Rupert D'Oyly Carte and the singers before each performance.

to the papers! Fire off postcards to the Directors! Become vocal on the subject whenever you have a chance! Don't quietly sit down under it!'

Her hearers seem to have gone on sitting down quietly. There is no hint in later issues of *The Gilbert and Sullivan Journal* of any campaign by slow-*tempo* zealots against Savoy Hill.

CHAPTER THIRTEEN

THE WIGWAM YEARS

TIMES WERE bad; and bad presaged worse. The Savoy season had opened two days before the onset of a New York stock exchange débâcle which bred financial panic, massive unemployment and much proletarian misery on both sides of the Atlantic. The fifty millions of invested capital which had sat in a row at *The Gondoliers* was, by paper reckoning, decimated overnight. On the surface bewilderment. Under the surface currents of anger.

In some places music was a poultice. One such place was South Wales. Here many pits and steelworks were idle or crippled. Moral mildew threatened whole populations. At Mountain Ash, near Pontypridd, Sargent used to conduct a festival choir of three thousand voices. Many of the singers were miners on the 'dole' or their sons and daughters. Those from outlying villages had paid a penny a week for fares to rehearsals. On the opening day, while waiting for the festival proper to begin, this giant choir and crowds inside and outside the hall passed the time by singing Welsh songs. As he drove over the ridge into the valley one June day at height of the depression Sargent heard the massed voices, seven thousand of them now, come up from below. He halted and marvelled. Given the malaise and penury of the times and, especially, of the Welsh valleys, what he heard was enough to wring any heart. We shall return to Mountain Ash.

The singular thing about Sargent's main enterprises, however, was that the Great Depression failed to put them down; they flourished in spite of it. Indeed, it was precisely in these years that he, as main lever, lifted one of London's great musical institutions out of the trough. The mid-1920s found the Royal Choral Society in a questionable state. As many amateurs as ever were keen to sing for it. Out of 800 or 900 singing members (today the typical strength is less than half of this), between 600 and 700, sometimes more turned up every Monday at six-thirty from the beginning of October until Easter or later for rehearsals in the concert hall of the Royal College of Music: so tight a fit that latecomers had to sit on the stairs at the back. But for one reason or another (classical music on the 'wireless' probably had something to do with it) the old, narrow range of choral classics no longer commanded so massive or as socially mixed a public. Except for *Messiah*, which still packed it, the Royal Albert Hall gallery was thinly populated on R.C.S. nights. Most of the Society's concerts, even *Elijah* nights, once an infallible draw, lost money cumulatively. There were deficits of up to £2,000 a season. Fees for conductors were for a time cut from forty to thirty guineas a concert. Some of the guests kicked. Others haggled. The management didn't budge. They could not afford to. Instead they went to bank for an overdraft, begged the Carnegie United Kingdom Trust unavailingly for a £1,000 loan and, early in 1925, spent a gloomy afternoon trying to think out other ways (none was found) of keeping the Society's head above water financially.

For three years (1925–28) Sargent took his turn at the rostrum with the Society's four other guests—Hamilton Harty, Eugene Goossens, Albert Coates and Dr. E. C. Bairstow from York Minster. Those three years were in some sense his probation. Taking into account the Ethel Smyth *Mass* of 1925, he conducted during those three years a total of twenty-one performances, among them three *Messiahs*, a Verdi *Requiem*, Beethoven *Mass in D* and an *Elijah*. At rehearsals the women singers smiled delightedly as soon as he showed his face. The men, especially those old enough to be his father, were almost equally pleased and possessive. His methods and disciplinary mannerisms never palled. When anything went wrong, an entry mistimed, say, or loss of pitch, he would go through motions of despair—'It's all over, this is the end, life is ruined, there's nothing more to live for, nothing to do except blow my brains out.' Everybody tittered and got the bit right next time. There were mock ferocities, too. In an Elgar piece, it is remembered, he asked the contraltos to make a slight breath pause in the middle of a certain phrase which was marked *legato* in their copies. Some luckless woman failed to pull up; her voice sailed through the gap to painful effect. Flinging out an accusing forefinger Sargent said: 'If any one of you hears your neighbour make this mistake again, give her a good kick!' He suited the words with a hacking motion of the heel. Everybody found the rebuke droll and amiable.

It soon dawned on the committee of management that in Sargent they had an asset of high potential. Early in 1928 Hugh Allen, who was one of their number, invited him on their behalf to become the Society's conductor-in-chief, a post vacant since Sir Frederick Bridge's retirement in 1921. The proposal was that each season he should conduct a minimum of four concerts and necessary rehearsals at a fee of £300; that he should have an assistant conductor; and that he should attend meetings of the committee of management. Sargent accepted. The third committee meeting he attended was the one at which Lord Shaftesbury contemptuously tossed aside Dame Ethel Smyth's letter calling Sargent a cad. By prearrangement he did not enter the committee room until this item had been dealt with.

His first full season as chief (1928–29) ended with a loss of over £2,000 on the Society's standard concerts. There was no hand-wringing, however. With Sargent's help the committee had tapped two healing sources of revenue: gramophone royalties and Coleridge-Taylor's *Hiawatha* mounted as an opera. Under these two headings the Society's 'take' that year came to nearly £4,000. After meeting the concerts deficit the committee were able to invest in Consols, an agreeable process which went on for eleven years and pays dividends still.

Of the two new money-getters *Hiawatha* was the bigger and steadier. For a fortnight every summer it crammed the arena of the Royal Albert Hall with melodious Red Indians and the rest of the immense building with ecstatic audiences. You paid half a crown for a gallery seat, half-a-guinea for a stall and up to four pounds for a box. Smiles and blessing came from on high. The weighty souvenir programme, to which concessionaires sometimes stuck 'sachets' advertising lilac scent, regularly carried stately page portraits of crowned heads in their capacity as patrons of the Royal

Albert Hall Corporation (which drew one third of *Hiawatha* profits) and the Royal Choral Society (which drew two thirds). The *Hiawatha* seasons were thus seen in by King George V and Queen Mary and seen out by George VI and Queen Elizabeth, Edward VIII, tense of face, hand on sword, making a transient appearance in 1936.

In all there were twelve *Hiawatha* fortnights. Sargent directed ten. (In 1933 and 1934, when he was ill, Geoffrey Toye and Albert Coates took over.) Profits down the years must have come to nearly £30,000. Without this lifeline and concomitant gramophone royalties things might have gone ill with the R.C.S. During the grim autumn of 1930 'series' subscriptions fell by half. Hitherto there had been concerts on Thursday nights and Saturday afternoons. The Society decided to cut out Thursdays and confine their activities (*Hiawatha* apart) to Saturday afternoons. There were some who wondered whether *Hiawatha* itself could stay the course. Early in the New Year (1931), all singing members were asked by the committee of management to guarantee the sale of tickets for the forthcoming June performances. It was put about that if advance sales did not reach £3,000 the performances would be dropped. Over 500 singers undertook to place tickets. They brought in guarantees of over £3,500. There was a gross profit on *Hiawatha* that year of nearly £4,000. The pessimists were confounded. Even the Great Depression seemed to be put in its place for a moment.

*

The *Hiawatha* seasons gave a stamp and flourish of their own to what may be described as demi-cultural life in London during the late 1920s and the 1930s. How they began and prospered and the way Sargent technically mastered and revelled in them are worth a closer view.

The idea originated with Thomas Charles Fairbairn, an English opera producer who, before the First World War, had prepared Wagner's *Ring* for an English provincial tour projected by an over-audacious German–Swiss impresario, Ernst Denhof. Meeting the composer of *Hiawatha*, Samuel Coleridge-Taylor, in London, Fairbairn put to him the possibility of *Hiawatha*'s being translated from the cantata platform to some vast hall where it could be

costumed, enacted, sung and danced amid props, scenery and dramatic lighting effects. Coleridge-Taylor seemed attracted by the
thought.

'But,' he said, 'what about Longfellow's words? They're mostly
in the past tense. In opera that won't do. Opera ought to be about
things happening here and now.' 'That's all right,' said Fairbairn.
'Where necessary I have changed past tense into present tense. It
reads quite well. Here's my script.'

The composer glanced at sample revisions. 'It's too late for
Longfellow to split on us now,' he laughed, handing the script back.
In principle he agreed to Fairbairn's project but died twelve years
before its first realization, which happened in 1924.

As early as 1920 Fairbairn had tried his hand in the Albert Hall
arena with productions of *Cavalleria Rusticana* and scenes from
Gounod's *Faust*. These whetted his taste and technique for handling
'lyric' crowds on a bigger scale. The scale he had in mind ruled out
a paid chorus. The problem was whether he could find hundreds of
amateur choral singers clever enough to wear costume convincingly,
rush about or stand still in the right attitudes at the right time, and
sing their parts without 'copies'. This last point he put to officials of
the Royal Choral Society. They replied as one man that there would
be no difficulty; the R.C.S. choir could probably sing the *Hiawatha*
choruses in their sleep already—if not they'd have them off by heart
in a month or so.

In those days no mammoth entertainment of a middle-brow
musical sort could hope for the right sort of backing unless it
carried the cachet of charity. It was arranged that the 1924 and 1925
Hiawathas should be in aid of the blind, for whom one third of the
profits were earmarked, this at a time when the R.C.S., itself a
sufficiently deserving cause, was driven to paring conductors' and
singers' fees and to dabbling in organ and choral 'recitals' because
these cut out the cost of bands and soloists. It was not until 1928
that the Society began to channel the biggest share of the profits
into its own bank.

The conductor in 1924 was Goossens. He used an illuminated
baton for one scene, which was played in total darkness—an enjoyable effect except when, as happened once, the lights refused to

come on again for an unconscionable time. On the first night
Goossens noticed many squaws and braves wearing spectacles or
wristlet watches or both. Sometimes, forgetting Fairbairn's present
tenses the chorus sang Longfellow's narrative tense, because this
was the one they were more accustomed to. These and other defects
were weeded out. Night after night the public sat open-mouthed.
The illusion of falling snow during the scene of Minnehaha's death
chilled everybody in a pleasant way; and Fairbairn's backcloth
became the talk of the town.

To begin with this ran to 10,000 square feet; later he put on an
extra two thousand. Using brushes with sticks ten or twelve feet
long, six men spent three weeks painting 'the world's biggest picture'
—a North American landscape with lake, pineclad slopes and snow-
clad mountains in the far distance. When the vast sheet was finished
Fairbairn had it taped to a pliable frame, hoisted by pulleys and
'anchored' to the Albert Hall roof which, the architects had assured
him, was of mild iron, finely smelted, and therefore capable, as few
roofs were, of taking the weight.* Slung from gallery to gallery at
the back of the platform, it completely masked the organ and the
organist—in 1924, as for decades, Arnold Greir. As well as seeing
nothing, Greir was cut off from much concomitant sound. 'I'm a
deaf man playing dummy,' he used to say.

During the run-up to Hiawatha's departure a point came at which
the choir sang unaccompanied. The timing of the funeral procession
hereabouts had everybody jumpy backstage. Then, as Hiawatha
sailed off to the west in his canoe, organ and orchestra came in
together with a sumptuous burst of tone. So that Greir should be
on the beat a spyhole was cut in the backcloth, somewhere in the
middle of the pinewoods. Here a sub-conductor was posted with a
long stick. At a signal from Sargent, whose rostrum and orchestra
were at the other end of the hall, the sub-conductor would tap on
Greir's shoulder or on his organ bench. This happened in the last
pages of the work. The cue was never known to fail. But at the end

* The backcloth has not been on public view since the latter part of 1939,
when Fairbairn took it to Australia. Later it went into a repository on the far
outskirts of London. In 1962 he had it out for inspection in a meadow. 'There
wasn't a single moth hole,' he reported.

6*

Greir always exclaimed: 'Thank God we all came in together—and finished together!'

Sargent's first *Hiawatha* season was in 1925. Goossens' name had again been pencilled in provisionally for this, but he had to decline because of a schedule which now included the conductorship of an American orchestra, the Rochester Philharmonic. It was left to Fairbairn to cast about for a substitute baton. A man of some versatility, he had conducted occasional opera seasons himself, including a run of *Tannhäuser* and *Aida* at the Excelsior Hall, Bethnal Green, in London's East End, where Wagner and Verdi alternated with professional Shakespeare nights, the whole at popular prices under the Bishop of London's sponsorship. At Bethnal Green his principal clarinettist had been the celebrated Charles Draper, the man who twenty years earlier had helped Thomas Beecham to found his first London orchestra, the New Symphony. He now recalled a talk he had had with Draper after one of the *Aida* rehearsals. Draper had been full of an extraordinary young man—'Sargent's the name' —whom he had encountered a week or two earlier at some Beethoven rehearsal, presumably in Leicester. 'He told me I was playing wrong,' said Draper—'and d'you know, the fellow was right!' One morning Fairbairn noticed Sargent's name on bills for the B.N.O.C. season at Golders Green. What Draper had said came back to him. Going out to the Hippodrome for one of Sargent's *Butterfly* nights, he was greatly taken by the newcomer's precision, pounce and suavity. Afterwards in the wings he introduced himself.

'Goossens,' he said, 'is off to America. So I'm looking for someone to conduct *Hiawatha*. There are fourteen performances starting in six weeks' time. Would you like to take over?'

'Wouldn't I!' exclaimed Sargent.

Arrangements were roughed out on the spot. Sargent didn't ask about money, a thing that impressed Fairbairn.

The 1925 run* went well but did little more than give Sargent an idea of *Hiawatha*'s possibilities. It was followed by a pause of three years during which the new financial share-out was negotiated. After

---

* Again Sargent found himself working with a ladies' committee straight out of Debrett and the College of Heralds. Presided over by Princess Mary, it comprised one duchess, one marchioness, four countesses and eleven baronesses.

this *Hiawatha* really came into its own—and Sargent into his. Coleridge-Taylor's tunes and the lusty or soulful choral singing were avidly enjoyed. So were the double casts of solo singers, most of them renowned, others recently risen on English stages and oratorio platforms—Harold Williams, Miriam Licette, Elsie Suddaby, Lilian Stiles-Allen, Walter Widdop, Parry Jones. . . . Among wigwams and campfires moved the Medicine Man, a part long played by the magnificently aquiline Chief Os-ke-non-ton of the Mohawk Tribe. Os-ke-non-ton wore a yard or two of feather head-dress and was stately and inscrutable. More opera-glasses were focused on him than on any other player. Then there were Fairbairn's picturesque contrivings. These aroused endless wonder. One triumph was the waterfall. He had begun with a waterfall painted on the backcloth but soon did much better. He had water piped up from fire hydrants to a high level whence it cascaded down a series of zinc chutes camouflaged as rocks and bushes, then disappeared through a hole in the platform. 'Where on earth does the water *go* to? people asked. Fairbairn had, of course, thought of everything. Swallowed by a cistern, the waterfall ran off into a natural watercourse under the Albert Hall cellars and reached the Thames in no time.

But there was a greater than the waterfall or even Os-ke-non-ton's profile. The pivot, common denominator and hero of any *Hiawatha* night was the conductor. From the start Sargent knew that here, if ever, was a prime opportunity for showmanship. He seized the opportunity with both hands, unapologetically. On showmanship he was always lucid and unequivocal. He sometimes argued thus: While there are much more important things in life and music, showmanship offers an innocent supplementary pleasure. It has always been in great demand among great masses of people, and there is no reason why artists born with the showman's talent (by no means a common one) should be shamed out of satisfying this demand by pundits who were born without it.

One thing the showman has to be sure of is that little things don't go wrong at the last moment and reduce his magic to common clay. Before every *Hiawatha* one of Sargent's aides, often a pupil of his conducting class, made checks in the orchestral area. This, with the conductor's rostrum, was under the royal box, at the far end of the arena from platform and backcloth. First, in case there had been any maldistribution by the librarian, the aide verified all band parts. Next he caused the orchestral desk lamps to be switched on and tapped each bulb under its cowl to make sure none was on the point of failing. Finally he tested a foot pedal on the rostrum which sounded the conductor's buzzer on the lighting switchboard backstage.

Having had his aide's report that all was well, Sargent would assume his white carnation, glance in the green-room mirror, touch his tie and shake down his cuffs. He made his entrance into the arena from below, up one of the remoter 'bull runs', as they are called. As he appeared all house lights came up, and a spotlight from the roof cocooned him on his brisk way to the rostrum. On opening nights he would mount the rostrum and raise his baton all in one striding, martial movement, plunging choir and band without pause into 'God Save the King'. This entry ritual, whdther the National Anthem intervened or not, invariably raised the roof. Nothing could have been simpler. Yet nobody had thought of it before. Nobody else, probably, would have dared to. The crowd were enchanted. The cheering over, Sargent would raise his baton again, this time in signal. Instantly all houselights and spots went out. The overture followed. It played for eight minutes in a blackness flecked only by the cowled orchestra lamps. Just before the end of the last bar Sargent pressed the foot pedal and sounded the lighting board buzzer. All house lights and 'floods' came blazing on. At the same time a great mob of squaws and braves rushed into the arena, squealing and howling, from all points of the compass. Then, as by a common impulse, they flung themselves on their faces before their tribal leaders and totems, freezing the hall to silence.

This may not have been opera as those understood the word who during these times were going to Covent Garden for Bruno Walter's *Rosenkavalier* or Beecham's *Ring*. But in the way of sweeping lyric spectacles London had seen nothing to touch either *Hiawatha*'s breathtaking start or much of what followed. The performances were regularly billed as featuring a thousand performers. Of these two hundred were dancers and a nominal eight hundred R.C.S. singing members got up as Red Indians. Braves and squaws used to come in at the end of the working day from offices, shops, timber yards, schools, hospital staff-rooms, factories and housewives' kitchens in all parts of Greater London and even from places deep in the Home Counties. Except on Saturday nights, when just about everybody put in an appearance and got into make-up, the average turn-up of singers was probably around seven hundred. For an hour before their first cue the bleak corridors beneath the arena were all bustle and keyed-up jollity. *Hiawatha* turned a disparate throng into a disciplined though seething family. Their pride in Sargent was their bond.

*

The second of the Society's new money-getters, as has been mentioned, was the gramophone.

Soon after Sargent's recording début with *Hugh the Drover* in the nightmarishly cramped studio at Hayes, acoustical recording gave place to electrical recording, and the grotesque trumpets into which artists formerly had to sing and play were supplanted by microphones. One charming thing about electricity and microphones is that they went or could be taken anywhere. The gramophone became footloose. The R.C.S. learned of a new race of musicians who trailed cables, wore headphones and talked in curt jargon about choral and orchestral scores which, it surprisingly turned out, some of them could read with the best. If allowed to trail their cables into the Albert Hall, it appeared, these men of the New Age would be able to record 'live' performances by mammoth choirs even with audiences present.

The thing sounded improbable and dreamlike. Eager technicians from H.M.V. label not only demonstrated that the thing was possible but, after satisfactory technical trials, offered the Royal Choral Society a royalty of ten per cent on the sales of any recordings they should make of the Society's performances. The Society happily accepted.

This had occurred two years before Sargent's appointment as conductor-in-chief. His first assignment under the agreement was *Messiah* on a Saturday in April 1926. Few in an audience which crammed the hall from ground to top gallery had any idea to begin with what was afoot, nor did many notice anything unusual.

Controlled and timed by Sargent according to a schedule worked out
with Fred W. Gaisberg, nominally H.M.V.'s chief recording
manager, actually one of Europe's most influential impresarios,
nine choruses were 'cut' that afternoon with a bonus in the shape of
'God Save the King' which, oddly, seems to have been sung at the
end of the concert. Gaisberg sat in a box overlooking the platform
and murmured telephone signals, or buzzed them, to a recording
team miles away on the top floor of Gloucester House, a business
block near the old Alhambra Theatre in Leicester Square. At that
time Gloucester House served as a recording centre for several outlying performance points. The *Messiah* choruses came in over a
hired Post Office telephone link and were cut on a pair of recording
machines, each taking over from the other. These were still run, as
they continued to be for a generation longer, on the weight, pulley
and clockwork principle. It is said that all nine numbers were
smoothly cut except the *Hallelujah* Chorus. On a 'full-close' chord
seven bars from home, an engineer, thinking the end had been
reached and very pleased, for the wax was running out, whipped
up the 'point', or stylus, exclaiming 'We've got it!' Actually he cut
out five terminal 'Hallelujahs' and a bit more.

Recordings from *Elijah* were made on a February afternoon in
1928. This time the audience were on the qui vive. Under the head-
ing 'An Item of Interest', a programme note warned them that the
Gramophone Company, as the H.M.V. firm still called itself, would
be making records during the performance. They were therefore
asked to refrain from coughing which, microphones being hyper-
sensitive, had been known to spoil many a record. This time the
performance was 'piped' to a newfangled recording van parked
outside the hall and jacked up against traffic vibration. Inside it were
twin recording machines which came into play alternately on buzz
signals from the recording manager, who sat with a field telephone
in front of Sargent among the violas and 'cellos. Sargent's score had
been 'plotted' so that the main choruses were divided into lengths
roughly equivalent to the maximum running time (4 min. 50 sec.)
of a twelve-inch wax. Upon nods exchanged by Sargent and the
recording manager—on this occasion young David Bicknell,
Gaisberg's eventual successor—depended the success of ticklish

co-ordination and split-second timings which prompted Sargent to exclaim long afterwards: 'God! The things we did when we were young! We wouldn't have the pluck even to attempt them now.' To ensure continuity in performances that spilled over from one side of a disc to the other, the cutting 'point' of one machine had to be lifted and the point of the other lowered within the space of one blank beat or bar selected beforehand. This and other niceties called for swift, cool co-operation on the conductor's part. Sargent revelled in the new technical challenges which 'live' recording threw up, just as he revelled in the liberating effect of electronic tape recording a generation later.

Of *Elijah* choruses thirteen waxes were successfully cut that afternoon. In the end H.M.V. put out eight of them. A little later that season he cut nine sides of *Hiawatha* at a R.C.S. concert performance (as distinct from an enacted one). He and his singers then moved to what became, Sundays apart, one of the most thriving recording studios in the world: Kingsway Hall, a Methodist mission on the rim of the West End theatre belt. At Kingsway he cut eight more *Hiawatha* sides. His singers sat facing the pulpit in reverse order with their backs to drapes of quilting hung from the balcony, the basses in front, the sopranos on the back rows. Sargent told the ladies that although their language was impeccable in the ordinary way it couldn't be denied that they were capable of 'blasting' in the acoustical sense. Neither the recording van nor Gloucester House came into the picture this time, the performance being transmitted to a new machine-room-cum-studio, the Lesser Queen's Hall (it was upstairs at the Queen's Hall proper), where much recording history was to be made. In the upshot one could buy (and thousands did) abbreviated versions of *Hiawatha's Wedding Feast* and *The Death of Minnehaha* for thirty-two shillings on sixteen sides. To this ready seller were added choruses from *Tannhäuser*, *Lohengrin* and *The Mastersingers* as well as a stunning Sanctus from Bach's B minor Mass. In the three seasons which preceded the Depression the Society's gramophone royalties came to £6,000. This meant more interest from more Consols. The Society was saved.

Recording from a platform and in the presence of an audience, with other people doing most of the technical donkey work, was one thing. Recording from a studio rostrum was another. Sargent's first studio assignment in the microphone era was with the Royal Albert Hall Orchestra. On a suite from Falla's *Three Cornered Hat* he cut fourteen waxes in one day. Eight were rejected and destroyed. The remaining six were passed, three of them for processing. This was tolerably good going. At his next session he cut eleven excerpts from Handel, Schubert and Walford Davies. All were rejected. A faulty transmission line between the studio and the machine room had something to do with the fiasco if, indeed, that is what it could be fairly called, for in those explorative days busy, unproductive afternoons were a commonplace of studio life.

One of the richest seams for record-makers was the Savoy operas. The clamour for these came from the ends of the earth: Australian back-blocks, African veldt, Canadian prairie and uncounted frontier and jungle stations, as well as from a sizeable section of the British and U.S. populations. Sets were on the market of nine complete Savoy operas which ran to twenty-two sides each and couldn't be called cheap since, with the pound worth four times more, they cost only a few shillings less than today's superbly realistic long-play versions on four sides. The sound was implausible. Obviously the time had come to re-do them before the microphone. H.M.V. and Rupert D'Oyly Carte approached Sargent. The upshot was that between 1929 and 1936 he recorded eight of the operas* with technical adroitness. Also with a kind of effervescent delight. It was as if Gilbert's words and Sullivan's music had been a treasure cave and he an exceedingly bright child who had suddenly stumbled upon it. In some ways it was 1926 and the Princes Theatre all over. There were overt grumblings about *tempi* by veterans of the Lytton–Lewis school or tradition. It is said that some recalcitrant went so far as to telephone Carte asking him to intercede. The stumbling block, inevitably, was one of the *Princess Ida* choruses. Carte took a taxi to the studio and heard the tail-end of the dispute between Sargent and a spokesman for the production side—'I repeat, you're taking it too fast, much too fast for the stage action.' 'But we aren't on the stage. We're making a gramophone record.' 'That makes no

* *Yeomen, Pirates, Iolanthe, H.M.S. Pinafore, Patience, The Gondoliers* (abridged), *Ruddigore* and *Princess Ida*.

difference. The music should be *coloured* by theatre.' Carte upheld Sargent and taxied back to the Savoy.

For *The Pirates of Penzance*, which was recorded at the Lesser Queen's Hall straight after the end of the 1929–30 Savoy season, a new deployment was tried: short, open-ended cubicles—one for principals, one for chorus, one for strings and one for the wind. Each cubicle had its microphone. A shirtsleeved Sargent on a high rostrum was the hub of everything and everybody. The first session began with a run-through of a projected take. At the end as many as could flocked after Sargent into the machine-room to hear the test wax that had been made. Listening to the playback with the score in front of him he noted faults of dynamic and balance. A second wax was cut to rectify the faults of the first. Halfway through a woman soloist came in half a beat behind. 'Stop!' shouted Sargent. There was no point in continuing with that one. A third wax was put on the turntable. During the brief wait for the red light and buzz he talked lightheartedly with his artists about the *tempi* of hacks he used to hire for a morning's ride in Richmond Park. This helped to keep the tensions down. Towards the end of the third wax, which went spiritedly and smoothly, somebody gave a sharp, loud cough. Sargent put his baton down and said over his shoulder, in the general direction of the cougher: '*You* have spoiled *that* one!' His tone was dry and damning. A fourth wax was fetched from the thermostatic cabinet. And so the session went wearingly on.

In the days before electronic tape any recording session was apt to be a bed of nails. Yet hundreds of performances came from them which have been reverently reprocessed and restored to the catalogues as landmarks of style and musicianly insight. Hence the Schnabel reissues in H.M.V.'s Great Recordings of the Century series (C.O.L.H. label). These include a Beethoven Piano Concerto No. 1 in C conducted by Sargent with the London Symphony Orchestra.

It is to this recording, presumably, that Gaisberg refers in an anecdote* which suggests that coughs, off-beat entries and other

---

* In his autobiography *Music on Record* (Hale, London, 1948) which, however, ascribes the incident to Beethoven's third piano concerto in C minor, which Schnabel recorded much later and with another conductor.

mischances were not the only problems a conductor had to face. Like many artists of ebullient and witty temperament, Schnabel had black interludes during which he would lament first, the day he was born, then, the day he became a concert pianist—specifically, a concert pianist with a recording contract chained to his ankle. Sitting down for one of the concerto takes, he grimaced with repugnance. 'O, why,' he asked rhetorically, 'am I *married* to this machine?'

'You're a lucky man,' countered Sargent. 'You can get a divorce tomorrow if you want to.'

Later, when all was set and the buzzer sounded, Schnabel threw up his hands mutinously, put on his martyr's look and groaned: 'I feel like Prometheus in chains. O, why do I make myself play down to this machine?'

'You do it,' explained Sargent patiently, 'for the same reason as the orchestra and myself do it.'

'And what reason is that?' asked Schnabel, suddenly curious.

'For money.'

There was a general laugh, in which Schnabel joined—with reason. If money consoled, he enjoyed rather greater consolation than Sargent whose fee at this time worked out at not more than £20 per concerto session. As a beginner some years earlier he had been paid as little as £10 a session.

It is not to be inferred from this exchange—into which elements of teasing and humouring should be read—that Schnabel and Sargent did not get on well with each other. By this time they were seasoned comrades, having been thrown together by two enterprises which, in wholly different ways, did much for Sargent's influence and prestige: the Robert Mayer concerts for children and the Courtauld–Sargent Concert Club. To these we now turn.

CHAPTER FOURTEEN

CHILDREN'S CONCERTS

FOR SIXTEEN seasons the London concerts of Robert Mayer—
who simultaneously promoted several like series in outlying
boroughs and provincial cities—were held at the Central Hall,
Westminster, another Methodist 'mission' which is put to secular
uses on weekdays. Sargent conducted all these London concerts up
to 1939, when they were interrupted by the war, except for the
first ones, an experimental set of three (1923), with Adrian Boult on
the rostrum for two of them, and the 1933–34 season, when he was
ill or convalescing. From all parts of Greater London and as far as
fifty miles out, groups of children who had been enrolled and mildly
indoctrinated in schools of all grades—preparatory schools, 'elementary' schools and public schools (including Westminster, which
regularly sent a hundred or two boys in silk hats)—flocked in on Saturday mornings for concert overtures, opera entr'actes, occasional helpings of oratorio, single movements or pairs from classical symphonies,
lots of standard concertos, a few out-of-the-way ones* and a sprink-
ling of 'modern' works, a category which then ranged back from
Walton to Debussy's *L'Après-midi d'un Faune*. At first there were
fifty in the orchestra, a variable personnel recruited from London's
three or four crack bands. The players had to be in their places for
rehearsal at nine on the dot, the concerts beginning two hours later.

The children paid a shilling a head at the outset. The hall could
hold 2,700. On the first Saturday, bedevilled by a transport strike,
only 350 customers turned up, and many of these were adults. The
'movement' quickly snowballed. From 1926–27 onwards the concerts ran to capacity, with few grown-ups in sight. Attendances at

---

* E.g. Haydn's *Sinfonia Concertante* for violin, 'cello, oboe, bassoon and
orchestra, heard in 1937.

the three pilot concerts of 1923, however, did not aggregate more than 2,000. Even when Central Hall threatened to give at the seams and there weren't enough seats for all would-be subscribers, a gap remained between takings and costs. The gaps were attended to by the Mayers. By the early 1960s, Sir Robert and Lady Mayer (he was knighted in 1939) were calculated to have spent £100,000 on children's concerts and related causes. Both were musically trained. Dorothy Mayer had sung professionally in musical comedy, grand opera and contemporary texts from Vaughan Williams and Holst to Stravinsky and Schoenberg. Born in Mannheim, Robert Mayer trained as a concert pianist (he remembers practising for hours with newspapers tucked under his elbows to strengthen his wrists) but, settling in London at seventeen, adjourned his musical ambitions to compile a fortune in the City, mainly on the copper market.

In New York soon after the First World War, he and Dorothy Mayer had been fired by the children's concerts which Walter Damrosch was then conducting at Carnegie Hall. Why not something of the same kind in London and other cities at home? Not one English child in ten thousand had heard a symphony orchestra, didn't know there were such things and, as matters then stood, probably never would: a sorry privation.

The pilot concerts of 1923 set the target and the method. At the first one Boult conducted a movement from a Mozart serenade to illustrate string tone; the Introduction to Act III of *The Mastersingers* to illustrate strings and brass combined; Beethoven's Rondino in E flat to illustrate the woodwind; and the third movement of Tchaikovsky's Symphony No. 4 to illustrate strings, woodwind and brass in alternation; and so on. After the third concert Boult went off to Birmingham to found and conduct a municipal orchestra there. The Mayers looked around for a new conductor.

Like everybody else they had heard much of 'this brilliant young chap from Melton Mowbray—or is it Leicester?' In the summer of 1924 they went to the Queen's Hall and heard him conduct his *Windy Day*. Afterwards they said, 'He's our man!' This happened on a Saturday. The following Monday they had him to dinner at Pagani's, a restaurant much used by musical eminences which became a legend long before Hitler's bombers blasted it out of existence. At Pagani's they explained their difficulty. They had booked Central Hall for eight Saturday morning concerts from October to June. Time pressed. With the opening concert less than three months off, they were without conductor, and no programmes had been drafted. Sargent took in the situation nimbly.

'As you'll understand,' they said, 'we need somebody who'll get on personal terms with the children, somebody who'll chat about the music they are going to hear—play the main themes beforehand on the piano and explain what the themes are about and how they're built up. Nothing schoolteacherish, of course. (Not that we've anything against teachers. They're co-operating wonderfully.) Something chatty and informal and funny.' They were sure Dr. Sargent could do all this without difficulty. Dr. Sargent was equally sure. He had done it for years already. What they had outlined was precisely how he had talked about music, illustrating it thematically at the piano, to boys and girls at the Melton Mowbray school.

By the end of the meal he and the Mayers had reached agreement. Or, as Robert Mayer put it, in the language of the City, they 'dealt'. Henceforth he was their conductor-in-chief. He began on 18th October, 1924. The programme that morning had a fuzzy line drawing of an orchestra, with the section-leaders numbered for identification. Before the main business (*Mastersingers* Overture, Scherzo and Nocturne from Mendelssohn's *Midsummer Night's Dream* music, Schubert's 'Unfinished' Symphony and Quilter's *Children's Overture*), he had his principals stand up successively and play the same tune so that the audience could scrape acquaintance with the different instruments, their 'personalities' and their functions. It is doubtful whether this departure from the plain line of symphonic duty pleased the leaders as much as it entertained the children. Accustomed to playing from band parts, they felt apprehensive when asked to play some snatch of melody, however familiar, from memory. At a later concert Sargent asked the leaders all round for a phrase from *The Minstrel Boy*. On learning before rehearsal what was in the wind some of them buttonholed him and asked that the bit should be written out for them. The first trombone, an artist of the first rank, asked to be conducted into the bargain. 'Would you mind,' he asked, 'giving me the upbeat and beating the first bar?'

As well as conducting eight or so concerts a year at the Central Hall, Sargent had charge up to 1930 of all the Mayers' outlying inaugurals. He thus gave the movement send-offs at Tottenham, Wembley, Wimbledon, Bethnal Green, Leeds—and Stepney. The Stepney offshoot was the earliest (1925) and the most daring. The inaugural concert and those that followed were at the People's Palace in the Mile End Road, a swarming Cockney neighbourhood more acquainted than most with hard times, under-nourishment and threadbare pallor. All things considered, Stepney was as remote as the moon from the refinements of classical culture. The first Saturday morning is well remembered. The hall was three parts full of urchins and bigger boys and girls who had paid fourpence to get in and, being a bit bewildered, were by Stepney standards, relatively quiet. Sargent bounded on to the platform with his elating smile and a 'Good morning, boys and girls!' which conquered them as surely as his 'Good morning, gentlemen!' conquered the D'Oyly Carte chorusmen.

But how would the boys and girls take J. S. Bach? The centre-piece of the programme was a movement from the E major violin concerto. It had been listed with some misgiving. Sargent opened with a talk on John Sebastian the schoolboy: over 250 school hours missed in three years, perhaps through illness. But, to make up for this, how industrious!—all those volumes of music belonging to his elder brother which, because forbidden to play them, he secretly copied out by moonlight, a task which spread over six months and did his eyes no good at all! The concerto soloist then came forward. This was Samuel Kutcher, who was to be leader of the Mayers' orchestra for many seasons. The music began. No whispering and wriggling in seats. Instead, utter absorption. 'If it hadn't been for the music,' Robert Mayer recalls, 'you could have heard a pin drop.'

The concerts in the Mile End Road were one end of the social gamut. As to the other end of it, Queen Mary arrived by pre-arrangement one morning in 1928, toque, lorgnette and all. Avoiding undue fuss, she came in by the back door of Central Hall in time to hear Schnabel take his eighth curtain call for Mozart's G major piano concerto, of which he had played not selected movements but the lot, and stayed on to hear entr'acte music from Schubert's

Rosamunde and the *Freischütz* Overture. Queen Elizabeth II attended her first Mayer concert when six years old. She was brought to Central Hall on that occasion—and on later ones with her sister, now Princess Margaret—by their mother, then the Duchess of York, who at this writing has been patron of the Mayer concerts for thirty years.

As winter followed winter, Sargent's fluency multiplying at the same rate as his commitments, he fell into the way of waiting until breakfast time on Saturday before preparing his explanatory talks on the morning's music. While he dressed and took coffee, he would have one of his pupils read articles from Grove and other histories about the composers involved and perhaps about the relevant pieces. He did not have to memorize facts and dates consciously; these stuck to his mind like adhesives. He was never at a loss for a word or a bit of playfulness. On all hands, even among hardbitten orchestral freelances, his extemporizations were allowed to be remarkably ready and telling. Usually his fervour caught up the entire hall, commanding rapt faces, intent eyes and not a few open mouths. There is record of one dissident. Sargent had been going on about the inexpressible loveliness of a harp solo in Debussy. A small boy's voice interjected: 'The man's mad.' Sargent gave no sign of noticing this. Probably he was too carried away to do so. Samuel Kutcher heard it plainly, however. Sometimes he was tempted to go on rather long. When this threatened, Mayer, posted at the back of the hall, pulled out a handkerchief and discreetly signalled with it to Kutcher who, seated within two armslengths of Sargent, would whisper at him to cut it short.

It had been worked out that, counting in explanatory talks and pauses between movements, an hour and twenty minutes was the absolute time limit for audiences including many below the age of ten and even as young as seven. Every extra minute invited inattention and wriggling and entailed delays in getting home for lunch and the ritual of Saturday afternoon games. It would never do to bore the little dears. One thing which, it was thought, would keep their minds from straying was what came to be known as audience participation. In other words, jingle singing. The idea originated not with Sargent but with Damrosch who, as the Mayers knew, had fitted nursery rhymes or jingles made up by himself to themes of symphonies and had them sung as mnemonics by young audiences in New York.

Among adults at a Mayer concert in January 1926 was a bland, solid gentleman in pince-nez who, while keeping a smile on his face, experienced an inward fury which, if he hadn't repressed it, would have resulted (so he confessed later) in his being thrown out for brawling. Like Sargent, Harvey Grace had been reared musically in the organ loft of a cathedral (Southwark) and, after charges in London and country churches, himself succeeded to a cathedral organ (Chichester). In 1926, however, he happened to be the editor of *The Musical Times* where, under the pen-name of Feste, he wrote one of the liveliest commentaries English musical journalism has known.

One thing should be made clear. Feste had nothing against children. To the contrary. He had a small boy of his own, 'Feste junior' as he called him in print, whose musical upbringing he recorded from time to time with affectionate drollery. (His uproarious account of young Feste's first threepenny mouth organ and his discovery of the chord of the dominant seventh before graduating to the shilling flute is worthy of the anthologies.) The programme included Bach's B minor suite for strings. Feste's first frown was provoked by talks interspersed between movements which, he complained, turned the suite into 'penny numbers' instead of permitting it to be taken in as an organic whole. What outraged him, however, was Sargent's treatment of the fugal movement. First he played the fugue subject several times on the piano. Then he bade the children sing it to the words: 'You *must* hear me tootle on the flute.' In his next *Musical Times* column he drove his resentment home with music type:

1

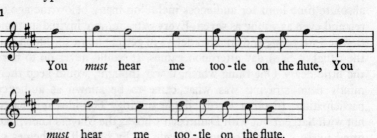

After Bach, Beethoven: the opening movement of the Fifth Symphony. The children were advised to think of the first two subjects as the Giant in 'Jack and the Beanstalk', a terrible fellow, and his Wife, a kind lady. 'And then,' added Feste, 'we all sang the following (all but me, that is: I was dumb with rage):

—and after several encores:

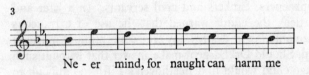

It would be long, feared Feste, before these nursery rhyme associations, so irrelevant to the music, were lived down in children's minds. In another context, while applauding Mayer's good works as big with possibilities, he predicted that the movement would miss its aim and even do harm if 'the more fussy type of "musical appreciation" enthusiast' were allowed a big part in its direction. 'The best place for him,' he added, 'is at the door, taking tickets.'

The dailies joined in the battle. A *Times* writer thought 'Fee-fi-fo-fum' for the first subject of the Fifth and 'the comforting ministrations of the ogre's wife' for the second were a wonderful help in leading from the known to the unknown and might set many a young mind on the road to both philosophy and music. In the *Morning Post*, Geoffrey Toye's brother Francis, author of a noted Verdi biography, asked which was the better, the jingle method or such analytical flummery as:

'Now, my dear children, this is the first subject, which you will kindly hum after I have played it on the piano. And this is the second subject, which you will treat in the same manner. Note the contrasting nature of the two themes, aptly illustrating the male and female principles of the universe. Your attention should now be drawn to the fugal treatment after letter X in the score; there is also an interesting example of an effective pedal point on the last page but three, while the ingenious use of the Neapolitan sixth at the beginning will not escape your notice.'

The most extraordinary thesis of all cropped up in *The Music Bulletin*, organ of the British Music Society. An editorial in the issue for March 1926 deplored the jingle method as developing 'nothing save the categorical sense, which is better developed by mathematics. Children's concerts on the present lines will only help to raise a nation of shopkeepers, bankers and civil servants.' In a later and more lucid article, the editor warned that the use of extraneous ideas as a mnemonic might destroy any true conception of music in the child mind. Should Dr. Sargent make answer that without such aids the average child would find Beethoven's Fifth too difficult to take in, an obvious conclusion was to be drawn, namely, that the Fifth was an unsuitable work for children's ears. That June the matter was turned over for free debate at the British Music Society's annual delegation conference. No resolution was tabled. Therefore no vote was taken. What the Society thought of Sargent's methods has not come down to us. Sargent himself put in an appearance, of course, and talked spiritedly. As he saw it, the only real difficulty in the way of children's concerts, there being few Robert Mayers about, was getting the money for them. Children were so much more responsive than grown-ups that they would certainly love good music if they had a chance of hearing it. Nothing but good could come of telling them about a piece or its composer so long as what was told whetted their interest. Nothing but harm could come of making the child's brain work too hard, 'since to know more about an art form is not necessarily to love it more'. Conventional symphonic analyses were as silly as plucking the petals of a rose to discover the secret of its scent.

This last point was irrefutable. Like Francis Toye's send-up of old-fashioned academic analyses it missed the point, however. The fact that dry-as-dust analysts were on the wrong horse did not prove that the 'jinglers' were on the right one. And it happened to be the jinglers who were on trial.

The controversy went rumbling on. Five years after Harvey Grace's assault, Sargent was heard on the air* in a not altogether clinching rearguard action. He said:

I have been criticized because I have on occasion set words to musical phrases which were not intended by the composer. . . . What I do is really quite harmless. . . . Where a piece is written in a very definite mood it is easy for the children to remember the tune if suitable words are put to it. For instance, the *Fingal's Cave* Overture of Mendelssohn has a little tune. . . , and I have repeatedly made the children remember it by asking them to sing 'How lovely the sea is'. Mendelssohn didn't have these words definitely in mind when writing the piece, yet one knows that he definitely had in mind how lovely the sea *was*, and so there can be no harm in labelling the little tune with those words.

Or take the *Mastersingers* Overture. It is simple to get children to grasp Wagner's polyphony if you get the three basic tunes into their heads. Tell them the story briefly. Get them to sing the opening theme to the words, 'Great Mastersingers of the town of Nuremberg'. The theme is then labelled for all time. The second theme, Walther's—here the words 'Eva I love' are absolutely right and will label it in their memory. The other theme is played by the brass when everybody is arriving for the festival. The words in this case are, 'Come to the festival of song today.' In this way, memorizing the tunes, a child can understand the whole of the counterpoint of the Overture.

But the anti-jinglers were persistent. At last the matter came to friendly discussion between Sargent and the Mayers. It was decided between them that jingles, 'having served their purpose', should be dropped.

In a wider sense than whether or not Beethoven's 'Fate' motif should or shouldn't be Fee-fi-fo-fummed, the issue of musical

* B.B.C. Music and Drama programme. VII: Talk by Dr. Malcolm Sargent on Music for Children, 17th July, 1931.

'appreciation' was and remains a vital one, involving as it does divisions of a philosophical kind as to the nature and function of music and the other arts. On these matters Sargent's considered attitude, while including an element of honest bafflement, had a lot in common with that of the young Ralph Vaughan Williams. In 1902 Vaughan Williams had written: 'The function of music is to be beautiful and nothing less—it cannot be more. . . . The emotion produced by music . . . is that which arises from pure delight in beauty; and that is the only true musical emotion.'* 'What is music?' Sargent was once asked in circumstances which gave him little time for reflection. He answered:

> That's a question I have asked myself a good many times without being able to solve it properly. Many times at rehearsals or concerts, perhaps afterwards to the leader, I ask: Why is this music so extraordinarily effecting? Why, for instance, are the first bars of the 'Unfinished' Symphony so very lovely? There's only one answer I can give, and I know it's not very definite or conclusive. . . . It seems to me there is something in the heart of humanity which is as deep and fundamental as the feeling of religion. It is this feeling of worship of beauty and love of Beauty itself. Music seems able to get at the spirit . . . without bothering about the [externals?] of it. Music is able in itself to express Beauty without any relation at all to the exterior world, whether of shapes or words and so on. . . . Music is fundamentally the essence of Beauty. I can say no more than that. . . . It is the soul of man speaking to the soul of man through sound.†

Again:

> I have spent a lifetime loving music and studying music and don't understand what music is. Music is a mystery. The more one studies music the more one knows about it *intellectually*, yes. By 'about' I mean 'round about' it. One learns the science of

---

* Quoted in *The Works of Ralph Vaughan Williams*, Michael Kennedy (Oxford University Press), 1964.

† B.B.C.: Any Questions programme, 21st September, 1941.

making music, one knows its construction, one learns its history and a thousand things. But the mystery of music is like the peace of God, past all understanding.*

Such reflections at a Central Hall Saturday morning would merely have made the young things feel lost and bewildered. What they revelled in, when occasion arose, was story telling based on 'programme' music. If a composer chooses to link his music with some narrative the commentator is morally free to go over the ground, with piano illustrations, in his own words and way. We can get an idea of what went on at programme music sessions in Central Hall from the transcript of a delightful Plain Man's Guide to Music which Sargent spoke, illustrated and conducted over the air in 1949.† Not only does the transcript show his method. It also preserves most vividly the man's mercurial high spirits and zest. The B.B.C. Symphony Orchestra were with him in the studio. The business in hand included Richard Strauss's tone-poem *Till Eulenspiegel*. Before conducting it he held forth from the keyboard. In the transcript his piano illustrations are described as 'Effects, piano'.

'Let's see,' he began, 'what a composer can do when he wants to portray a character. . . . Till would be represented in England probably as somebody rather like Puck, mischievous, couldn't be naughtier in fact. But you can't help loving him. Real rogue, scamp, vagabond—and an adorable creature. Not malice but mischief is what makes him behave so badly. (Effects, piano.)

'That was simply an introduction, saying: "Listen, this is a little story for you." Then we get the character of Till himself on the horn. (Effects, piano.) Very gay and roguish tune. He's enjoying himself hugely. . . . More mischief making. (Effects, piano.) You hear that many times. Now off he goes on a horse. (Effects, piano.) Galloping away, looking for adventures. Soon finds one. Lands himself into a market place. Looks round and sees a terrible big stall loaded with crockery. A lot of old women selling the stuff. He charges his horse right into it and there's a dickens of a crash. I needn't describe it on the piano—you'll hear it all right on the orchestra.

* B.B.C. Light Programme, 3rd May, 1949.
† B.B.C. Light Programme, 2nd December.

Well, having made himself a thorough nuisance he gallops off. Looking round again he sees a monk. He goes up and tricks the monk, pretending to be extremely moral. This is Till preaching. (Effects, piano.)

'Now here comes a flourish all on its own. (Effects, piano.) Here we are. Always puts his tongue out at the wrong moment. (Effects, piano.) But he's not without his little moments of contrition. (Effects, piano.) His tears, I'm afraid, aren't quite sincere. (Effects, piano.) "I'm so sorry, I am really. But I'm going on just the same as before." He looks round and sees a very pleasant young lady worth making eyes at. (Effects, piano.) Completely conceited, satisfied, cocksure of himself. Well, he soon leaves her. (Effects, piano.)'

And so the tale and the piano bits went on. Argument with the old pedagogues . . . Till's anger. . . . 'But off he goes whistling down an alley. . . . He's on top of the world. Big climax to show everything's to his heart's content. . . . When suddenly, listen. Great crash of chords. . . . Obviously—the heavy foot of the law. A policeman with very large feet! Till puts his tongue out. . . . They chase him. . . . And then Till gives rather a squeal. . . . They've got him at last—and the poor little chap's feeling really contrite. . . . He's taken before a judge who condemns him to be *hanged*. . . . He's made the "big drop". . . . His soul rushes out and up. . . . But he finds he's gone to the wrong place and comes down. . . . And our story's over. . . . Don't worry, though. In case you should feel disheartened it isn't *really* true, you see. Just a story. And I (the story-teller, that is) hope you've enjoyed it. . . .'

Between 1924 and the spring of 1939, Sargent did nearly a hundred Mayer concerts at Central Hall and well over a hundred if the Stepney and other 'inaugurals' are added. Purists nagged at him for permitting applause between movements. To these he replied: 'With young children it's absolutely essential they should have a chance, after sitting still for ten minutes, to clap and relieve muscular tension. And why shouldn't they clap if the music's marvellously performed?' Similar considerations made him and the Mayers chary of complete symphonies and concertos, especially during the early seasons, when single movements or not more than two out of four were the general rule.* Schnabel, who gave several concerto performances for the Mayers, always without fee (a sacrifice in his heyday of £300 a time), challenged this policy and went so far as to call it nonsense. 'I will undertake,' he said, 'to do a complete concerto, Mozart's G major (K. 453), without boring the children for a moment. I could make it come off all right, just you see!'

He kept his word in 1928 at the concert which Queen Mary attended. Sargent cheerfully co-operated. Between the first movement and the second and the second movement and the finale, he extended the pauses from the customary few seconds to over half a minute so that the children could have 'release'. What Schnabel didn't want was applause. 'Why break Mozart into three pieces?' To tell the children not to clap was out of the question. At Mayer concerts children were never told *not* to do things. That was one of the rules. . . . All went well. During the pauses the children stirred and whispered, but only a little. Gripping the sides of his stool tensely and looking ahead with sternness and concentration, Schnabel *willed* them into silence. It is to be admitted, however, that what lay within Schnabel's power was hardly feasible for all artists and all occasions.

Twice Sargent devoted whole mornings to a conspectus (thirteen numbers) of *Messiah*, making no secret of his conviction that, given equal musical sensitivity, Handel's music necessarily means less to sceptics than to believers. As he put it thirty years later: 'Handel was fanatically inspired. He was a complete believing Christian. . . . Now, the sequence of texts would be really, I think, quite meaningless to one who's ignorant of Christian theology. . . . The fullest appreciation of the words and music of *Messiah* can only be realized by a true believer, by one who really knows what is being talked about.'

The *Messiah* mornings at Central Hall were precursors of a more swarming one at the Albert Hall soon after the war. There he conducted another *Messiah* abridgement for an audience of children. Before picking up his baton he asked how many had not heard a

* The ratio of complete symphonic performances to 'selective' ones and a general survey of his Mayer programmes at the Central Hall will be found in the Appendices.

note of the music. Four or five thousand put their hands up. Sargent mentioned this some days later at a B.B.C. Brains Trust session. He added: 'They adored every minute of it. They showed that by their silence when listening and their applause afterwards and by their letters. It isn't true young people can't take the best things first time. They usually do.'

To which Cyril Joad: 'When children like, or appear to like, the kind of things Sargent thinks they *ought* to like because they're good, they're doing what children so often do, saying things that will please their elders.'

Sargent: 'Not true, not true!'

Joad's judgments were not to be taken lightly. Not all of them amounted to much. But millions hung upon his every word. From the relative obscurity of a women's college where he taught philosophy and psychology, Joad's ready omniscience on the B.B.C.'s Brains Trust lifted him for a few years during and after the war to the rank of Britain's loved and leading oracle. When he gave public lectures mounted police had to clear a way for him through ecstatic crowds. Affectionate theme of music-hall jokes, popular songs and one of the Food Ministry's wartime recipes ('Joad in the hole'), he was popularly reputed to know something about everything under the sun and beyond it. Over the air Joad and Sargent were amiably at loggerheads for years. Some account of their dissensions will be found in a later chapter, 'The Brains Trust'.

CHAPTER FIFTEEN

COURTAULD-SARGENT

PEOPLE SAID at the time and have been saying ever since that Mrs. Courtauld was the 'making' of Sargent. There is something in this. Although she died little more than two years after they were first in the public eye together, it is equally true, however, to say that Sargent was the 'making' of Mrs. Courtauld. But for his high-strung energy and talent, it is unlikely that her name would be niched as it is in the country's musical history.

Elizabeth Theresa Frances Courtauld was the wife of Samuel Courtauld, the rayon millionaire; brisk and grey-haired, given to lawn tennis, trout fishing and camping holidays as far afield as the Rocky Mountains. She had a knack of organizing people, benevolently bossing them and getting things done. During the First World War she turned her Essex home into a military hospital and worked as a nurse in one of its wards. For a while she was on the transport strength of the War Office, driving generals about in her own motor-car. The war over, her mind turned, as did that of her husband, to aesthetic causes. While Samuel Courtauld was buying Manets, Renoirs, Cézannes and Van Goghs for his immediate pleasure and that of friends, though ultimately for the nation's, 'Lil' Courtauld busied herself for six bountiful years with grand opera and symphony concerts. Without making any public song about it, she went first to the rescue of an institution which, between the wars, was for ever on the point of giving up the ghost and pulling itself down, namely, the Royal Opera House, Covent Garden. Calling herself the London Opera Syndicate, she spent nearly £50,000 of Courtauld money on three international seasons (1925–

1927) which are remembered among other things for Bruno Walter's *Der Rosenkavalier*, *Ring*, *Fidelio*, *Figaro* and *Don Giovanni*, for the glory of certain German voices (this was the heyday of Lotte Lehmann, Elizabeth Schumann, Frida Leider, Lauritz Melchior, Friedrich Schorr) and, not least, for Mrs. Courtauld's tireless ubiquity. Credited by her extremer admirers with being Covent Garden's ruler as well as good fairy, she scouted for singers, personally engaged several who took her fancy, picked or endorsed the operas they sang in and determined many other things, down to the aim and tone of publicity hand-outs. While the Italian side of her seasons was well cared for, her predilection seems to have been for German artists. Her critics made much of this.

Shortly before the end of the 1927 season, the Courtaulds let it be known that they had had enough. Why was not divulged. The Courtauld syndicate moved out. Another syndicate backed by another rich person moved in. If Mrs. Courtauld had suffered any disillusionment on the score of opera, her zeal for music in general remained untouched. She looked around for new burdens and out-lets. 'What other musical cause can I help or start?' she asked. The answer was supplied by her friend Artur Schnabel. One day he arrived hotfoot at the Courtaulds' town house in Portman-square full of a musical adventure which had befallen him in Berlin. For the first time in his career he had played all thirty-two Beethoven sonatas at a series of seven concerts. The remarkable thing was not the marathon itself but those who attended it, most of them manual workers and their families, people who, unable to afford concert tickets in the ordinary way, paid token prices for them under the block-booking arrangements of the thriving Volksbühne organiza-tion. The Volksbühne's purpose was to further proletarian culture in the great German cities.

'Why not,' suggested Schnabel, 'start something of the same kind here?'

Mrs. Courtauld kindled at once. For months she talked the idea over with her husband, the Mayers and other friends. Sargent was brought in as consultant at an early stage. She decided to act. Again Samuel Courtauld brought out his cheque book. Comforted by what the Courtauld archives describe as 'a small endowment fund', she

booked the Queen's Hall for six dates between October 1929 and
April 1930, hiring the London Symphony Orchestra to play at all
of them, with the proviso (startling in a town where the rule was a
single rehearsal 'on the morning') that each concert should have
three rehearsals at least. Financially this was a good thing for the
L.S.O. Of the L.S.O. directors she demanded in return that they
should drop the notorious 'deputy' system. Under this system, more
properly described as licensed lunacy, a regular player, having
attended rehearsals and earned fees accordingly, could, if some
more advantageous offer turned up in the meantime, absent himself
on the night, his place being taken by some colleague, usually of
inferior capacity, who not only came in raw to the conductor's
specific requirements but, when there was new music in the programme, precariously sightread his way through it. In her talks with
the L.S.O. Mrs. Courtauld made it clear that the 1929–30 season
would only be a start. She undertook to subsidize at least two seasons
more. Taking into account other regular bookings on which they
could depend, the L.S.O. thus seemed assured of mild prosperity
for three years, a matter of high moment at a time when adversity
was creeping up on symphony orchestras from below. Apart from
the general 'depression' and consequent box office blight, the coming
of the 'talkies' had dispersed sixty cinema orchestras in Greater
London alone, where hundreds of musicians were on the dole.
Throughout the country 10,000 were estimated to be out of work
or not earning enough to pay their rent.

What of the prospective audiences?

In the space of a few years the dissemination of classical music
over the air and on the 'new' gramophone records had enormously
sharpened the demand for 'live' performances among a whole
population of modestly-off people who, if they wanted to hear
Beecham conduct Mozart or Rachmaninov play in one of his piano
concertos, had to queue early and long at the gallery entrance for
relatively meagre allotments of two-and-fourpenny, three-and-six-
penny or five-and-ninepenny seats. Mrs. Courtauld resolved that
this new and expanding public should have a better deal.
These were her prices for a series of six concerts in the Queen's
Hall:

1s 6d (i.e.	9s for all six) for seats usually sold at									2s 4d
2s 6d (,,	15s ,,	,,	,,	,,	,,	,,		,, ,,		3s 0d
3s 6d (,,	21s ,,	,,	,,	,,	,,	,,		,, ,,		5s 9d
5s 0d (,,	30s ,,	,,	,,	,,	,,	,,		,, ,,		8s 6d
7s 6d (,,	45s ,,	,,	,,	,,	,,	,,		,, ,,		10s 6d
10s 0d (,,	60s ,,	,,	,,	,,	,,	,,		,, ,,		13s 6d

Sets of tickets at these prices were obtainable through membership of musical societies, welfare groups and cultural clubs connected with banks, stores, assurance offices, civil service departments and the like. Mrs. Courtauld and her friends wrote down as many sizeable and suitable employing organizations as they could think of on the spur of the moment. Working without professional publicity from a room in Portman-square, she and her secretary looked up addresses in the telephone book and sent out a circular inviting spokesmen of selected organizations to a meeting a few days later. Of those invited fifteen turned up. They brought with them a dozen other interested parties. Between them these thirty or so delegates represented a music-hungry mass of teachers, shop assistants, bank-tellers, civil servants, clerical workers and so forth, as well as their wives and children, for these, too, were potentially roped in by The Concert Club, as the project was first called. The meeting was held early in July (1929). With the opening concert less than four months away, little time was left to work up the block bookings on which the system would depend. Mrs. Courtauld defined her scheme in a pointed phrase or two. 'There must,' she said mildly, 'be many people with musical tastes similar to mine. I don't want a concert all to myself. If there are people who want to hear what I want to hear, that is, the best and *only* the best, we can all enjoy ourselves, and the artists will not be paralysed by the stupidity of a "fashionable" audience.' Before the meeting she had expected to sell perhaps 500 serial tickets. The actual take-up that night was 900. This meant not only that 900 serial tickets were sold but also that The Concert Club had 900 founder-members—a promising foundation. By the eve of the opening concert, the membership stood at 1,700. The list had to be closed for the season. Would-be members were turned away by the hundred. Taking into account sections of the stalls and the grand circle which were reserved for the general public—and promptly taken up—the Queen's Hall was booked solid for the first night and for every succeeding Courtauld night (131 in all) until the series ended in 1940. Mrs. Courtauld had tapped a mass appetite for good music whose extent she had hardly surmised. There was only one way of coping with it. Henceforward each set of six concerts (sometimes increased to nine a season) would be given in duplicate (one year they were triplicated), the same artists performing the same programme on successive nights so that all who wanted seats should be satisfied.

*

For some pages Sargent has been waiting in the wings so that the reader might form some idea of the kind of audience in store for him. It was a younger audience than typical of the Queen's Hall, unpretentious socially but musically fervent and increasingly shrewd. School teachers were preponderant, accounting for nearly half the membership from the start. Adaptable to 'musical democracy' no less than to musical committees made up of duchesses, Sargent's alert charm and technical gifts made him an obvious choice for the new rostrum. Mrs. Courtauld had first seen him in action with one of the student orchestras at the Royal College of Music and had looked in also at some of his public concerts, including Mayer mornings.

As to what followed there is an account by the late Cicely Stanhope in the Courtauld archives. Miss Stanhope was secretary of the concerts from beginning to end and had much to do with their organization in a wider sense. Out of sheer devotion and to save the cost of a press agent, she took on most of the publicity work herself. It was she who wrote the press hand-outs and saw to their placing. She attended to advertisements also, deciding on lay-out and revising proofs. During the preliminary months, according to Miss Stanhope, Mrs. Courtauld discussed with her various conductors. At first Adrian Boult was favoured. 'But,' continues the account, 'she decided to pick someone who would do "exactly" what she wanted and what she told him to do, so she chose the comparatively unknown young Malcolm Sargent. This choice gave him a unique opportunity denied to other young conductors.' The programmes for the first three seasons (1929–31) were, adds Miss Stanhope, chosen by Mrs. Courtauld, often with advice from Schnabel and Bruno Walter, another frequent visitor to Portman-square. After Mrs. Courtauld's death, which happened on Christmas Day 1931, Samuel Courtauld took charge. Henceforth, says Miss Stanhope, programme timing was a matter of constant argument between him and Sargent, Courtauld's view being that no concert should run for more than two hours, namely, ninety minutes for the music and thirty minutes for applause and interval. The series continued for eleven seasons and cost Courtauld £15,867 altogether, equivalent to £120 per concert. Throughout that time, continues the account, it was Miss Stanhope's job to find out from a firm of concert agents what artists were available and if any new works were likely to be finished in time for performance. 'Then there was one meeting with Sargent for which I had to have ready all the details about possible artists, fees and suggested programmes. At this meeting the programmes were decided for the season. Sometimes Mr. Courtauld told me to engage some special artist. He ruled that Malcolm Sargent should never conduct more than three or four times a season.' All this suggests that Sargent's authority as musical director was strictly limited.

At this stage the title was still The Concert Club. 'Mrs. Courtauld,' commented Miss Stanhope, 'intensely disliked personal publicity and was over sensitive about it for fear it be thought her musical ideals weren't serious and that she was only splashing money about.' Robert Mayer pointed out to her that the title she had chosen was vulnerable as well as colourless. He had changed the title of his own organization to The Robert Mayer Orchestral Concerts for Children on being reminded that there was nothing to prevent the original style (Orchestral Concerts for Children) from being appropriated when the time was ripe by some commercial promoter. She saw the point. The Concert Club became the Courtauld–Sargent Concert Club, a form shortened on hundreds of hoardings and in thousands of mouths and minds to the Courtauld–Sargent Concerts. Henceforth Sargent's name was to be almost as widely canvassed as that of Beecham himself.

The first newspaper handouts announced that out of the first six concerts he would conduct the inaugural one and three others. The remaining two concerts were to be taken by Otto Klemperer, who would be making his London début with the first performance in this country of Bruckner's Symphony No. 8, and Bruno Walter, who was down for the second English performance of another German classic which did not fully come into its own with English concertgoers for another generation or more, Mahler's *Das Lied von der Erde*.

At two of his concerts Sargent was to accompany Schnabel in a total of four piano concertos. Already Schnabel was a power and a legend in the land. Some may have thought that, with two pairs of concertos and such a counter-personality on his hands, Sargent was in danger of being overshadowed. Others took the line that he was an excessively lucky young man and that, if anything, he had been awarded a premature apotheosis. Chief among the disparagers was a close and lasting friend of Schnabel's, Walter James Turner, poet, playwright and critic, son of a pro-cathedral organist. Unhampered by any excess of technical knowledge, Turner wrote about music with racy dogmatism week by week in *The New Statesman*. No sooner had Mrs. Courtauld's first circular reached the newspapers and fourteen weeks before Sargent lifted his baton on her rostrum, he came out with an article so withering that it may have rebounded in the young man's favour. Bruno Walter, wrote Turner, was down for one concert, Otto Klemperer for another.

But what [he went on] is to happen at the remaining four concerts? Nothing but tragedy!—the tragedy of lost opportunities, of wasted money—the tragedy, indeed, which almost inevitably results when a well-meaning, public-spirited amateur tries to help the cause of art. In short, Dr. Malcolm Sargent is to conduct the remaining four concerts. The fact that this bitter pill is sweetened by the engagement of Artur Schnabel to play two pianoforte concertos at two of these concerts does not make matters better. Why should Mr. Schnabel have to carry the weight of two orchestral concerts on his shoulders?

I have nothing against Dr. Sargent; he deserves his chance among other young English musicians, but these concerts, I take it, are planned with the idea of giving, for once, the very best that can be got, not with the idea of giving young English musicians the opportunity to show their deficiencies and get experience. There are plenty of other concerts throughout the country where our young conductors can exercise themselves. . . . A series of concerts backed by Mrs. Courtauld is quite sufficient to give Dr. Malcolm Sargent a wholly fictitious reputation which will be an obstacle to his own progress and to the progress of music in general. Dr. Sargent is young, and what Dr. Sargent and all our other young musicians and amateurs of music need is to learn of the heights in front of them instead of being assisted to crow more loudly on their miniature dunghills. . . .*

Turner ended with a bland 'practical suggestion'. If Mrs. Courtauld and Sargent were really sincere and disinterested in their love of music, they would take two concerts away from Sargent and give them to Felix Weingartner, 'unquestionably the greatest living conductor of Beethoven' who, now nearing seventy, would not in the course of nature have many more years in which to show London what Beethoven's music was *really like* when played in the finest classical tradition.

A riposte over Robert Mayer's signature appeared in the *New Statesman* a fortnight later. Weingartner, he pointed out, became Kapellmeister at Mannheim at 29, having been invited to an equivalent post in Berlin when 28. Furtwängler had been appointed to the Gewandhaus Orchestra of Leipzig at 33. 'What,' he asked, 'would have become of them and other great German conductors who have helped to bring music in Germany to its present pre-eminence if they had been denied a chance owing to their youth? Mr. Turner says that our conductors have many opportunities to exercise themselves throughout the country. The few permanent orchestras outside London have permanent conductors already. Therefore, where are those opportunities? . . . The fact that one conductor will rehearse all these concerts and conduct four of them should make for a fine ensemble and bring them nearer to the level attained by the great Continental orchestras.'

* *New Statesman*, 13th July, 1929.

Turner continued the battle in a footnote. To be sure, Sargent was neither too young nor inexperienced. But at present he was nothing more than 'an average Kapellmeister'. (For Turner, as for many English writers of the day, 'Kapellmeister' was a wholly stigmatic term.) He would benefit far more by acting at least four times out of six as assistant to Weingartner than by conducting so frequently himself at these concerts.

By the end of the first season Turner had changed his tune a little. Sargent, he wrote, had given 'a magnificent example to young English musicians. Himself a musician of experience, he nevertheless accepts as colleagues other conductors and works as hard for their success as his own. . . . A musician who shows this spirit also shows that he is a man of real ability, above pettifogging jealousy.' On issues of greater moment, however, Turner's scepticism remained. After crying up the Berlin Philharmonic Orchestra and crying down London's three principal ones—the London Symphony, the B.B.C. Symphony and the Royal Philharmonic Society's —he expressed grave doubt as to whether a first-rate orchestra could ever be set up in this country if its training were left entirely to any living English conductor.

'If we are to have a first-rate orchestra in London,' he shrilled, 'then let the B.B.C. engage Mr. Klemperer . . . for three years.'

This was written in the autumn of 1929. Turner could not have been expected to foresee how sweepingly he was to be confuted three years later by Beecham's founding, with Sargent's aid, of the superb London Philharmonic Orchestra. It was certainly true that the Courtauld–Sargent concerts, while crowning a young British conductor and conferring something like security upon a British orchestra, gave much time to foreign scores nobody had heard before and put a good deal of work and extra kudos in the way of performers from abroad whose names were to resound, or already did so, throughout the world. The concertgoing public on the whole were delighted. Not so the English musical establishment or an important wing of it. The president, past-president and president-elect of the Incorporated Society of Musicians put out a statement (*Musical Times*, 1st December, 1931) lamenting the idea (widely held in this country, they alleged) 'that only a foreigner can possess the true

7*

qualities of a musician; that a foreign composer must of necessity be superior to our own musicians. . . . It is in no way reasonable that foreign artists of no repute and of mediocre attainments should be employed in this country when there are so many of our own musicians who lack employment.' The signatories added a startling recommendation. Foreign performers visiting these shores must be made to declare their earnings *here* and not be allowed to leave 'until the appropriate Income Tax has been paid'. Arnold Bax, a future Master of the King's Musick, whose Symphony No. 4 was to have its first performance under Sargent at a Courtauld–Sargent night in 1933, weighed in with a brusque commination. 'Foreign artists?' he inquired. 'Why, I would keep the whole lot out for ten years. The only result of our generosity is to make some of the foreigners who come here insufferably arrogant. The pianists criticize our orchestras in a way they wouldn't dare to do in their own country.'

These and like strictures applied, in so far as they were valid, as much to other promoters—the Royal Philharmonic Society, for instance—as to Mrs. Courtauld and her advisers. For want of any corporate defence Mrs. Courtauld spoke up in her own behalf. From what turned out to be her deathbed, she wrote (*Daily Telegraph*, 11th November, 1931) that the first two seasons of Courtauld–Sargent concerts had cost £12,307. Of this 19 per cent went to foreign musicians (reduced to 14½ per cent when taxes, rail fares and hotel bills were deducted) and 51 per cent to British musicians. The remaining 30 per cent was accounted for by hall-hire, advertising, administration, etc. She named only one foreign artist. Artur Schnabel got £200, she disclosed, for playing twice over (12th and 13th January, 1931) in three piano concertos: Schumann's, Mozart's (K. 467) and Beethoven's *Emperor*. On this she made no comment. That an artist of Schnabel's eminence should play at the rate of about thirty-three pounds a concerto obviously spoke for itself.

Even so, some who could not be reproached with xenophobia felt that he and the Courtauld–Sargent management were perhaps over-reaching themselves. At six concerts, most of them during the early seasons, Schnabel appeared in fourteen concertos. Ten of these, between October 1929 and December 1931, were with Sargent. At the opening concert he did Beethoven's No. 4 and Brahms's No. 1, with Mozart's G minor Symphony intervening. His second and third concerts consisted of concertos and nothing else. At each he played three. His first 'triple' comprised Beethoven's No. 3, Mozart's K. 466 and Brahms's No. 1. The programme of his second 'triple' (12th and 13th January, 1930) is detailed above. There followed another pair: Beethoven's No. 1 and Beethoven's Fantasia Op. 80 for solo piano, chorus and orchestra. What aggravated Schnabel's excess in the eyes of people who thought him guilty of it was that at least one of his 'triples' was originally announced without detail. The Courtauld–Sargent prospectus simply said: 'Three concertos for piano and orchestra: Soloist Artur Schnabel.' It was not until a much later edition came out that subscribers knew which three they were going to hear.

The composer Constant Lambert, then writing brilliantly on music for *The Nation and Athenaeum*, said on the strength of the first prospectus that the series might be fairly described as conventional Celebrity Concerts; concerts, that is to say, which pandered to the public's greater interest in musical personalities than music itself. The people who had bought tickets for the concert at which Schnabel was to play in three unspecified concertos were presumably more interested in Schnabel's personality than in what he played. In any case, added Lambert, concertos were notorious for the amount of inferior music they contained. 'The idea of three piano concertos in an evening,' he concluded, 'is boring and repellent to the sensitive musician.'

Already well on the way to acceptance as English music's appeal-court president, Ernest Newman took up Lambert's complaints and elaborated them zestfully. The public not having been told in advance which concertos it was paying to hear, the assumption was that anything Schnabel chose to offer should be regarded as good enough for it. Schnabel was a great artist 'in his own sphere'. That had to be acknowledged. Nobody had greater admiration for him than Newman. But it was time to call a halt to current deification of Mr. Schnabel—a deification that was rapidly making him supremely ridiculous. It was not for Mr. Schnabel to become the arbiter of English musical life at the urging of admirers with more zeal than discretion. We had been able to do our thinking for ourselves, he concluded, before Mr. Schnabel honoured these shores with his presence and would continue to think for ourselves when he had left them.*

After the first of the three-concerto concerts Newman complained of the 'particularly atrocious' cadenzas which Schnabel had loosed upon a defenceless audience. The time had come, he added, to launch his long-meditated appeal for a fighting fund for the S.P.C.C. —The Society for the Prevention of Cadenzas to Concertos. When some correspondent rebukingly cited the authorship of the cadenzas, he replied that, not knowing whom they were composed by, he was able to see them for just what they were, 'whereas the victims of superior knowledge fell adoringly, as, of course, they would do, as soon as they learned they are by Beethoven. Is it not about time we got rid of this cringing attitude towards the classics? . . . I must repeat that the cadenza to the Beethoven concerto was poor stuff and the cadenza to the Mozart even poorer.'†

Undeterred by Lambert, Newman and other critics who had taken a similar line, Schnabel pressed for yet another all-concerto programme in the 1933–34 season. This time he would play three by Mozart. Samuel Courtauld at first liked the idea. Then he cooled off. The Courtauld archives have a reproachful letter of 8th March, 1933, from Schnabel to 'Dear Sam' which, while admitting that three Mozart concertos on the same evening would be unusual, rails at the 'ignorant depreciation', 'cheap prejudice' and 'snobbish preconceptions' which had hindered wide acceptance of these masterpieces in the concert hall. The time had arrived to act and fight for undervalued treasures. If some critics had their way in this and like matters the musician's life would be impoverished to the level of a shabby provincial schoolmaster's.

In the end Courtauld had his way. Schnabel never again played more than two concertos, whether by Mozart or anybody else, in the same Courtauld–Sargent programme.

*

* *Sunday Times*, 23rd November, 1930.
† Ibid, 16th March, 1930.

In debates which touched him nearly as musical-director, Sargent took no public part. In private he assumed, and possibly felt, an amused tranquillity about the Turner onslaught. When meetings were held at Portman-square of club members' delegates he was always at Mrs. Courtauld's side and had the job of answering delegates' questions. Miss Stanhope allows that members enjoyed their discussions with him, 'which were often lively'. Of 132 Courtauld–Sargent concerts he conducted about half. Other conductors who came in as guests, some when he was ill in 1933–34, included (in addition to Bruno Walter and Klemperer) Beecham, Georg Szell, Erich Kleiber, Robert Heger, Carl Schuricht and Fritz Stiedry. With certain of the guests he was involved in matters of technical preparation. Sometimes, in letters to Miss Stanhope, he jibbed at their requirements. When one of them submitted an orchestral specification not only for flageolets (nobody had any of *those*!) but for two bass clarinets as well, he contended that bassoons would do just as well as the latter; also they would cost less. Another guest approved of a rehearsal schedule, then asked to have it altered so that he could be free on Sunday. This, judged Sargent, was very naughty. What was the dear man's religious persuasion that Sunday rehearsals should be so repugnant to him? No, he insisted, the schedule must stand. It involved sessions on Sunday morning and Sunday evening. No one *liked* two rehearsals on the same day, but this gentleman had put up with it hundreds of times. When a third guest raised a similar difficulty he scoffed at distinguished foreign visitors who at home conducted nine hours a day in their opera houses but were frightened at the thought of doing more than three hours over here.

So much for what went on behind the scenes. From the Queen's Hall rostrum he radiated personality even when his back was turned to the audience almost as potently as to his Promenaders at the Royal Albert Hall decades later. His repertory—samplings of which are given in Appendix Two—was in essence typical 'Sargent'. He remained conspicuously loyal to Elgar and revelled, as he was to do for the rest of his life, in William Walton and Holst. After hearing him conduct *The Planets* in March 1931, Holst wrote to his daughter: 'This week your Pa has become a Gay Young Thing. It's chiefly the

fault of Mrs. Courtauld and Malcolm Sargent, who did the complete
Planets last night, with a delightful supper at which her (and
his) stories of . . . [a celebrated composer, apparently] were as good
as her champagne. And dear Malcolm had three splendid rehearsals
during the week. He's been longing for years to do *The Planets*
complete. . . .'* The Holst suite had come at the end of a programme
which included Paul Hindemith playing solo in his Viola Concerto
No. 2. This novelty was likened by critics to a toy Tower Bridge
built from a Meccano set (Richard Capell), a flat pancake which
Toscanini himself couldn't have turned into a *soufflé* (Herbert
Hughes), and patterns cut from a busy stencilling machine (Eric
Blom). Two months later Sargent shared the platform with Igor
Stravinsky, whom he conducted two nights running in the *Capriccio*
for piano and orchestra. These were its first performances in
England. Insular taste had not yet adjusted itself to Stravinsky's
neo-classicism. That was clear from the tepid first-night applause.
'Utterly frivolous, saucy, flippant', 'Superficial music, of course'
were typical phrases read at breakfast tables next morning. The one
thing that perturbed Stravinsky was a bill he received from a
London firm of piano dealers for transporting the piano on which
he played *Capriccio* from their warehouse to the Queen's Hall and
back again. Nothing like this, he said, had ever happened to him
before. He had no intention of paying the bill and begged Mrs.
Courtauld not to be inveigled into paying it for him. At both performances he and Sargent were obviously on good terms. Their
handclasp at the end was cordial.

During the early seasons many complimentary things were
written about Sargent's skilled beat, contagious vitality and the
effect of these things on orchestras. After the opening concert of
the second series Newman wrote that under his baton the London
Symphony Orchestra 'once more showed that it is a far surer instrument than it has been in the last season or two'. Presently, however,
there was a certain clouding over. Of his *Don Quixote* (R. Strauss)
at the beginning of the 1931–32 season, Newman said it suffered
woefully by comparison with Beecham's performance of the same
score a week earlier. 'Sargent's *tempi*,' he went on, 'were not so much

* *Gustav Holst* by Imogen Holst (Oxford University Press), 1938.

fast as fussed and flurried. The work lost most of its dignity and—till we came to the finale—its pathos. To make Sancho Panza gabble at that pace is to deprive him of the stolid rustic sententiousness that is the very essence of him.' Of Sibelius's Symphony No. 4, which had preceded the Strauss, the critic of *Truth* owned that it was energetically conducted but added: 'The danger of such methods is that muscle tends to take the place of mind. Rigidity and over-emphasis and a lack of unity as between conductor and soloist [Piatigorsky had played solo 'cello in both *Don Quixote* and the Dvořák concerto] characterized the whole concert.'

Towards the end of the same season he did an *Enigma* Variations which came under the guns of Eric Blom. 'What,' asked the future editor of Grove IV, 'is happening to this conductor? The London Symphony Orchestra, which progressed so remarkably under Sir Thomas Beecham, plays with Dr. Sargent as though it fretted under the task. In the *Enigma* Variations he seemed to be hectoring and worrying the performers, with the result that this beautiful master-piece seemed crude and superficial. In the matter of *tempo* there was exaggeration of most of the composer's directions, the *presto* swings making up for what was lost on the *adagio* roundabouts, and in the matter of phrasing there was stiffness and surliness. Almost the whole work sounded as though played against the grain. Perhaps the orchestra knew as well what was wanted as the conductor appeared to do and resented not being allowed to give it.' (*Birmingham Post*, 22nd March, 1932.)

It was not the first time such points had been made against Sargent, nor was it to be the last. But on this occasion other factors than strictly musical ones were involved. *What is happening to this conductor?* Three things were happening which Blom either did not know about or didn't make full allowance for. Those things were overwork, over-tension and the onset of grave illness.

CHAPTER SIXTEEN

COLLAPSE

HE WAS working and living voraciously, 'much hated by men for his professional success, his success with women and his wonderful tailoring.' These are the words of a loyal and shrewd friend who saw much of him in Belgravia, country houses and circles that were consciously cultural. A thing ruffling to musicians of the kind who think compartmentalized careers the best was the number of conflicting compartments he could live in at the same time. A Brahms–Beethoven night at the Queen's Hall would be followed by a *Mikado* night at the Savoy, this by an afternoon of B minor Mass at the Royal Albert Hall, this again by some party in Chelsea where, having roped in old Ben Davies and Edmund Burke for name-part and Mephistopheles, he would sit at the piano and conduct a scene or two from Gounod's *Faust* for the love and fun of the thing, singing in some of the 'uncast' bits himself. Or he would dart off after lunch to some unlikelier assignment still: to the People's Palace, say, where he once took massed 'mothers' meeting' choirs through folk-songs, hymns and fragments of oratorio. Most of the singers on this occasion were grandmothers.

'I've heard better voices,' he conceded. 'But they sing with a spirit and intention which would have put some professionals to shame.'

Or perhaps to Uppingham in the depths of Rutland, for a daylong final rehearsal and performance of *Elijah* or *Messiah* with a choir of four hundred drawn from the little town itself and twenty environing villages. The Uppingham dates were a survival from his Melton years. A local enthusiast rehearsed the singers throughout the winter; but even when absent 'Malcolm' (as they still called him among themselves) was the compelling personality, the one who invisibly kept them at it. Of his Rutland Festival Choir, as they called themselves, he used to say the singers were anybody and everybody, from the ploughboy to the squire. 'Lady So-and-So and the Dowager Lady Whatshername come with their cooks and house-maids,' he vaunted. Once he used them as a stick with which to beat others. A rehearsal is remembered of Elgar's *The Music Makers* with the Leicester Philharmonic Society. The men singers fumbled one of their entries so grossly that Sargent flared into anger, an unusual thing with him. 'Not long ago,' he said, 'I was rehearsing Upping-ham Choral Society [a section of the Rutland Festival Choir] in this very passage. They are villagers, men who work on the land. They did this well. I come to Leicester where the standard is supposed to be higher. You sing it wretchedly. Stupid!'

The De Montfort Hall continued to see a lot of him. Every winter he took some or all of the Leicester Symphony Orchestra's concerts. Impulsively generous in money matters ('A lot came in and it all went out,' says one who, for a while, had knowledge of his budgets), he was reluctant to part with anything that had been his musically. Professional voracity led him, while conserving old territories, to take on more. Somebody ran into him on a northern railway platform at three in the morning, bright as a button. The night before he had done Brahms's *Requiem* in the local town hall. It had gone very well. But he had to get back to London for a rehearsal at ten with the British Women's Symphony Orchestra. 'They call themselves "the B—— Women", and they're most promising. Nowadays you get women players in the Proms orchestra and in the B.B.C. orchestra— an unheard of, splendid thing!' To the Bradford Festival Choral Society, whose concerts and rehearsals had, since the mid-1920s, entailed a hundred or two rail journeys, half of them night ones, from London and back, he now (1932) added another relished bur-den of the same kind, the Huddersfield Choral Society, all of whose concerts he undertook on the basis of at least two rehearsals per concert.

Bradford, his first big choral appointment in the provinces, merits a further note as showing his easy adaptability in money matters. The original arrangement was that he should conduct the

Society's three concerts a season plus three rehearsals per concert, an annual total of twelve dates. His fee was to be 150 guineas a season, or little less than thirteen pounds a date. He made his first bow with the Society in November 1925 with the B minor Mass. He had not been with the Society long before hard times involved them in reduced public support and money difficulties. Towards meeting these the singers agreed to increase their annual subscription from five shillings to seven and six. On hearing of this Sargent said: 'That's very generous of the singers. I must do something to help. I will reduce my fee from one hundred and fifty guineas to a hundred guineas a season. All I ask in return is that my rehearsals be cut to one per concert—the final rehearsal, that is.' His offer was thankfully accepted. Preliminary rehearsals were attended to by somebody on the spot, as at Uppingham. He was taking one third less money for much less work. But the story did not end there. His fee stayed at a hundred guineas a season, until, through pressure of foreign engagements and B.B.C. work, he resigned from the conductorship in 1951. By that time foreign promoters were paying him up to four times as much for a single concert.

With northern choral singers, a race not disposed to gush over 'foreigners' on sight, his touch was as certain and winning as with those of the Royal Choral Society. The women singers fluttered over what came to be known as his Raymond Massey look. ('In fact,' testifies a noted portrait-painter, 'he had a distinctly monkeyish look in the 'twenties and 'thirties. What of that? He enchanted everybody.') Women choralists and men alike were lost in admiration or the lucid professionalism that underlay his charm. That he should have been called in for the Leeds Triennial Festival, once a choral stronghold of Hugh Allen, was foreseeable. His début there in October 1931 almost outshone his Courtauld–Sargent achievements and was to have perhaps more enduring results. For the first time he came into direct, day-to-day collaboration with Sir Thomas Beecham, the Festival's conductor-in-chief, at whose word, frown and wink everybody trembled, tittered or rejoiced.

The young William Walton had recently completed *Belshazzar's Feast*, a piece found daring not so much because of its purely musical facture as because its text was from the Bible, whence it followed that the whole work fell into a category, that of oratorio, which conventional progressives had scoffingly discarded decades earlier. It was Beecham who decided to put *Belshazzar* into the festival programme. Not that he had any intention of conducting it himself. Untried and unproved scores on such a scale were not to his personal taste on occasions of pomp. The 1931 'Triennial' was one of his Delius obeisances. He treated himself to *The Mass of Life* and gave *Belshazzar*, as well as the B minor Mass, to Sargent as his appointed second in command.

The preparation of the first *Belshazzar* performance was the subject for over thirty years of one of the oddest canards in English choral history. It was said that after an abortive run through of their parts the festival chorus pronounced them impossible to sing and told Beecham they had no intention of going on with the work; that in face of this revolt or strike Beecham sent Sargent north post-haste to bewitch the rebels and knock sense into them; and that Sargent made them see the point and fall in love with the work almost before getting off the train. This story circulated in London so persistently and with such seeming authority that Walton himself accepted it for decades. A number of 'Triennial' veterans who took part in the first *Belshazzar* were consulted recently. All had highly articulate memories of the performance and its preparation; and all dismissed the revolt story as fiction. It is likely that some of the older singers muttered resentfully about the score's irregular metres and other hazards. A Leeds newspaper reported, indeed, that the whole choir had been in a state of 'anguish'. To this suggestion the veterans reply as with one voice: 'Rubbish! We all enjoyed learning the *Belshazzar* music.' The possibility is that the fiction may have been put about by Beecham himself either as a joke or as 'cover' for saddling Sargent with *Belshazzar* in the first place.

On the composer's calculation the first performance lasted ten minutes longer than it should have done. He was jubilant, nevertheless, and with reason. Amid happy dins at the end he was gestured up on to the platform by Sargent for handshakes, beaming and back-slapping. No other baton in the land could have welded Walton's choral and orchestral forces or wielded them with such adroitness or with greater faith in what the music was about.

Henceforth *Belshazzar* was distinctively a 'Sargent score'. For him it was proof that the age of epic art was not ended.

Two nights later the festival ended. More happy dins. This time they were presided over by Beecham. He gestured Sargent up from the stalls, just as Sargent had gestured up Walton. Together they shared the cordiality, pandemonium and glory. What else did they share? What else had they in common? Extremely little. This may be said of any pair of contemporaneous conductors since conducting first found acceptance as one of the executive arts. Beecham's characteristic statements on Sargent tended on the whole to ironical understatement. 'Pretty good. Can show these imported medio-crities, these damned foreign batons, a thing or two.' This of Sargent the all-rounder. On Sargent as a handler of choruses his accolade was absolute: 'He is the greatest choirmaster we have ever produced. Choir conducting is one of the most difficult arts. Myself I can only bring it off occasionally—sometimes in the last Act of *Die Meistersinger*, for example. But Malcolm always does it. He makes the b——s sing like blazes!'* Of Beecham Sargent said at one of our early meetings (spring 1951): 'You ask me how Beecham gets what he wants from an orchestra. A man like Beecham—if there ever has been another man like him, which I doubt—gets what he wants by devilish brilliance. Beecham is not merely witty. At times he's almost cheeky. He has a tremendous assurance that might almost be mistaken for mischief.' When I showed him a transcript of what he had said he revised the last two sentences. 'No, let's say instead: "Beecham is not merely witty. He has also a Svengali-like assurance which at times borders on the mischievous."' The manners and tactics of the two at orchestra rehearsals, and up to a point, the response and feeling they got from orchestra players differed sharply, as will be evident from later chapters. In the early 1930s, however, a situation developed which brought their interests and ideals into exact focus.

*

* As reported by Lord Boothby, B.B.C. 1 Television, in birthday tribute, *Sargent at Seventy*, 22nd April, 1965, Beecham did not actually say 'beggars' but explained Boothby another word 'rather like it'.

The orchestra at the 1931 Leeds 'Triennial' had been the London Symphony, a name still much in view from Courtauld–Sargent billings. When the L.S.O., a self-governing 'co-operative' reformed itself in 1929, aiming at a permanent personnel as against the exasperating flux of the deputy system, Sargent foresaw a brighter future for London orchestral music generally but had certain reservations. Somebody asked him whether the co-operative principle on which the L.S.O. ran itself was the one best calculated to get the finest players. 'I would not say that,' he replied. 'Whatever may be true of politics, I believe that in art the best results come from dictatorship. . . . A band like the L.S.O. needs a permanent chief musical director who would not necessarily conduct all or even many of its concerts but would ensure the discipline that visiting foreign conductors cannot impose.'

By the end of the second Courtauld–Sargent season, the Courtaulds and their musical director alike were in a state of simmering disillusion. The orchestra's playing personnel had not turned out to be as stable as promised and, at best, included a residue of inferior players who of themselves were enough to preclude the sort of ensemble inculcated among London connoisseurs by such visiting orchestras as the Berlin Philharmonic and the Philadelphia. As has been told in detail elsewhere* Mr. and Mrs. Courtauld asked Sargent to form a new and truly permanent orchestra of picked players. They undertook to spend £30,000 on the project to start with. Seasonal deficits would be met as required. Feeling the need for maturer counsels, Sargent broached the proposal to Beecham. Between them, in the late summer of 1932, they founded the illustrious London Philharmonic Orchestra, having ditched the recalcitrant L.S.O. and won over the cream of its players: a coup of untold artistic benefit which, however, bred lingering resentment and recrimination. Called to sit at Beecham's right hand and named on L.P.O. letter headings as its auxiliary musical director, Sargent helped Beecham with auditions, the picking of players and 'bedding down' rehearsals. They planned to share schedules between them, each making his own contributions to the L.P.O.'s pool of

* *Thomas Beecham: An Independent Biography* by Charles Reid (Gollancz), 1961.

engagements. The first schedule of a hundred or so concerts was commented on by Sargent with jubilation. Under Sir Thomas the L.P.O. would play for the Royal Philharmonic Society, in the Royal Opera pit during the international summer seasons, at a main series in the Queen's Hall on Sunday afternoons, in the studios of the Gramophone Company (future E.M.I.), with whom comforting contracts were negotiated, and on tour in all the big provincial concert halls. Under Sargent they would play at three main series—the Courtauld–Sargent concerts, the Royal Choral Society concerts and the Robert Mayer concerts for children. One thing that filled him with hope, he said, was that the new orchestra included a large number of talented *young* musicians. For their auditions he and Beecham had profitably rummaged the junior end of every leading provincial orchestra and the top layers of all music colleges of note.

The L.P.O.'s explosive and brilliant inaugural under Beecham (it began with a *Carnaval Romain* Overture which had people standing—some of them on their seats—to cheer) happened on 7th October, 1932. Three days later Sargent conducted the orchestra for the first time in a Courtauld–Sargent programme that included Debussy's *La Mer* and Strauss's *Till Eulenspiegel*. A fortnight afterwards he introduced the L.P.O. to the Royal Albert Hall and the Royal Choral Society; there they made their début in *Elijah*. Aided, though not determined, by radio and recording engineers, English orchestral music had entered upon a phase of energy and musical refinement which, in thirty or forty tradition-forming years, helped to raise London's status from third rate to that of 'Europe's musical capital' in the judgment of some foreign observers.

It might have been supposed that in the autumn of 1932 Sargent had enough on his hands. It is in the nature of much to want more, however. Around this time he was approached by the Australian Broadcasting Commission. Would he (they asked) be interested to visit Australia to set up a symphony orchestra, conduct launching concerts in Melbourne and elsewhere and act as their adviser on programme planning, choice of a permanent conductor and so on? Sargent was cockahoop. After working out a provisional timetable with the A.B.C. he went in December to the committee of the Royal Choral Society and sought three months' leave of absence. The committee agreed that he be allowed to accept the offer on the understanding that before leaving he should organize the musical side of the next *Hiawatha* production, fixed for 5th to 17th June and that he should conduct the first few performances before handing over to some deputy conductor of equal capacity to his own. This last proviso aimed high. At that stage the committee seems to have had no substitute in mind. They decided to remind the choir of the seriousness of the Society's prospects should the next *Hiawatha* prove a failure: this, apparently, by way of assuring in advance the singers' goodwill towards whoever stepped into Sargent's shoes.

Arrangements with Australia were completed early in the New Year. The plan was that he should sail to Sydney early in June, completing the journey to Melbourne by air and rail. The plan had to be discarded. He was not to make the journey until 1936, over three years later.

*

As has been said, what worried the R.C.S. committee was how the 1933 *Hiawatha* would fare. They might have done well to begin worrying earlier. The first public sign that they had a sick man on their rostrum occurred during the *Hiawatha* of 1932.

After the first act one evening Sargent made his usual spotlit exit for the interval across the arena and down the 'bull-run' farthest away. Arnold Greir, already down from the organ console, saw at a glance that he wasn't well. His face was drawn with pain. 'He didn't stagger,' says Greir. 'Sargent wouldn't have staggered even if dying.' (This was born out to the letter in the same hall thirty-five years later when, seventeen days before his death, feeble and unassisted, he made his way to the front of the platform and uttered what he must have known was to be his farewell to Promenade concerts and 'Prommers'.) In the artists' room he lay down on a sofa. He had a grey look and admitted to pain. At that time Greir was the Society's honorary secretary as well as organist. He had a decision to make. 'You can't possibly go on,' he told Sargent. 'You aren't going to do any more. You are going home to bed.' But that meant a substitute. Who was going to take over Acts II and III? Sargent made a suggestion or two. Could somebody get hold of Sir

Thomas? Or Sir Henry? Either might just possibly be in town and free. Futile telephone calls were made. In the midst of them a young man came into the room with the score of one of the *Hiawatha* acts under his arm. He was in full evening dress. Muir Matheson was then twenty-one, a conducting pupil of Sargent's and a future deputy of his on the *Hiawatha* rostrum. He often attended Sargent's *Hiawatha* nights. Because of the 'social' nature of these occasions and the parties that followed he usually wore a dinner jacket. On reaching home that evening from Elstree, one of the film studios at which in the future he was to conduct hundreds of orchestral sound tracks, he learned that his dinner jacket had been borrowed by his brother. There was nothing for it but to put on a tail coat and white tie. Already he was Sargent's *Hiawatha* understudy. During the weekend he had been studying Act III, which explained why he had the score under his arm.

'You'd better go on, Muir,' said Greir. 'In fact you'll have to go on.'

One of the vast ballet interludes that night was led by Hermione Darnborough, who danced the Spirit of Spring. A minor production detail was that on her first entry she should curtsey to Sargent, who responded with a smile and a bow. Miss Darnborough, who had heard nothing of the emergency, was astonished at the last moment to find herself curtseying to a tailcoated Matheson. He was her fiancé. This was his first *Hiawatha*. He did not know the work well. The singers and the orchestral players did, however. There were no mishaps. Meantime Greir had motored Sargent home and to bed.

From this precursory attack, whatever its clinical nature, he seemed to recover. Within days he was resiliently busy again. It was not illness but other commitments, including the setting up of the L.P.O., which kept him from the D'Oyly Carte rostrum that autumn. Even so, he felt a pang. He wrote to Rupert D'Oyly Carte saying how much he loved the Sullivan operas and working for him and suggested that when he had a free night they should go to one of the Savoy performances together as a 'treat'.

He began to be dogged by abnormal temperatures. He opened the fourth Courtauld–Sargent season with a reading of 100 degrees. This was also the night of his début, mentioned above, with the

L.P.O. A few days earlier a pathologist had taken a blood sample. The test had negative results. Two other doctors whom he consulted were as mystified as the pathologist. Apart from the high temperature he felt well. He put down the trouble, such as it was, to an insect bite.

Life as well as music continued at a sharpening tempo. On *Hiawatha* nights, in this loggia and that, he usually had a scattering of guests, socially eminent people for the most part, some of whom pursued musical culture not so much from inborn fervour as because 'dear, splendid Malcolm' had charmed them into it. Ushered and shepherded by one or other of Sargent's assistants, the guests would meet during the intervals for cocktails in a reception room alongside the Albert Hall board room. These gatherings were almost as minutely prearranged as rehearsals and rehearsal tactics; not a thing was left to chance. Most *Hiawatha* nights ended with a party at Wetherby-place, with Malcolm and Eileen as hosts. More than once Henry Sargent and Agnes Sargent came up to hear their son conduct. Afterwards they mixed with his fashionable friends. He made his mother and father known to great names with scrupulous and affectionate formality and saw to it that they were made much of.

Agnes Sargent was shy and enraptured. Henry Sargent chuckled a lot and told funny stories as of old. Most of the Courtauld–Sargent nights ended with champagne parties at Portman-square. At first Mrs. Courtauld made a point of inviting society friends as well as avowedly musical people. Among the musical guests were austere minds who feared that extraneous pressures might deflect her concerts from the original ideal. Nothing of the kind happened. It was the 'society' people who changed course. Classical music suddenly bored them. They deserted it for some newer fad. After this the Portman-square parties were smaller and better.

Whatever their size or type, parties found Sargent in his element. His talk was inexhaustibly bright and won infatuated attention. It ranged widely. He would talk drolly about riding misadventures in Richmond Park; of the hack which swung its head round to see who was on its back, then, having assessed the rider's temperament, dashed off in all directions at once. His privileged visits to the

London Zoo were another recurring theme. There was a cage where Lord Auckland had eight wolves boarded out. He was allowed inside and played with them, let them put their paws on his shoulders. He had been in a cage with tigers, too. 'If they've just had a meal and you show you aren't afraid they'll curl up and lie on their backs like kittens.' Some of his extra-musical interests may have made musical puritans bridle. In those days the Royal Albert Hall put on professional boxing among other entertainments. He was often at the ringside and boasted that he rarely missed an outstanding match if he could help it—even though he had been conducting *Gerontius* or the *Saint John Passion* music under the same roof the previous afternoon. There was no doubt as to the genuineness of these tastes. But his exulting in them was accounted for partly by his wish to free himself from the notion, then widespread, that musicians, especially choral conductors from the organ loft, were people of constricted ways and stuffy tastes. On champagne, while never abusing this or any other liquor, he was uninhibited and ceremonious. On his son's christening day he opened a bottle in the kitchen for the servants. He would gleefully tell how the charwoman, professedly a teetotaller, said, 'No, really, I never touch a drop!' took her glass with alacrity and emptied it at one draught. Joad might dismiss champagne as 'a species of sour ginger beer'. For Sargent it remained to the end of his days the queen of drinks. He spoke up for it over the air at a time (December 1941) when champagne, like other Edwardian luxuries, was beginning to be scowled upon by some thinkers as the vestige of a culpable and doomed social system.

Life was gay. Not getting to bed until three in the morning was delightful. But the high temperatures continued. He was losing weight. Sitting in his bedroom at Wetherby-place while he dressed for a concert—'We're going on to a party afterwards. Why not join us? It'll be fun!'—Herbert Howells noted his thinness. His temperature always went up to 100 degrees around half-past five. He would go on to the rostrum in this state and conduct with fierce energy. He sweated more freely than hitherto. By the end of the concert his temperature would be down. Then, in tingling form, he would change for the night's party. People marvelled at his freshness on the rehearsal rostrum at ten the next morning.

'Why go to all these parties?' asked Howells. 'Are you running after these famous people? It is they who ought to be running after you.'

Sargent laughed. 'I go to parties,' he said, 'because I like them. You think going to parties is a hard life. It isn't hard at all. You ought to come with me to a few. You'd see.'

Only one thing was to be seen that counted: the thinness. Bouncing determinedly into the New Year (1933), he coped in mid-January with another heavy Courtauld–Sargent programme, triplicating Berlioz's *Harold in Italy* (soloist Lionel Tertis), Mozart's Sinfonia Concertante (K. 364) (soloists Albert Sammons and Tertis) and *Belshazzar's Feast*. A week later he played a piano concerto, one of the Mozarts in A flat, with the L.P.O. for the first time, Sidney Beer conducting. At the end the audience went on applauding inordinately. They hoped that, disregarding the convention usually observed by concerto soloists, he would come back and play something more. He smilingly declined.

Again he was in pain, abdominal pain. And again the doctors, having taken further blood tests, did not know what to make of it. This was towards the end of February. By now he was being kept to his bed at Wetherby-place. He had visitors from morning until night. Prince George brought azaleas. On the same day his place was taken at a Robert Mayer children's concert by Adrian Boult. He had conducted his last concert of any kind for nearly two years. Early in April he was taken to a nursing home at Princes Gate, still in Royal Albert Hall 'country'. At last the diagnosticians discovered what was wrong.

On a Friday early in April he was operated on by Sir Thomas (soon afterwards Lord) Horder, in his day physician-in-ordinary or extraordinary to five English monarchs, for a tubercular abscess on a gland in the lower part of the body. The operation was a difficult and taxing one. For a few days the nursing home bulletins had a dubious ring. 'As well as can be expected' was a persisting note. He had been near to death. Musical friends when he began to receive them knew he might be saying farewell to professional music-making if not to them. To his friend from boyhood Thomas Armstrong he said: 'I don't know whether I'm going to conduct any more, but I have no complaints. It has been a wonderful life.' He read a good deal in the Bible and discussed favourite texts with likely and unlikely listeners. An old aunt who had not been noted for special kindness wrote him a letter of surprising comfort. He replied cheerfully and stoically. Things hadn't really been too bad, he said. 'My dear Malcolm,' she returned, 'I'm delighted to find that you've discovered, as we all do in time, that life is not a joy ride—it's a try-out. As long as you look on this world as a place you are sent to as a sort of school then, in one way, the worse it is, perhaps, the more worth while it is.' As he grew stronger alarmed emissaries came in from musical societies near and far. What was to happen to the concerts he was down to conduct next winter? The Royal Choral Society, shrugging stoically, deleted him from their *Hiawatha* publicity drafts little more than a month before the annual run was due to start and brought in Geoffrey Toye, the former D'Oyly Carte baton. His absence from the Royal Choral Society's regular concerts and from the Courtauld–Sargent promotions among others meant a spread out of work among Beecham, Boult, Harty, Albert Coates, Hugh Allen, Leslie Heward, Landon Ronald, Julius Harrison. . . . It is doubtful whether one musician's sickness had ever caused quite as much commotion and reshuffling before.

His Leicester friends were especially glum. One of them came up with news that Karl Russell, feeling that his music shop was not getting enough glory from the Leicester Symphony Orchestra, had decided to withdraw his patronage. There was no one now to pay or guarantee the orchestra's bills. Sargent fixed a bedside meeting between the Leicester emissary and the concert agent, Harold Holt. He waved them hospitably to a cabinet loaded with gin and whisky, drinks which he rarely touched even when well, and said to the man from Leicester: 'You see how I am. I shan't be able to conduct you next winter and I don't know when I shall be with you again. But I'm sure Mr. Holt will work something out.' What Holt did was to take over the orchestra temporarily and merge its concerts with his former 'celebrity' series. The first concert under the merger was conducted by Albert Coates to many empty seats; the body of the De Montfort Hall was not more than a third full. After the con-

cert Holt joined with Coates in a telegram to Sargent telling him
what a good orchestra he had built up—and again muttered asides
about 'lousy Leicester'.

Australia was not as easy to relinquish. He had a passage booked
in S.S. *Mooltan* and meant to sail on 4th June. He expatiated eagerly
on the restorative effects of a long sea journey. With Lord Horder
at the decisive consultation was Sargent's doctor friend Harold
Furness ('Grumps') from Melton who, since their early meetings,
had graduated as an amateur conductor from Gilbert and Sullivan
to oratorio and was now in charge of Malcolm's old choir, the Melton
Choral Society. It seems that Horder considered Sargent fit for the
voyage and tour.

'But would you countenance it,' put in Furness 'if Malcolm were
to tour Australia as a member of a Rugby football team?'

Horder: 'Why, no. But surely there's no comparison.'

Furness: 'Have you ever seen a conductor at work?'

Horder: 'I've been to concerts, of course.'

Furness: 'No, what I mean is *really* at work—rehearsals morning
and afternoon and performance at night?'

Horder: 'Can't say I really have.'

Furness: 'Well, that routine's just as demanding, it takes just as
much out of a man, as if he were touring as scrum half.'

Rather more than a fortnight after the operation, Melbourne
learned that Sargent had cancelled the visit to enable him to make a
complete recovery. The Broadcasting Commission announced they
were not entering into negotiations with any conductor for six
months. (Oddly enough *The Times* did not report the cancellation
for another ten days, when it appeared under a Melbourne dateline.
It almost seemed as if there had been reluctance to release the news
at home.) Sargent was distressed at having to call the project off and
seems at first to have thrown a minor tantrum. According to a contrite letter to Dr. Furness dictated from bed it had never entered his
head that the Australian journey would have to be put off. This had
come to him as a shock. Having always felt well, he had assumed
there could be nothing wrong with his health. Horder had explained
to him, however, that, in work and play alike, he had been living on
excitement; that he had never given himself the chance of seeing

how he could get on without excitement—any more than a man who
always drinks whisky tries to find out whether he can do without
that. But, concluded the letter, he had learned his lesson. Henceforth his attitude and behaviour towards life would totally change.
If he failed in this he would be unworthy of anybody's friendship
and affection.

For all the pace at which he had been living and his attention to
the social flourishes, or perhaps because of these things, Sargent was
a relatively poor man. He earned a good deal, though never hugely,
and what he earned he spent promptly. 'I've never had a head for
business,' he once told me. 'I've always been extravagent. Always
gave money away, threw it away.' The children were the first
problem. Peter, seven years old, was sent to a preparatory school in
Hertfordshire run by a friend of the family on a 'pay when you can
—don't bother now' basis. Eileen busied herself with a girls' school
at Bexhill where she hoped to get Pamela, now nine, admitted on
similar terms. Friends rallied. Hugh Allen put his shoulder to the
wheel and, when necessary, to doors. On his motion the Royal
Choral Society made a grant of £200. The Schnabels, who had been
looking for temporary living quarters in London, took the Wetherby-
place house for a year, servants, piano, library and all. This was a
help. Although he conducted no Courtauld–Sargent concerts at all
during the 1933–34 season and only two the following winter, that
of his first Australian visit, Samuel Courtauld went on paying his
seasonal fees as usual. There were whip-rounds among choral
singers and orchestral players in sooty northern concert halls,
London rehearsal rooms, and mellow assembly halls where *Messiah*
alternated with *The Gondoliers* and hunt balls. On the one hand there
were florins and half-crowns. On the other hand there were substantial cheques. Robert Mayer, Samuel Courtauld and a third party in
the City put down five hundred pounds each. The money that came
in proved almost startlingly the affection, for it was nothing less,
which Sargent had won among people of extremely diverse types
and fortune. Every penny of it was needed. The surgical operation
and eighteen months in English and Swiss nursing homes, clinics
and sanatoria were made possible, as he acknowledged later over
the air, by the charity of friends. It is unlikely that without their

provision he could have been restored to a full working life.
Nor were the attentions he received limited to monetary help. He
spent most of the summer which preceded his leaving for Switzer-
land in a fashionable sanatorium in Hertfordshire. It was put to him
that, having been cut off from it for so long, he might care for an
afternoon of 'live' music. The idea enchanted him. Samuel Kutcher,
who had led for him devotedly at the Mayer concerts, at the Three
Valleys Festival in South Wales, and at a number of *Hiawathas*, had
founded a string quartet which won high prestige. One hot day he
motored down to the sanatorium with his three co-artists—Frederick
Grinke (second violin), Raymond Jeremy (viola) and Douglas
Cameron ('cello). They found Sargent lying on his back in the
garden, stripped for the sun. He was carried indoors. They set up
music-stands in his room and played a movement of a Borodin
quartet, the whole of Ravel's and the slow movement of Haydn's
Emperor, the one which treats the main theme of the Austrian
national anthem in variation form. He had been consulted on this
programme beforehand. It made his eyes shine with tears.

Generous by temper, he properly prized generosity in others. It
was his delight later on, become relatively rich, to do deeds of
private charity—not only because charity is good in itself but also
as a memorial to the succour he had himself experienced. In a sense
his generosity was gratitude. And this is a suitable point to mention
examples of it.

Several cases are known of his helping young couples, one or the
other of whom showed musical promise, to marry and start a career,
something which, for want of money, they had little chance of doing
unaided. He would say to them: 'Don't set up house on the "Never".
You'd find it a millstone round your neck. I will lend you whatever
you need and you can pay it back to me by an agreed date in instalments without interest.'

Some of his gifts were delightfully imagined. A penniless boy
student who occasionally acted as his amanuensis married a penniless girl student who eked out by selling programmes and ushering
at the Royal Opera House. One Christmas when out of the country
Sargent telegraphed the young husband saying that a table had been
booked at the Savoy for himself, his wife and a third party (also a

student). The husband was to act as host. It had been arranged that he should sign the bill in Sargent's name.

A musical administrator died of cancer. Sargent paid for the daughter's education. Another old musical friend lay on what was clearly to be his deathbed. He paid a trained nurse to live in, ensuring the old man something near comfort during his last days. A leading contralto of former times in one of his amateur Gilbert and Sullivan companies lost her husband suddenly. The news reached him in London. His was the first telegram of condolence to reach her. Afterwards Mrs. ———— learned that on the same day he had sounded an intimate friend. 'How is she going to be placed for money?' he had confidentially asked. 'Please find out if I can help.' As it happened, help was not needed. But the prompt and tactful offer of it was acknowledged to be 'Malcolm all over'.

To solace another lingering and mortal illness, that of a friend who had done him a great service decades earlier, he put himself and his secretaries to endless trouble with piano agents, second-hand shops and auctioneers. The sick man had a loved piano. Unable to play it any longer, he remembered the automatic player attachments of his youth. Would it be possible to get hold of one? Egged on by Sargent six dealers of one sort or another joined in the hunt, all to no purpose. Such attachments, they reported in the end, were obsolete and in any case did piano actions no good. Why not, it occurred to him, send gramophone records instead? It would be an easy matter for him as well as a great joy, he wrote to his friend's wife, to send as many records as her husband fancied. One recording he sent was his own of Benjamin Britten's *Young Person's Guide to the Orchestra*—modern music, he admitted, but fascinating; a 'hit' wherever he had conducted it; and a striking example of modern scoring. Not long after this he learned that his sick friend, whose home was in a small Midlands town, had no automatic long-play equipment. Writing to the nearest big gramophone shop, he bade the manager bring his friend's wife in by taxi, a double journey of thirty miles, so that she could pick the latest in radiograms and take it home with her. He had thought, he said, to give her peace in forty-minute stretches—and there she was changing records still! As far as he could make them so, these were works of stealth. When

(a) Christening party for Alastair Hamilton, May 1941. *Left to right*: Sir Arthur Bryant, Dr Malcolm Sargent, Miss Vivien Leigh, Lt. (now Sir) Laurence Olivier, R.N.V.R. and Hamish Hamilton

(b) With Sir Laurence Olivier after their investiture as Knights Bachelor, Buckingham Palace, 1947

With the King of Denmark at a reception of the Anglo-Danish Society,
London, September 1955

somebody went round during a rehearsal interval on 'pay packet' day, collecting for some player or ex-player who was ailing and in need, he had a genuinely furtive way of taking a five-pound note from his wallet. Always he would enjoin the collector to come to him again the following week and for as long as the problem lasted.

During that first long illness he received, as he was later to give, with grace and was resolutely gay. Propped against pillows or up and about in a dressing-gown, he dominated sick-room parties with a return of the old virtuosity and saw much the same people as on *Hiawatha* nights. Someone met Hugh Allen coming away grumpily from his convalescent quarters.

'I've been to see The Boy,' he said, 'but the room was full of duchesses. I couldn't stand it and came away.'

It was decreed that he should complete his cure at Montana (Valais), on a sunny, dry ledge six or seven thousand feet up, over-looking the Rhône Valley. While Sir Thomas Beecham and the Royal Choral Society were preparing a *Messiah* for his benefit at the Royal Albert Hall under Hugh Allen's brusque impulsion, he left for Montana on a November afternoon. He had caused the press photographers to be warned in advance ('the sort of thing one doesn't do,' commented a fellow conductor whose code on personal publicity was to avoid it whenever possible); the smile he gave them from his wheel-chair was that of a mischievous small boy on his way to a treat. One of his rich friends had personally reconnoitred Montana to make sure that no comfort or attention should be wanting. The plan was that he should stay there until Easter or a little longer, a matter of five or six months, lying on his back most of the time, forgetting concert-schedules, programme-plans, orchestral-specifications and, above all, the urge to *achieve*. At the end of three months he wrote home that he seemed to have been away for years. To liven things up he started a curling competition in the sanatorium corridors. Bedpans were used as curling stones. In the interests of healthful repose all round the staff put a stop to this.

Late in February came the news of Elgar's death. Fired by grief and made eager by it, he wrote letters to Courtauld and Miss Stanhope suggesting a memorial performance in Queen's Hall of *Gerontius* in April for Concert Club members only. Either because

8

of practical difficulties or because of a doctor's veto, nothing came of the idea. In his absence there were memorial concerts by the Royal Philharmonic Society at Queen's Hall and by the Royal Choral Society at the Royal Albert Hall, Boult and Landon Ronald conducting. Within four months of Elgar's going two other English composers died: Delius and Holst. Sargent's chance came in the autumn, when he conducted a memorial to all three, consisting of *The Planets* and the *Ode to Death*; *Songs of Farewell* and the 'Cello Concerto; and *The Music Makers*.

This was the concert that marked his reappearance on the Albert Hall platform. He had already reappeared there as a member of the audience. Early that summer, at a time when few people knew he was back in London, he joined a party in the royal box for a *Hiawatha*. His portrait appeared in the programme alongside that of Albert Coates who, explained the caption, would be conducting all that year's *Hiawathas* in view of Sargent's continued illness. During the second interval Charles Fairbairn, having noticed Sargent, had one of his spot men focus on the royal box. All heads turned that way. Clapping began. Sargent came to the front of the box and bowed. The clapping turned into an ovation.

Hugh Allen had seen everything, including the instruction to the spot man.

'You shouldn't have done that,' he frowned at Fairbairn and walked off without saying why.

CHAPTER SEVENTEEN

GENTLEMAN v. PLAYERS

THE CURE had made him look younger. Again his smile, his litheness and his straight back were those of a boy. With the old fever gone his energy had a core of tranquillity not evident before. He had a career to refashion, new platforms and publics to conquer. The Australian offer was reopened. He now planned to be there in 1936 for concerts in most of the State capitals. Before that there would be *Hiawatha* again.

When *Hiawatha* rehearsals came round, involving him with the orchestra and different groups of singers in three-session days, young newcomers to the cast were staggered at the amount of work he got through. 'Dr. Sargent,' said a baritone fresh from the Royal College, 'we're amazed at your stamina. How do you keep it up night after morning and morning after night?'

'Simple!' he replied. 'I have a gift. Every afternoon I can sleep for a quarter of an hour, lying flat on my back. That sleep to me is gold. If I couldn't do that I shouldn't be with you here today.'

He said something of the same kind to his Leeds friends. Another triennial festival was on the way. It was here that he made his first professional reappearance in the summer of 1934 at Beecham's right hand. Rehearsals began in July. In Leeds Town Hall his three hundred and fifty singers, picked after ruthless auditions, greeted him with explosive affection. An artless and moving account has come down from one of the women singers: 'We were all terrified when he fell ill. Now he's back we're overjoyed. It's so exciting . . . I've often gone to rehearsals tired after my day's work, wishing I hadn't to go. But once you get there every bit of tiredness disappears. His enthusiasm makes *us* enthusiastic. And he's so gentle. I feel I could sing for Dr. Sargent even if he didn't beat time at all. His expression itself is enough to tell us what he wants. The chorus get more out of it than those who just sit and listen. If I wasn't in the festival choir I'd have to go right away from Leeds until it was over.' For Sargent the Leeds singers were 'glorious, unique voices. Among the great choirs of the world they rank as the Pyramids do among the world's great monuments. Their energy is colossal.' But he owned that they were not always absolutely on the note in the mornings. How could they be expected, after three or four days' full rehearsal, to sing perfectly in tune always at morning concerts, bearing in mind the exacting programmes they had sung the night before—and, often, the afternoon before as well? In short, the chorus had too much to do. His words were heeded. Three years later their burden was lightened and rationalized.

Meantime they did nobly by Liszt's *Christus*. This, the first production in England of Liszt's oratorio, was received with a fair amount of scepticism; the Liszt revival and vogue were ten or twenty years off. Although Sargent made substantial cuts the performance went on for two hours and a half. After the final rehearsal malcontents forecast that this first performance of *Christus* would be the last. 'There was never a greater mistake,' he retorted. 'I have myself arranged for future performances of it. For choral societies *Christus* is a find. They tell me the tickets aren't selling well. If Leeds people stay away they don't know what they're missing. It's beside the mark to say *Christus* must be poor stuff because it has been neglected. After all, Bach's B minor Mass was on the shelf for a hundred years.'

It cannot be said that his championing secured for *Christus* much of a place in the repertory.

The festival that year was ill attended. An all-Bach concert had been arranged to satisfy a supposed or actual clamour for Bach's music. Sargent conducted it. For the first time in the festival's history hundreds of seats had been set apart at a low price, six shillings. Many of these were empty. Even Beecham could not be sure of filling the hall and lashed out at 'rotten' audiences. 'To have to play to six or seven rows of empty benches,' he said, 'is an insult to artists. I am not coming here again. And I shall tell other artists not to.' (Like more than one Beecham threat, this came to nothing. He and his orchestra, Sargent as well, were back in 1937.) To meet expenses of seven pounds a performing minute, private guarantors, who had paid £900 in 1931, brought their cheque books out again.

Sargent did not see the justice of private subsidy. He began to speak up in favour of public ones. In the manner of one thinking aloud he supposed it 'the wild dream of a mad musician' to suggest that the festival deficit might be met by the levying of a special rate (it need only be infinitesimal) within the city. A lot of people loved music who had little money. He would like to see sections of cheap seats allocated for their benefit. Three years later the corporation complied to the extent of putting up a guarantee fund and letting the festival managers have the Town Hall rent-free. He was to revert often to the theme of State or municipal aid for music—but, as we shall see, only after his intervention in another aspect of musical economics had embroiled him with musicians of various ranks and kinds in a quarrel that took long to forget.

A few weeks after Leeds he was received with happy tumult by his Courtauld–Sargent and Royal Choral Society followers. With the R.C.S. singers he embarked on ten rehearsals for a performance of *Belshazzar's Feast* which on paper looked like making the galvanic Leeds *première* of 1931 seem small beer. At Leeds there had been a choir of three hundred. The R.C.S. strength was 850. The performance came off early in the New Year (1935). The choral climaxes were sweet and earthshaking. Sometimes, unfortunately, they half swamped the orchestra. The following season he made a double-bill of *Belshazzar* and *Gerontius*, an exalting afternoon. Then, at a Courtauld–Sargent concert in April, came William Walton's Symphony in B flat minor, still in three movements only; the finale was not yet off the slipway. From the *Times* man, Capell (*Telegraph*) and other key critics he won compliments on a reading of signal insight and warmth. Certainly he was capable of soaring on symphonic occasions—given the right symphony, although here his effective range was limited. It was his *Belshazzars* and *Gerontiuses*, his *Messiahs* and B minor Masses which marked him off from all other batons. These were the scores which gave him pre-eminence of a sort never known before and made other choral practitioners, however skilled and gruffly imposing they were, seem drab by comparison. No writer has better described the nature of his sovereignty on choral platforms than Bernard Shore: 'You have only to see the eyes of a choral society screwing into him like a thousand gimlets to know what he means to them. He is hypnotic .... He plays upon their imaginations and minds like a mesmerist.'* Accompanying standard choral classics was not, in the ordinary way, a task that orchestral players relished. A week of oratorio and the like at churchly music festivals made them feel like bondsmen. Yet every man of them rose to the precision and fire with which Sargent, on his great nights, unleashed tons of choral climax, with squelch of full organ, thunder of kettle drums and belch of brass thrown in for good measure. In these matters, as Beecham acknowledged, nobody came near him.

*

Here we come to a line which traversed Sargent's career and perhaps his psychology like a geological fault.

He loved choirs. And choirs loved him. But what of his orchestral players?

Most of the choralists, superbly trained as well as dazzled by him, were amateurs. His orchestral players on the other hand were professionals, members of the toughest and most sensitive professional tribe the arts have ever known; laconic and, after their fashion, cynical; committed to rehearsal drudgery and concert stresses or boredoms; but given to dreaming about great music as well as publicly making it; men with ideas of their own, often implacable, about the speeds at which the stuff should go, how the louds and softs should be graded, how this melody and that should be phrased to bring out its full beauty. Every new conductor who appeared before them was tacitly up for judgment and stayed under critical scrutiny for the rest of his days.

How did they judge Sargent?

One thing is certain. They never fell at his feet as the choralists did. As professionals they could not have been expected to. The choralists, incidentally, vastly outnumbered them. Orchestral

* *The Orchestra Speaks*, by Bernard Shore, Longmans Green, 1938.

players in the symphonic sense of the term were numbered in hundreds. Of choral singers on the other hand, Sargent used to boast that he once conducted four thousand in a single week, none of them twice over. There were other differences apart from number. Choral singers were Sargent's subordinates because they weren't qualified to be anything else. Orchestral players were his subordinates, in the first instance, as a matter of discipline. It did not follow that they were obliged to accept him as musically their superior. Many players have eyed the rostrum ambitiously. Several have reached it and acquitted themselves there to music's gain as well as their own. Sargent's contemporary John Barbirolli, once among the Queen's Hall 'cellos, is a case in point.

Another factor that makes for rough passages or smooth at rehearsal sessions is relative age. As principal viola in the B.B.C. Symphony Orchestra and in other capacities Bernard Shore observed Sargent at close range throughout the 1920s and 1930s. Towards the end of this term he wrote: 'Conductors under the age of thirty-five or forty are not popular with a first-class orchestra. For some reason the players resent being handled by a young man and would rather have an experienced man of mature years rather than a youngster, however brilliant.'* Mr. Shore did not mention names. The cap was there for any taker. On the B.B.C.'s famous Brains Trust Sargent came near to saying the cap had once fitted him. What Mr. Shore had written was, he said, 'awfully true. We have all [known of] it until the age of forty. . . . The old orchestral player rather resents a young man coming in with new ideas about things he has worked at for years with older conductors. . . . Certain jobs are jobs of experience, and age will count. In these jobs you often find that the physical power of the person remains.'

When Sargent said this he was fifty-one years old. Ten or eleven years earlier his line on orchestral players had been less circumspect. At forty he could be offhanded to the point of rashness.

Something has been said in an earlier chapter of a brush with a clarinettist in the British National Opera pit and a measure of alienation which this caused. Twenty years after his *Mastersingers* experience he had recurring quarrels with leading players in the

* Ibid., p. 26.

reconstituted Liverpool Philharmonic Orchestra. After most of these episodes he would break down and cry, usually in the privacy of David Webster's home. Webster, now Sir David, who later became general administrator of the Royal Opera House, was then chairman of the Liverpool Philharmonic Society and the main begetter of wartime symphony concerts which won renown far beyond Merseyside. When Sargent broke down Webster would adopt the paternal manner typical in a relatively young man trying to help a senior in distress. Come now, he would say, this would never do! Why take a tiff so much to heart? Sargent's reply was that certain orchestras (he did not specify which) had given him a bad time as a young man, the paradoxical outcome being that he was unpopular with orchestras, not they unpopular with him. He made similar avowals to other friends. Rehearsal clashes a decade or two earlier had bred in him a certain uneasiness on orchestral rostrums. This sometimes betrayed him into a breezy schoolmasterish manner and what they conceived to be perfectionist niggling which put players on edge. There was an intermediate phase when, thanks to his first great public successes, this maladjustment had righted itself painlessly. There is nothing like acclaim for enabling a man to get on with people. Until well into the 1930s the newly-formed or upgrowing B.B.C. Symphony Orchestra invariably welcomed him with open arms. Usually they did their welcoming and he his radio conducting in Studio Ten, of receding memory. This was an improbable cave, roomy and well equipped, partly inside and partly hugging an arch of the old Waterloo Bridge. From its earlier uses or independently of them, Studio Ten was known as the Pickle Factory, the Wine Vaults or the Fleapit. At rehearsal break players could get from it into a contiguous pub, The Feathers, on either of two levels. This was not the least of its charms. The studio was so big that players and staff brought in their wives, friends, relations and broods uninhibitedly without getting under anybody's feet. Few rehearsals were without mixed unofficial audiences. Occasionally a rat would run along a wall pipe to which the conductor usually had his back turned. Nobody seemed to mind.

To this curious cellarage Sargent brought 'a breath of fresh air', as more than one veteran has put it. It was not only that he could be depended on to sparkle at ten in the morning like a painless firework. If unaccompanied by sheer musical acumen his gaiety would have palled quickly. But with cheerfulness went a technical alertness, a mental ubiquity on detail, which no other English conductor except Henry Wood and few foreign ones had ever paralleled. Nothing was left to chance. It wasn't enough to make a point conversationally. The point had to penetrate. Coming to a double bar and *da capo* sign, most conductors would simply say either, 'We do this repeat' or 'We don't do this repeat' and leave it at that. Occasionally it would happen that a player didn't hear because he wasn't paying attention or because the conductor hadn't made the point incisively enough. On the night the inattentive player would commit a wrong entry, unnerving everybody and humiliating himself. Sargent always gave instructions of this kind with sufficient emphasis, though without raising his voice, to make it stick in eighty or a hundred minds. Having made the point, he would say, 'Mark it in!'; and pencil stubs would come from eighty or ninety desk ledges and mark in accordingly. The opening bar of many a piece was approached as mantraps are approached. If there were initial rests, he would make it plain whether he was going to 'beat' them or whether he meant to 'give them for nothing'. A case in point was the opening of Bizet's *L'Arlésienne* suite. This starts on the third beat. 'I won't beat the first two beats,' he would say. 'I'll give you those two beats and come in on the third. Like this.' Here he would demonstrate with the stick rather as Henry Wood used to do in like cases. 'Now mark that in your copies.'

There was nothing innovatory or unique about any of his methods. The difference was that he applied them more insistently and effectively than most other conductors. He trusted his players ninety-five per cent of the way. Since the remaining five per cent of the way was all pitfalls, the players were glad of the security he gave them by refusing to take things for granted. Reverting to Bernard Shore's dictum, it is true to say that as an under-forty Sargent was not only *not* disliked by the generality of players but on occasion won admiration from seasoned men and tyros alike.

His fortieth birthday fell in 1935. The orchestral scene was sunny for him. Before another year was out much of the light had gone.

8*

*

Sometime during 1935 the London Philharmonic Orchestra in the person of Beecham, with Sargent very much at his elbow (in managerial matters he spoke freely of 'we', 'our' and 'us'), suddenly got rid of eight players, some because they were not quite so good as they had been, the rest because other players who were 'a little bit better' (Sargent's phrase) had been found to take their places. Like most other institutions, orchestras are subject to certain laws of competition and, if they have any money to buy talent with (there wasn't a great deal of it about in the mid-1930s), naturally go out for the best that offers. They cannot afford to be deterred by the thought of displacements that will inevitably follow. However, sacking men because you have no choice is one thing. Parading the fact is another.

On a certain Saturday in June 1936, Sargent being happily engrossed with his annual *Hiawatha* run, the *Daily Telegraph* carried a humane and admirably reasoned article by Ferruccio Bonavia, one of their staff critics, about retirement pensions for orchestral musicians. Before settling down to musical journalism and music teaching (he wrote chamber music as well), Bonavia had played among the Hallé violins in Manchester during Hans Richter's day. It was under Richter that the Hallé Society's pension scheme started; and it was this scheme that he commended to other orchestras and patrons. During the weekend a *Telegraph* reporter sought Sargent's opinion on the matter.

Orchestral pensions? By all means, Sargent replied. He was a humanitarian and loved his fellow man with the best. 'But,' he went on, 'there is a snag. As soon as a man thinks he is in his orchestral job for life, with a pension waiting for him at the end of it, he tends to lose something of his supreme fire. He ought to give of his lifeblood with every bar he plays. Directly a man gets *blasé* or does not give of his very best he ought to go. It sounds cruel, but it is for the good of the orchestra.' It was at this point that he cited the L.P.O. sackings. His tone was that of one who briskly retails the economic facts of life to softies who shy away from them or are too dim to take them in. In a general way, he concluded, he was in agreement with the idea of a pension scheme; but the pensions should be on the basis of one-year contracts, renewed only if the musician retained his finest form, and payable 'only at the end of the musician's life, when he has poured out ungrudgingly his whole strength'.

What this amounted to was that Sargent approved of pensions and damned them in the same breath. In one sentence they were a bad thing; in the next they were grudgingly agreed to be, in their way, perhaps, meet and just, yet on the dangerous side, a matter Saint Cecilia herself might have thought twice about.

In the fortnight that followed he was jumped on in the *Telegraph* by letter writers and by other interviewees with a unanimity that must have perturbed him, although he gave no outer sign of this. His main fear—that, with pensions in prospect, players would slump back in their seats, sending orchestral standards to pot—was disposed of by a simple consideration. Under any properly devised scheme the conductor would retain the power of sacking backsliding players, who would at a stroke lose their jobs and either forfeit their pensions or have them commuted. Among those who jumped on him were the heads of the country's two main teaching institutions. From the Royal College of Music and the Royal Academy of Music Sir Hugh Allen and Sir John McEwen wrote to the Editor in grave deprecation. They were joined by a third musical knight, Dan Godfrey, the Bournemouth conductor, who thought, as they did, that no man plays the worse for knowing he'll have something to fall back on in his old age. Three eminent English string players reproved him. Lionel Tertis, the violist, agreed with Sargent that the player should give of his lifeblood and added that he was only too willing to do so. 'But,' he added, 'some conductors reduce him to stone, and from a stone nobody can get blood.' Albert Sammons, the violinist, who had once led for Beecham, dwelt on overwork. How could players give of their best if, in the hope of putting something by against hard times, they had to scrabble for extra assignments and tire themselves out? Arthur Catterall, leader successively of the Hallé and B.B.C. orchestras, lauded orchestral players after thirty years among them as sincere, accomplished artists, 'well able to teach many conductors their job. They will put up with anything so long as they are happy with their conductor and his leadership gives them artistic satisfaction.'

Finally the great Fritz Kreisler spoke up. 'I am sure,' said Kreisler, 'that musicians the world over play the better for feeling secure. The idea that one must starve to be a great artist is out of date and quite wrong. Whoever says a man plays better for feeling insecure does not understand musicians. As a youngster I was badly off for a time; but I had a great deal of hope, and that carried me through. It is different when you are young. The more secure a musician feels the happier he is and the better he plays.'

Sargent was routed. He either didn't see or wouldn't admit this. Fighting back in follow-up letters, he complained that his critics were putting the cart before the horse and making him a scapegoat for a deeper disarray in musical organization. First things first, he exhorted. Before setting up pension schemes for old players the country should buckle to and set up civic orchestras for young ones fresh from music college. If that were done pensions would follow without difficulty. He would even be prepared to cede three-year contracts—but only for top players; for rank-and-filers one-year contracts would do.

Again, however, he took back with his right hand what he had given with his left. He fatally added that the feeling of instability about where next year's bread and butter was to come from had made many an artist give continuously of his best.

This last sentence and the one about the player's lifeblood were never forgotten. Most players now in their middle fifties or over bear witness to the bitterness which Sargent's opinions provoked in bandrooms all over London. They put it thus: 'Here was the man we had had whip-rounds for when he was ill three years earlier. We all cheerfully paid in our five bobs or what-not. By way of thanks we got a reminder that it was the breadline for us if we weren't good boys.' At one point in the debate Sargent had spoken, a little belatedly, of his wholehearted admiration and respect for British orchestral players and claimed they were his great friends. In the summer of 1936 and for many years afterwards this claim had a hollow ring. Clippings of his pronouncements in the *Telegraph* were carried in scores of wallets and are remembered to have been stuck up on many a rehearsal board before Sargent occasions with the 'lifeblood' and 'bread and butter' phrases underlined. In one of the orchestras there was a wag who sometimes brought out a collection box in the bandroom and rattled it sardonically in allusion to the whip-rounds of 1933. The box contained a button and a French halfpenny.

It could not be said that orchestral players were among the world's affluent. Rank-and-filers in the freelance pool were paid something like twenty-five shillings all-in for rehearsal (morning) and concert (usually the same evening). For a recording session the pay was twenty-nine shillings. If he could rely on being booked regularly for six concerts a week, the rank-and-filer might venture to get himself a family and try to bring it up; but there were not that many concerts to go round. In London there were only two orchestras that paid regular salaries: the B.B.C.'s and the London Philharmonic. Star players made their own arrangements and were said to get up to £1,000 a year. In the case of the L.P.O., the orchestra with which Sargent had most to do, rank-and-filers got eight pounds a week and no more whatever the week's assignments happened to be, whether symphony concerts, opera, ballet, broadcasts or recording sessions. It is evident that no family man could hope on such terms to save up against encroaching senility.

But the money aspect of the debate was not the one that rankled most. What really hurt was Sargent's implication that orchestral players were a lower musical breed, a sort of superior artisan; his blindness to the fact that, in general, their devotion to great music, amounting with many of them to reverence and delight, was no more determined by cash considerations than a conductor's readings should be (and Sargent's never were) by the knowledge that crowned heads are listening to him.

It was after his discomfiture on the pensions issue that Sargent became increasingly assertive on the need for subsidies. Beecham having publicly recoiled at the thought of artistic enterprises controlled by some government department or other on the strength of the public money it was handing out, Sargent leapt into print (*Times* letters) with a scheme for concert grants on a 'pound to pound' basis. He gave an example of how this would work. A municipality would guarantee a fund of, say, £500. To this the Government would add another £500. With the resulting £1,000 it would be possible for the town concerned to run cheap orchestral concerts on a substantial scale at negligible cost to individual taxpayers. While the Government might be allowed to vet balance sheets the scheme would remain essentially free from central control, the thing Beecham so dreaded.

It may strike the reader as curious that Sargent should have pressed for the public subsidizing of music at a time when he, conspicuously, as well as everybody who went to the Courtauld–Sargent concerts, were benefiting from a highly successful form of non-State patronage which, bearing in mind the trend towards 'monolithic' industrial structures, had an important potential for the future. It is hard not to conclude that his motives were mixed; that he was preaching the subsidy principle partly in expiation; that, having spoken so mistakenly about orchestral pensions, he wanted to put himself right and be loved again. But did he *know* he had made a mistake? If so, what sort of mistake was it?

In conversation during his last decade to an old friend who happened also to be an influential musical organizer, he said of the *Telegraph* interview: 'It's one of the things I wish I had never said.' He added, however, that he hadn't changed his mind a bit. He still thought a musician played the better for not knowing where next year's bread and butter was coming from. He took the same line when negotiating his 1962 tour of Australia and the Far East with the L.P.O. To a spokesman of the L.P.O. management he said: 'If one gives musicians too much security, they'll not be on their mettle. They'll sit back and you'll not get the best out of them.' Again his view was contested. 'Chaps give of their best under a good conductor,' he was reminded, 'because they love music and they love their jobs.'

The mistake he owned to was one of inexpediency only, the mistake of telling the world gratuitously what is in one's mind. The effects of it were evident for thirty years. No biographer can avoid the conclusion that, among English orchestral players, Malcolm Sargent became in 1936 the least liked conductor of his generation and eminence. There was to be little change in their attitude until his last, mellowing years.

CHAPTER EIGHTEEN

PALESTINE AND THREE VALLEYS

LITTLE MORE than a week after the last public exchanges in the pensions debate he sailed for concerts in New Zealand and Australia. These were his first assignments abroad. Henceforth and increasingly he is of international status. So many of his doings overlap, repeat and interlock that chronology throws its hands up in despair. His future career must to some extent be set down not in the order of happening but according to theme and place. It has therefore been found convenient to group the Australian tour of 1936 and those of 1938 and 1939 in a chapter of their own. Meantime we follow him to Palestine, among other places. Occupied by the British under a mandate which at this time had twelve more years to run, Palestine (now the State of Israel) was already a troubled country but a resolutely evolving one. Sargent had often talked of holidaying in Palestine, for him above all else the Holy Land—'a holy land,' as he put it, 'for people of more than one religion and for people of more than one trend of thought.'

Early in 1937 he conducted in London a performance of the Beethoven violin concerto with Bronislav Huberman as soloist. Of Polish origin and Jewish blood, Huberman was a virtuoso of the first order and, more remarkably, a visionary with energy and practicality enough to make a noble vision come true. Summoning from all parts of Europe refugee and other musicians, some of them displaced by Nazi racial laws, others available for different reasons, he had built up in Tel Aviv one of the most extraordinary orchestras in history. Speaking many tongues, very few knowing Hebrew, the players dribbled into Tel Aviv in the late summer of 1936 and rehearsed under sub-conductors in a rickety pavilion that survived from a recent international fair. If the weather was wet rehearsals had to be called off because rain came through holes in the roof. By December the orchestra was ready for a baton regarded by many as the greatest in the world as well as the most formidable one ideologically. In a second exhibition building which had been rainproofed and adapted to seat three thousand, Arturo Toscanini conducted the inaugural concerts of the Palestine Symphony Orchestra (now the Israel Philharmonic) in a gesture of faith and defiance which rang across the world in more than the musical sense. Toscanini's had been the culminating act but Huberman's the genitive (and more important) one. When Huberman arrived in London to rehearse the Beethoven, Sargent said how he admired his achievement.

'Would you like to come out and conduct us?' Huberman asked.

Sargent said he would like nothing better. A formal invitation came within a matter of days. He accepted at once, cancelling a number of alternative dates.

Here a digression.

The year 1937 was Coronation Year. The musical season coincided with the crowning of King George VI and his Queen. Music played its part in solemnities and jubilation both at home and overseas. The arrangement was that Sargent's concerts in Jerusalem, Tel Aviv and Haifa should be Coronation concerts with official backing and pomp. A few days before flying out to Palestine he took part in a great Coronation concert at home, one of five conductors who laboured through an all-English programme which, being of the sort customary on these occasions, is almost as tedious to recite as it must have been to hear: Stanford's *Songs of the Sea*, *Blest Pair of Sirens*, Holst's *Jupiter*, a Vaughan Williams antiphon, a Bantock hymn (to Aphrodite, it is true), things by Quilter, Sullivan, Smyth, Edward German. . . . On the platform a mere thousand singers and players. This cheese-paring was handsomely made up for a year later when, by Royal Command, he conducted in the Albert Hall two thousand voices all at once. Most of these singers had come in groups of four to six from every corner of Great Britain, the pick of 260 choirs whose joint singing membership ran to half a million. For want of room on the platform and its terraces, which were preempted for a giant orchestra and a great battalion from the Royal

Choral Society, all the incoming singers were posted to the arena—and filled it. Again there was a procession of conductors to the rostrum. As a treat for the multitude, however, it was decided that Sargent and Sir Henry Wood should make a ceremonial entry together. They got an ovation that raised the roof. That night assorted batons conducted nearly thirty pieces, many of them snippets, from *Summer is icumen in* and the *Agincourt Song* to the *Beggar's Opera* Overture (in Frederic Austin's version) and Elgar's *Imperial March*. Most of the time the mammoth choir sang in sections. Now and again, however, everybody joined in. Whenever this happened Sargent was the one in charge. He conducted with his face to the arena-choir and maintained with both arms a widely ranging beat that was equally clear to the players and singers behind him. The entire mass had been as easy to handle, he exulted afterwards, as a choir of twenty. For Parry's *Jerusalem* at the end the two thousand were reinforced by the immense audience, making seven thousand voices in all. The King and Queen stood up in the royal box, a row or two of courtiers behind them, and sang like everybody else. Sargent was in his element, face wet with patriotic tears. Long afterwards he counted this among the most memorable concerts of his career. *

*

A few days later he was ensconced in Government House, Jerusalem, guest of the High Commissioner, Sir Arthur Grenfell Wauchope. Already his comings and goings bore something of the exalted stamp which was to earn for him the title of Britain's Ambassador of Music. When he announced from Government House two days before the event that he had decided to substitute Mozart's G minor for the *Jupiter* Symphony in his opening programme the tidings smacked almost of State business. With the G minor as its

---

* His considered list of 'most memorables' makes instructive reading. It included two other Albert Hall nights—a concert in 1928 to mark the tenth anniversary of the First World War Armistice ('the dear old King [George V] and Queen [Mary] and the whole court were there,' he used to say); and his seventieth birthday concert in 1965, when he conducted three crack choirs in three Te Deums— and a concert for the Red Cross in Sydney, Australia, two months after the outbreak of Hitler's war, when his baton was auctioned, fetching £108.

centrepiece, the programme which he played at all four concerts
(one in Jerusalem, one in Tel Aviv, two in Haifa) took in Elgar's
Introduction and Allegro for strings and two Delius pieces—an
Irmelin entr'acte and a dance from *Koanga*. Most music-lovers in
Palestine knew little about Elgar and Delius. In a talk for the
Palestine broadcasting service he did what he could to enlighten
them about both. He conceded without apology the imperialist
streak in Elgar, describing him as a sort of musical Kipling.

His first rehearsals were, up to a point, an exercise in snaffle and
curb. There had never been such a body of string players at any
time anywhere else in the world. Between them the players spoke
half a dozen languages, each his own and usually no other. How they
managed to understand Sargent was and remains a mystery. Seven
out of his eight 'cellists had been principals in important European
or American orchestras. It was much the same with the other string
departments; most of the players had been leaders or had played in
string quartets. In the end he was to say he had never heard better
string playing in or from any part of the world. In the beginning,
however, the players' egocentric eagerness amounted to a handicap.
'There is,' he reported, 'almost an excess of good musicianship. Too
often a conductor has to excite players to get the best out of them.
But here the players are excited before we begin, all full of warmth,
eager to give of their best. So much so that the conductor has to tone
down their individualism. If anything, he has to say, "Steady now,
steady!" If you collect the best players from the best football teams
it doesn't follow you've got the best team ever. Football stars have
to train for team work. The same applies to an orchestra.' At one
rehearsal he went so far as to reprove them. 'It is right,' he said, 'that
you should love playing music; but you should love music more.'

He opened at the Edison Theatre, Jerusalem, with 'God Save the
King', followed by *Hatikvah* ('The Hope'), the Palestinians' national
anthem, played with a verve that gave his audience gooseflesh; it
had never occurred to Palestinians, least of all the musical ones, that
their national anthem could be made to sound, as one Jewish critic
put it, like a movement from a symphony. This feat at the beginning
of the concert perhaps had something to do with the noisy jubilation
at the end. Sargent was recalled nine times by an audience that

included everybody of consequence. The High Commissioner was there; so was the General Officer Commanding in Palestine, Lt.-General Sir John Dill. During the first tour and later ones, Sargent was made much of by those running the country. Lowlier people made even more of him. Of his two concerts in Haifa the second was for manual workers only. Men got tickets for themselves and their families through trade unions at cut rates. That night the Armon Theatre was packed. The standing ovation at the end was more striking in its way than his gala reception in Jerusalem five nights before. When, during a later tour, one of his rehearsals in Tel Aviv was interrupted by clangours from a shipyard nearby, somebody went out and asked if work could not be stopped until after the rehearsal. The yard workers were paid by the hour. They agreed to forgo their money in return for free tickets for the concert.

Sometimes noises off were more disturbing than pneumatic riveting. Racial tension bred riots. There were armed skirmishes almost daily. During the slow movement of a Beethoven symphony a burst of machine-gun fire was heard from outside the hall: a hold-up by Arab terrorists, presumably. 'I have never known Beethoven sound more impressive,' Sargent claimed. More than once he and his players travelled from one town to the next escorted by armoured cars. At home the newspapers carried a story that they had been ambushed. Somebody mentioned this to Beecham. 'I never read the newspapers, my dear boy,' he drawled. 'What happened?'

'Malcolm was ambushed by the Arabs.'

Beecham stroked his beard. Then: 'I never knew the Arabs were so fond of music.'

From his 1937 tour he flew back home in time to take final rehearsals at the Three Valleys Festival, Mountain Ash. Here he was sure of the deepest and most adoring ovation of all.

*

The three valleys were those of Aberdare, Merthyr and Rhondda, South Wales. Mountain Ash was in the first of these valleys, a mining township with a population of something over 30,000, mostly miners and their families. It clung to a steep mountain slope in a fashion that symbolized what was going on in the minds of most of the people who lived there; they, too, were on a slope, that of industrial decline, which was bringing privation and care to unnumbered hearths. Edward VIII had visited the region when Prince of Wales. Shocked by a scene of dereliction and desolation, he had said: 'Something must be done about this.'

There was one thing that could be done at little cost. More music could be brought into more people's lives. Although not much of a cure for economic evils, music was a considerable solace against them. Set up in 1930 by the Welsh National Music Council, the Three Valleys Festival, with its multiple choirs totalling three thousand voices, flourished beneficiently for ten years. During most of that time Sargent was its idolized conductor-in-chief, so much the darling of the stricken valleys that, after one of his concerts, a mob of young devotees waited for his motor-car in the valley bottom and hauled and pushed him to his hotel as a conquering hero. There can be no doubt that in communities where, at one time or another, as many as seven men out of ten were idle and pithead gear was falling to pieces, the Three Valleys Festival and the excitements that preceded as well as attended it were a factor towards social cohesion during disintegrating years.

One reached Mountain Ash by rail from Cardiff. Beyond the town of Aberdare the valley narrows, so that its floor is not more than a hundred yards wide. Trains bound for the festival hugged a stream fouled by dirt from colliery tips. At festival time the straggling main street, not more than the width of two 'buses, was hung with bunting and crowded with townsfolk in their best clothes. From the main street spread side streets with parallel rows of miners' cottages terracing the mountainside. Where the shops ended a steep byway which tested legs, lungs and low gears led to turnstile gates and the festival Pavilion. This was a huge stone barn of a place. Built for the National Eisteddfod of 1905, it had been used in the interim for boxing, all-in wrestling and 'wild beast' shows as well as for music.

It was on the strength of its Pavilion that Mountain Ash had been picked as the festival's annual home and headquarters. There was room on its platform for eleven or twelve hundred singers and an orchestra of seventy or eighty. The floor and galleries could seat four thousand and often did. Outside there were grounds where ticket-holders used to parade before the concerts. Loudspeakers hidden in trees relayed the music to hundreds who had either been barred by Full House notices or couldn't afford the admission prices. These were humane enough: ten shillings for four concerts or eight shillings for three. There were unreserved seats at a shilling for those who turned up early enough. The inside of the Pavilion had a bleak look which garish paper decorations did little to correct. Most of the seating was wooden benching. For the rest there were unupholstered chairs, including a few rows of superior ones at the front for important visitors—'the ones in fur coats', as the locals said. In one way or another several notables did their duty by Mountain Ash. There were heartening speeches on the closing night by such grandees as the Marchioness of Bute and Viscount Tredegar. For one of Sargent's big nights the Baroness de Rothschild flew over from Paris.

Platform 'rises' and choir benches had been put in as a complimentary gesture by the local colliery company. On them sat women singers in white blouses and dark suits and men singers in dark suits, white shirts and black bow ties. The alternative choirs of the Three Valleys Festival (three thousand all told but never more than eleven hundred in action at once) took in teachers and other professional people as well as railwaymen, 'bus crews and other workers whose jobs were relatively stable. But one third of the singers are reckoned to have been from out-of-work miners' families, including many heads of such families. These, too, had their dark suits and white shirts, retained against all economic odds for weddings, funerals, chapelgoing and the like. The black bow ties were said, perhaps as a wry joke, to be handed down as family treasures from father to son.

The great choirs of Mountain Ash were made up of little choirs who had practised for months beforehand in a dozen outlying villages and small towns.* In several villages the singers used to pay a few coppers a week in advance for coach tickets to some central point, usually a sizeable chapel in one of the valley towns, for mass

* The list of tributary choirs for 1937 makes poetic reading; Abercynon, Abercwmboi, Aberdare, Cilfynydd, Cwmaman, Ferndale, Merthyr, Mountain Ash, Nelson, Treforest and Ynysybwl.

rehearsals. Some of these were taken by Sargent. He exulted in the lustre and power of his Welsh voices. 'Listen to my tenors,' he would bid. 'Every one of them has a good top B flat.' Once a rehearsal had got into its stride and their voices were limbered up they never wanted to stop. He would start rehearsing a thousand singers at two in the afternoon and go on with one short break until nine at night. Even at that hour voices would be raised in jovial protest. 'Can't you put us through another chorus or two, Dr. Sargent?' he was asked.

An incidental aim of the Three Valleys Festival was to 'improve and refine' Welsh choralism. That was the official phrase. The verb which Sargent used was 'quell'. He set out to 'quell the native enthusiasm' of Welsh choralists and teach them to sing sensitively while losing none of their old fire. In this he claimed to have succeeded. Under his spur and teaching his singers graduated with growing cohesion and polish from *Messiah* and *Elijah* to the Requiems of Brahms and Verdi, *The Music Makers*, the 'Dona nobis' and 'Sanctus' from the B minor Mass and, finally, *The Dream of Gerontius*. After the last *Gerontius* rehearsal he had particular praise for their Demons' Chorus—'so technically difficult a piece that it was once considered almost impossible to perform even by the most skilled and experienced choirs.'

The people behind the festival were high-minded and hard-working. Some of them, however, were inclined to use such chilling words as 'education' and 'educative'. Educating young men and young women into loving music seems as redundant a cause as educating them to fall in love with each other. All they need is liberal opportunity of hearing good music well performed. If the appetite is there devotion follows. Much was made—and certainly it was a striking thing—of the gradual improvement in audience behaviour and outlook at Mountain Ash. During early festivals the audience would break in with frantic applause before the end of all the big *Messiah* choruses and would crack nuts, suck oranges and chatter during the 'Pastoral Symphony'. As the years went by the crudity of such goings-on became self-evident; good listening manners evolved of their own accord. At the same time a taste developed for the orchestral classics in communities which up to then had regarded singing as not merely enough but as all in all. As early as his third festival, Sargent ventured on Haydn's *Surprise* Symphony. The crowd drank it in. 'Two years ago,' he commented, 'it would have been dangerous to do any symphony by Haydn. They would have been restless. Tonight they were spellbound.'

Altogether the Three Valleys festivals were a seminal chapter in his career. He taught the valleys much. The valleys taught him something in return. He never forgot the evening when he stopped his motor-car to hear the song of thousands come up the mountainside as if in greeting. He pulled up and listened, marvelling. It was as though the very spirit of Wales, the spirit of a people acquainted with beauty and hope and pain, was walking the hills. Before the end of every festival he would put on a boiler suit and helmet and be taken down some pit in a fold of the hills where coal was still being got. At the coalface he would talk with men who, it sometimes happened, had sung for him the night before. In the dim light all he could see of their begrimed faces was the gleam of eyes and teeth —enough to show that they were smiling with delight and that music made them his equal: not to say him theirs.

CHAPTER NINETEEN

SORROW

HE TOOK a greater delight than most grown-ups in children: all and any children, not merely his own. Perhaps he saw more deeply into their innocence. In his mind, as in Wordsworth's, they were an intimation. Where children trod there the clouds of glory trailed. Whether they came in their thousands, as happened at the Robert Mayer concerts, on in ones and twos, he knew infallibly how to talk to them, make them laugh and feel at ease.

One encounter was to be remembered for a long time. His friend and colleague at the Royal College of Music, Herbert Howells, had a small boy, Michael. One day Michael went with his father to Sargent's orchestral class. He watched and listened avidly. At the break he was taken into the conductor's room. Tea was being handed round. Sargent asked if he was enjoying himself. 'Oh, yes!' What had interested him most? The trombones. 'Please,' he asked, 'why aren't your trombones all the same length?' This enchanted Sargent. He almost spluttered into his cup. Yet he did not give the little boy the feeling of being laughed at. In simple language he described the difference in compass between bass trombones and tenor ones and explained what trombone slides were for. Michael went back for the second half of the concert with a learned feeling. Four years later poliomyelitis struck him. He died after as many days. He was ten years old.

For months Herbert Howells was a sick man. He continued with his work at the College as professor of composition but, apart from lessons, did not want to meet people, still less talk to them. Sargent saw how he was suffering and helped him as much as a friend could.

He and Eileen had him round at Wetherby-place and did their best
to take him out of himself. One night Sargent prevailed on him to
come to a party. On the way their motor-car was held up at Hyde
Park Corner. Suddenly Sargent looked at his friend, and his eyes
were filled with tears. 'You mustn't get me wrong about taking you
to a party,' he said. 'If this happened to either of my children I'd
be in a far worse state.'

Some months after this, in the summer of 1937, the Sargents
holidayed with friends at Portofino Mare, Italy. They stayed in a
hillside villa overlooking the sea. For the two children, as for the
others, the first part of the holiday was halcyon in a broiling way.
Everybody swam, lay about on the beach, played tennis. Pamela was
now fourteen. Peter eleven. She had dark hair and exceedingly dark
eyes. Quick of mind and body, she was in many ways a small femi-
nine counterpart of her father, with similar contours of face and
the same fine-boned hands. She took dancing lessons. These meant
much to her; there was talk of her becoming a ballet dancer.

Late one afternoon Sargent came back from tennis and found her
shivering and feverish. Peter had taken off his pullover and wrapped
it round her. They had been in the sea. Afterwards they had sun-
bathed on the torrid sand. The shivering fit had come upon her
suddenly. Soon there were other and more disquieting symptoms.
Her arms went numb; she could not move her fingers. A local
doctor called in an Italian specialist, Professor G., who chanced to
be holidaying nearby. Professor G.'s diagnosis confirmed everybody's unspoken fear. It was poliomyelitis, the dread infantile
paralysis. The immediate need was for a serum injection. The
clinics and hospitals of the province were scoured by telephone that
night and the following day, a Sunday, to no purpose. By Monday
it was clear that no polio serum was to be had within convenient
range. A supply was flown in from Rome. Meantime Professor G.
had given Pamela an injection of his daughter's blood; she had been
treated for polio ten years earlier.

For three days and nights Pamela suffered atrociously. Nobody,
her father wrote to a friend, could have suffered more. At one stage
the legs, arms, chest walls, abdomen, voice and eyes were all
paralysed. It looked as if she was going to die. Suddenly she rallied.

Life crept back along nerve and muscle until only the legs and upper arms remained inert. The doctors comforted the mother and father with a proverb—'The worse the better'. They began to hope. From the onset 'Pamela has been angelic', added Sargent's letter, '—no whimperings and not one tear.'

There had been no case of infantile paralysis at Portofino within living memory. Pamela had already made friends there, and her illness brought sorrow to many. In the village church girls of the village prayed for her, and Masses were said in her intention.

Of Eileen's anguish and his own Sargent wrote little in his letters to friends. There was no need to. The sweat of anguish was there between the lines. So far there had not been much shadow in his life. By this time his illness, which had brought him near to death, was as if it had never been. The one earlier grief had been his father's death. But this had been long awaited. Henry Sargent had been ill for twelve years with cancer, the disease that was to kill his son. During those twelve years he had undergone many operations, most of them minor ones which had to do with an aperture in the gullet and the fitting of a tube for drinking. Suffering did not douse the old spark. When he first managed to drink through the tube they had congratulated him.

'One swallow,' he had faintly croaked, 'doesn't make a summer.'

Malcolm had been at his bedside when he died in January 1936, seventy years of age. He left little money and the knowledge in many hearts that the world would never see anybody else quite like him. Nor would the world see anybody quite like Pamela. But Pamela was only a child.

One morning in mid-September she was carried down by mule-track from the villa to the nearest point on the main road. Here an ambulance was waiting to take her to Geneva. Thence she travelled by night express to Paris. Another ambulance awaited her there. At Le Bourget she was lifted into a chartered 'plane. And so to a nursing home in Kensington. Her father and mother were with her on all stages of a journey made less harrowing by the sweetness of her courage. Slowly her condition improved. Presently she was able to walk a little with sticks and could get into and out of taxicabs unaided. Stairs were too much for her. Sometimes her father took her to the theatre. He used to carry her into the stalls. In the theatre, as outside it, they were moved by the same things and laughed at the same things on much the same note. They were fellows in laughter and in compassion. Whenever his thoughts were free he gave the whole of his mind, will and spirit to Pamela. The alchemy of suffering and pity had turned affection into a father-and-daughter idyll. However they begin, idylls do not last long.

*

A fortnight after the journey from Portofino he and Beecham began a week's orchestral rehearsals in London for yet another Leeds Festival. Sorrow was now lodged with him for ever. Even the idyll did not cure that. Outsiders suspected nothing, however. His back was straight, his smile prompt. Everything about him seemed to denote a man making the most of the best of possible worlds.

In programmes that were either all his own or shared with Beecham he conducted that year nine major works. Some of them refreshed a personal repertory which was beginning to look a bit jaded. Berlioz's *The Childhood of Christ*, a score which might have been expressly designed for him, was prominent among these. Eighteen months earlier he had introduced it at a Courtauld–Sargent concert, apparently on Samuel Courtauld's urging. At that time *The Childhood* as a whole was little known. Researchers for Courtauld–Sargent had been unable to trace the date of its last previous performance in this country. Courtauld had recommended a full-scale revival on the strength of isolated numbers which he had heard sung at a private concert in the house of some musical peeress. The 1936 performance in the Queen's Hall and the 1937 one at Leeds made *The Childhood* in a sense Sargent's fief for a while. Three other works on his list were the sprawling and splendid Busoni piano concerto, the one with the choral finale (Egon Petri, an eminent Busoni disciple, played the solo part); a new choral piece by Walton, *In Honour of the City of London*; a year-old piece by Vaughan Williams, *Dona nobis pacem*, which was not quite as liturgical as the title conveyed, having a text compiled from miscellaneous sources, including the Books of Jeremiah, Isaiah and Micah, Walt Whitman's *Drum Taps* and John Bright's 'Angel of Death' speech in the House of Commons during the Crimean War; and a Rossini charmer, the *Petite Messe Solennelle.*

While rehearsing this last he pulled up a woodwind group and had them replay a four-bar phrase two or three times. He asked one of the players to hand up his part. After a glance he said, 'A wrong note. I thought as much.' He scribbled in a correction. 'What a marvellous ear!' the choralists whispered to each other.

With the Verdi Requiem and Elgar's symphonic study *Falstaff* he had marked successes. His Brahms Symphony No. 4 did not carry quite the same conviction. Many years afterwards he said, 'I was ten years a conductor before I dared to touch any symphony of Brahms'—a quick aside which the biographer had no chance of following up. He made the same point, without elucidating it, in his presidential address to the Incorporated Society of Musicians, London, in 1957. He then said that he studied the Brahms symphonies for ten years before feeling he would be justified in putting on a performance of any one of them. He went on to say sharp things about 'any young conductor' of that time, the mid-1950s, who, when asked to do a Brahms symphony, promptly agreed, went off to hear it on the gramophone, came back and did a bad imitation of whatever recording he had heard. If we date his career from his début at the Queen's Hall with *Windy Day* (1921), it may be inferred that he did not touch any Brahms symphony until the early 1930s. With the Sydney and Melbourne orchestras in 1936 he had done No. 1 and No. 4 respectively. His first Brahms symphony at a Courtauld–Sargent concert was No. 3. It came as late as November 1937.

For Sargent to own himself intimidated by any music was unusual. What had made him shy away from Brahms? The relative austerity of the man's symphonic thinking? The weight and texture of his orchestration? As to the latter, it is known that sometime in the 1940s he went to work on the band parts of Brahms's No. 1. During a rehearsal with the London Philharmonic Orchestra it emerged that he had modified some of the brass scoring in the finale. At rehearsal-break the horns and trombones got together and vowed to play 'what Brahms had written and nothing else'. The phrase comes from one of the players involved. After a verbal tussle, during which feelings ran high, the players were talked into doing as Sargent wished.*

It is not suggested that anything of the kind happened during the preparation of No. 4 at Leeds. His fluent baton, the quicksilver of his thinking, the adroitness with which, off the rostrum, he graded and distributed his charm (for he did not confer its fulness on all and sundry) carried away or mightily impressed more people than ever. At concerts conducted solely by Beecham he usually sat in the balcony with the Princess Royal's party from Harewood House. That year there was a second princess on hand: Princess Helena Victoria. Watched with awe by many and with faint deprecation by a few, at least, of his fellow musicians, he talked volubly and gaily during the intervals with both princesses, a countess or two, the odd marchioness, Baron Franckenstein (the Austrian ambassador) and many others highly-born. It may be questioned whether any English conductor before him had behaved with quite such ease in such circles. His bright amiability put routine courtiers in the shade. This was no crime. It was the exercise of an unusual social gift. In some musical quarters such gifts were not readily forgiven. As Sargent's friendships were cemented in noble and royal milieux, so did resentment increase among those who considered, not altogether rationally, that the highborn were of their nature musically dumb and that the best thing for a musician of talent to do was tour an ivory tower and keep himself to himself.

Although they constituted a solid anti-Sargent lobby for thirty years, the musical 'democrats' and deprecators were relatively few. The adorers swamped them. On the last night at Leeds in 1937 Sargent listened from a doorway recess in the stalls to Beecham's final showpiece, the Coronation Scene from *Boris Godounov*. After a swelling ovation for Beecham at the end a cry of 'Malcolm, Malcolm!' went up from the chorus and spread through the hall. When signalled up to the platform by Beecham he had difficulty in freeing himself from a throng of girls who were after his autograph. Again the companion of princes and princesses had shown himself a musician for the multitude—that quasi-anonymous multitude

* This was not an isolated case. He is alleged to have 'improved' several other scores besides Brahms's No. 1.

whence he had himself sprung. It was in social ubiquity, perhaps, that Sargent's uniqueness lay. We are not to forget his humorous boast at seventy—'I have friends in high places, friends in low places and friends in between!' No other musician of his time gave so much delight on three levels at once or got more delight in return. He never wanted for incense.

*

The ache remained. Would Pamela get better? Could she long survive? These were the thoughts that gnawed.

Whatever she asked for he gave her. She never asked for what was beyond his capacity to give. One of her dearest wishes was to go to a certain finishing school in Kensington of which her friends had told her. By this time the war was on and the School evacuated to Hartland Abbey, a mansion in the West Country near Bideford. Sargent went down and talked with the headmistress, a woman of perspicacity and wisdom. He touched on the possibility, remote as it seemed then, of his daughter's dying. The headmistress answered that Pamela would be welcome in any case. Sooner or later everybody had to witness death; and, as to the girls in her charge, how better could they first encounter it and learn to understand and accept it, than if it came to one they all knew and had made friends with?

So Pamela was taken down to Hartland Abbey. She had a room of her own and many visitors. Although spending much of her time in bed, she contrived to attend some of the lessons. These included musical appreciation. She was as intent on music as she had been earlier on dancing lessons. Her musical instinct was sharp and evolving. She was able to put in a little piano practice. What her companions remembered most, however, was not so much her quick mind and talents as a quality of spirit that expressed itself more often than not in gaiety. She never had the air of a distraught, pathetic thing.

As we shall see, anxiety bit more deeply into her father than any but his intimates ever knew. In public he continued insouciant and pouncingly efficient. Yet the substance of the man was changing under anguish. He had always been compassionate. His compassion now needed new outlet. From this time on he made a point when he was abroad of visiting polio wards and talking with the sufferers there. What Pamela had undergone and what he had suffered vicariously enabled him to give a grain or two of comfort. Talking to a sick stranger is no small test of personal quality. He came through the test well because his concern was so full-hearted. Here was someone whose words, since he knew what suffering meant, had some balm in them. At home his voice was heard over the air in appeals for the crippled, the maimed and the needy. Compassion became insistent, almost passionate. The listener was not cajoled or wheedled at. He was almost hectored at times. . . . Incurable cripples were holding out their hands beseeching help. Some could not even do that. 'So,' he would say, 'out with your cheque books, you with hands that can write and hearts that can feel! And, while you are giving, give more than you think you can afford.'

One lesson which these piercing, splendid words brought home was that music is not, as some have taken it to be, a fenced-off domain for elect souls to lose themselves in, accounting the rest of the world and the rest of life well lost. For Sargent a suffering human without a note of music was as momentous as a suffering human with a head full of it. This impartiality had always been latent in him. Pamela's suffering made it more fruitful.

CHAPTER TWENTY

ANTIPODES

WE COME now to the first Australasian tours. In 1936, 1938 and 1939, he spent an aggregate of eight months in Australia and one month in New Zealand. During that time he drilled and helped to build up State symphony and radio orchestras; inculcated new standards of choralism; conducted seventy concerts in six State capitals; and acquired a fervid new public.

For all this he was paid handsomely in pounds sterling as distinct from the Australian or New Zealand pound, which was one fifth lower in value. In 1936 for the Australian Broadcasting Commission he conducted fourteen public concerts at £100 a concert; in 1938 twenty public concerts at £115 each and four Young People's concerts at £25 each; in 1939 twenty-three public concerts and five Young People's concerts for an inclusive fee of £2,500. On top he was paid first-class overseas fares as well as all fares for travel within Australia. In 1936 alone his travel bills covered 4,000 miles, including 3,300 miles by air.

To ultra-refined minds the money earned by eminent musicians is an unseemly topic. In Sargent's case it is a topic worth dwelling upon as showing, among other things, the different values placed on his services at home and abroad. One hundred pounds sterling during the late 1930s was equivalent in purchasing power to about £400 at the time of Sargent's death. On home platforms during the late 1930s he never commanded a 'standing' fee of £100-plus, or during the late 1950s and the 1960s anything like £400. Certain foreign batons did much better. The one who did best was, of course, Arturo Toscanini. Conducting the Philharmonia Orchestra at the

Photo: Keystone

With Queen Elizabeth the Queen Mother at diamond jubilee function of
the London Symphony Orchestra, Royal Festival Hall, May 1965

(a) After television recording, London, October 1959,
with diva Maria Callas

(b) With Eileen Joyce, the pianist, after concerto performance Harringay
Stadium music festival, London, June 1947

Royal Festival Hall in 1952, Toscanini cleared £1,000 a concert. Then and later Sargent was prepared to conduct a dozen orchestral concerts at that price, as is shown by a contract he signed in 1958, the dozen concerts listed for him on that occasion comprising six in the provinces, which brought in £300, and six at the Festival and Royal Albert halls which were worth £700. During his last phase he was obliged to go to America for massive fees of the kind which tempted von Karajan to London.

*

The 1936 tour lasted three months. It had taken over a year to plan. Planning entailed much more than saying: 'I'll conduct the following pieces with this orchestra and that choir on such and such dates in cities as under.' From a distance of 12,000 miles he checked on local instrumental resources in the light of the scores he was to conduct and arranged in several cases that preliminary rehearsals should be taken by recommended sub-conductors who, it was understood, should stand down (which they did cheerfully enough) as soon as he took the limelight. He usually saw to it on his last night in any city that these self-abnegating gentlemen came on to the platform for a spell of limelight and an ovation on their own account.

His first assignments that year were in New Zealand. It had been his intention to take a month's music-free holiday there before moving on to Sydney, New South Wales. When New Zealand's broadcasting powers heard of this they prevailed on him to under-take three concerts in Wellington, the capital. It was agreed that for one studio concert and two in public (these also to be broadcast) he should be paid between £250 and £300 by the joint promoters—the National Broadcasting Service, the Royal Wellington Choral Union and the Wellington Symphony Orchestra. Leaving England on 4th July, 1936, he travelled via Quebec and Vancouver, coming ashore from S.S. *Aorangi* at Auckland early in August. His three concerts in Wellington, with rehearsals before and between, occupied twelve arduous days. 'I came to see your country, not to conduct,' he told someone, 'and I find I haven't a minute to spare.'

His orchestral repertory covered Mozart's G minor Symphony

9

(K. 550), *Fingal's Cave*, Schubert's 'Unfinished' Symphony, Glazounov's *Serenade Espagnole*, the *Oberon* Overture, ballet music from the Albert Hall *Hiawatha*, Elgar's *Pomp and Circumstance* March No. 1, the *Londonderry Air* (arr. Grainger) and Schubert's *Marche militaire*. The schedule included one piano concerto, Rachmaninov's No. 2. Vocal pieces he conducted were: madrigals by Dowland, Weelkes, Ford and Morley, *Blest Pair of Sirens* and *Elijah*, which, of course, had an evening to itself. The scheme had a familiar ring, that of his apprentice years in Leicester and Melton. The orchestral playing must have sounded much the same. Everybody was keen, everybody tried hard, some had talent. Certain of the orchestra's most skilled players were from the De Luxe cinema band. Between his own rehearsals Sargent made a point of attending one of theirs. The occasion developed into a concert for his benefit.

'Tell us what you'd like us to play, and we'll play it,' they challenged.

He chose Nicolai's *Merry Wives of Windsor* Overture, the second Hungarian Rhapsody of Liszt and the *Knightsbridge* March of Eric Coates.

'Excellent, first class!' he pronounced. 'You are one of Wellington's musical assets.'

Between rehearsals a mayoral reception was given in his honour. From this occasion and the rehearsals excited accounts spread through the city of the visitor's professional brilliance, his friendship with the Gloucesters and the Kents, his unending flow of talk, his sense of fun and his winning ways. Everybody who was anybody in Wellington made a point of seeing and being seen at his concerts. Some came just for the music, or for the music as well. The concerts were held in the town hall at lenient prices: 2s, 3s and 5s 'plus tax'. In the five-shilling seats most of the men wore dinner jackets; most of the women were in furs. The hall lamps were of the kind that dazzle without giving enough light, the seats hard, the ventilation inadequate, the acoustics capricious. Matting was laid to mute the over-resonant aisles. In the presence of so illustrious a guest some Wellingtonians were a little ashamed of their principal concert room. A thing that bemused them all, since they had neither seen nor imagined anything like it, was Sargent's fluent left hand.

After the opening concert a local critic wrote that, while the right hand beat time, the left hand 'painted in the picture, put in the highlights, delicately applied hairlike line upon hairlike line, made broad sweeps of colour, fashioned delicate traceries and applied dainty touches, all with the surety of a master.' For *Elijah*, with a choir of three hundred, there was so great a crush at the doors that it took the crowd an hour to get in. A troop of 'society' girls sold programmes with their names printed in them and were supposed to show people to their seats. They had a bewildering time. The concert began a quarter of an hour late, with the Governor General and Lady Galway in the ceremonial seats. It ended in frenzies of shouting and clapping. In the days that followed singers and players were limp and happy. Where, they asked each other blankly, as so many others had done before them, did Dr. Sargent get the energy that took so much, to such wonderful effect, out of his performers?

During the free time left to him after *Elijah*, he had a gold medal pinned to his lapel, which made him a life member of the Royal Choral Union; accompanied a deputation to the Ministry of Internal Affairs with plans for a vast musical festival in 1940, New Zealand's centennial year; and, with Lady Galway, climbed the national war memorial campanile to inspect its carillon. After ten minutes at the practice clavier, he played *Annie Laurie* and *The Londonderry Air* for the whole city to hear. The carillon was not played by hand alone. It was also roll-fed and could be played mechanically. This induced one of Sargent's schoolmasterish moods. Warning the carillon's custodians not to use the mechanical player, as they were evidently inclined to, for relatively complicated pieces, he pointed out that carillon bells were majestic things and the apparatus that controlled them elephantine. 'You mustn't,' he said, 'expect an elephant to gambol any more than a double-bass fiddle to skip about like a piccolo.' Slow tunes were the thing, with a bass line only as accompaniment.

He burned to leave something more tangible behind him in Wellington, a community still hit by trade depression, than the memory of three concerts. His chance came when the Broadcasting Service asked him to conduct a fourth. Of what followed he gave

an exultant account to an English friend. His first Wellington concert, he said, had been such a sensation that the others sold out, over
a thousand being turned away at the doors. Asked to conduct an
extra concert on the Sunday night before his departure, he discovered that by law no admission charge could be made at the town
hall on Sundays. Knowing that the event would be a 'pandemonium'
success in any case and wishing to raise money for the unemployed,
he declined to have anything to do with the project unless standard
prices were charged. The Prime Minister, none other, asked to see
him. As a result 'the law was altered'. The rush to the box office was
such that half an hour after the plan opened not a seat was left.

A lightweight programme in the chockablock town hall that
Sunday night was dominated by the Grieg piano concerto. A slim
girl with auburn hair and a white dress played the solo part. Her
name was Eileen Joyce. Born on the fringe of the Tasmanian bush,
daughter of a none too successful mining prospector, she had taken
her first piano lessons in Boulder City, Western Australia, at sixpence a time. Her talent was unmistakable. It had blossomed from
a vacuum. The Wellington concert marked her first appearance
with Malcolm Sargent. She was to appear with him in many other
concerto performances in England during the war and after it,
mostly at the Promenade Concerts. Here a glance ahead. When she
found herself scheduled for the Grieg concerto under his baton for
the 1955 season she jibbed because, having played in it at the Proms,
usually for other conductors, six times almost in a row, she wanted
to give it an extended 'rest'.

'Why the Grieg?' she asked the B.B.C. 'I've got seventy concertos
in my repertory. Let's do something else.'

Sargent was invoked. He spoke to her on the telephone, using all
his charm:

'My dear Miss Joyce, I *beg* you to play the Grieg.'

'But I don't *want* to play the Grieg again. I want to play something different—Beethoven's G major, for instance.'

'A splendid idea. We'll do the Beethoven next year. But this time
the Grieg just once more, please! You play it so beautifully.'

In the end Eileen Joyce submitted. Few of either sex could
withstand Sargent's cajolery. While escorting her on to the Proms

platform that year he said, 'This is going to be your best performance ever.' He often made this prediction to his solo artists. It elated some. Others it made jumpy.

*

Two nights after this farewell concert he sailed in S.S. *Niagara*. As she steamed down Sydney harbour on 5th September, 1936, in blue, blazing weather, the city, or what he could see of it, looked less festive than the day. The immediate impression was of water-front shacks with corrugated iron roofs. Beyond this squalid fringe lay much official and private opulence. He tasted both kinds to the full. Having some aversion to hotel life, he sought desirable invita-tions with disarming candour if these did not come his way on the desirable host's or hostess's initiative. In city after city he was put up and fêted either by State governors or by people well up in Commonwealth society who had a lot of money and considered themselves under some obligation to help the arts. He trod guber-natorial lawns and the pile of private drawing-rooms with springy gait, turning over in his mind the winning or audacious things he would presently be saying to pretty, handsome, rich and important people. His audacities usually took the form of 'blue' stories. ('I know people say I like parties and women and *risqué* jokes,' he once confessed, 'and so I do, up to a point. But these things aren't my life, although it's fun to let people believe they are.') His impro-prieties, as another age (his own) called them, slightly embarrassed some. Most hearers were shocked in a mildly pleasant way. They told each other delightedly that Malcolm had a streak of the naughty small boy in him. Their delight was understandable; 'naughtiness' enhanced his charm. In Australia, as wherever he went, his spell was all but infallible. Official receptions in his honour had the bright tension of first nights; even the gatecrashers hung on his every word and twinkle. He was the most courted and fought-for guest music had ever known. To have Malcolm under one's roof for the week-end was a social plume of great price. The qualification 'all but' is used above. His infallibility was not absolute. One case is known of a hospitality bid going awry. When a much later Australian visit was being planned he telegraphed a certain State governor thus:

'Should so appreciate staying Government House during my forthcoming tour. . . . Dates as follow. . . . Attic will do.' An aide telegraphed back: 'Sorry, attic full.' Most grandees, however, were ready at any time to offer him a wing. He was much wooed at the official receptions. Down the Australian years he was accorded dozens of these. Always there was a massed opulence of flowers. Amid parchment lampshades, banked gladioli, profusions of peach blossom and crystal bowls where camellias and rosebuds floated, he met hundreds of people who were mad about music and didn't get enough of it and hundreds more who apologized for being three parts tonedeaf. When bishops and colonels and attorney generals and men with half a million sheep to their name didn't know the first thing about sonata form and made a clean breast of it, he would turn with alacrity to other topics. On zoos he was sprightly. How different Australia's zoos were from London's! 'In London Zoo,' he once reflected, 'the animals are lean, cadaverous. Even your carnivores look contented. But what magnificent vitality they have! Let me make a confession. If I were an animal, do you know what sort of animal I'd like to be? I'd like to be a leopard or a jaguar hunting through the jungle at night. The excitement of the chase would more than make up for the danger. . . . Still, one of the loveliest creatures I saw at Taronga Park [the Sydney zoo] was a koala. There it snuggled in the crook of a tree, enjoying the sun and munching a gum leaf. What an ecstatic expression it had! No old gentleman in a London club with a fat cigar and a glass of Napoleon brandy could have looked more pleased with life.'

*

On Sargent nights the auditorium of Sydney Town Hall was always full. Hundreds were turned away. Bearing in mind that the hall seated something like 2,500 and that the president of the New South Wales Musical Association put the city's true musical public at 2,000 or less, it followed that at least one fifth of the ticket buyers were there, in the president's words, for social cachet or from curiosity. Sydney was not alone in this sort of division and ratio. For most of this century the world's great conductors have been voted to pre-eminence by the world's capital cities almost as much for their profiles, gestures and 'dynamic' as for their strictly musical attainments. What marked off Australia's cities from those of Europe and America was the lack of a well-rooted musical tradition. There hadn't been time enough to send roots down. Until the Australian Broadcasting Commission (founded in 1932) began to concern itself with musical promotion there was relatively little symphonic music to be heard; and as a rule that little was neither stylishly nor confidently played.

During his three pre-war seasons Sargent visited Sydney, Melbourne, Brisbane, Adelaide and Perth. He conducted a total of sixty five concerts, including twenty each in the first two of these cities. Twelve of his concerts were wholly or in part choral and will be discussed in a later chapter. The programmes of his orchestral concerts are summarized in Appendix Three.

Getting the best out of five strange orchestras made up partly of semi-professionals, i.e. players for whom symphonic music was a sideline or a second job, taxed Sargent to the hilt and won him the warm regard not only of the paying public but also of the players themselves on account of new ensemble standards to which he trained them. As has been said, his visits were made on the initiative of the Australian Broadcasting Commission. During the 1932–33 season the Commission had set up in Sydney and Melbourne concert orchestras, each of twenty-four players, which were optimistically described as sufficiently big to perform 'the smaller works' in their original form. For special occasions the strength of either was augmented to between forty and fifty and, for visiting conductors of note, to seventy-five, about enough to cope with the standard classics. Up to 1936, when the Commission completed its plan for permanent concert orchestras in all five States, few of the musicians had played together; such corporate training as came their way had been sporadic. In 1933, when Sargent was ill, his place had been taken by Sir Hamilton Harty, conductor successively of the Hallé and London Symphony orchestras. After giving five concerts in Sydney and four in Melbourne he reported that conducting Australian orchestras was as exciting and uncertain as driving an old motor-car at seventy miles an hour. George Szell, now of the Pittsburgh Symphony Orchestra, was another guest. Of the orchestra which he found in Adelaide (1938) he said: 'Between the best they can offer and the least that I am prepared to accept there is an unbridgeable gap.' He reconciled himself to the gap, nevertheless, and is considered by Sir Charles Moses, at that time general manager of the Broadcasting Commission, to have coaxed some respectable performances out of them.

Like certain other visiting conductors before and after him, Sargent found himself taking section leaders and other key players from city to city. Outside Sydney and Melbourne there wasn't enough orchestral talent to go round. The extreme instance in 1936 was Brisbane. He was scheduled for a concert in the City Hall: Schubert's 'Unfinished', *The Music Makers*, *Blest Pair of Sirens*, *Barber of Seville* Overture and *The Ride of the Valkyries*. For this he had to import twenty-two players, ten of them from a military band. Flying in from Sydney he rehearsed his disparate particles until, after a fashion, they fused. The process spread over three days. One Schubert phrase he sang illustratively a dozen times over and had it repeated as often by his players. Their twelfth attempt appeased him. 'Lovely, perfectly lovely!' he exclaimed. 'If I can get this effect on the night I shall be satisfied. It's now one o'clock. Shall we go on?' A dozen or two voices promptly shouted 'Yes!' as eager for more as his singers of the Three Valleys. In between orchestral rehearsals he drilled the Brisbane choir—'I've wound you up emotionally,' he told them on the eve of the concert. 'You will sing magnificently'—ate bêche-de-mer soup for the first time, went on an excursion through the bush to a paradisal surf-beach and watched a whale disporting itself inshore. His appearance on the City Hall platform was the signal for cheers. There was even greater clamour at the end. Both ovations were led by his singers and players. It was a night long remembered in Brisbane. The report which Sargent turned in to the Broadcasting Commission (see below) claimed that hard work had ensured 'a good concert'. But he warned that unless additional players of merit were imported and retained it would be impossible to form a sizeable orchestra in Brisbane of acceptable quality.

Transfers and switchings of key players from city to city sometimes entailed the relegating of local first-desk players in favour of more skilled outsiders, a delicate operation which Sargent seems to have managed with diplomacy, leaving no sore heads behind him. In their attitude to visiting Englishmen, especially those with a crisp English accent and manners, Australian musicians were as detached and quizzical as most of their fellow countrymen. For his first Sydney rehearsal he arrived lithe and blithe in a superbly cut suit with the usual buttonhole. Nobody on the band floor had ever before seen a conductor wear a red carnation to rehearsal. Some of the players stared amusedly and said things to each other out of their mouth corners. Across the way from the Piccadilly Arcade, where the rehearsal took place, was the noted Marble Bar. As usual the brass section—most of them remembered as 'old toughies'—went over in a body for a drink at break. On the way they passed a street barrow loaded with toffee apples, Australian version, hard, red and shiny. After the break they reappeared with toffee apples in their buttonholes. Sargent doubled up with laughter. Throughout his life he took jokes at his expense with grace.

From the start, however, he was the disciplinarian. Instruments had to be clean. An elderly tuba player had sprayed his instrument with 'silver frost' to save the trouble of polishing it. 'Good God!' exclaimed Sargent, 'what's that made of? Cardboard?'

Only one clash of a serious kind is recalled. While rehearsing the César Franck symphony in Melbourne he pulled up a hornist and asked for a different nuance. The hornist treated the request with 'dumb' insolence and, when the request was repeated, open insolence. Sargent said quietly: 'I think you'd better go.' The player packed up and went. Sargent's firmness was admired. Again in Melbourne the 7/8 metre in the *Perfect Fool* ballet music went off the rails. He had expected as much. Halting the shambles, he bade his players: 'All say after me: *This is very difficult, this is very difficult.*' Seven syllables to the sentence inured them to seven beats to the bar. They chanted the sentence with delight. Someone coming away from the rehearsal said: 'He's treating them like schoolkids, and they're loving it.' He taught players how to sit—he could be scathing about violinists who played with their legs crossed or slumped against their chair backs—and how, in acknowledging an ovation, to stand up at his signal as one man, making a well-timed bow. He

9*

insisted that all players should be settled in their places, instruments tuned and silent, before he made his entry for rehearsal. (In this respect the discipline which he imposed without much difficulty in Australia sometimes eluded him at home where instrumental moo-ings and twitterings were apt to persist until the moment he picked up his baton.) To say that he was loved by Australian players during his early visits would be to gush. The impression of Sir Charles Moses after thirty years was that he won their respect and admira-tion. It was in later years that these feelings warmed to affection. 'Sargent,' he summed up, 'saw it as his job to get the best from his players. This meant discipline. He did not feel that he should be matey with his players any more than a captain should be matey with his crew. Australians, who are notoriously matey, might have been expected to be irritated by this precise Englishman. They were not. They found in him a painstaking, though never finicky, pro-fessional. Sir Malcolm knew what he wanted from an orchestra, and he got it. Australians admired him for this.'

*

At the end of his 1936 visit Sargent dictated for the Broadcasting Commission a report in which he assessed each of the five State orchestras and drew general conclusions.

He found the Sydney and Melbourne string sections excellent in the main; they had flexibility, tone quality and a sense of 'colour'. This praise did not apply to the double-basses who, not only in these two cities but throughout the Commonwealth, 'do not regard themselves as artists' but simply as men whose job it was to lay an inflexible foundation for the orchestra. In all the orchestras he had met it was desirable that throughout the strings a discreet balance should be kept between the enthusiasm of youth and the experience of age. If and when it came to offering permanent contracts, old string players who were 'dried up musically' should never be engaged save as a last resort, he counselled.

Summarizing his findings Sargent was sanguine about Australia's orchestral future despite the weak areas: horns, oboes and bassoons. There were enough excellent players of these instruments for one orchestra. To find enough for two (presumably in Sydney and

Melbourne) would be difficult. Finding enough for all five State orchestras was, as things then stood, out of the question. The problem could be solved by importing a dozen players or more; but this course, he imagines, would be 'a diplomatic mistake'. The only other way out was to have horn quartets in all States coached by the Broadcasting Commission's crack hornist (presumably Mr. Woolfe of Sydney) and all oboe–bassoon groups by visiting players from England—if any could be found who were free for such work.

The question of importing key orchestral players was one on which the Musicians' Union of Australia might be expected to have well defined views. The matter did not come into open debate until the National Orchestra experiment under Sargent's direction in 1937.

*

The suggestion that a National Orchestra of Australia should be got together by the Broadcasting Commission originated with Sargent and was put by him to Charles Moses. The Commission decided that such an orchestra should be recruited for his 1938 visit and that he should conduct it at three concerts in Sydney town hall. His other nineteen concerts that year were to be with pre-existing State orchestras as before. The project was announced as an 'experiment', nothing more. When it was over key players who had been brought in from other States would go back, happily stimulated, and pass on to their home colleagues any new technical notions or aesthetic verities they had acquired. Another object the Commission may have had in mind was to give Sargent and Sydney's musical public a brief treat by heaping up the best on one plate. The best turned out to be not so much a nationwide creaming off as a merger of Sydney's and Melbourne's top orchestral players. Lionel Lawson, of Sydney and Edouard Lambert, from Melbourne, were co-leaders. After attending two rehearsals a *Morning Herald* writer said that, while the players of each city were out to prove themselves as good as the rest and probably better, their emulation remained healthy and good-natured, with never a hint of rancour. The Commission had been worried lest certain section leaders should feel outraged when called upon to take second place. In the event the players concerned accepted their demotion calmly, even smilingly. The *Herald* writer put this down to Dr. Sargent's 'extraordinary tact'.

The three 'national' concerts that September were billed as a Sargent Festival and as a milestone in Australia's musical history. There were to be a hundred players on the platform. In Sydney, as throughout the Commonwealth, seventy-five or thereabouts had been the limit previously. The Sargent Festival opened with Strauss's *Don Juan* and ended blazingly with the Act III Entry music from *The Mastersingers*. Symphonies played at their three concerts by Malcolm's Hundred, as someone called them, were Beethoven's Fifth, Elgar's No. 2 and Berlioz's *Fantastic*. To these were appended a *Firebird* Suite, Rimsky's *Scheherazade* and two *Lohengrin* preludes as well as standard *Mastersingers* excerpts. Ovations on all three nights reached pandemonium point. They were focused on Malcolm. To most of the crowd in the town hall he meant as much as the composers he was conducting, perhaps a little more. Australian orchestras and choirs looked upon him as 'something heaven-sent', his rehearsals as 'a revelation'. These were his own words in a letter to the Furnesses. His audiences, he added, sat spellbound through the music. Then they *shouted*. To attend a single concert people would travel two hundred miles through the bush. Back home they would tell their neighbours how worth while it had been. All this, with ideal technical conditions—he always had as many rehearsals as he wanted—had been a great incentive to do his best; he had, in fact, never done better work, he concluded. A year later he was quoted as saying that the National Symphony Orchestra's playing had been 'equal to the best in England', a claim which could only be construed as putting it on the same level as the London Philharmonic Orchestra during Beecham's prime.

But the main problem still nagged: how to set up not a single permanent orchestra of high quality but two or more. One way, said Sargent, would be for the Broadcasting Commission to pick promising young players, send them to finishing courses in Europe's musical academies and get them temporary desks in Europe's great orchestras. After two years away they would be under an obligation to return to the Commission's own orchestra as players and teachers.

To stiffen Australia's orchestral ranks with twenty such seasoned players would take perhaps ten years. This was a long time to wait. What was to be done in the meantime?

In an address to The Millions Club, Sydney, Sargent advised the Broadcasting Commission to import at once expert teacher-players from Europe for the horn, oboe, bassoon and viola departments in particular. He added: 'The development of orchestral talent in Australia is being retarded by union regulations which prevent the employment of skilled performers from overseas. Sections of the Sydney orchestra will never achieve the skill of which they are capable so long as union regulations prevent their getting special training on their instruments.' That the Commission should import players had already been advocated by Harty and Szell, the latter remarking that it was precisely through a parallel influx from Europe that great American orchestras had achieved their 'paramount standard' and become self-supporting. Both Harty and Szell, however, had put their ideas forward in private memoranda which did no more than glance at the hostility of the Musicians' Union.

For a conductor to rebuke even covertly the M.U. of his own country is unusual. To rebuke semi-publicly the M.U. of a country at the other side of the world to which he has been invited as a guest conductor smacked of temerity. Yet in the brief shindy that followed Sargent came off without a bruise. A statement put out by the Australian Musicians' Union denied an allegation (made by someone else) that in the case of foreign musicians a five-year residential qualification, as against six months in the case of British subjects, was imposed under Union rules before membership was granted. It was admitted, however, that membership had been denied outright to foreigners during the post-1929 economic crisis. Those years had been endured with bitterness and are talked of by Australia's orchestral veterans to this day. Musicians who had been driven to playing in the streets, for such cases were known, were apt to argue that the new orchestras set up by the Broadcasting Commission should, since they were paid for out of Australian pockets, be the preserve of Australian artists and that foreigners should be refused work permits accordingly.

To what extent this attitude coloured official Union policy is hard to determine thirty years later. A point not publicly canvassed at the time is that during the 1930s the Union discriminated financially in favour of its own; it required of any foreign musician who was granted membership an entrance fee of 20 guineas as compared with £5 from entrants born in Australia. All the plain music lover asked for was the best orchestral talent that he, and through him the Broadcasting Commission, could afford, wherever that talent came from. He might have added that, by keeping down performance standards, narrow protectionism drove customers away from the box office and must ultimately be to the detriment of Australian-born players. Espousing Sargent's address to The Millions Club, a leading article in the *Sydney Morning Herald* contended that Australia could still get many outstanding players from Vienna, Berlin and Munich and branded Union opposition to any but British importees as 'invidious nationalism', an unworthy and deplorable thing.

That Sargent was not caught by the coat tails and dragged into the cogs of a controversy which he helped to publicize is in itself testimony to the special position he had so quickly won in public regard. He could fan a dispute yet remain above it.

*

In one or other of six cities during his pre-war tours he conducted Verdi's Requiem, *Gerontius* (twice), *Belshazzar's Feast* (twice), *Elijah* (three times), *The Creation* and *Hiawatha's Wedding Feast*. As a rule his soloists were meritorious Australians. No glittering names appeared on the hoardings to take the shine from his own. For the Verdi Requiem he found himself saddled with a luckless tenor who had trouble with his upper register, skirted disaster twice and ran into it once. An audience that was listening to Sargent with all its eyes hardly noticed. At the end they joined the choir in 'For he's a jolly good fellow.' Next morning the *Sydney Morning Herald*'s critic reflected that if Sargent's standards could be maintained local choral societies need no longer worry about half-empty houses. Every date would be a sell-out. In Brisbane, working ferociously hard yet buoyantly, he conducted three orchestral

concerts and an *Elijah* in eight days. On *Elijah* alone, taking choir
and orchestra in alternate sessions, he worked for three days at the
rehearsal rostrum or in private with the soloists from ten in the
morning until ten at night. As his tours continued such feats were
repeated all the way along. They left case-hardened experts open
mouthed.

Even Sargent's superhuman energy would not, in the time at his
disposal there and elsewhere, have been fruitful without spade-
workers. The most compelling spadeworker of all lived and reigned
in Melbourne. George English, remembered by old friends as a
'natural' musician, came to prominence in 1931, when he conducted
a choir from the postal institute in Bach's B minor Mass. He was of
dark complexion and had a strikingly saturnine look. When singers
mistimed an entry or were guilty of watery tone, he would rap the
rostrum and stare at them witheringly through steel-rimmed spectacles. In such situations he did not say much or anything. The
stare sufficed. He was the sort of person to whom others automatically pay attention. His singers trembled and thought the world of
him. English was the man chosen by the Broadcasting Commission
to set up and prepare a Sargent Choir, as it was called, of 250 voices
for *Gerontius*. Elgar's oratorio was not unknown in Melbourne.
There had been an indifferent performance of it early in the century
and a good one in 1934 by Bernard Heinze. Many of the singers who
were to serve Sargent were thus singing it for the second time
within a couple of years. Even so, English devoted five months to
working it up. Perhaps he underestimated the psychological stress
that this entailed. Whatever the reason, the singers lined up for
their first rehearsal with Sargent apprehensively. In the first 'Kyrie',
with its alternating full chorus and semi-chorus, they quickly lost
pitch and went on losing it. English was standing by. Some of the
singers glanced at him covertly. The glint behind his steel-rimmed
lenses was almost sinister. They imagined how he would tear them
apart when he had them to himself. Sargent did not interfere. He
let them sing to the end. Then he began talking quietly, not about
pitch, not even about the music, but about the words and the
heights and depths of their beauty.

'Now,' he said after a pause, 'we'll try again.'

At the second attempt the 'Kyrie' went beautifully, with dead-centre pitch. Even George English smiled relief.

Three rehearsal sessions of three hours each on one day ended with the orchestra wilting, for they and Sargent had been at it longest of all. During the last hour he warned the double basses that he was going to beat the orchestral introduction to the Angel's Farewell six quavers to the bar, although the part is written in three crotchets. So they were to watch out. Some of the players were too tired to take in what he was saying. They came in prematurely on his second quaver beat instead of his third. 'Men have been shot for less,' he quipped. The double-basses hadn't a laugh left in them but managed a weary smile. Trying again, they took his beat correctly. His jesting rebuke had got the rehearsal round a psychological corner. On the night, off the platform and on it, everybody was ecstatic. Afterwards the choir took supper as guests of the Broad-casting Commission. When the time came for speeches English referred to the *ad hoc* status of the Sargent Choir.

'Do you want to break up?' he asked.

Two hundred and fifty voices shouted 'No!'

It was George English, again, who prepared *Belshazzar*, which had two performances in successive years. After 'pencilling' the first of these, for 29th September, 1938, Sargent began to hesitate. Might not some of Walton's choral writing prove too tricky for the Melbourne singers? Might it not be too aggressive harmonically and rhythmically for the audience? Some seasons earlier, when Bernard Heinze had introduced Walton's Symphony No. 1 to Melbourne a number of regular concert patrons protested orally or by letter against its 'unintelligibility' with the spluttering indignation proper to people who, having paid for a pleasurable time, fail to see the point. It was being put about that by comparison with *Belshazzar* the symphony was 'kindergarten stuff'. Several months ahead of the concert date he told the Broadcasting Commission that if they, too, had any doubts he would be prepared to substitute some other oratorio. The Commission's music department set his mind at rest. The preliminary rehearsals were going well, they reported. When Sargent took over he found that English had imparted the root of the matter. The performance ended with what had by this time become the standard Sargent ovation, prolonged and thunderous. Whether the audience had the root of the matter in them is, however, another thing. Melbourne's first *Belshazzar* coincided with the signing of the Munich pact. A noon edition of the Melbourne *Argus* with one word, SETTLED! in outsize type on its front page carried inside a third of a column headed TRIUMPH FOR DR. SARGENT. Much other home news had been crowded out. As after the Leeds performance of 1931 the night was described on all hands as 'electrifying', by this time almost a statutory adjective for *Belshazzar*. But in Melbourne the voltage was greater because of the euphoria brought on by the day's news. People thought the nations had been reprieved.

A little earlier the baritone's *quasi recitativo* had sounded in their ears: 'And in the same hour as they feasted came forth the fingers of a man's hand. And the King saw the part of the hand that wrote. And this was the writing that was written: "Mene, mene, tekel, upharsin." ' The King—and others—had been weighed in the balance and found wanting. What most people in Melbourne and most people the world over took for a reprieve was the writing on the wall.

*

Nurtured by various talents, though by none more than Sargent's, something of a concert boom overtook Australian cities. When plans opened for his Sydney concerts and those of other European eminences people would wait an hour or more on three flights of airless stone stairs at the Broadcasting Commission's booking office in Market Street. At the top of the stairs a man and a girl behind a counter coped as best they could, during the boom's early weeks, with a demand for single tickets that far outran the supply. Over 2,000 seats at the town hall were ordinarily set aside for season ticket holders. This left only five hundred seats for people who wanted to attend this concert or that. There were loud grumblings. The Commission replied that but for season ticket sales it would be impossible to arrange for musicians of Sargent's standing to visit Australia at all. Every surviving official who had much to do with Sargent's early seasons testifies that no other visiting conductor at that time could compete with him in the art of 'pulling people in'. Other batons may have been his equal musically. But, in the words of Charles Moses, 'he made music *look* great as well as sound great.' As a result he was the object of something like mass infatuation or, at all events, a middle-class one. To see his tails, carnation and smile, to nudge each other admiringly at the ceremonial precision with which he took his 'calls' and had others on the platform take theirs: for such felicities as well as for what they were going to hear more people travelled greater distances than they had for any other performer except Nellie Melba.

Before he was halfway through his 1936 tour a 'Keep Sargent' movement developed. As in the case of the B.B.C., the Commonwealth's Broadcasting Commission worked under the Postmaster General's authority. Was the P.M.G. aware, asked the Leader of the Opposition during a Senate session in Canberra, that a considerable volume of opinion in Australia favoured retaining Dr. Sargent and that representations had been made to this effect to the Broadcasting Commission? The Postmaster General, while mentioning that such matters were determined without ministerial sanction, promised to look into it. Negotiations with Sargent had, in fact, already begun. On the day of his first *Gerontius* there he attended a meeting of the Commission's managerial board in Melbourne. He was asked whether he would consider extending his current tour (1936) for some weeks. He replied regretfully that this was out of the question and showed them his diary. Due to sail from Fremantle on 2nd November for uncancellable concert in London on the 30th. Five *Messiahs* to conduct up and down the country before Christmas. Total of sixty other concerts before the end of May. Diary entries included even the times of the trains he was to catch. Pressed by Charles Moses for future tours of not less than four and up to five months, he promised that as soon as he got home he would see what could be done about shedding some of his commitments in the Commission's favour. Upon this assurance the board adjourned to the town hall and heard his *Gerontius* as a body.

In the end he declined the invitation for 1937. Coming back in 1938 and 1939 he gave Australia in these two visits an aggregate of thirty-two weeks. In a letter to Charles Moses he stressed that he

was in wholehearted agreement with the Commission's policy and
judged they had it in their power 'to make Australia very definitely
of supreme importance in the world of music.' He dreamed aloud
of clearing seats from the town hall floors of Sydney and Melbourne
for Promenade concerts on Queen's Hall lines at which Prommers
would pay a shilling a head for complete cycles of the Brahms and
Beethoven symphonies. With the blessing of the outlying mayors
concerned, he took the Sydney orchestra into industrial suburbs.
Were the proletariat ripe for symphonic music? Had middle-class
infatuation begun to percolate down? His first 'industrial concert'
was in Marrickville town hall. There were many empty seats. One
possible reason for the poor attendance is touched on below. As to
its main items, Tchaikovsky's *Pathétique* and Poulenc's two-piano
concerto, the programme was identical with one which had packed
Sydney town hall and set it aroar five nights earlier. It must not
be overlooked that all the time he was reaching potential as well as
actual music lovers over the air. In 1932–33 the Commission had
started off with a perhaps a million and a half regular listeners.
In the year we have reached (1939) the figure stood at four and a
half millions and was rising sharply. In 1967, the year of his last
visit, the total was over nine millions and took in the bulk of Australia's population. As in all countries classical music had a low
listener-rating. But those who listened regularly were without
doubt a cultural spearhead. The procedure worked out for the
1938 and later tours was that he should conduct roughly the
same programmes in Melbourne and Sydney, the first half of
each concert being broadcast from one city, the second from the
other, or vice-versa, with three other State capitals completing the
pattern.

*

One reason for the empty seats at Marrickville was that people who
might have sat in them preferred to stay indoors alongside their
radio sets for more important matters. The war was a month old.
In Marrickville what Hitler was up to had greater impact than
Tchaikovsky and Poulenc. Sargent had been in the country since
18th July. The third of September had found him in Melbourne,

the guest at Government House of the Governor-General and Lady Gowrie. He had arranged that night to attend a charity film gala. With other English notables he was asked to appear on the stage and say a patriotic word or two. He complied briskly, though with a heavy heart. As he recalled years later, there was a complete blanket on news from England. Had the bombing begun? In his mind's eye he pictured the Albert Hall a smoking ruin. Four months earlier he had conducted a *Gerontius* there, part of the London Music Festival backed by the B.B.C., with 900 choice and superbly trained voices from the Royal Choral Society and his choirs in Huddersfield, Bradford and Croydon. Toscanini had been there. At the end, overwhelmed by the beauty of the score and its performance, he had embraced Sargent. Would he ever conduct *Gerontius* in the Albert Hall again? Would there be an Albert Hall to conduct in? One comforting thought: if anything hideous had happened to London it was unlikely that Eileen and the children would have been involved. Before leaving England in June he had seen Lord Horder, now a close friend. Horder had promised that the moment war seemed imminent he would see them evacuated to the country. Thinking of this, he shrugged off his gloom. Two nights later he conducted his second Melbourne *Belshazzar*. This may have been the concert at which somebody suggested he should repeat the National Anthem at the end. He declined on the ground that to play it once more, having opened the concert with it, would merely remind the audience of external stresses and strains of which they had been temporarily relieved. He added later that German music 'can give us relief and escape from our emotional burdens as surely as British music or any other sort of music can, so long as it is good music'. This is a point he elaborated several times. During the last days of futile peace negotiation he had conducted music by Mendelssohn, Brahms and Haydn, Elgar, Delius and Vaughan Williams before two thousand schoolchildren. 'Look at your programmes,' he had told his audience. 'You will see that, by a happy coincidence, three of the six composers we are hearing today spoke English and three spoke German, one of the three being Austrian, another a German Jew. God forbid that on account of nationality anybody should think Elgar a better composer than Brahms or Brahms a better composer than Elgar—or forget that in music all these great men spoke a common language.'

In speaking up for music of 'enemy origin'—which had come under a wrongheaded though partial ban in Britain during the Kaiser's war—Sargent spontaneously took a line which was being taken uncollusively by most musicians outside Nazi or Nazi-controlled territories. The declaration of war caught him midway through a schedule of over a hundred performances, one half of which—by far the weightier half—were of German and Austrian classics. Neither he nor anybody else thought for a moment of taking the German and Austrian pieces out and putting English, French and Polish compositions in. 'We disapproved forcibly,' he said, 'when Hitler suppressed music and poetry written by Jews. Why should we be barbarous, too? Haydn and Beethoven had nothing to do with this war. To deny ourselves the solace that, say, the music of Richard Strauss can give would be cutting off our noses to spite our faces.'

*

Although he supposed Eileen and the children to be safe, he strained for home. With the war only three days old the Melbourne *Argus* mused that if his plans for the future were knocked askew by the international situation it might be that England's loss would turn out to be Australia's gain. 'Music lovers hope,' added the article, 'that if the crisis permits it the Broadcasting Commission will sponsor additional performances of British choral works under Dr. Sargent's direction.' The Keep Sargent campaign was on again. On the day this appeared or soon afterwards the Broadcasting Commission asked him: 'Will you consider signing a new contract and staying on in Australia indefinitely? There'll be no difficulty about your family. We'll bring them out to stay with you in safety.'

Sargent thanked the Commission but said 'No'.

It was now his turn to put a question. 'May I,' he asked, 'be released from my remaining commitments here'—sixteen concerts—'and may I go home by the first available transport?'

He was told with regret that the balance of the contract must be honoured.

Sailings and civilian passages had been so diverted or curtailed by war exigencies that he could not in any case have hoped to get away by the end of October as he had originally planned. With droves more in like case he put his name down for the first available air flight and occupied himself with concerts in aid of the Red Cross. He conducted two of these, one in Sydney town hall, the other at Government House, Melbourne. At the Sydney concert, after conducting such back-straightening or ennobling pages as the *Cockaigne* Overture, the *Enigma* Variations and Sibelius's *Finlandia*, he turned round and told the audience to their joy that the evening had raised over £1,000. This was the occasion when somebody put up his baton for auction, raising another £108. People went home feeling grim and gay. Few had paid scholarly attention to the music. It was not a night for either scholars or connoisseurs. But backstage a woman struggled through a congratulatory mob. 'Thank you,' she called as soon as within earshot, 'for the *Enigma*, especially the "Nimrod" part. It makes Hitler look *silly*.' Then she struggled back the way she had come.

*

His flight voucher came through a few days later. He reached London on 27th November, 1939, by a devious, strategically-dictated route in dangerously bad weather. The day was a Monday. A week the following Wednesday he conducted his first orchestral concert in wartime England. The orchestra was the London Philharmonic; place the Central Hall; starting time 12.30 p.m. He began with some Handel–Harty and went on to the Serenade for Strings. While these numbers were afoot the audience steadily grew as people dribbled in for lunch break from the offices and shops of Westminster. Some brought sandwiches and ate them while listening. Many smoked. There were arms around waists, heads leaning against shoulders. By one o'clock, when he started on the César Franck symphony, the audience was quiet and fairly stable. Except between movements the doors stayed shut.

Barrage balloons hung ponderingly in the London sky that day. In Western Europe real war had not begun. There was a faintly nightmarish sense of waiting for and wanting it. There was a sense, also, that the world and the people in it had in some way changed. Music making and some of its incidentals were among the things which, for worse or better, would never again be quite as everybody had known them.

CHAPTER TWENTY-ONE

THE 'BLITZ' TOUR

CALL-UP, EVACUATION and the black-out paralysed public music-making for a while. But music was a public need; and the need had to be met. Orchestras which had been thrown into disarray picked themselves up and set about earning what was at first a meagre living. Evening concerts continuing under ban, afternoon ones took their place on Saturdays and Sundays; and on weekdays there was lunchtime music of quality in London and other cities. In the West the 'real' war was yet to begin. During the last month or two of the war's 'phoney' phase Sargent began to busy himself with the London Philharmonic Orchestra, newly become a self-governing body and soon, through Beecham's departure for America, to be without a permanent conductor. In London and the provinces he did twenty or thirty concerts with them in the first half of 1940. His fee from the L.P.O. at this time and for some seasons after was twenty pounds a concert, a big come-down from what Australia had paid him. But he was not the man to think wistfully on such things, especially in an embattled Britain. The war was his cause, music his mission. In his mind the two things went together. They were not going together as fruitfully as he could have wished, however. He sensed in the country a stronger and wider appetite for the classics than had ever been known before. But music was not being presented on the scale or with the sort of flourish it deserved.

One day in late spring after the 'real' war had begun and France was crumbling his telephone rang. A voice said this was Jack Hylton, and would Dr. Sargent be interested in taking the London Philharmonic Orchestra out on the road for twice-nightly concerts in variety theatres up and down the country, playing classical music all the way—not all of it *too* heavy, of course? The idea was that the L.P.O. should fill the bill in every town. There was no question of sharing the show with conjurers and red-nosed comics. The voice had a north country accent and wasted no words. Sargent warmed to it. He replied that, yes, he was very interested, and when could they start? He had never met Hylton but knew of him as a highly successful dance-band leader whose music, it was true, he no more cared for than for that of dance bands generally. What he did not yet know was that Hylton, the son of a Bolton millhand, had taught himself to play the piano when a child. At twelve he had begun earning his keep as singer-pianist with a pierrot troupe and had once been a cinema organist. A year or two older than he, Hylton dabbled later in opera, ballet and Shakespeare and promoted extremely prosperous 'musicals' in the West End and elsewhere. Before speaking with Sargent he had had meetings with Thomas Russell, the L.P.O.'s new business manager and the committee of management. In the provinces, it seemed, variety theatres were as much in need of talent as orchestral players were of concert dates. The 1940 Hylton tour, a model for those of later wartime seasons, was planned to cover ten cities, the first city on the list being Glasgow, where the Empire theatre was booked for the six days beginning 12th August. The nine other cities were: Manchester, Liverpool, Birmingham, Coventry, Newcastle, Leeds, Bradford, Edinburgh and Sheffield. Who should be the principal conductor? Several names came up at the early conclaves and were rejected, after a quick review, in favour of Sargent, not because his musicianship clearly outrivalled that of all others but because of his 'svelte figure, incisive manner and conscious showmanship . . . the enthusiasm he so easily displays and arouses, [his knack of making] audiences feel at once that they are in for a good time and [his introductory talks from the rostrum], which created a favourable atmosphere for the music that follows.'* Another point that weighed was Sargent's exceptional efficiency, his ability to think out beforehand the endless detail entailed by a fourteen-weeks tour in what amounted to circumstances of emergency. Russell added that where other conductors left much to chance and often seemed

* *Philharmonic Decade* by Thomas Russell (Hutchinson), 1945.

blandly unaware of detailed responsibilities, Sargent systematized everything in a practical way, saving time and trouble for all concerned. With him as assistant conductor went Basil Cameron who, as the schedule worked out, usually relieved him on Fridays and Saturdays. Eric Coates, too, sometimes gave a hand, conducting programmes of his own light music from the *Three Bears* suite to the *Knightsbridge* March and *Summer Days*. Two concerts daily, making twelve a week, was not the L.P.O.'s absolute ceiling. Occasionally a third concert starting at 1 p.m. was superimposed on those beginning at 3.30 p.m. and 5.45 p.m., bringing the week's total to thirteen, fourteen or more. (See Appendix Four.) Sargent's preternatural energy would have been equal to the entire schedule if his engagement book had not divided his attention both on this tour and a later one between the L.P.O. and other promotions and loyalties. By this time he was installed as conductor-in-chief and musical adviser to the Hallé Orchestra, Manchester, a post which he had accepted before leaving for Australia in 1939. The following season witnessed the beginnings of a wartime and postwar association with the Liverpool Philharmonic Society's orchestra which, under his direction, was to acquire national ranking and something like international prestige. By Christmas 1940 he had brought the Royal Choral Society out of the brief hibernation forced upon it by evacuation and other disruptions; and he contrived to put in as many spick and span appearances as ever with his Huddersfield, Bradford and other choirs. But all this was not enough. With the 'real' war little more than a year old he began regular guest performances with what came to be known as the B.B.C.'s Brains Trust, extemporizing comments running to scores of thousands of words on topics ranging from boomerang throwing, whether Caruso's voice really did shatter wineglasses and the funny feeling a water divining rod gives when it starts jerking in your hands (one had jerked in his) to the status of trade unions under nationalization, stock-exchange 'gambling', the future of small businesses and Christian faith considered as a 'cradle gift'. Of these side lines or main lines more will be said. For the moment it is enough, perhaps, to say that during 1942, his first full year as a Brains Trust oracle, with over 13,000,000 listeners in this country alone attending to his every syllable and sentiment, he con-

ducted on his own calculation* the equivalent of one symphony or
choral concert a day; all this, so far as the public could see, without
fluster or fret and certainly without mental tarnish. Nor did he depend on nostrums. Those who were close to him report that he never
took so much as an aspirin tablet.

*

Jack Hylton excelled at publicity among other things. No sooner did
the Twice Nightly Tour (later renamed the Blitz Tour) begin than
the entire country seemed aware of it despite graver matters
that weighed on all minds. Parading Beethoven, Tchaikovsky and
even Bach (for Sargent's arrangement of the Air for the G string was
not overlooked) where Robey and Lauder, Tilley and Little Tich or
their emulators had trod was, according to all the peacetime rules,
asking for box office trouble on a massive scale. But these, like so
many other peacetime rules, had been mysteriously superseded. At
Buckingham Palace Sargent was received in audience by the Queen.
On his assuring her that none but good music, 'Grieg to Beethoven',
would be played she wished the venture every success. On the Sunday
the orchestra were due to leave for Glasgow there was a final rehearsal
in the concert hall of the Royal College of Music. It was a sunny,
sweltering day; one of the vital early days of the Battle of Britain,
with anti-aircraft guns keeping up a greater thunder than had been
heard before and air fights spreading to the capital. Towards the end
of the day news came in of enemy fighters shot down in vast numbers.
The night train from King's Cross got the orchestra to Glasgow at
breakfast time. It had not been possible to send anyone ahead to fix
accommodation. The players scattered to seek lodgings individually
or in groups, instrument case in one hand, suitcase in the other. Each
man had with him as well as a tailcoat two dress shirts and two white
ties which by the end of the week had toned to off-grey. That afternoon the curtain rose for the first house with the seventy players in
position and ready-tuned on a rostrum with ceiling and side flats
which had been specially built to correct the acoustics of open stages.
Their first programme that day was: *Carnaval Romain* (Berlioz),
The Londonderry Air, Tchaikovsky's *Romeo and Juliet* fantasy, the

* Quoted by Berta Geissmar in *Baton and Jackboot* (Hamish Hamilton), 1944.

William Tell overture, the *Carmen* prelude, *Tales from the Vienna Woods* (J. Strauss) and *Finlandia*. Before the interval Eileen Joyce appeared in a pretty dress and played two or three pianoforte *soli*, as the bills spelled them. 'Why not *solos*?' asked a wag in the *Glasgow Herald*. '*Soli* is no doubt more elegant, but it will cause bewilderment somewhere about the fourth row of the gallery.'

Complete sets of programmes for this time are hard to come by, but the specimens already quoted may be taken as typical. What may be called 'fringe' pieces included as well as the *Blue Danube* Waltz and *Tales from the Vienna Woods*, the *Rhapsody in Blue* of Gershwin and Ravel's *Bolero*, both of which Sargent showed some disinclination to conduct, and the *Poet and Peasant* and *Morning Noon and Night* overtures of Suppé. In his preparatory talks Sargent made much of the Suppé items. He would slap the score and say of *Poet and Peasant*, for example: 'This work has been played on everything from the mouth organ to the Mighty Wurlitzer. At last you're going to hear it as the composer wrote it!' Against this it was contended by old orchestral hands that Sargent presented not authentic Suppé but inflations and adaptations intended for small ensembles. Symphonies on the 1940 tour were, or included: Beethoven, Nos. 5 and 7, Tchaikovsky, Nos. 4, 5 and 6, Schubert's No. 5 and the 'Unfinished', and Dvořák's 'New World'. Overtures, suites and miscellaneous numbers ventured as far as Rimsky's *Scheherazade*, the *Irmelin* prelude, Beethoven's *Egmont* and *Leonora* No. 2, *Casse-noisette* and the *Boutique Fantasque*. Much play was made with martial numbers such as *Finlandia*, the 1812 Overture, *Pomp and Circumstance* No. 1, *The Ride of the Valkyries* and Berlioz's *Rakoczy* and *Trojan* marches. What he gave the ten 'twice-nightly' cities had much of the old Sargent ring, in short, and did not depart in any sensational way from what he had been giving to his audiences in Australia.

The Glasgow concerts were a sell-out and drew 30,000 people, which was said to be record business for the theatre. Sargent was in a state of brisk, approving glee. The seating in most variety theatres, he told an interviewer, was more comfortable than in most concert halls; he hoped 'twice-nightly' tours had come to stay. In one theatre a stage hand said to him, 'You know, Doc, you're going over real big. Your only rival in the music halls is George Formby.' This he quoted

with a satisfaction deeper than pride, for it seemed to support a
quasi-mystical conviction of his that the stresses and sorrows of war
were enabling fine music to sink into simple hearts which had up to
then been impervious to it. Working-class men and women hearing
symphonic music for the first time had, he insisted, been 'greatly
impressed'. He cited the case of a fifteen-year-old boy in the Manchester Palace gallery. He had gone there because he always went to
the Palace on Monday night. Expecting the usual string of variety
turns, he had been so delighted by Sargent and the L.P.O. that he
returned every night for the rest of the week. 'For the first time,'
Sargent triumphed, 'hundreds of humble galleryites normally entertained by conjurers, contortionists and red-nosed comedians will
listen for an hour to heaven-sent music.' What in peacetime had
seemed a luxury entertainment for the cultured few proved in wartime to be 'a necessity, a really refreshing food for the ordinary man
and woman in the street'.

In the opinion of certain other observers, many people went to
hear the L.P.O. in 1940 for a more prosaic reason. As music-hall
'regulars' and victims of habit they were prepared, for want of a
palatable alternative, to put up even with symphonic music. Few of
these pretended that Sargent did what Lauder and Marie Lloyd had
done for them. In Edinburgh one Saturday, after the Largo of the
New World symphony, an old woman in a shawl found the cor anglais
lament too much for her and shouted down from the front row of
the gallery, 'Play something cheery!' Sargent good-humouredly
shouted back that she'd find the next movement cheery enough. She
wasn't there to confirm this, having been invited to leave.

The orchestral boom that began to develop during the Battle of
Britain undoubtedly responded in part to genuine new musical urges.
Certainly it was naïve though creditable in Sargent to hope, as he
once did over the air (New York to Australia, 'Transpacific Call',
1st June, 1945), that after the war music and the other great arts
would bind people and nations together through their mutual love
of the beautiful and make them so understand one another that war
would end and peace prevail for ever. Yet musical taste and even
modest musical scholarship were cropping up in the most unexpected places. Travelling from one Lancashire town to another the

orchestra found their concert cancelled because bomb blast had damaged the roof of the hall and snow was melting on to the platform in cascades. Sargent took two committee men for drinks into a modest public house. A man in overalls and muffler, ready for late shift on some engineering floor, paused with a pint of beer halfway to his mouth and asked, 'Are you Dr. Sargent?' When told this was so he entered upon a knowledgeable analysis of Beethoven's Symphony No. 7 as conducted by Dr. Sargent in a B.B.C. broadcast. Some of Dr. Sargent's *tempi* did not please him at all. Why should he (and certain other conductors, for that matter) make every *diminuendo* an excuse for a *rallentando*? Sargent listened courteously, spoke of how conductors were apt to feel their way more deeply into the classics after years of experience, and congratulated his critic on his familiarity with a masterpiece. The critic shook him by the hand, finished his pint and made off.

This Lancashire date had been scheduled among consecutive 'one-night stands' that were inserted between the orchestra's Monday-to-Saturday runs on their twice-nightly list. It was not the only 'one-night stand' which ran into trouble that entailed cancellation or late starts. Once the instrument van got hopelessly misrouted and couldn't be found. On the Lancashire moors Sargent's motor-car stuck in a snowdrift. The day after two motor-coaches with the orchestra on board were fogbound for hours. In towns crammed with blitz evacuees from other districts the players slept in station waiting-rooms or the floors of the town hall where they had played.

If Sargent selflessly scurried all over the country and worked like one possessed, the same or more could be said of his players, who incurred certain hardships which he was spared. As well as hunting for lodgings (during the first variety tour only, at any rate; later on an accommodation-fixer went ahead), they had to pay for these out of their earnings: seven pounds or seven pounds ten for 'back desks', eight pounds five for sub-principals and as little as nine pounds ten for principals. After the last house on Saturday they would pile at midnight or later into a train for London, however far away London might be; for, under a contract negotiated with Harold Holt before the war, the L.P.O. were responsible for a Sunday afternoon series at the Royal Albert Hall and feared that if they broke the contract some other orchestra, probably the London Symphony, would step in. Sometimes a saloon coach was booked for the orchestra. Invariably they found it full of snoring soldiers. If there were no serious delays on the way owing to raids or troop movements they reached London in time for breakfast at eating places in Upper Regent Street and ten o'clock rehearsal at the Queen's Hall. They would converge on the Albert Hall after a midday meal which some were lucky enough to snatch at home. For the Albert Hall concerts they changed into 'morning' suits. Wardrobe niceties, including the laundering of dress shirts and ties, were exasperating but, for boiler-suited warworkers in the top gallery, part of the show and value for money. The Albert Hall concerts brought in an extra two or three pounds a week for most of the players. Certain Sundays later in the war are incredulously remembered when they squeezed in a second concert in the early evening at a Golders Green cinema before catching the midnight train for whatever provincial city came next on the list.

Of the ten cities on Hylton's music-hall round in 1940 or later, six —Birmingham, Liverpool, Coventry, Glasgow, Manchester and Sheffield—were, as ports or armament centres, priority targets for the Luftwaffe. In these six cities and their environs nearly 11,000 civilians were killed by the spring of 1941 in night raids by forces of up to five hundred bombers. As guest conductor at this period with the Liverpool Philharmonic Society and as conductor-in-chief and musical advisor to the Hallé Orchestra, Manchester, an appointment of which more will be said, Sargent had many additional calls to the north-western sector of what came to be known as Britain's Front Line. Excitements came his way which, in general, are difficult to date and place after nearly thirty years partly because, in the tumult of the times, some musical archives were neglected, others destroyed, others again dispersed.

It is known, however, that he was in Manchester on 22nd December, 1940, and witnessed the first of two severe raids on consecutive nights. An hour or two after he had conducted a Hallé *Messiah* enemy parachute flares lighted up the city like day. Then the massed drone of bombers was heard. Their main mission was to burn the city out. Showers of incendiary bombs came down all night. Sargent joined firewatchers on the roof of the Midland Hotel and kicked fire bombs down into the street as they landed. Not all the city's buildings were similarly patrolled and protected. Empty shop and office blocks became monstrous torches. To these were added one torch more monstrous still, for it was not fed by tangible wealth alone. A few hundred yards away the Free Trade Hall slowly flamed its heart out. Next day only the outer walls were standing. The inside was a mould of smoking rubble. This did not mean an immediate musical privation. The hall had been closed to the public as an air raids precaution on the outbreak of the war. Sargent's *Messiah* the previous night had been sung in a 'super-cinema'. In a longer view the situation was disquieting. The Hallé Orchestra was destined to be a nomad and short-term lodger for eleven years in the city which had bred it.

Twice that winter when on northern rostrums he heard bombs explode and shrapnel from anti-aircraft guns pelt the roof while the smell of burning buildings snaked in from across the road. On one of these occasions he warned the audience that they and he and the theatre might all be blown sky-high. But, he added, there were certain things that would last for ever. 'This,' he said, picking up the score of Beethoven's Symphony No. 7, 'is one of them.' Beethoven's music was indestructible. What better could they do than play and listen to it now? Sargent once asserted of that night's Seventh that no orchestra had ever played so well and that no audience in his experience had ever listened so 'intensely'.

When shrapnel from anti-aircraft batteries was raining upon pitchblack streets and surface shelters were the only ones within reach, audiences usually stayed on, with official approval, in the relative safety of public auditoriums or their cellars until the 'All Clear' went at one or two in the morning. Staying on with them, Sargent and the orchestra would begin a second concert when the first one ended. This meant a new programme; it would have been poor psychology to submit the public again to the pieces they had just heard. While the librarian was sorting out new band parts and distributing them among the stands the orchestra would play light classical pieces from memory, sometimes with their leader taking a relief turn on the rostrum. They called this busking. As had been seen at the children's concerts, individual players shrank from standing up in public and playing anything without the 'copy', but when all seventy were in it together the case was different. During these busking interludes the audience occasionally felt they should have a say in what was to be played. One night there were calls for *The Blue Danube.*

'But I don't know it,' objected Sargent. There were jocose encouragements from players such as: 'We know it.' 'We'll play. You follow us!' Sargent preferred to send across to his hotel for the score and turn his baton in the meantime to something else. The truth is that he was always chary of conducting from a blank desk.

*

During these years he was for ever shuttling between the North or the Midlands and London. In pinched, frustrating times his comings and goings were charmed and privileged. A jargon phrase current in Whitehall distinguished between Very Important Persons and the rest. In the matter of wartime travel Sargent was high among the V.I.P.s. He could always be sure of a 'sleeper' for over-night railway journeys. Always he was carried to and from his concerts in a hired limousine, often driven by the same chauffeur. As in peacetime he wore a red carnation during the day, a white one at night. Even if he had not been doing the work of two men or more, nobody would have grudged him these comforts and trappings; they had come to be expected of him; they were an applauded part of the Sargent 'show'.

Many of his visits to London had to do with the Royal Choral Society. His determination to bring the Society into action again met at first with little but long faces. Hundreds out of the choir's strength of nearly a thousand had left London. Everybody's address seemed to have changed. Nobody knew where anybody was. As seen at R.C.S. headquarters the difficulties seemed insurmountable. It was decided, however, to attempt a *Messiah* at Christmas (1940). The appointed day was a Saturday; place, the Queen's Hall. An advertisement was printed well in advance asking as many members of the Society as possible to attend a rehearsal at twelve noon on the day of the concert. Pessimists said it was a forlorn hope. They were wrong. Two hundred and fifty singers who had seen the

10

advertisement or heard about it turned up in good time. Their voices were rather rusty, in Sargent's phrase. In soft passages they tended to go flat, in loud passages they were coarse rather than brilliant. Having sung *Messiah* under him twice a year for anything up to fifteen years, they knew the score inside out. So, instead of taking them through choruses, he dismissed the orchestra and had the choir practise unison scales for three quarters of an hour. Then he packed them off to lunch with a warning not to take the bloom off their voices by talking too much. The concert began at 2.30 p.m. By this time another fifty singers had signed on. In the end there were three hundred singers on the platform, as many as the Queen's Hall could comfortably take. 'Packed house, wonderful performance,' said Sargent on the morrow.

An incidental reason that prompted Sargent to do what he could to revive choralism did as much credit to his heart as to his head. Most English solo singers of note had depended largely on oratorio and, in lesser degree, on grand opera for their livelihood. The onset of war brought both forms or media to a dead halt. Given the spirit and social flux of the times it did not seem altogether certain that much would be heard of either again. It seems to have been in response to an approach by out-of-work singers that Sargent engineered his Christmas *Messiah* and certain other choral productions that soon followed it. When the day came for his first wartime performance of the B minor Mass, for which three hundred and fifty members of the Royal Choral Society mustered, he tested their alertness at rehearsal by instructing the organist *not* to give them the note at the beginning. Then he said: 'I'm going to depend on you entirely. Take your courage in both hands. I want you to sing the chord of B minor out of your heads.' The chord with which they responded was tested on the rehearsal piano. Every note was dead centre. . . . And so to a historic *Dream of Gerontius*.

On the afternoon of 10th May, 1941, he conducted this at the Queen's Hall with the R.C.S. and, as soloists, Muriel Brunskill, Webster Booth and Ronald Stear. A moonlit night followed. For five hours waves of Nazi bombers showered incendiaries and high explosive on the heart of the capital. Many famous buildings were hit—Westminster Abbey, the Tower of London, the Royal Mint, the War Office and the British Museum among them. But two were completely destroyed. One was the House of Commons debating chamber, the other the Queen's Hall. Sargent visited what remained of the latter two mornings later. Within a ring of calcined walls he noted eerie details. In what had been the dress circle there were thousands of seat springs from burnt-out chairs. Where the organ had stood there were stumps and lumps of melted organ pipes. After *Gerontius* many members of the London Philharmonic Orchestra, in expectation of a rehearsal there the following morning, had left their instruments in the band room, now a squalid refuse dump, with here the carcase of a double-bass fiddle and the stringless remnants of a harp, there a buckled kettledrum with a set of cymbals nearby which would sound no more. (During the next month or two the L.P.O. were overwhelmed by personal callers, telephone messages and letters [there were three thousand of these] offering replacements as gifts or on loan or for sale—enough instruments, after the best had been selected, to meet the needs not only of the L.P.O. but also of prisoner-of-war camps, to which many were sent through the Red Cross.)

The last words sung in the Queen's Hall had been the Angel's 'Farewell, but not for ever! Be brave and patient on thy bed of sorrow; Swiftly shall pass thy night of trial here, And I will come and wake thee on the morrow!' To which chorus and semi-chorus had responded with an Amen that swelled, then softened out of hearing though never from the memory of some who were there. For Sargent the music and the poetry were in mystical accord with the day and its morrow; they presaged that after anguish all would come well. Although his body stayed unscarred by the blitz, he had not gone untouched in other ways. His house had been blasted by high explosive. Afterwards he had seen the mangled body of a neighbour dug from the dusty chaos that had been her home. It had taken the rescue squad three days to reach her. But in Newman and Elgar lay an abiding answer to many questions and salve for much pain. Or so he thought when he had a moment to stop and think.

CHAPTER TWENTY-TWO

LIVERPUDLIAN

AFTER HIS Kensington house had been blasted he found himself new quarters a mile or so to the east in Chesham-place: smallish bed-sitting room, bathroom and very small kitchen in a stylish block of flats. Eileen had gone to live in the Buckinghamshire village of Denham, away from the blitz zone. Sargent had sent much of his music library there for safety. Peter was at Eton; Pamela, as has been said, an evacuee at finishing school in Devonshire. It would have been possible, say those who remember it, to put the entire Chesham-place flat inside his music room at 9 Albert Hall Mansions. The bed-sitting room had two divans flanking a circular table at which he and his secretary did their work. There was no piano. The kitchen, of a kind known as 'kitchenette', became his working library. Shelves intended for pots and pans were stacked with 'current' scores and others scheduled for some months ahead. Never so much as a cup of tea was brewed there. Breakfast came up from the restaurant below where, occasionally, he ate during the day. For much of the week and in the aggregate for half the year or more, he was the better part of two hundred miles away from Chesham-place.

For a while Manchester (the Hallé Orchestra) and Liverpool (the Philharmonic Society) shared his services. In the beginning Manchester, where he made his Hallé début with the B minor Mass in January 1935, had more of his time and reacted touchily when he identified himself with other orchestras, especially 'interloping' ones. As well as an orchestra the Hallé Concerts Society had a choir and Manchester itself a choral tradition that ran deep. The difficulty with traditions that run deep is that they are apt to disappear from

sight and mind. For decades Manchester had supported with ease
two *Messiahs* a year on consecutive nights at the Free Trade Hall.
But something resembling a choral slump was at hand. A time came
in the mid-1930s when the year's second *Messiah* entailed 'ghastly'
financial failure. The oratorio had to be relegated to a single date.
With Sargent's coming, however, that single date took on new
moment and lustre. In a season when Henry Wood conducting the
Verdi Requiem only half filled the house and Beecham in a typical
Haydn-Rimsky programme lost hundreds, Sargent's *Messiah* made
a profit of £267.* His repertory in Manchester had fairly wide span.
While dealing liberally in box office certainties—Beethoven and
Tchaikovsky, Wagner and Brahms—he conducted also much
Sibelius, Elgar and Debussy, revived *A Song of the High Hills* and
Sea Drift, and put himself down, or let others put him down, for
several more recondite things (as Manchester then considered
them), including the Walton Symphony. This latter (1938) drew a
meagre audience: no fault, it would seem, of Sargent's but rather the
sort of thing that happens when programme-planners take an over-
sanguine view of majority taste and listening habits. About the
personality and musicianship of Sargent majority taste had no doubt
at all; he was greatly to its liking. And he was greatly to the liking
of Hallé committee men. Hamilton Harty had left Manchester in
1933. For six years the Hallé was in the hands of guest conductors,
Sargent among them. It occurred to some of them at last that it
might be no bad thing to ask Sargent to become conductor-in-
chief.

To ask was not, of course, to have. In a memorandum to his
fellow executive members Philip Godlee, later the Society's extremely able chairman, pointed out that if Sargent accepted it the
job would involve residence in Manchester; and Sargent had too
many irons in the fire to permit of that. 'I doubt,' he added, 'whether
Manchester could ever be his chief interest. The conductor of the
Hallé Orchestra should not spend half his life in railway trains.' The

---

* For this and much else about Sargent's relations with Manchester I have
drawn upon Michael Kennedy's admirable *The Hallé Tradition*: *A Century of
Music*, Manchester University Press, 1960.

truth was that Sargent did not mind trains in the least; overnight sleepers had become so much a part of his life that he might have felt in mild disarray if deprived of them. The executive committee plucked up courage and made their offer. To the surprise of a few and the delight of everybody, he accepted. His appointment was announced early in 1939. He took over as conductor-in-chief on returning from Australia late that year and stayed until the end of the 1941–42 season.

To what extent did he feel himself committed? In private he made it clear, as Godlee had surmised he would, that he could never regard the Hallé as his first professional charge. Apparently the title of 'permanent conductor' was tentatively mentioned to him at one point. He would have nothing to do with it. Before the war he had conducted up to eleven out of the Hallé's twenty concerts in Manchester. At the end he was taking not more than eighteen out of twenty-four; this because of 'other irons in the fire'. Some of these irons were noted jealously. During his twice-nightly tour for Hylton he brought the London Philharmonic Orchestra to the Hallé's very doorstep and also, an equally grave matter, to Liverpool, long a preserve of Manchester orchestral players. Twice in 1940, by letter or by deputation, the Hallé players complained to a sympathetic executive committee that their chief conductor's close connection with and propaganda for the L.P.O. were calculated to damage Hallé interests. Sargent lost no time in meeting the committee and the players. At a joint meeting he gave assurances, talked everybody round, charmed birds off trees.

In helping the orchestra through its material difficulties he was ardent and outspoken. For want of a sizeable and suitable concert hall the Hallé played throughout his tenure on Sunday afternoons in such theatres and cinemas as happened to be rentable. One such theatre was the Opera House, Quay Street. When, in 1942, the Opera House management declined further 'lets', Sargent told his last audience there that if Manchester would not provide them with another temporary home he would conduct the Hallé on street corners if necessary. This did not come to pass. The Hallé hobbled on in one alternative theatre, two suburban cinemas and the remote King's Hall, part of the Belle Vue amusement park. It was to the

King's Hall that Sargent took *Messiah* for some winters. There were six thousand seats in concentric rings and an arena which at other times was used for circus shows, all-in wrestling and political rallies. Sargent's dressing-room had Ringmaster's Office painted on the door, a detail that delighted him. As the years went by and counter-attractions returned, *Messiah* rehearsals and performances some-times overlapped circus seasons. He used to swear that one year, while the audience were applauding and he taking his bow, he could see out of the tail of his eye through canvas flaps into the elephant stable. Three elephants were there. Taking the applause as intended for them, they were bowing their heads and 'lolloping' their trunks as they had been trained to. If some of his stories are to be credited, the arena was not always salubrious when the orchestra arrived for 10 a.m. rehearsal. 'More *sostenuto*, trombones,' he once directed; 'take a deep breath.'

'You wouldn't ask for a deep breath,' replied a trombonist, 'if you were sitting over this sawdust.'

*

In the matter of Christmas *Messiahs* and certain other musical matters, Liverpool behaved more boldly during the early war years than the sister and rival city of Manchester. Two or three months before the war began the local Philharmonic Society had opened its splendid new Philharmonic Hall, whose only defect was that, with a public capacity in front of the platform of just under 2,000, it could have done with 500 seats more. There had been some talk in September 1939 of closing the hall down because the state of war made that seem the right thing to do. Under the Society's vigorous and far-sighted new chairman, David Webster, a stop was put to all such nonsense. Instead of being closed to the public and requisi-tioned for war stores as the Free Trade Hall had been, the Phil-harmonic Hall not only stayed open but luckily survived to house an immensely greater number of concerts than had ever been dreamt of in peacetime.

Sargent's share of engagements with the Liverpool (later Royal Liverpool) Philharmonic Orchestra during his six years as principal conductor totalled 720, including over a hundred recording sessions for august labels. He ranked high among those personalities and talents who, whether through gramophone recordings or other channels of prestige, achieved for the Liverpool Philharmonic Orchestra the status of a national one, thus ensuring when the time came (as it soon did) a sharp if unproclaimed rivalry with the Hallé Orchestra as revitalized by John Barbirolli. One advantage enjoyed by Liverpool and, incidentally, by Sargent was the swarm of uniformed men and women of all Services and of most Allied powers, as well as of Great Britain, who passed through the port or served on Merseyside, then the Admiralty's controlling centre for the Western Approaches. It was from the Forces that much of the new musical public came and among them, perhaps, that the war-time concert boom originated. Sometimes uniformed people were let free into the Philharmonic Hall, or part of it—usually the seats behind the orchestra; more generally they paid a nominal fee. And, no matter what the Luftwaffe was up to, *Messiah* continued to be a double date. Billed for a performance of *Messiah* with the Phil-harmonic choir on a Saturday afternoon in December 1940, Sargent agreed at the committee's request to do a repeat 'for the Forces only' on the Sunday afternoon following. The dates fell just after Christ-mas. During the week before Christmas there were heavy raids two nights running and a minor one the night after. Fresh from his experience of the Manchester blitz, Sargent arrived in Liverpool to find much rubble, dishevelment and resolve. Hundreds had been killed, thousands made homeless. At the Adelphi Hotel, his 'north-ern headquarters', two hundred bedrooms were unusable from blast. Sung almost before the dust had settled, his two *Messiahs* that year were technically as secure as anything heard in peacetime and had other qualities that were either conferred by the stress and menace of total war or imagined because of them. The printed Liverpool programmes of that time carried a routine note in heavy type saying that in the event of an air raid alert during the concert the audience would be warned of it by the continuing glow of an amber light on the conductor's rostrum. Anybody who so wished might leave; but, 'as the music will continue without interruption, will those who are leaving do so as quietly as possible.' It was probably one of these 1940 *Messiahs* Sargent had in mind in a broadcast five years later* when he spoke of 'frequent alerts during the performance'. Nobody in the audience stirred. Every listener was so much in the grip of great music and great words that wars, wounds, fears and conflagrations might never have touched or neared them. Never, swore Sargent, had he heard anything sung with greater conviction. 'The choir might have been singing *Messiah* for the first time.' But then, he concluded, in England during the war people so often got the feeling that they might be singing a piece for the *last* time that they were inspired to make a better job of it than usual.

A year later Liverpool went one better. The usual full rehearsal with orchestra on Saturday morning was followed not only by public performances of *Messiah* on the Saturday and Sunday afternoons— these, claimed Sargent, were sold out to the ordinary public within an hour from the opening of the box office—but also by a third repeat at six on Sunday afternoon solely for men and women in the Services, who would otherwise have been crowded out altogether. During the afternoon performance the manager of the hall was called out by the police to advise on an extraordinary emergency. The building was under siege, all exits blocked, by Service people of every arm and nearly every nation in the 'Grand Alliance', a disquieting situation considering that air raids were still a possibility. Patiently the crowd was sorted into queues so that the afternoon audience could get out when the time came. That night the 'all Forces' audience paid sixpence a head; which is why Sargent called this his 'Woolworth *Messiah*' and gloried in it. He used to say that admirals and generals as well as privates, naval ratings and 'Wrens' (Women's Royal Naval Service) paid their sixpences at the doors and that in defiance of licensing regulations the crowd occupied every foot of seating space, stairs and gangways included. Taking the Saturday morning rehearsal into account, choir, soloists and orchestra were giving their fourth performance in two days. In the case of professionals they were giving it free; all had been persuaded by Sargent to forgo their fees. He knew they were dead tired, he

---

* The broadcast was 'Transpacific Call' from New York to Australia, 1st June, 1945. It identified the occasion as Christmas 1941, but by then the 'blitz' was over. Liverpool had had no raid to speak of for eight months.

10*

had told them that morning. Then a joke. 'I have ordered ambu-
lances to take you home. If necessary I will order hearses for your
dead bodies! But I know I can depend on you for a tremendous
performance.' He must have got what he asked for. At the end he
came off the platform much as he did after his first *Choral* Symphony at Leicester seventeen years earlier, all exaltation and tears.

*

For years it seemed that nobody in musical Liverpool could put a
foot, sixpence or semibreve wrong. Events and wellwishers conspired consistently in favour of the Philharmonic. The municipality
bought their hall for £35,000, let them play there for nothing and
undertook to pay a subsidy of £4,000 per annum in perpetuity.
Even a kick could turn out to be a blessing in disguise. Liverpool
had never had what could be truly called an orchestra of its own.
For generations what was known as the Orchestra of the Liverpool
Philharmonic Society included a high proportion, often a pre-
dominance, of players from Manchester. Conversely, players from
Liverpool were to be seen with the Hallé Orchestra. Owing to a
shift in musical politics which need not be narrated here, these
interchanges came to an abrupt end early in the war. For different
reasons and with different timings, Liverpool and Manchester,
considering that no man should serve competing masters, barred
outside freelances and required exclusive service from their players.
In this way Liverpool first, Manchester a year or two later, achieved
orchestral autonomy.

In Liverpool there had been a Merseyside Symphony Orchestra
which, founded and conducted by the violinist Louis Cohen, gave
'popular' concerts at a seaside resort, New Brighton, and later more
serious ones on Sunday nights at Liverpool's St. George's Hall.
Taken over and initially augmented to sixty players, this was the
first Liverpool Philharmonic Orchestra to deserve the title literally.
Under guest batons and that of Louis Cohen, it so expanded in
quality and number that by 1941 Sargent was entrusting it with
Beethoven's *Choral* Symphony and Elgar's A flat. As to concertos
of his choosing, it accompanied not only the 'standards' but also
Beatrice Harrison in Elgar's 'cello concerto and Lionel Tertis in

Walton's viola concerto and *Harold in Italy*, both on one afternoon. From Sargent's assiduity as a guest conductor it was clear that he had taken to Liverpool. Liverpool reciprocated and wanted to make sure of him. In May 1942 a committee of the Philharmonic Society offered him the post of principal conductor with a schedule of eighty to a hundred concerts a year in and out of Liverpool at a fee to be negotiated. The project was mulled over for a couple of months. One of the Society's requirements was that he should undertake not to conduct other symphony concerts within a hundred miles of Liverpool except those for which he had been engaged before May. Manchester lay well within the hundred-mile limit. Clearly the proviso was aimed at the Hallé Orchestra. Sargent accepted the offer. His appointment caused something like consternation in Manchester.

Owing to tenacious claims by the B.B.C. Northern Orchestra on the services of half its players, the Hallé Orchestra found itself cramped and crippled. There was a macabre possibility, as things then stood, that C.E.M.A., the forerunner of the Arts Council of Great Britain, would actually prefer the Liverpool Philharmonic Orchestra to the Hallé for a sponsored series of summer concerts under Hallé noses in Manchester itself. As Philip Godlee foresaw, this would have meant dissolution. He acted quickly. The Hallé Orchestra was turned into a permanent orchestra, its players on a 52-week contract. And, as a riposte to Sargent's appointment, John Barbirolli was brought back from the United States to be the Hallé's permanent conductor and musical director. For six years he had been Toscanini's first successor with the New York Philharmonic Symphony Orchestra. Godlee received many congratulatory messages on his 'capture' of Barbirolli. One of the first was from Sargent. In return Godlee chivalrously stated the Hallé Society's wish that Sargent should conduct their orchestra 'on many occasions'.

*

While Barbirolli brought his depleted orchestra up to strength the hard way, i.e. by scouring the country for likely players at a time when man power and woman power were being roped into the

Forces and the arms factories, Sargent and his Liverpool friends were reaping the benefit of a windfall without precedent.

As soon as the war began, and in accordance with plans laid long before it, a dozen or more of London's best orchestral players made for a mansion at Evesham, Worcestershire, which had been taken over by the B.B.C. Here they formed themselves into the B.B.C. Salon Orchestra, sixteen strong, whose purpose was to discourse light music and arrangements of classics, thus consoling the country at large against the massive air raids which were expected any minute. Three years later the B.B.C. decided that the Salon Orchestra had served its purpose and gave the players a month's notice. On the day the notices were served most of the players gathered in a saloon bar on the outskirts of Evesham. One of their number, who months earlier had received an indirect invitation to join the Liverpool orchestra any time he felt like it, put in a telephone call to his friend Henry Holst, then principal violin and leader of the Philharmonic.

'If the offer's still open,' said the caller, 'I'm going to join you. Perhaps some of the other boys will be interested if there are jobs going.' Holst passed on the news to David Webster, who put in a return call to Holst's friend the same evening.

'You'll be most welcome,' Webster said. 'Tell the other chaps not to do a thing until I come down. I'll be with you tomorrow.'

As a result of Webster's visit Liverpool acquired a nucleus of players (some were teacher-players and skilled in chamber music as well as orchestral work) who had been principals under Beecham or were eminent because of other appointments and experiences. Among them were Anthony Pini ('cello), Reginald Kell (clarinet), Arthur Ackroyd (flute), David Wise (violin), John McCarthy (oboe) and John Alexandra (bassoon). Other section leaders or sub-principals of distinction came in later. From the autumn of 1942 the Liverpool Philharmonic Orchestra became an instrument of consequence. Before taking his first rehearsal with them that autumn as their chief conductor, Sargent gave an inspiriting speech of welcome. He ended, however, on a note that chilled some: 'We'll see how you get on this first season. We shall probably have to make changes.'

'Why did he have to say that?' asked a player of his desk mate. The other, one of the newcomers from Evesham, replied: 'That's Malcolm's way. He gives a brilliant speech and drops a brick at the end of it. It always happens.'

That first season Sargent conducted ninety-seven concerts or recording sessions for the Philharmonic out of a grand total of 155; next season (1943–44) 140 out of 233. He never again touched his 1943–44 total but for six years averaged well over a hundred engagements a season, including dozens of children's concerts and as many as thirty a year for audiences of soldiers, airmen and arms workers under the aegis of C.E.M.A. or its twin organization E.N.S.A. (Entertainments National Service Association). He used to tell with relish of excursions at night through a pitchblack countryside to remote underground factories where youths and young women worked in shifts round the clock filling bomb and shell cases with high explosive. With specially formed touring groups from the orchestra he would play Rossini, Grieg, Schubert, Suppé and Delibes in thronged, respectful canteens. His schedule outside Liverpool took him to relatively small towns which had never had a symphony orchestra in their midst before. To the regular Saturday and Sunday concerts in Liverpool evening series were presently added. Outside and inside the city an orchestra which once had given a mere dozen concerts a season, to an aggregate audience of ten thousand or so, stayed busy throughout the year and played to an aggregate of over 350,000.

Even when planned with one eye on the box office his Philharmonic programmes could be piquant. Tchaikovsky's B flat minor piano concerto and *Casse-noisette* by all means; before and after these, however, came Shostakovitch's Symphony No. 1 and *Firebird*. An all-Beethoven programme included the *Emperor* Concerto and the Seventh Symphony to be sure; but you got the Grosse Fuge and the Rondino for Wind Instruments on the same afternoon. He and his committee had ears for contemporary music as well as dug-in classics. It was under Sargent in the Philharmonic Hall that Bartók's *Concerto for Orchestra* had its first performance in Britain. New English works came up in something like patriotic profusion. In Manchester he had done Edmund Rubbra's Symphony No. 3 and

Bliss's *Morning Heroes*. To Liverpool he brought Michael Tippett's
Symphony No. 1 and his oratorio *A Child of Our Time*, Vaughan
Williams's Symphony No. 5 in D, Bax's No. 3, Ernest Moeran's
G minor, Sinfonietta and 'cello concerto. Benjamin Britten he
saluted in good time with productions of the *Sinfonia da Requiem*,
the *Serenade* for tenor, horn and strings (twice: with Peter Pears and
Dennis Brain), the *Peter Grimes* prelude and interludes and *The
Young Person's Guide*, a work which he took to his heart. He conducted many choral concerts—*Belshazzar*, *Gerontius*, B minor Mass
and so on—sometimes with the Liverpool Philharmonic choir,
sometimes bringing over his Huddersfield one, at other times using
an amalgam of the two.

It has been said that he made of the Liverpool orchestra an
instrument to be reckoned with, peer during the war and for some
years after it of the best the country had to offer. Most of his players
were northerners whose pre-war symphonic experience had been an
incidental fringe to day-by-day work of a humbler kind. Within
recent memory Liverpool had boasted fifteen restaurant and teashop
bands, mostly trios or quartets, and, going back a little further,
cinema bands by the dozen. It was the best players from these who
traditionally served the Philharmonic Society, finding deputies for
their day-to-day jobs when symphonic duty called. The incursion
of players from London via Evesham heightened their sense of
prestige and, as many a veteran acknowledges, made better orchestral
players of them.

Sargent worked the orchestra hard at rehearsals, which were
doubly taxing for men who had been on firewatch all night. But they
marvelled at the mathematical clarity of his beat and were appreciative of his demonstrations in advance of how he was going to beat
this tricky bar or that. Sometimes they took a surreptitious look at
his conducting scores. Here, too, was something to marvel at: blue
and red pencil marks all over the place, rings round some phrases,
long lines with arrow heads interconnecting others. A Sargent score,
observed one veteran, was like a London Underground map. 'Lines,
lines, lines—you always knew where to change from Bakerloo to
Central.'

As happened in the case of more orchestras than Liverpool's, the first 'honeymoon' phase was followed by a detached and critical one. He could be very kind. Everybody agreed on that. There was an occasion when, the orchestra having a Blackpool concert, he called an early rehearsal so that they could get away in good time to a circus nearby; he had bought seats for all eighty. But also he could be furiously disapproving. Hence his 'black looks', as the Liverpool contingent called them. One day the principal bassoon did not turn up at rehearsal. Sargent asked the second bassoon (Liverpudlian) if he would be so good as to take over. In a broad Lancashire accent the second bassoon said all right, he'd have a go; but he didn't want 'any black looks nor any bloody messing about, neither'. By 'messing about' he meant being pulled up and told to play something in a different way. The main work in hand that morning was *The Planets*. During the bassoon solo in the *Saturn* section, which is subtitled The Bringer of Old Age, Sargent rapped the rail and asked Mr. X if he couldn't take the phrase in one breath instead of two. 'But,' objected X, 'this tune's supposed to be about an old man, and I'm making it sound like one!' Sargent and every player on the platform except X, who permitted himself a tolerant smile, laughed for minutes over this.

'Black looks' did not always have so agreeable a sequel. In a Suppé overture one of the 'London boys', as the locals called them, had a conspicuous solo. Sargent interrupted him, saying: 'I would like you to play it like this'—and sang illustratively. Mr. Y, as we may call him, played the solo again exactly as before.

'You are still not doing as I ask,' complained Sargent.

'No,' retorted Y, 'and I don't intend to.'

Sargent pressed his point a third time, to be told: 'I have always played it like that. I am not going to alter it for anybody.'

Sargent had no choice but to drop the matter and shrug. More than once his differences on musical and disciplinary issues resulted in emotional breakdown. One of these involved his first 'cello, Anthony Pini, who more than once played solo in concertos under his baton. The piece in rehearsal was a symphonic poem by Smetana. In a passage for the 'cellos marked *piano* the 'cellos behind Pini played loud and were not corrected from the rostrum. At the first halt Pini asked Sargent whether he really wanted a *forte* when the score said *piano*. This is what followed, according to converging memories of people there. At first Sargent ignored the question even when it was repeated. Finally, in a sharp tone, he said: 'I will look after that. It is not for you, sitting down there, to be the conductor. To conduct you need special qualifications. Your job is to look after your own part.'

'But,' objected Pini, 'they were playing too loud. Are you going to let them get away with it?'

Without further ado Sargent threw down his baton and walked off, leaving a startled buzz of conversation in his wake. After a while Henry Holst, the leader, who had been discussing the incident with Sargent offstage, returned and said to Pini, 'He wants to see you.' Pini complied. Sargent's first words when he entered the conductor's room were: 'I feel very disappointed and hurt.'

'Well, so do I,' returned Pini. 'You seem to have no idea how players feel.'

At this Sargent burst into tears. After a moment or two he said, 'I feel better now. Let's forget all about it.' Whereupon they shook hands.

As has been noted in an earlier chapter, Sargent was in the habit of carrying his woes to David Webster's house and there weeping anew over rehearsal skirmishes. Quarrels and walkings off on the part either of players or himself recurred occasionally almost to the end of his career. They were symptoms of an ingrained incapacity to win much more than watchful neutrality from even well-disposed players. Was he, during those war and immediate postwar years, made more sensitive and hurtable than usual by overwork? His engagement diaries of the period are nightmarishly overcrowded. The dozen or so choirs and orchestras which he conducted regularly in widely spaced towns and cities up and down this country were not the whole tale. The 'ambassador of music' thesis had begun to catch on. As a result he was to the fore among those whom the British Council deputed to wage Britain's 'cultural war' in neutral countries.

He flew twice to Sweden (November 1942 and September 1943) and once to Portugal (January 1943). Conducting the principal native orchestras, he was received in both countries with ecstasy by

crammed houses. His new secretary Mrs. Chapman was confidentially briefed beforehand about one of these trips. He took the night
train to Scotland, precise destination unknown, with a stack of
scores. Next day she received a laconic telephone call from nowhere: 'Well, I'm off. Thank you for packing my things so nicely.'
This meant he was about to climb into the bomb-rack of a Mosquito
for an unescorted flight across the North Sea and over Nazi-occupied
Norway to some Swedish airfield. Although there were no bombs in
it, his section of bomb-rack was so small that he had to sit with his
knees to his chin. He clutched to his chest a Walton score and an
Elgar score which he had thought to study on the flight and felt
airsick. In Stockholm and Gothenburg, Lisbon and Oporto, he
conducted five concerts or more at each visit. His repertory, although
not all-British, since it contained things by Brahms, Dvořák and
Saint-Saëns, was a showing of the flag. Massive audiences were
treated to the Walton Symphony, Rubbra's No. 3, Vaughan
Williams's No. 5 and Tallis fantasia, *The Planets*, *Brigg Fair* and
two other Delius pieces, Britten's *Sinfonia da Requiem*, the *Enigma*
Variations and (in Portugal, at any rate) the Elgar 'cello concerto,
for which Suggia came out of her retirement to play the solo part.

He was given to understand everywhere, not only by winks and
nods, that Great Britain was admired and loved. When he entered a
restaurant in Gothenburg the band struck up *Land of Hope and
Glory* and followed it with *Tipperary*. In Lisbon, where for five
concerts he had ten days of rehearsal with the Portuguese National
Symphony Orchestra, the theatre where he conducted them was
packed for his last programme an hour before starting time. At
rehearsal the big swagger of trombones in the *Cockaigne* Overture
so warmed up the rest of the orchestra that players began surreptitiously giving him Britain's V for Victory sign with forked fingers
while he returned the compliment with his left hand. Sticklers for
protocol would have called this imprudent behaviour in a neutral
country—not that anybody rebuked or repented it.

That orchestral music could be effective propaganda had occurred
to the Germans as well as to the British Council. Sargent was preceded in Sweden by Furtwängler (plus the Berlin Philharmonic
Orchestra) and followed by him to Portugal. In one or other of these

cities their sojourns overlapped. Furtwängler knew Sargent from meetings while on conducting missions to London before the war. Wishing to meet him again, he sent Sargent a message asking if this would be feasible. Sargent returned a negative answer, and, when Furtwängler sent a further message assuring him that he was not a Nazi, replied with a note saying that, while he had always admired Furtwängler as a man and as a musician, henceforth he would admire him as a musician.

Never were days more crowded and exhilarating. From his first Swedish trip he reached London at 9 p.m., dictated a sheaf of telegrams to cities far and wide, repacked his suitcase, filled another with band parts (he often supplied these from his library and got hire fees from promoters for doing so), took yet another northbound train at 11 p.m. and was back in Liverpool next morning with the usual chain of rehearsals and concerts ahead of him. He was as buoyant physically and mentally as eager as anybody had known him; and so he remained throughout years of scurry when his apparent object was to be in three places at once. But anguish suddenly struck. It had to do with Pamela and was never wholly to leave him.

CHAPTER TWENTY-THREE

THE DEATH OF PAMELA

ER FIRST eighteen months at Hartland Abbey were an
interlude of tranquil, slow recovery. She was gay; and her
gaiety had a quicksilver in it which sickness never dulled.
This was the quality in her, unforced and vernal, that is most
remembered and with something like awe. Everybody at the school
and many connected with it outside were her friends. To the more
intimate among them she would talk about her father. She saw
plainly that there were two sides to him. About his precisions of
wardrobe, glossed hair, buttonhole and smile, his shrewdness in
gauging applause, the practised suavity with which he took his
platform calls and, in considered order, summoned his singers and
players to take theirs: about these and other tricks and tactics she
laughed affectionately. That was the showman side, the one that
dazzled those who knew him from a distance and noisily adored. The
'Papa' side differed so sharply from the public one that nobody
who knew both sides equally well (few did) could help feeling a sort
of amused delight. When he came to Hartland his platform attitudes
peeled off of their own accord. His affection was simple, impulsive—
and wholesale. He was out to make not only Pamela happy but every
other soul under the roof. He became something between father and
uncle, coeval and brother, or all four at once, to the entire community. In the Hartland drawing-room he played Beethoven and
talked about him to a throng of girls, equally riveting those whom
music ordinarily bored and others who were making it part of their
lives. After the music he would do conjuring tricks. Calling for
everybody's concentrated gaze and silence, he would balance a slim
stick on his forefinger, then shift the stick to some level surface and

make it balance there all on its own 'by sheer power of thought', as
he maintained.

The school had an excellent music mistress whose musical appreciation classes were attended by Pamela so long as she could get
about. While taking after her father in looks, gaiety and much else,
she was never judged, presuming complete recovery, to have the
makings of a professional musician in her. Music was among subjects
that her sharp intelligence took in its stride. Not that the process
stopped there. When, taking piano lessons, she first spelled her way
through a Bach two-part invention or a Haydn sonata, she uncovered
truths that went deeper than any accessible to mere brightness of
mind. With these adventures went routine keyboard exercises that
were intended in part as a therapy for an arm which polio had
weakened. Sometimes she sang in the girls' choir which her father
had not so much launched as precipitated. This happened during
one of his early visits. 'Why don't you form a choir?' he asked the
music mistress.

'I hadn't thought of it,' she replied, 'but I'd love to.'

'Let's do it right away. Get your best singers together tonight, and
I'll give you a send-off.'

In the drawing-room thirty or forty girls were sorted into groups
for part singing and put through exercises and sight reading. As usual
Sargent's briskness gave to the enterprise an air of novelty. It was as
though a girls' choir had never happened before. He rebuked
blunders in the drollest way, and got discipline and strict attention
without seeming to insist or impose. He prepared or conducted them,
or, given time, did both, in music by Pergolesi, Schubert, Mozart
and others which he arranged for female voices if they had not been
composed for that medium in the first place.

How he found the lighthearted stamina for these addenda to a
career which already seemed overcrowded to bursting point will
never be understood even by those who knew most about his current
working days and those which were planning for seasons ahead. Off
he would go from Devon into the Midlands or to the Pennines. In
far-off concert halls he would solve imperturbably and on the spur of
the moment hitches and mishaps that would have made any other
man scratch an ear or fume. During an oratorio performance in

Lancashire his contralto glanced up at him helplessly when the time came for her first entry. She had brought on the wrong copy. Taking in her plight at a glance, he stopped the performance, walked off swiftly and came back with the right music. He handed it to her with a comforting pat on the back which is recalled with shining eyes by every woman choralist who was there. A simple enough thing. But who else would have thought of it? Somewhere else in the North he conducted much of a *Messiah* with his collar sprung loose. His disregard of its flappings is one of the town's legends. At Preston Mr. P, the concerto pianist, did not appear at the rehearsal. He was still missing when the concert began. Nothing had been heard from him. Sargent, although in the dark like everybody else, told the audience that Mr. P was on his way—he gave the impression almost that he had seen Mr. P coming round the corner—and that the night's symphony would be played in the first half instead of the concerto. Mr. P's train had made a detour because of bombings. When he did appear, a little breathless, the applause he got, like that which followed his performance, was all the warmer for Sargent's fatherly aplomb in handling the emergency.

Returning to Chesham-place in February 1943 from his Portuguese trip he found himself unexpectedly, owing to some wartime exigency, without a private secretary. The table in his bed-sitting room was so loaded with letters which the hall porter had taken in day by day for weeks that some of them had slid off and were littering the carpet. Although the day was Sunday he started to hunt for a new secretary. By telephone he enlisted the help of a dozen friends. One of these, whom he did not reach until Monday, knew 'just the person'. A friend of hers, Anne Chapman, young, cultivated and intelligent, to whom the reader has had an advance introduction, had thought of taking a job related to the war effort, being newly free to do so, and had come up from the country to look for one during the weekend. Through this intermediary Mrs. Chapman got Sargent's message the same night and telephoned him next day to say she was interested. 'Good,' said Sargent. 'Get into a taxi and come round rightaway.' The bed-sitting room was as cluttered as a transit camp. There were trunks from the Portugal trip, one of them open and half unpacked; also a model galleon in silvergilt filigree—'Isn't that nice? They [the orchestra] gave it to me in Lisbon.' Then to business.

'Have you ever had a job before?' 'No.' 'What can you do?' 'I can write shorthand and type and have German, French and Spanish'. 'Do you know anything about music?' 'I'm not musically trained, but I love listening to it.' 'That's all that matters.' 'I ought to tell you I have the offer of another job, with the American Red Cross in Grosvenor-square.' 'I'll give you three minutes to make up your mind about this one.' 'All right, I'll take it.' 'Splendid. We'll make a start on this stuff' (indicating the mound of correspondence). 'Please take a telegram. To Arthur Heap (he's honorary secretary of the Bradford Festival Choral Society; you'll find him in the address book there)—"Regret can't arrive until six-twenty. Please start rehearsal at four hours. Two trumpets, three trombones essential." '

This first interview, offer and acceptance, with discussion of terms, took little longer than its telling.

As the whirlwind began, so it went on, with the Engagement Book an increasingly complex jigsaw, its main entries four or five concerts a week with attendant items such as rehearsal orders confirmed, train-times checked, hire cars hired, sleeping compartments reserved, day carnations and evening ones ensured, telegrams sent, telephone calls put in to choirs in weaving towns, worsted towns, steel towns, pottery towns. The reign of his manservant, the unruffled, omniscient Oliver, was not yet. Up to a point he looked to his own valeting. From a scribbled list which has survived from late 1943 it is clear that after four years of denuding war, with paint flaking even from royal façades and an entire population darning and patching, and 'making do' he could, when it was fitting, travel a morning coat, grey waistcoat and grey tie as well as an extra lounge suit (striped) and evening dress for the rostrum. (It is true that he, too, had recourse to clothes menders. Having reduced a three-piece suit to two pieces for repair of the trousers, he used to boast he was the only man who always sat on his waistcoat when out to lunch.)

Any few hours snatched in London away from score-study, rostrum, rehearsals and business matters of several sorts were spent in table talk that made the clock hands move faster. Wherever he sat as host or went as a guest there were no longueurs. His talk had incomparable urge and verve and warmth. Although not unique, his humour was somehow all his own. And he didn't often stop to take breath. All faces round the table were always turned his way. He rarely used irony and never showed anger. If he had somebody or something to condemn a glint of indignation might show; but his typical way was to condemn with an appealing smile, the appeal being to good sense and rightmindedness. Music critics? 'Let me tell you where they go wrong.' An argument would follow about anxious scribblers, eye on clock, head full of deadlines, so worried about what they were going to write that they couldn't listen to the music or, anyway, enjoy it.* Crooners (a contemporary race of 'pop' singer)? 'They aren't singers, they can't sing. All they can do is hum. We can all do that. They walk on the stage or recording floor with this awful sort of telephone thing in their hand, trailing a long tail or ribbon or rope behind them and produce a toneless, falsetto note which the telephone thing turns into a lovely, Caruso kind of sound. I've been to recording sessions that were shameful to see. Once upon a time if you hadn't a voice you couldn't sing. Now you can sing even if you can't. I would like to see every crooner simply wiped off the stage and all stage microphones done away with.' Funny stories which many a raconteur might have thought tepid came with piquancy from his mouth. 'The headmaster produced the cane and said, "Do you know what this is?" And I said, "Yes, sir, we have met before." And the headmaster said: "Bend over. You are now going to meet behind." ' He could recite preparatory school 'cracks' of this kind, while ingeniously applying them to adult dilemmas, with an uncanny flash of twelve-year-old charm which, since he didn't 'put it on', was one of the things people liked about him. His charm and fun were in no ways at odds with the hour. With the war going well for the Allies on all fronts, the whole country was avid for fun and charm on credit account, in expectation of victory. Zest was in the air. Sargent breathed in more of it than most. It sharpened his sense of transient beauty.

On a day of sun and snow he burst into the Chesham-place flat

---

* He put this idea forward once in a B.B.C. broadcast, overlooking that it is dull performances of dull music that make words harder to find; a fine performance of a masterpiece makes them flow.

and told Anne Chapman to put on her hat and coat quickly; he wanted to show her something. A taxi was waiting. They drove to Hyde Park Corner. From a pavement by St. George's Hospital he pointed to the quadriga on the arch at the top of Constitution Hill. 'That is what I wanted you to see,' he said. Snow and sunlight had turned Peace driving four horses and chariot, as viewed from a chosen angle, into the semblance of a gigantic butterfly in pale gold. 'I noticed it on the way back from the club, and simply had to have another look,' he explained, and watched absorbedly until the sun-gold faded. Even when beauty meant menace the zest for it went on. London and southern counties came under 'pilotless' bombardment. When the alert sounded he would chase up to the roof to spot flying bombs in the sky over Kensington or on its horizons. He saw many by day and watched the tree of smoke that rose when they dived and detonated, and many by night, when they moved down the sky with tails aflare like red stars. His excitement was that, again, of a twelve-year-old.

*

By this time, however, anguish was at hand.

Early in 1944 Pamela's condition had begun to decline. The specialists, Lord Horder among them, pronounced that, while there had been no recurrence of the old trouble, there were grave 'complications'. Rest was imperative. Piano lessons and singing in the choir had to be given up. She stayed in her room, in bed for most of the time, and received her friends there, blithely. Her friends, as has been said, were many, so many, indeed, that she became more decisively than before a focal point for the school. They noted that as she weakened and came under physical duress the essential Pamela stayed strong. Whatever she suffered, whether of pain or foreboding, she was never seen in tears or with a long face. Some on the staff who did not use such language lightly spoke and speak still of her spiritual radiance. At last Horder told her father that Pamela was dying. It was not known how long she would live. She might linger on for months. Or it might only be for weeks. In any case she was beyond recovery.

On being told this Sargent returned to Chesham-place in a

torment of grief. He went into the bathroom and, burying his face in a towel, wept endlessly. 'It's all up with Pamela,' he sobbed.

The storm passed but not, as yet, the torment. He willed himself back into the career-whirlwind, came and went as unceasingly as before, afraid now, perhaps, to pause, since pausing meant brooding; bowed and beamed on familiar rostrums with the wonted dins of adulation in his ears. When the ovations ended, the hall empty and he back in his hotel room, the anguish would flood back. Travelling south on an early train after a Saturday night concert in Leeds to a Sunday afternoon rehearsal in Leicester, he chanced upon Herbert Howells at breakfast in the restaurant car.

'Herbert, I envy you,' he said. 'Why envy me, Malcolm?' 'Because Mick died after three days. Pamela is in the seventh year of her suffering.' To ease his spirit, Howells had written *Hymnus Paradisi* to his boy's memory. For twelve years he showed it to no one. When at last Sargent received the score and played it through on his piano he was wrung inexpressibly. The performances he conducted of it in London, Leeds and Huddersfield were considered to bear the mark of a deeper apprehension than musicianship alone can teach. . . .

The goad of the engagement book was almost a balm. He might be free of anguish for the whole of an intensely busy morning and afternoon. Evenings, if free, were an ambush. The anguish lay in wait.

In a Knightsbridge restaurant he was telling his companion about his current budgerigar (he always found it hard to live without one); how it adored the noise of the vacuum cleaner ('which I simply cannot stand!'); and how, when the thing was switched on, it immediately burst into song. In the middle of a sentence tears overtook him. He buried his face in his napkin as he had used the towel on that first black day and wept uninhibitedly, as a stricken Sicilian peasant might weep. The waiters knew and liked him. They turned the other way with concerned faces as though mourning themselves.

By one of nature's consolatory paradoxes, the calmest times for him were when at Pamela's bedside. Towards the end he spent every day there that he could snatch from his preposterous work-schedule. Father and daughter talked at ease, often smilingly, of small things and last things. Pamela knew she would not live long. The thought of death did not frighten or chill her. She was precociously wise, as those often are whose term is short. Her inborn faith was irrefragible and twin to that of her father.

Sometimes while she slept he worked at her bedside, writing case on knee. His task, bred of sorrow and reflection, was the orchestrating of the accompaniments to Brahms's *Vier ernste Gesänge*, the *Four Serious Songs*, whose Biblical texts pass through the darkness and gravedust of Ecclesiastes to the great affirmation of Corinthians: 'And now abideth faith, hope and charity, these three; but the greatest of these is charity.' While at work on the transcriptions he thought of voices which were apt or, better still, preordained for Brahms's line and the thoughts it carried. Two new young contraltos of exceptional quality came especially to his mind: Nancy Evans and Kathleen Ferrier. Soon after the war both were to sing the main rôle in the first (Glyndebourne) production of Benjamin Britten's *The Rape of Lucretia*. And both were to be in at the birth of the Brahms–Sargent *Gesänge*. He had lightheartedly undertaken to conduct fifteen symphonic programmes, well laced with concertos, on fifteen consecutive days in Liverpool during the summer of 1944 as part of a 'holidays at home' campaign prompted by the fact that civilian war workers could not spend their holidays anywhere else. Billed as 'For the Man in the Street', the concerts were informal, smacking of what was sometimes called the New Democracy. Smoking was allowed during the music; you could buy a single seat for as little as eighteenpence and spam sandwiches at the interval. As it happened, Nancy Evans, in addition to being highly talented, was a Liverpool native. The first performance went to her. She sang the *Gesänge* on a Thursday night, following a Handel organ concerto, the Bach double violin concerto and a fragment of *The Creation*. At the piano rehearsal a day or two earlier, as at the rehearsal with orchestra and most of the way through the first half of the concert, Sargent was composed, bright and normal. By the end of the *Gesänge*, however, his face was streaming with tears. Miss Evans, who knew that Pamela was seriously ill though not that she was dying, sensed the truth and later, the truth having been confirmed, sent a note of sympathy round to the Adelphi Hotel. After the concert, outwardly tranquil once more, he introduced Miss Ferrier to Miss Evans in the artists' room at the Philharmonic Hall and made some joke about how hazardous it was to make two contraltos known to each other. Kathleen had been in the audience at his invitation because he had her in mind for the second performance and wanted her to get the measure of his scoring.

With the Man in the Street concerts out of the way he sped south and spent another weekend at Hartland. Pamela's condition was still inclined to fluctuate. Minor improvements alternated with flaggings and relapses. He returned from his weekend saying: 'We talked for hours. It has been wonderful. We had a wonderful time together.' Again she had spoken of her religious faith and, with resignation, of death. But uncertainty harrowed him still. Death might be months or only hours away.

He took the accustomed night train for a few duty days in the North. On one of those days, 23rd August, 1944, Pamela Stephanie Sargent died suddenly. He was reached by telephone in Liverpool. The voice from Hartland said she had died peacefully. The news felled him morally. He had thought himself girded and prepared. He was wrong. Anne Chapman met him off the 'sleeper' from Liverpool next morning. She had never seen a person so desolate, nor did she conceive how anyone could recover from such desolation. It was evident that he had been weeping all night. The tears had dried on his face. The ramrod back was bent with grief. It had become an old man's back. After five days he straightened and stayed straight until, twenty-three years later, mortal sickness bowed him for the second and last time.

Pamela was buried in a village churchyard near Hartland. Afterwards her father went to the piano and played through the *Four Serious Songs*, music of the shadows to words of pessimistic undertone yet aureoled with hope. The day was a Friday. On the Saturday afternoon Kathleen Ferrier sang the second performance in a studio-broadcast from Manchester with the B.B.C. Northern Orchestra, Julian Harrison replacing Sargent. Kathleen was to make the *Four Serious Songs* peculiarly her own, enduing them ultimately with a tenderness and light bred in part of suffering. Here a digression or, more exactly, a pendant to the story of Pamela.

Sargent had first met Kathleen after a Hallé concert at which she had been present late in 1941. Alfred Barker, then leader of the Hallé, for whom she had sung with a seaside orchestra of his own, introduced her, saying: 'This girl has a *voice*.' Sargent auditioned her in May 1942, himself at the piano, in an otherwise deserted Manchester hotel lounge which, although thinking it ill suited to her voice, she was obliged to accept since there had been no time to book a studio. At the finish, as we learn from Winifred Ferrier's biography of her sister,* he told her she had a great future but that she would find it difficult to get on unless she settled in London. At Chesham-place a day or two later he said to Mrs. Chapman in the manner of one who cannot wait to unburden himself of something momentous, 'I've heard a wonderful voice. The name is Kathleen Ferrier. Please put it down. Get her booked for *Messiah* with the Royal Choral Society.' He then dictated a letter on Kathleen's behalf to a London concert agency who auditioned her and put her on their books. Five months later, the day being Christmas Eve 1942, Kathleen with her sister, having left their home in Carlisle and moved south, took over a flat on Hampstead Hill which became the base of a career which, though cruelly short, was to span continents. While waiting for the flat to be made ready she stayed with musical friends in Edinburgh. Her hostess, Mrs. Maitland, chanced to turn up an old copy of the *Four Serious Songs*, which meant much to her. At that time Kathleen knew nothing of them. She tried them through, writes her sister, and sang them over and over again. 'Mrs. Maitland went out for an hour or two. When she came back Kathleen was still working at them, enthralled.' The Manchester broadcast on the morrow of Pamela's burial came two years later. By that time she possessed the music in its depths and heights, though not in the sovereign and luminous way that came later.

Someone wrote of an early London performance by Kathleen of the *Gesänge* that in them her voice had a curiously compelling and *moral* quality; while listening to it the hearer felt it was high time he started leading a better life. The idea was akin to some which

* *The Life of Kathleen Ferrier* (Hamish Hamilton), 1955.

Sargent often expressed. As was his way when a concert notice took his fancy, he sent the critic a postcard of agreement and thanks. On the elevating influence of music he was insistent. Notions of this kind might be 'dated'. But truth was one thing, fashion another.

'The classics,' he said to me in 1961, 'are spiritual highlights in a person's life. When you listen to them you go away feeling better. Or perhaps not better. As one man said to me—he was a little working man—after a *Gerontius*, "I love Elgar's music. It makes me go away feeling I'm a very *bad* man." '

'And modern music?' he was asked.

'The music of the moderns, most of the moderns, anyway, is of a different type. Beecham used to call it "music of intellectual manufacture". Some people get the same sort of mental stimulus from it as from playing chess. It's not like looking at a blue sea or a blue sky.'

Thus, Kathleen Ferrier, as he and many more heard her, was a proponent of music's ethical sway. Not that this was a matter they reverted to when the *ernste Gesänge* or *Messiah* or the B minor Mass were in rehearsal. On these occasions the rock bottom verities are kept not on the tip of the tongue but at the back of the mind. In Kathleen Ferrier's view, Sargent did not see as deeply into some kinds of music as certain other conductors: Bruno Walter especially. But she enjoyed working with him as few singers did. Warmly assessing his human quality, she laughed about his showmanship with an indulgence that had something in common with Pamela's comprehending affection. She was not as young as Pamela when she died, but equally her death was a grievous cutting off. She sang to the world, as distinct from the 'parish', for less than ten years. It should have been twenty years, thirty years. Without Malcolm Sargent's encouragement in 1942, however, the world would have had to make do with even less.

*

There is a second pendant to the events of 1944. It concerns Nancy Evans. Her singing career had taken a rather different course from Kathleen's; for several years she devoted herself in greater degree to the new upsurge of English opera. But during thirteen consecutive Promenade concert seasons she often renewed the link with Sargent, who conducted her in chansons, Lieder and song cycles. Her daughter Helga was taken to hear Mama sing from the age of three. One year she was taken round as usual to the artists' room at the Albert Hall to be made a fuss of. Her mother was disturbed to find her running a temperature which had come on during the concert. The little girl, six years old now, clung to her in a distraught way. Sargent looked on with concern. He had Helga drink some of the special orange juice which he often took after conducting and whispered, 'You must get her to a doctor.' That summer there was much polio about. Clearly he had this in mind. Since Pamela's death, indeed, polio had rarely been out of his mind. Helga was taken home and put to bed. Next morning a telephone call came from Sargent's office. 'Sir Malcolm has been wondering how Helga is,' said the secretary. 'He says he can't go out to the rehearsal until he knows.' Helga, as it happened, was herself again. The ailment had been of little moment. Sargent, saying how relieved he was, started the day's work. This happened at the height of the 'Proms' season, when professional preoccupations might excusably have driven everything else out of his mind. No other soul knew anything about his concern except Helga's parents. Far from being averse to publicity, he pursued and cultivated it untiringly in career matters, even tactlessly. He was of the sort who say: 'You can quote me as saying . . .' to newspaper writers before they have sought his opinion. But about the golden side of him, as it has been called, he never breathed a word or hinted that go-betweens might murmur one. There were matters on which gossip and print would have struck him as obscene.

CHAPTER TWENTY-FOUR

BRAINS TRUST

IN THE ordinary way conductors are directly known more or less, as distinct from being known about, by a relative handful, such being the ratio of earnest concertgoers, operagoers and musicians to the population at large.

In the case of Sargent the ordinary way and ratio were startlingly superseded during the war. From 1941 and until near the end of that decade his guest performances with the B.B.C.'s Brains Trust, as it quickly came to be known ('Any Questions' was the original title), carried his voice to half the firesides of the land. It cannot be said that half the firesides of the land were burning to hear him on the compass of the valveless trumpet in Beethoven's day, a topic on which he ventured once: but, inevitably, most of the questions that came in had to do with other matters, many of them weighty (e.g. 'What are the five attributes of a full and happy life?' 'Why do we want the British Empire to go on after the war?'), a few of them freakish or flippant (e.g. 'How does a fly land on the ceiling?' 'Can you tell me why a woman always has cold knees?'); and Sargent, although the Trust's 'music man', addressed himself to non-musical themes like everybody else round the table. With women listeners especially he was the Trust's most popular guest.

His rise to fame from mere celebrity came to him disconcertingly after a concert one Sunday afternoon outside a stage door in the Potteries. A girl was waiting with an autograph book. 'You Dr. Sargent?' she asked. He nodded smilingly. She looked sceptical. '*The* Dr. Sargent?' He nodded again. 'Dr. Sargent of the Brains

Trust?' she persisted. He nodded a third time. 'All right, I'll have
your autograph,' she conceded.*

From the moment of his début (recorded 27th June, transmitted
29th June, 1941) he knew that this was a medium and a task for
which he was shaped by nature and training. The mental challenges
were sharp and, for that, the more stimulating. He found himself
disputing with men and women whose academic rating made him
look, on paper, at least, like a self-educated boy and with others
formidably seasoned in political or other debate. At the Brains Trust
table he sat with scholars, poets, sages, historians, editors, economists
and administrators, some of them past Ministers of State or future
ones: Herbert Samuel, Bertrand Russell, Gilbert Murray, Lord
Elton, A. L. Rowse, Dr. Moore of Harrow, William Beveridge, the
'two Barbaras' (Wootton and Ward), Kingsley Martin, Julian Huxley,
Walter Elliot, Geoffrey Crowther, Quintin Hogg, Jennie Lee,
Ellen Wilkinson. All, except the lionesses, were lions. Sargent
entered their den with a calm sprightliness that made even the
lionesses feel at home if they were 'guesting' for the first time and
felt apprehensive.

Before sessions everybody used to be lunched by the B.B.C. at a
hotel in Bloomsbury, where Cyril Joad (whom we have met in an
earlier chapter) and Sargent habitually limbered up by quarrelling
on the first topic to hand and exchanging 'cheerful insults'. It was
usually Sargent who won, says Howard Thomas. During the early
days, before transfer to a dungeon at Bush House in the Strand,
the sessions were held in a small studio some floors below ground
level at Broadcasting House. Nothing went out 'live'. Every session
had to be recorded on film and steel tape and transcribed overnight for the wartime censors who cut out anything judged to be
against security in time for the transmission two days or more later.
From almost repressed beginnings (a mere half-hour on Wednesday
afternoons) the programme rose to peak-time runs of forty-five
minutes on the two best days of the week. It attracted up to a
thousand listeners' questions a week (as well as four times that

---

* This conversation is quoted in *Britain's Brains Trust* (Chapman and Hall)
1944, by Howard Thomas, producer of the programme, whom I follow on
other historical points also.

Sargent often played piano in chamber music. Seen here at concert in
Guildhall, London, January 1956

Kathleen Ferrier, one of the great contraltos of the century, whom
Sargent 'discovered' in May 1942

many letters) and was soon being heard regularly by thirteen and a half million, many of whom tuned in also to the routine repeat transmissions.

For Sargent self-dissemination on so grand a scale was a heady experience. Talking his way into people's hearts had always been a passion with him. Indulging that passion, he now had millions for table companions. Off and on it seemed as though Britain herself had turned her head his way and was listening engrossedly.

Now as to what his talk was about.

We deal first with musical topics.

*

On music he and Cyril Joad were at amiable loggerheads from their first meeting at the microphone in June 1941.

Men serving a balloon barrage in the North of England asked: 'We are told you have to be educated up to classical music. How do we begin?'

Sargent: 'The first step is very easy. Listen to it. Listen with a completely open mind. Don't have any preconceived ideas that it's going to be awful or difficult. You'll find that the best classical music is extremely easy to listen to. . . . It is classical because it has stood the test of time. Had it been difficult to listen to it probably wouldn't have got very far. It all comes back to what a real British working man said over his drink in a bar not long ago. He had been to a music hall and found himself listening to a symphony orchestra for the first time. And he had liked it! He said he had become "a bloomin' 'ighbrow"!'

Joad: 'I demur. Dr. Sargent thinks it much easier than it is. I dare say it's easy for *him*. . . . But if you happen, like me, to be musically obtuse . . . you'll find that no music worth hearing ought ever to be heard for the first time, because it'll bore you to tears. . . . Up to twenty-one I never really liked anything but popular songs. . . . And then it so happened that in my rooms at Oxford I heard a young man next door practising over and over again the third movement of Beethoven's *Pathétique* Sonata, Op. 13, No. 8. . . . The first way to learn to like a piece if you're musically stupid like me is to hear it repeatedly—six times, twelve times, twenty times, and then it'll penetrate the thick ramparts of your soul.'

Sargent: 'You listeners at the other end, take not the slightest notice of anything you've heard. (Laughter.) Dr. Joad is that sort of man. Against him I've got to say that for twenty weeks we've been giving symphony concerts in the music halls. I've inquired at the box offices and I've been told that the same sort of people are coming to the gallery who went to hear the comedian or see the contortionist. And they loved it! You see, Dr. Joad is the sort of person who tells you the opus number and the key signature of a rondo. Now, I'm not in the least like that, nor need you be at all like that. I don't *know* the opus numbers. At least, I've forgotten them. And they're not essential. So much that Dr. Joad said was grand from his point of view. But I assure you he isn't quite the man in the street.'

A R.A.F. wing-commander stationed in Dumfries thought composers seemed to have gone at a tangent off 'the normal, traditional lines'. 'Is it,' he asked, 'all a leg-pull?'

Joad: 'My guess is . . . that posterity will regard our generation as having its leg pulled by Mr. Britten, Mr. Tippett and Mr. Bliss and all the rest of them. . . .'

Sargent: 'Well, I must take exception to [that]. Quite definitely modern composers are not leg-pullers. It is not an easy thing in music to pull a leg or crack a joke, because it takes so long to write it down. A man writing a symphony may take over a year on the job. To keep yourself in a leg-pulling mood for that length of time shows the sort of brain that probably wouldn't bother with composition at all. There's something rather cranky about that sort of noddle. . . . The stress of classical beauty in music [reached] a point where only supreme genius could attempt to carry on the same line. The result was that most people of [, I wouldn't say] no genius at all, . . . but certainly of good talent felt the shortest way out of the difficulty was to write something original, in that it could not be said to copy anything . . . There has been this search for originality, which I think is very distressing and a blind alley, a great mistake. Composers attempting to be original rather than follow on tradition . . . are, the best of them, absolutely sincere. And I think that some of the

composers mentioned by Dr. Joad will actually—that, well, quite
the reverse will happen to them. . . . It will be discovered that they
weren't leg-pulling at all. We shall think we were perhaps too staid
in our judgment and too stereotyped in our knowledge completely
to appreciate them in their own time.'

*

On the conductor's art—and pretensions—he had two entertaining
tussles with Joad.

The first was prompted by three cooks of the Women's Auxiliary
Air Force at an air station in Buckinghamshire. Their question read:
'We know the conductor's a sort of inspiration to an orchestra. But
is he as important as he looks?'

Sargent: 'Oh, I hope he's much *more* important than he looks. . . .
He's the one man with the whole script, whereas the other people
just have single parts. . . . The leader, for example, may have fifty
bars "rest" to start with. That is simply Number 50 with a sign
underneath it. At the first rehearsal he knows nothing about what is
happening. The conductor must decide beforehand how the piece
is to sound. He goes there with the authority of being the "producer". . . . At rehearsal he sets to work to make the orchestra play
and achieve the effects he has already imagined in his own mind from
the score. This entails a great deal of practical knowledge. He must
know what the strings are capable of doing; how best [to direct their
bowings]; and the breaths, the breathing, of the woodwind. . . . One
mind must be there to see they all work together to achieve what the
score lays down. At the concert, as compared with the rehearsal, he
must add something more. Because some conductors get a perfect
rehearsal and not so good a performance at the concert.'

Joad: 'You hear people say they're going not to a Mozart or
Beethoven concert but to a concert conducted by Toscanini or
Beecham or Barbirolli or even Sargent. Does it make all that
difference? One day I arranged for a party, mostly women, to be
present at a gramophone recital. They were people who laid very
great emphasis on the comparative merits of conductors. I arranged
for a series of orchestral pieces to be played to them on a first-rate
gramophone. Then I asked them: Who was the conductor? The

degree of error they made was in excess of chance. They got it wrong more often than they would have done if they had merely guessed.'

Sargent: 'I know this horror people have of hearing "Toscanini's Beethoven's Fifth" or whatever it is. . . . But it's simply a quick way of saying he's conducting this work by Beethoven. I've not tried it on the gramophone myself. But I do know this, I'd have no difficulty, listening to a Mozart symphony, even one I'd not heard any of them do, in distinguishing between Toscanini, Beecham, Boult and Wood. I'm certain I would get it right.'

Joad: '*You* would, but——'

Question Master: 'That means the difference is there. . . . I shouldn't be surprised if next week we get a question from three conductors asking what's the difference between three cooks.' (Laughter.)

Six months later a Mr. Peacock asked: 'Should the musical conductor be *unseen* by the audience? Is it not possible for the audience to enjoy the music without his. . . .' (General laughter prevented the monitor from hearing the rest of the question.)

Sargent: 'Obviously it's quite possible to enjoy music without watching the gymnastics of the conductor, because music can be enjoyed over the radio and with the gramophone. But a good many people for some reason get a great deal of extra pleasure when they see the conductor. They seem to think his gestures *convey* something to them. And that may be possible. After all, the conductor's gestures are intended to convey his feelings with regard to the interpretation, so it's not really unexpected that they should convey the same thing to the listener. If anybody finds the conductor a nuisance, as many people do, I say: Close your eyes. That's a perfectly good way of hearing—the very best method. You needn't put the conductor underground or hide him as if he was a thing to be ashamed of. Let him stay there and do as he likes. Just close your eyes and listen.'

Joad: 'For my own part I very much like the concealment of conductors. What matters about music is not so much how it's played or who plays it as what is played. A great many of my friends wax eloquent and enthusiastic over different conductors. "Is Sargent better than Beecham?" "Is Beecham better than Sargent?" and so on. My own view is that they couldn't really tell a ha'porth of difference between them if they didn't know who it was. I should very much welcome the experiment of concealing both Sargent and Beecham and Toscanini and all the rest. I could then say to my friends: Who was the conductor that time? And I wouldn't mind betting a hundred to one that a good many of them would get it as wrong as right.'

Sargent: 'Actually it depends on the keenness of their hearing. It's quite easy for anyone who knows music well to tell which of the three of us was conducting the particular thing, because we each do certain things in different ways. I'm very flattered they haven't yet decided which is the best so far as three of us are concerned or [the better of the two] so far as Beecham and I are concerned. On the last point I should have thought there wasn't any doubt. I entirely agree with Dr. Joad that you listen to music and don't look at it. But most people seem to *want* to look at something, and probably the least offensive thing they can watch when the music is taking place, the most musical thing, may be the gestures of the conductor.'

Question Master: 'Very sporting of Dr. Sargent. . . . Most people would say if we can hear Sargent we don't mind whether the band's there or not.'

*

Transmission of Brains Trust sessions by short wave brought in questions from oversea. A listener in Christchurch, New Zealand, wrote: 'Some of the sentiments of our National Anthem are out of date. Should it not be rewritten?'

Sargent: 'No!

> O Lord our God arise,
> Scatter his enemies
> And make them fall.

'That is the verse that everybody hates. It goes on:

> Confound their politics,
> Frustrate their knavish tricks. . . .
> God save us all.

'The point being that if their politics *are* bad, if they *are* against the King, if their tricks *are* knavish, then they *should* be confounded. This verse entirely echoes the spirit of any thinking person who is also religious. There's nothing wrong in the lines as they stand.'

Joad: 'Well, sir, I would like to say No to that. Part of the verse is stupid and part of it is wicked, and it's a pity to go on perpetrating what is both stupid and wicked.'

(Joad was not alone in his revulsion. Sargent refused to be deflected, however. 'You'll notice,' he said on the B.B.C.'s Light Programme in June 1949, after conducting a Royal Birthday tribute to King George VI, 'that we have sung the complete version of the National Anthem. Always it has been the tradition of the Royal Choral Society to sing all three verses before commencing any of their concerts . . . I confess I had many protests with regard to the second verse. . . . So far as I am concerned and so far as the Royal Choral Society is concerned, we will always wish to ask God's help that the enemies of the King may be scattered and that any knavish tricks they may wish to indulge in may be frustrated.' In performance he often as it were italicized Verse 2 by having it sectionally sung. This he managed to especially striking effect at a concert in Malta by inter-Services musicians to mark the coronation of Queen Elizabeth II in 1953 [see Chapter 28]. While the first and third verses were sung by everybody in the hall, audience included, the second verse was entrusted to the choir alone, the singers being 'commandos' and sailors of the Mediterranean Fleet, all in uniform.)

*

A civil servant wrote from Colwyn Bay that, while fond of most other kinds of music, he did not 'appreciate' symphonies and, as a rule, found them boring. What could he do about it? On this occasion Sargent had as co-guests Will Hay, the comedian, and Jennie Lee, M.P., who twenty years later became Britain's first Minister of Education and Science with 'special responsibility for Arts and Culture'.

Sargent: 'It's a matter of time and patience. The difference between a symphony and an ordinary piece of good music is merely length. In a small piece an idea is simply stated and the piece is over. In a symphony a statement is made and then developed. It's rather like the difference between a short essay and a book. A newspaper article may interest you, while a long book on the same subject may bore you. It's you who are wrong, not the piece. [Touching on the same subject in a later broadcast he said: 'The most civilized man would be the one able to sustain the most supreme emotion for the longest time. Most people peter out. I mean, many people find Schubert's 'Great' C major Symphony too long. It simply means that *they* are too short.'] The civil servant who asks this question, obviously of an inquiring nature, feels this to be all wrong. But there's no reason, given opportunity of hearing symphonies and reading something about their form and getting some musician to take him through them and show him their logic, there's no reason, as I say, why he shouldn't come to love the biggest form of orchestral music there is.'

Will Hay: 'I'd say a person who doesn't like a symphony is inclined to be of the impatient type. Perhaps if he developed a little patience it would help.'

Jennie Lee: 'Not altogether. You're more likely to tell a person's income by whether he likes symphonies or not. There's a great number of people in Great Britain a long way yet from enjoying music of that kind because they've not had the education and opportunity.'

Sargent: 'I'll take up that point if I may. The question is whether a rich man has more opportunity of enjoying symphonies. I'm sure that, according to Miss Lee's ideas, he's *less* qualified to understand great music because, as a rich man, he's had less opportunity of experiencing life as it is.'

*

Many of his thoughts on musical criticism had a dissatisfied tone; as came out when the following was put:

'A music critic recently referred to a concerto as having "dazzling colour", "sincere sentiment" and "pungent wit". Is this sense or nonsense?'

Sargent: 'How awkward this is! I read so many criticisms and can't make out what they really mean. Trouble is you've got to describe music to the ordinary person reading the paper through the medium of words, and it just won't work that way. *Dazzling colour?* He obviously meant a very brilliant sort of orchestration. Instead of saying "orchestration" he said "colour". It's a standard [practice] nowadays if you're talking about music and you really want to get away with it to say, "The line is wonderful and the colour is marvellous." And so on. The words have to do with painting. But looking at a painting you talk about the "harmony", the "counterpoint" and so on. The point is that no one can understand what you mean. Other people can't contradict you, and with luck you may pass as a knowledgeable person on the subject. *Sincere sentiment?* I don't know! I can't think of a concerto with sincere sentiment. *Pungent wit?* That puzzles me. The idea of wit in music is a thing I've never been quite able to see. If you make a joke the thing's done quickly. But the whole process of music is length—the actual putting of it down. I've never believed people who see great jokes in music. The better the joke the worse it was to have committed it, because there it stands for all time. People have seen it thousands of millions of times, and it's really not very good. I think this criticism's meant to be sense, and I certainly have no right to say it's nonsense. But I will say that a lot of criticism does get very complicated, because they use words that refer to some other art, that of painting or literature, and they do rather muddle up the ordinary reader with regard to the music actually involved.'

Michael Ayrton, the artist: 'With one destructive blow Dr. Sargent has dealt death to Haydn, to Mozart's "Musical Joke", to music of Erik Satie, to a good deal of Chabrier . . .'

Sargent: 'I refuse to admit I've dealt a death blow to Haydn or any of these people, or tried to. When they were being funny they were not at their best. And music—which is possibly the greatest of the arts—is not at its best when it's using one of the least important sides of artistic enterprise; any more than you'd say . . . slapstick comedy or even first-class farce [represents] the art of writing for the theatre at its best . . . The worst bits in *Romeo and Juliet* and *Hamlet* are the funny bits. I still say Haydn was not at his best when he was writing 'Farewell' symphonies. That symphony remains today because it happens to be very good music most of the time. But the joke at the end when people just walk off is not the most important part of it, and it hasn't lived, I think, because of that. I don't believe the wit of some of the moderns will live very long. I'm all in favour of it as a pleasant form of entertainment. But it isn't music at its greatest.'

Ayrton: 'I'm tempted to cross swords violently with Dr. Sargent who, having asserted that music is the greatest of the arts, [tries] to demonstrate that the more comic and witty sides of music are a low form of musical art. In all other arts comedy plays almost as distinguished a part as tragedy. . . .'

*

As will be seen in later chapters, Sargent was sometimes adversely criticized by orchestral players for his 'improvements' to or alleged tamperings with the scoring of classics. The issue was raised by the following question:

Were the same varieties of musical instruments we hear today in use when the great symphonies of Beethoven and Mozart were originally performed? If some instruments familiar to us were not then known, what authority issues permission to arrange or interfere with the work of the masters?

Sargent: 'Some varieties were known, others were not, and those that were known were often different from those we have today. The organs of the day were different. We should hate the sound of them now. Mozart wrote one symphony, the G minor, without clarinets, then, having got hold of clarinets and talented players, he rearranged it and brought them in to great advantage. . . . The people who like to hear *Messiah* performed "as it was done originally" have my sympathy as connoisseurs or collectors. But so far as the music is concerned I have no wish to hear it as he first heard it. The organ would be terribly out of tune, the [scoring] was very sketchy, most of it being filled in by him at the harpsichord or organ. The wind instruments were thoroughly out of tune. The balance of the choir with the orchestra differed so from what we have today that there were more in the orchestra than the choir. There's a letter he wrote after the first performance with regard to a later one. In it

he says he would like twelve more oboes in the orchestra because the
choir was so small! In other words, the oboes simply doubled the
soprano parts. . . . The arrangements we make today we *have* to
make because the circumstances are so different. . . . We always try
to make them to the advantage of the work. We do what we consider
the composer might have done if he had been placed as we are today.
The good arranger does nothing in the way of composition. He
doesn't really add anything to the thing. He does, however, take
advantage of certain instruments we now have which we believe the
composer would have used had he got them.'

(The 'realization' of Handel's *Messiah* was a subject to which he
often reverted in conversation and at least once in print. His basic
contention was that in Handel's day conditions of performance were
determined not by what the composer would have liked but by what
forces were available. These varied according to time and place—
e.g. four oboes for the first *Messiah*, twelve additional ones for a
later performance. There were, he would add, no big amateur
choirs in those days capable of singing difficult music. At the Dublin
première he had to make do with fourteen men and six boys.
Whereas at the Handel commemoration in Westminster Abbey a
quarter of a century after the master's death *Messiah* and other works
were sung by a choir of about 300 voices, with an orchestra of 250 in
support. Joah Bate, who had got up this force and who conducted it,
'had known Handel well and respected his wishes'. From this
Sargent deduced, precariously perhaps, that for *Messiah* Handel
would have rejoiced in a choir of several hundred well trained voices
at any time, if only they had been there. Sargent's own introduction
of clarinets to supply certain 'organ chording effects' he admitted
to be an anchronism. To conductors who reproached him for this he
replied with a *tu quoque*, saying they were anachronisms themselves,
direction in Handel's day being not from the rostrum but from the
keyboard. Like Beecham he twitted purists who year after year gave
Messiah with 'the original accompaniments—all different!')

*

From Handel to Beethoven.

Dr. Moore, of Harrow: 'Sargent, do you think that probably we can do better justice to Beethoven today than could have been done in his lifetime?'

Sargent: 'Well, I'm sure the playing even of amateur orchestras today is much better than orchestral playing was in his day. The wind instruments must be much more in tune now . . . I should imagine woodwind intonation was extremely faulty. Our ears being more trained, we should find it disturbing today. Two extraordinary things. . . . Trumpets were able to play only certain notes. Same with the horns. In Beethoven you will come across successions of four chords. Three of these chords will include trumpet and horn notes because those notes could be played on those instruments. But in the fourth chord notes were missing because those instruments couldn't play them; they weren't available. From Wagner's and Weingartner's arrangements onwards, everybody has added notes we feel sure Beethoven would have put in had they been available then. If you take two C's in octave on the first and second trumpets that was O.K. But the next chord has a note which the first trumpet couldn't play without jumping an octave and a ninth to get it!'

*

On jazz, swing and related styles of music the man who years later had an unprecedented youth following at the 'Proms' was peremptory.

From a pilot officer, R.A.F.: 'Isn't it time serious musical people took more notice of the best kind of swing music?'

Sargent: 'Speaking not as a highbrow but as one who's intensely fond of dancing and who listens with the greatest interest to any kind of music, swing included, I must say I have watched with the greatest horror the retrogression that has taken place in dance music in my time. . . . But I know that few of these jazz bands rehearse at all. Most of it is extemporized. At any moment the trumpet or [say, the clarinet] is just given a sign by the conductor, and then he does what, I think, is called a "break"—plays variations of his own which can never be repeated exactly on any other occasion at all—not even by him. Which is a good thing! . . . I respect exhilaration in music as I do that of whisky or champagne. But it's not the serious musician's job to take great interest in this thing. . . . It achieves its

own end, which is catchpenny. . . . It's not really worthy of very
serious consideration. . . .

'Most of these tunes [in the arrangements that come up] hardly
last a week. If I go the following week I hear the same band playing
them in a different way. The man isn't capable of repeating them the
same way. . . . It has become a very poor show. . . .

'The art of making popular music, a very important one, has
become, as I said catchpenny. We've got this idea of sudden success.
We've got to make a tune catch on immediately. . . . These tunes
are . . . all in the same rhythm. . . . It's a terrible sign of poverty.
The playing can be marvellous. The technique of these people is
extraordinary. I take my hat off to them. I'm not a highbrow. I love
dancing. I love dance music. But I want it to be something that
will last for more than a night and more than a week. A good tune
should still be a good tune in ten years' time. . . . We've got back to
the primitive things. Rhythm is the most primitive of all musical
sensations. You find it in the complete barbarian. . . . The thing is
absolutely machine-made. The conductor could be a metronome
and be quite perfect. . . . It's a form of intoxication that takes you
out of yourself but . . . probably throws you back in the end on
your worse self. . . .'

*

On matters outside music his opinions were sometimes shrewd,
sometimes naïve and often at odds with the received opinions of the
hour, not to say those of the half-century. He was ready to put his
finger in any pie; even in the dread pie of economics.

*

Questioner: 'Is the profit motive the principal thing that makes
people enterprising, and is it a good idea?'

Sargent: '*What can it profit a man if he gain the whole world and
lose his own soul?* The person who's out to make money, if that's
what we mean by a profit, may find that instead of getting a profit
he has got a loss. I'm embarrassed in dealing with this question,
because I'm doing a job which to me is my greatest happiness.
Whether earning my living at it or not, I'd still wish to be doing the

job I am doing. Whereas a man working in a sewer—well, it would be rather hard for him to say the same thing. What really matters is motive. Take the coal-mining industry. There seem to be three conflicting reasons for coal mining. . . . On the one hand we're told we mine for coal so that the owners of the coal shall make a big profit. On the other hand we are told by the trade unions that we mine for coal so that the coal-miner in the bowels of the earth shall get large wages. It seems to me that the real reason for coal mining is that the cold man may get warmth.

'If the motives behind work were for one's fellow creatures, then half the problems would be solved. Ideally no man should have to work just to make money. The ideal trade union would exist to see the workers did the most for their fellow creatures for the least money. Mind you, the fellow creatures, the people they're working for, would see the workers got the most money possible! We should have a Socialism that was a spiritual one, working entirely on its own. The man who's speculating and buys shares one moment and sells them the next and has done nothing but make some money for himself cannot be defended at all, I think, on any reasonable grounds. [He reverted unluckily to this theme a little over a year later. A question having been put, 'Is the Stock Exchange really necessary ?' he contended that it would be a good thing if people putting their money into business or trade 'through the Stock Exchange' should be obliged to keep it there for two or three years, so that, instead of its being immediately 'sold away' as a gamble, it could reach the industry for which it was intended and 'get down to the workmen'. 'Sargent,' commented the Editor of the *Economist*, who was a fellow guest, 'has the queerest idea of what goes on in the City.'] All work should be done for a disinterested motive. Obviously the wage must be provided by the fellow for whom you work, and he should like providing it.'

*

On nationalization he squared up to Emanuel Shinwell, soon to be Minister of Fuel and Power in the first post-war Labour government, and did not, all things considered, come off badly.

Questioner: 'Output of coal has decreased owing to absenteeism.

If the miners can't be made to work in wartime, how could they be made to work under nationalization, should this be introduced?'

Shinwell: 'Given more congenial conditions in the pits, assurance of regular employment and the knowledge that they are working for the community and that nobody's taking an undue share of the swag: given this, I think there'll be little absenteeism; there'll be increased production.'

Sargent: 'Is it possible to nationalize an industry without also nationalizing the trade union . . . as has more or less had to be done in Russia? If you nationalize or subsidize an industry must you not at the same time ensure that the wages shall not continue to go up? Because if there is a subsidy [you get] a vicious circle. The moment there's more money the instinct of the trade union would be to earn it with less work; and so we go on for ever and ever.'

Shinwell: 'I'm bound to say I think Sargent mistaken in assuming you must subsidize a nationalized industry . . . I reject the conception of subsidies as applied to nationalized industry, or indeed any industry. And I'm opposed to nationalization if it means trade unions controlled by the State. . . . The trade unions must remain independent bodies, whether working for the State or for private employers.'

Sargent: 'I'm still questioning Mr. Shinwell. Surely the security a man [got from nationalization] would be the fact that he'd know there could be an unlimited subsidy, whereas when working for a private employer he doesn't know whether the man mayn't go broke and be unable to pay his wages. I'm sure the feeling of many men in the street is that nationalization comes first of all to industries that need to be subsidized to make sure a man gets a good living wage from a job that isn't necessarily profit-making. In many people's minds, rightly or wrongly, the two things are linked together, and I don't think this can be waved away by saying they aren't.'

Shinwell: 'And I say that if you operate a great national industry or service on efficient lines you don't require to subsidize it at all.'

*

From economic generalizations to their humble applications.

Questioner: 'Can you suggest a solution of the problem of the blind-alley occupation, such as errand-boy, boot-black, news-vendor?'

Sargent: 'If everybody blacked his own boots you'd soon do away with boot-blacks. With regard to errand-boys and news-vendors, I believe there are famous newspaper owners still living who started their lives selling papers on the streets. I see nothing against any boy being an errand-boy or newspaper-boy. There are many more unhealthy jobs than that. A smart boy who, as soon as he leaves school, starts running errands isn't necessarily damned for life. I don't see why it [should be] a blind-alley occupation.'

Joad: 'Sargent says he doesn't know what a blind-alley occupation means. It means an occupation you follow for a year or two after leaving school, when your labour is cheap and anybody will employ you. Then you get thrown out of it on to the industrial scrap heap. . . . In other words, it doesn't lead anywhere.'

Sargent: 'I don't know why Dr. Joad is so angry with me. I entirely agree that through education the boy can step further. What we haven't discovered is how to do away with the errand-boy and the newspaper-seller. I don't believe you can. My point is: Don't make his job a blind-alley one! Let him do it as a part-time job while he's still carrying on his education. Somebody has to run errands. Somebody has to sell newspapers. It doesn't mean a boy's necessarily out and finished after two years . . . if we help him.'

*

It was a time of heightened, even bristling class consciousness in some quarters. The following came up at a session in which Bertrand Russell took part:

Questioner: 'The man who cuts my hair addresses me as sir, but presumably he doesn't "sir" the dustman. Am I worth more than the dustman? If not, shouldn't we discourage this preferential mode of address?'

Russell: 'In England a person with a larger income is addressed by a person with a smaller income as "sir". This is not the case in America. In that respect the Americans are to be preferred to ourselves. I hope we shall imitate them.'

Sargent: 'I disagree. I'm all for levelling up politenesses—but not impolitenesses. It's very convenient for the hairdresser to say "sir" to anybody who sits in his chair, because he probably doesn't know his name or occupation. He's not in any case going to say "Mr. Dustman" or "Mr. Solicitor". I'd say when the hairdresser is dressing the dustman's hair he calls the dustman "sir". And when the dustman is collecting the hairdresser's rubbish he calls the hairdresser "sir"! It's just a convenient word used by the person employed to the person employing him. I see no reason to get rid of it at all. . . . "Sir" can be used by anybody to anybody to whom he feels inclined to use it—and the more people he feels inclined to use it to the better person he probably is.'

*

Questioner: 'In a democratic age should tipping be abolished?'
Sargent: 'Oh no, no! Everyone should tip more. We each tip in a democratic age, everybody equal, we all tip everybody as often as possible. I'm all against this "politeness" business. If we are democratic, let's do the best thing all the time and not all decide to do the worse thing, or nothing at all.'

*

Questioner: 'Should education improve manners, and if so why hasn't it done so?'
Sargent: 'It hasn't done so because it hasn't been good education. "Manners makyth man" puts the cart before the horse. A good man will produce good manners. It's fatal to teach children manners as such. I'd teach a child to get up and open the door for his mother not because it's a good thing and "good manners" to open the door but because he would naturally wish to show his respect for her. I would say also to the child: "If by any chance you'd rather not open the door for your mother, then for heaven's sake don't have "good manners" and be hypocritical. Just don't do it. Sit tight and wait for a better frame of mind." We should always teach manners by teaching the reasons for them. Which is Christianity in small doses. . . . Teach the reason. Good manners will follow.'

*

Questioner: 'What is your definition of a snob?'
Sargent: 'Snobbery doesn't apply only to the upper classes. At

the moment there's more snobbery from below than ever existed in the upper classes, although the war has killed off snobbery to a very great extent. I've met all the classes . . . and know them pretty well. There's still more snobbery among the ordinary middle class in small towns—the distinction between the person with one maid or no maid or two maids, for example—than there has ever been in the lowest classes or in the upper classes. It's just as snobbish to consider the charwoman more important than the duchess as it is to think the duchess more important than the charwoman. In *Pygmalion*, I think, Shaw defines a gentleman as "a person who shows equal courtesy and civility to all classes". And it is true. Any form of class distinction at all, whether in favour of the lowest class [or any other] is snobbery. Snobbery . . . can work from either end . . . I have known snobs who were just armchair snobs—the old lady who sits there and just talks about [eminent] people; she knows her *Debrett* inside out—it's her fund of intellectual amusement. We must remember the bore, a great snob he was, who walked into his club and was greeted with, "Hullo, how's the duke?"

' "The duke? Which duke?"

' "Oh, any duke!" ' (Laughter.)

*

International politics and the war's moral aftermath often came up.

Questioner: 'Is it possible to re-educate the Japanese so that they can ultimately be accepted by other nations?' (The Japanese had surrendered two months earlier. Bertrand Russell was a fellow guest on this occasion.)

Russell: 'I haven't the slightest doubt it's possible.'

Sargent: 'You can educate fleas to perform quite decently in public. You can educate cats and dogs to be house-trained. I am certain that, [coming] to human beings, the Japanese—if you could get fundamentally at their religion, at their philosophy, you'd make a whole difference. If we *can't* educate them, then obviously what we do is use lots of atomic bombs, because there's no sense in keeping a race alive who could be a menace in a world which we've got to improve, if we could not believe they would eventually become more decent people.'

Russell: 'I'm a little alarmed at the idea of the use of the atomic bomb. If we say "Our way of life is best, you've just got to learn it—if you don't you'll be atomized"—when we say that, it's just as bad as when Hitler and the Japs say it.'

Sargent: 'If we say everybody's belief is as good as everybody else's, then we're striking at fundamental truths, and that I can't agree with. There must be some standard. You cannot say, "You, who have entirely opposite standards, which I believe to be quite immoral and against all one's convictions, you are equally worthy to bear the missionary spirit throughout the world." With that I just don't agree. I'm not saying we *should* use atomic bombs against the Japanese. But I did say that, if we felt it was not possible to re-educate them, then we might be justified in this extreme measure.'

Russell: 'Force plays its part so long as war is going on. When war is not on it seems to me the proper method is persuasion. That's a different thing from destroying them utterly. You have a right to insist on being able to put persuasion before people.'

Sargent: 'Professor Russell . . . wouldn't attempt to persuade a person if he knew it was not possible to persuade him.'

Russell: 'But we don't know that.'

*

What brought out the warmth in Sargent and, as some will think, his sagacity were questions that touched or fringed on faith and morals.

Questioner: 'What is superstition?'

Sargent: 'Superstition, it seems to me, is when you're afraid the thing *might* be true. . . . It probably isn't so. But it might be. And you tell yourself "If it's true I'm in the cart unless I do some particular thing. It may be true that going under a ladder brings bad luck, so perhaps it's better for me not to go under the ladder." And so on. It's important to distinguish between superstition and faith. In faith you feel that *it is* but cannot logically prove it in your own mind or to the satisfaction of anybody else's. In your heart of hearts you feel the thing *is* true, not that it *might* be true. That is faith. Superstition is the reverse.'

*

Questioner: 'Can one believe in ghosts and apparitions?'

Sargent: 'For my part I believe in future life entirely. . . . As ordinary believing Christians we have the warning that necromancy, which is dealing with "familiar spirits", is to be ranked with murder and other sins as worthy of hell. I for my part am willing to take that as a fairly sensible ruling. I have no wish to deal with either a "familiar" or "unfamiliar" spirit. . . . There have been churches who say: "This is of the Devil. You must 'prove' the spirits to see if they are good or evil." I have no wish to prove spirits myself. I believe they can be there either for good or for evil. . . . I have no longing to meet a ghost. I should hate to. . . . And so, I leave it entirely alone. . . .'

*

Questioner (boy of 11): 'Why should I learn history? What's the use?'

Sargent: 'I sympathize with the questioner entirely. I think what's wrong is who has been teaching him. . . . The whole point of any education is simply to avoid having to learn "by experience". We all seem to think that experience is the best teacher. But it's only the best teacher for fools. The wise person says, "Let me look at the experience of other people and see what happens if a man does such and such a thing. They don't in that case have the worry of making their own mistakes. We should all become better statesmen and better stateswomen. . . . We can only avoid mistakes in thinking or action by seeing what other people have done, where they have done the right thing and where they have failed. That's the thing history can teach us.'*

*

Questioner: 'If I'm permitted to send one book in one volume to a British prisoner-of-war in Germany, what should I send?'

Desmond MacCarthy, the literary critic: 'Spinoza, *War and Peace* . . . a complete Shakespeare . . .'

---

* The question recurring eighteen months later, he summarized his position thus: 'It's only the fool who learns at the school of experience. The clever person learns at that school of the other fellow's experience.'

John Betjeman, the poet: 'The works of Chaucer. . . .'

Helen Kirkpatrick, the journalist: 'I should send a Bible.'

Sargent: 'Oh yes, I back up Miss Kirkpatrick. The Bible gives you everything you can possibly want under almost all circumstances. You've got your history, your poetry, your philosophy. You've got solace, you've got inspiration, and you've got characterization. . . . Many different styles. Magnificent literature. And divine inspiration behind it all. . . .'

*

Questioner: 'If you were a fairy godfather at the christening of a baby girl, what five attributes would you bestow on her in the hope of ensuring her a full and happy life?'

Joad: 'Well, number one, good health. . . .'

Julian Huxley: '. . . I put health and energy at the top.'

Commander Campbell: 'I should put health first most decidedly.'

Sargent: 'Health? I've known many people who were healthy and extremely selfish and unsympathetic. I'm not sure we haven't all seen people much improved by certain bouts of illness. I would not be brave enough to wish that any godchild of mine should be, throughout life, healthy. The child might miss something that is learned only through some sort of affliction.

'There are three things I would be brave enough to ask for. One is simply kindliness, the real art of loving one's neighbour as oneself. . . . Another is a sense of humour, which means placing a relative value on oneself, so that even in one's greatest tragedy there's still something that makes one smile, and you see that relatively [the tragedy] is not important. The third thing is the first thing, really—the gift of faith, ordinary Christian faith. I've discovered that people who have it—there's nothing really in this world that can really affect them at all. All the other things may be useful—beauty and so on. Or they may be snares. I don't know. Given faith life, can remain an exciting adventure. And even death can lose its sting.'

The same question was given a repeat run two years later. W. L. (later Sir Linton) Andrews, editor of *The Yorkshire Post*, was at the session.

Andrews: . . . 'Self knowledge, self-reverence, self-control' (a citation from Tennyson).

Sargent: '. . . Self this, self that, self the other. One so often hears "To thine own self be true" quoted as if it were from the Bible. Actually they were words put into the mouth of a doddering old man. They are not from the Bible at all, and they are not essentially true. "To Thine own self be true, and it follows as the night the day thou cans't not then be false to any man." That's obviously *un*true. Hitler was true to himself and false to many other men. If the person concerned was absolutely perfect, that would be different. But to say the same to the average person, a person who should really be denying himself, a person who knows that most of his own self is pretty rotten and is trying to improve that self . . .! No, we've got to be very careful here.

'The fundamental qualities I would like to find in a child—the second of them would simply be the endeavour to love his neighbour as himself. With that quality he couldn't go far wrong in his actions towards his fellow creatures; he would be faithful to his ideals, kind and sensitive to other people's wishes. Whether he were successful or not in business wouldn't matter, because he would have done a good job of work. But all this would be preceded by *the* fundamental thing which I would like any child of mine to have. That is simply the ordinary Christian faith. With that there can be no harm mentally come to him or harm spiritually come to him. His life becomes a great adventure, his death an even greater adventure. . . . In fact it is all summed up in the First Commandment: "Love the Lord thy God with all thy might." '

*

The two foregoing passages are quoted from Brains Trust transmissions on 22nd December (repeated 27th), 1942 and 20th November, 1945. Some admirers regard them as Sargent's noblest public performance in any medium.

CHAPTER TWENTY-FIVE

KNIGHT BACHELOR

D URING the six years leading up to and including 1950, his career ramified and his circumstances changed out of knowledge. While keeping faith in Britain with a dozen or fifteen choral and orchestral societies (the Leeds Philharmonic Choir was his newest acquisition) as a juggler keeps balls in the air, though rarely as many, he flew with suitcases full of scores and band parts— Elgar, Beethoven, Tchaikovsky, Sibelius, Vaughan Williams, Delius, Walton, Holst, more Elgar and Elgar again—to Scandinavia, the Peninsula, Greece, five Australian States (a jubilant return), South Africa and South America, paying excess baggage fees of up to £50 for a single trip and five times that amount when he toured a continent. From embassies and official residences he wrote spirited despatches for the briefing or first-hand information of favoured gossip writers at home. He told of admission prices raised, houses sold out, disconsolate hundreds turned away and worshipping throngs at stage doors. Without exception, he conveyed, his concerts were triumphs. Not personal triumphs, to be sure. Triumphs for British music, rather. Judicious showmanship helped the wider cause. Whenever it was feasible he had himself caught in a spotlight for his first entry, the auditorium lights being simultaneously dimmed. Cocooned in a white blaze, he would leap to the rostrum and summon up the opening drum roll of the National Anthem, British or vernacular, with an imperious baton salute that gave people gooseflesh all the way from His Majesty's Theatre, Perth (W. Australia), to the City Hall, Johannesburg, and beyond.

At home, the *Hiawatha* pageants having been abandoned for good, his spotlit appearances at the Royal Albert Hall were now

332

limited in the ordinary way to three carol concerts with the Royal
Choral Society each Christmastide. If an additional chance offered
he jumped at it unblushingly. In the summer of 1948 he conducted
at the Royal Opera House a dramatized, mimed, sung and danced
version of *The Pilgrim's Progress* at sixteen crammed performances,
all standing room taken, to an aggregate of 32,000 (twice that
number were unable to get in), including a bigger ratio of bishops,
deans and archdeacons than the theatre had ever before seen. Not
only did he conduct the music. He had also chosen and adapted it
for the theatre's chorus and orchestra, number by number, according to the script's dramatic moods and exigencies, from the works of
two composers, Bach and Gluck. During the rehearsals he told
Frank Ballard, Covent Garden's veteran 'machinist' that he proposed to make his entry each night with spotlight on him down the
centre aisle. Frank Ballard had been reared in a staid tradition.
He spluttered at the idea. It was in any case an impracticable one.
The dome spotlight's limited angle of play ruled it out. A compromise was arrived at. Sargent should be spotlit from the dome
on making his entrance not down the aisle but through the customary door into the orchestra pit. Ballard assented but was un-
appeased. He wondered what the world was coming to.

Before passing to a detailed account of his professional doings
abroad, certain other happenings at home and elsewhere may conveniently be touched on here.

Intimate friends had been aware for some time that all was not
well between himself and Eileen. None were surprised when it
became known in mid-August, 1946, that a decree nisi, dated
25th February of the same year, dissolving the marriage had been
made absolute in the Royal Courts of Justice. Eileen Laura Harding
Sargent was petitioner, and the grounds cited were desertion. In
Sargent circles it had been expected that the decree would be made
much of in the newspapers. For one reason or another, among them
shortage of newsprint and the brevity and formal nature of the proceedings, the item was minute; it caught so few eyes and was so
rarely if ever adverted to in print that Sargent was surmised by
many admirers to have been a bachelor then and for ever. A week
after the promulgation of the decree, Eileen wrote to a friend that

this was the very sad end of a chapter; that she had been at fault in marrying a genius; that she would remember only 'the Happy Times' and hoped she and Malcolm would always remain good friends, since life was so short and they had been through so much together.

It was around this time that he left Chesham-place for a some-what bigger flat elsewhere in Kensington, a semi-basement. You went down steps from the street into a hall which had been turned into a dining-room. His bedroom-workroom had one small window, a divan, a desk and a wardrobe. He once contrived, by taking some-thing out, to insinuate a piano. His music he kept in a windowless box room, where Peter sometimes slept when on leave during his last months with the Royal Naval Air Service. His private secretary did a lot of her work at a little desk in the corridor. The furniture wasn't his and didn't look as though it might be; there were arm-chairs in red plush. A daily help who didn't always turn up and meals from the kitchen upstairs as and when wanted (rarely) completed the amenities of what Sargent laughingly called his 'hovel'.

*

Suddenly everything changed. The early summer of 1947 brought a translation of environment and station. A cultured woman friend whose charm, adroitness and lightest word carried weight in Down-ing Street and higher places still, had urged upon Clement Attlee, the Prime Minister, that something ought to be done to secure official recognition of Dr. Sargent's services to his country through music at home and away. There was no dallying. He appeared among new knights bachelor in the 1947 Birthday Honours and in all the newspapers next morning, looking ten years younger than his age according to some, quite fifteen, according to others. In so far as politics had relevance the knighthood was an added reason for his smiling upon the Labour government. He had been in Australia when the new administration came to power. At one of the innu-merable luncheons in his honour he told fellow guests that the election results did not worry him at all, because the Left had always been out to help the arts. The outgoing government, he said,

had spent a mere £175,000 a year (through C.E.M.A.) on backing
three thousand concerts. 'Nothing like enough!' he exclaimed.
More was on the way, however.

That Sir Malcolm Sargent, Mus.D., F.R.C.M., bearer of honorary degrees from the universities of Oxford and Liverpool, should
live down a basement flight amid red plush armchairs would not
have seemed fitting, if they had known about it, to his thronging
admirers, who thought of him as a story-book prince and expected
him to live rather like one. The season of his knighthood was the
season also of his removal to No. 9, Royal Albert Hall Mansions,
an eyrie dominating the Park and the Royal Albert Memorial; also
the roof under which he was to die. He had no furniture to take
there. His income was growing. But there had been heavy calls upon
it, some of them heavy ones; and always he had lived and given
open-handedly. Up to this point his earnings had been in the range
of £10,000 to £12,000 a year. There was never a lot of money in the
bank. No. 9 was furnished to a large extent by friends; by one friend
in particular. Opulent, solid and 1930-ish in tone, the new interior
hit off with nicety his taste and personality. Whether at table in the
dining-room that overlooked the park or darting with eager smile
and word from group to group of cocktail party guests, or upstairs
in the library, listening with hands clasped under chin to test
pressings of his newest gramophone recording—whatever he was
about and in whatever part of it he chanced to be, No. 9 matched his
talk and alertness and the cut of his clothes as decisively as if the
work of a theatrical designer.

One room, set apart for an office, was big enough, as presently
proved, for two assistant secretaries and their machines as well as
for the private secretary. Anne Chapman had left for an appointment in the Consular Service; as has been mentioned earlier, she
remained a friend and confidante of 'the Maestro', often exchanging
letters with him, for the rest of his life. Her place had been taken
during the last months of the semi-basement régime by a girl newly
out of the Women's Royal Naval Service, Miss Sylvia Darley. She,
too, was with him to the end, a personal assistant of increasing
influence in matters of administration and liaison. She became his
right hand, a kind of unofficial manager and self-trained publicity

agent, as widely reputed behind a hundred platforms as her principal was in front of them. A noted English impresario has testified that whenever he rang No. 9 to inquire whether Sargent had a free date for, say, a year or two years ahead, it usually happened that he got no further than Miss Darley, 'who would say it was all very well and they'd have to see.' When the time came for seeing, she saw clearly and shrewdly. Sargent delegated much liaison work to her. Among promoters and musical committee men far and near she was accepted as a person of consequence. 'The *éminence grise* of Albert Hall Mansions' was the phrase used of her by an orchestral veteran who from the mid-1920s and, during his last two decades, knew Sargent more intimately than most. The phrase defined her well. Not that there was anything *grise* about Sylvia Darley except in the metaphorical sense. She had pretty hair. Then, as later, *éminence rousse* would have been nearer the mark literally.

Another who must not pass unnoticed is the equable and homely Oliver, who came to No. 9 the same year as Miss Darley. Oliver's special gift was that of being versatile and thinking little of it. In the early 1920s he had been a family chauffeur at Melton Mowbray. One day his own 'people' not having come down to Melton by the usual London train, he gave a lift to one who had, Edward Prince of Wales. No car was waiting for the Prince. Oliver and his car were momentarily at a loose end. What more natural than that the Prince should jump in? 'Were you in the Army?' he asked. 'No, in the R.A.F.,' said Oliver. 'Right!' returned the Prince. Those were the only preliminaries. When hearing Sargent at the parish church organ in those times, it never entered Oliver's head that, a generation later, Dr. Sargent would be Sir Malcolm and himself Sir Malcolm's manservant. At first he attended to the cooking as well as to his master's clothes. Towards the end (he retired the year before Sargent's death) the kitchen became too much for him, for he was older than Sargent by two years. On occasion he would still turn out one of his specialities, however. At steak and kidney pudding with oysters and mushrooms he was a dab. The wardrobe side of his work was onerous. A conductor working at Sargent's pace and travelling up to 40,000 miles a year does not wear clothes out; he devours them. At any one time Sargent had six evening dress suits in his wardrobe. Each cost £75 and lasted not more than five years, sometimes less. During Oliver's eighteen years at No. 9 Sargent got through about twenty-five 'tail' suits. What made them go so quickly was the sweating, especially at summer concerts and in sub-tropical climates. After a sweltering night it would take a suit three or four days to dry out at the proper slowness. 'And then,' Oliver used to observe, 'foreign valeting is so bad. Suits come back shiny.' As well as black tail suits his master had six tropical outfits, white dinner jackets and all; and there were always a dozen day suits on hand. Laundry was a pretty problem. In hot weather he would put on five shirts and five collars a day—one of each before rehearsal, after rehearsal, before the concert, during the interval and after the concert.

Briefing hire-car drivers was another job. Before the Brains Trust and the knighthood had accentuated his fame Sargent could leave the Albert Hall in tolerable security. By the time he took charge of the Promenade Concerts (1950) the case had altered. Every night insatiable knots of young people would wait at the artists' entrance with programmes and miniature scores for autographing. As soon as he came out they would crush in upon him with supplicating eyes and hands and slowly move with the grinning, struggling prisoner in their midst across the sixty yards that separated him from home. Often he found other knots barring the doorway and inside it crowding the hall. More than once Oliver had 'a bit of a job' to get him free. Because of these trials the dodge was worked out of having a motor-car drawn up before the end of a concert and barriers placed across the pavement so that the Idol could get away without being involved in a jovial scrum. The routine was to drive into Kensington Road and make off in the direction of Knightsbridge, 'giving the impression that the boss was going out to dinner'. Then back to No. 9 after a detour long enough for 'my children', as he came to call the young Prommers, to have dispersed. Like every other notable who has been affectionately mobbed he was scared and delighted. These occasions may have been a triumph for British music or for whatever pet choir he chanced to have been conducting. But there is no doubt they were a triumph for Malcolm, too.

That he should be adored as much by droves of boys and girls under or little over twenty as by mature ladies on the front row of famous amateur choirs was nectar for a man in his fifties, conscious of new tangents and stirrings that were alien to him. Adrian Boult brought back a concert version of *Wozzeck* to the Albert Hall, where he had venturesomely done it before the war. This time he had a more perceptive and responsive public, including a good proportion of under-twenty-fives. To Berg and others of the 'second Viennese school' Sargent remained unresponsive. Of *Wozzeck* he once said something which at first sight is hard to credit: 'The difficulty is that I can't enjoy the music, because I find the story so distasteful.' That a man of such charity and human 'resonance' should have been blind to the compassion that informs Büchner's text is not, perhaps, as surprising on reflection as it may seem. To some natures and in some situations, like, far from being attracted to like, recoils as from a stranger. On the new popular music he continued prim and unbending. At the height of the Frank Sinatra hysteria he said more than once that young girls who swooned to Sinatra's singing should be spanked by their mothers. He maintained that the new sort of 'pop' number 'kills itself stone dead very quickly', and boasted that when a dance band leader wanted to swap orchestras with him for a day or two his reply was: 'I can quite see why you should want to conduct mine but not why I should want to conduct yours. If you've got a Rolls-Royce, why swap it for a Ford?' In Australia and elsewhere he talked about a brewers' experiment or project at home: halls seating two or three hundred where young people could drink and listen for half-hour stretches— separated by fifteen-minute intervals (necessary for recuperation, it appeared)—to classical music by, say, a string quartet or a solo pianist. Music of this kind, he thought, was much less likely to make young people 'untidy in their loving' than the music of jazz bands.*

To what extent did he seriously attend to music outside his 'perimeter'? At first among young people and gradually among some of their elders, the Beatles 'pop' group began to possess the

---

* Quoted by *The Argus*, Melbourne, Australia., 14th June, 1945.

world's ear in 1963. Nearly four years later, two months or so before the final illness struck, closing the perimeter of his taste for ever, he said he was one of the few people in the world who had never heard a note of Beatles music. He seemed to plume himself on his immunity. By this time the Beatles were beginning to be gravely analysed and lauded by music critics of standing. By then it was too late for him to open his mind. Even if there had been all the time in the world one doubts whether he would have done so. In music his attitude to worlds other than his own was one of defensive, almost touchy incuriosity. Some of these worlds were nearly the whole world to young people of the 1950s and 1960s. By adolescent and post-adolescent standards he was, in the cant of the day, a 'square'. It made little difference. An exception to new sociological drifts, he was one of the few elders in the public eye who rode high and immune above what came to be known as the Battle of the Generations.

The younger end of the 'Proms' public, upon whom this judgment is to some extent based, were themselves exceptions and offered limited criteria. But they were not sealed off from the rest of their generation; they came under natural opinion-pressures from their coevals. This made their roaring ovations for Sargent pleasantly anomalous. Since before these youngsters were born, hostile orchestral players had called him 'Flash Harry'. The 'children' adopted an adverse nickname and shortened it to 'Flash'. 'We want Flash, we want Flash!' they would chant on the first and last nights of the 'Proms'. A time came when, on one of these last nights, he gave a speech, saying: 'It is forty-five years since I conducted my first Promenade Concert.' As he left the platform some youngster shouted: 'Good night, Grandad!' and the cry was gleefully taken up. The young crowd in the arena called him 'Flash' and 'Grandad' because they thought the world of him. When masses of people think the world of somebody a nickname or a fireside name becomes a need.

As a public figure is loved, so is he hated, by the sediment of crackpots. From time to time there were malignant, threatening letters. At least once the police were invoked, and plain clothes officers kept guard outside No. 9. Threats bred of psychic upsets denoted the same thing as the adoring scrums and shouts. They were adoration inverted.

*

He began his international gaddings before the war was over, though the end of the fighting was in sight. Early in February 1945 he flew on an official 'facility' flight to New York and flew back a month or more later, suffering near-suffocation on one of the journeys because of faulty oxygen supply.

This was his first professional sight of America. His mission was with Toscanini's orchestra, the N.B.C. Symphony, in a broadcasting studio which Toscanini frequented much, H8 at Radio City. Here, in the presence of a 'captive' audience, after a luncheon in his honour at which he stressed how symphonic music had blossomed in Britain during the war ('at first a necessary *moral* builder, now performed on a bigger scale than ever in peacetime'), he conducted the first of four Sunday afternoon concerts over the air, his programmes being devoted—Sibelius's first symphony and Dvořák's seventh (D minor, Op. 70) apart—to English music—the *Cockaigne*, *London* and *Wasps* overtures, the *Perfect Fool* ballet music (which Olin Downes in *The New York Times* found 'very bourgeois'), the viola concerto of Walton (with William Primrose) and the violin concerto of Elgar (with Yehudi Menuhin). The studio audience received him warm-heartedly from the start, although Downes judged him not to have quite got the measure of the orchestra, or the orchestra his, in the Dvořák symphony at the first concert, a performance said to have been rough in tone quality and episodic rather than sustained in line. In the end, said Downes, he was conducting with far more control and mutual understanding and finally gave the impression of conspicuous gifts. Of the Elgar concerto Menuhin remembers how quickly and completely he won over the players at rehearsal and how stylishly they responded. Thirteen years earlier Menuhin had for the first time played in the concerto under its composer, a revelatory chapter. Looking back, he considers that around the time of this New York performance, Sargent was 'next best to Elgar in this work'. Sargent might have thought that was putting it mildly. On the violin concerto and Elgar generally he regarded himself as an authority, one upon whom the mantle had fallen. When rehearsing he would sometimes introduce points of phrasing and accent which were neither laid down by the text nor corroborated by players who had sat under Elgar's baton and remembered the minutiae.

'Yes, that's all right,' he would say if anybody demurred. 'I had it from Elgar himself. He once said, "My music is always safe with young Sargent", then went off to the races, leaving a rehearsal in my hands.'

Three months after leaving New York he touched down in Melbourne, following a flight which a string of mishaps had lengthened from eight days to nineteen. He was four days late for his first rehearsal and hoped this would be a record for the rest of his life. He was to conduct twenty symphony concerts, mostly in pairs of repeat programmes, in five State capitals under the auspices once more of the Australian Broadcasting Commission.

It was the late 1930s all over again. Melbourne, its auditorium and orchestra, its warm-hearted audiences and other old friends, had changed so little that he might, so he said, have been there only the week before. Some things that remained the same might have been changed to music's advantage. Woodwind sections were still under-provided and undertrained. 'Your orchestras,' he said, 'could do with more strings, but there's no point in bringing that about until your woodwinds have been strengthened.' Australia's policy, he tartly advised, should be to ban the export of her best theatrical and musical artists and think about raising the ban on the import of good ones from overseas.

This was said after an early rehearsal in Sydney. Yet the performance he got nine days later from the Sydney Symphony Orchestra of Elgar's E flat Symphony (No. 2) won praise from a penetrating and seasoned pen. 'A noble, strong and deeply moving interpretation,' wrote Neville Cardus, who was at that time the *Sydney Morning Herald*'s critic. 'Dr. Sargent rose to the height of his theme. I have never heard him conduct anything so eloquently and simply. . . . Here was truly interpretative art. As an Englishman who heard the first of all performances of this work thirty-four years ago, I confess to having listened last night with fresh ears and a quickened appreciation.' The following concert in the Sydney series brought up Sibelius's Symphony No. 1. Over this Cardus shook his head. He had reason to. It was a slovenly business in part. What no critic and exceedingly few people off the platform could have been expected to know at the time was how the slovenliness came about.

Section by section, privately as well as in full rehearsal, the orchestra had worked at the score unsparingly and well. A performance to match that of Elgar's E flat was confidently hoped for. A few minutes before the concert began news reached Sargent that his first clarinet had been taken ill. So the first clarinet part was taken over by second clarinet, who had to play intricate and liberally nuanced music at sight. By chain reaction the second clarinet part, also a difficult one, was transferred to third clarinet, who sight-read with a borrowed instrument and had to transpose part of the way. For anxiety Sargent had never before experienced anything to touch this, and nothing quite like it came his way again. He told his players afterwards that they had done magnificently in the circumstances. This was no hyperbole. They had managed to keep together, in a manner of speaking. They felt like men reprieved.

Between mid-June and late September (1945) he conducted four pairs of concerts in Sydney, three pairs in Melbourne, two pairs in Adelaide and four unpaired concerts spread over Brisbane and Perth. His symphonies, apart from the Elgar and Sibelius mentioned above, were Beethoven's Fifth, Tchaikovsky's Fifth, Brahms's No. 2 and No. 4, Schubert's 'Unfinished' and 'Great' C major, and Dvořák's 'New World' and No. 8 (G major, Op. 88). With two exceptions the concertos, overtures and 'make-weights' generally were, like the symphonies, routine Sargent repertory. The exceptions were the Khachaturian piano concerto, with William Kapell, and Stravinsky's *Capriccio* for solo piano and orchestra (the work in which he had conducted its composer at a Courtauld–Sargent concert), with Nöel Mewton-Wood, a young artist who, born in Melbourne, had already made his name in London as a specialist in contemporary music.

For Sargent, generally speaking, contemporary music stopped at Dover and, when it came to typical programmes, comprised at the outside a score or so pieces by Vaughan Williams, Holst and

With Sibelius at his home near Helsinki, Finland, in 1956, the year before
the composer's death

After conducting the première of Ralph Vaughan Williams's Ninth Symphony for the Royal Philharmonic Society, London, April 1958. *Left to right*: M. S., Thomas E. Bean (manager of the Royal Festival Hall), R. Vaughan Williams, Mrs Myers Foggin (wife of the chairman of the R.P.S.) and Ursula Vaughan Williams (wife of the composer)

Photo: Erich Auerbach

Walton, with a fringe of Bax plus *The Young Person's Guide*, which recurred nearly as often as the *Perfect Fool* ballet.

*

No sooner was he back in London than his shuttlings resumed. To the Graz Festival (1946) in Austria he contributed two programmes, one with the Vienna Philharmonic Orchestra, the first historic Continental orchestra he ever conducted, who played Delius's *Paris* for him and Elgar's Introduction and Allegro, with three genuine Viennese professors in the string quartet. The second programme was with the Städtische orchestra of Graz, whom he conducted in Vaughan Williams's Symphony No. 5 in D minor, a work listened to more in politeness than rapture. That August he opened Lucerne Festival, conducting the festival orchestra in the Introduction and Allegro, the *Perfect Fool* music and Shostakovitch's Symphony No. 1. Later during the half-decade, which would weary the reader if traced chronologically, he took Vaughan Williams's *London* Symphony and Walton's *Sinfonia Concertante* (solo pianist, Phyllis Sellick) to Brussels to play with the Grande Orchestre Symphonique; introduced Bax's Third Symphony to the Oslo Philharmonic Orchestra in Oslo; did Rachmaninov's Symphony No. 3, Haydn's No. 86, Beethoven's Fifth and Vaughan Williams's 'Tallis' fantasia with the National Orchestra of Spain in Madrid and—after a brief Portuguese round, comprising Lisbon, Oporto and Braga—took the same orchestra to Gibraltar where he conducted them in a flying boat hangar adapted to seat 1,400.

He was invited back to Austria, billed this time for Vienna, not with the Philharmonic but with another illustrious orchestra, the Vienna Symphony. He resolved that Vienna should have its first hearing of Elgar's E flat. If Sydney town hall, why not the Grossermusikvereinsaal? That the Viennese had hitherto failed to honour what was, he insisted, music for all time, 'music which has made history', had never failed to surprise him. It was put to him on behalf of the Viennese that, in England reciprocally, not much attention had been paid to certain great Austrian symphonists of Brahms's day and later. In reply he professed to admire Bruckner

12

and Mahler, a position not altogether borne out by later practice
and allusions, but could not resist adding: 'To my mind—and note,
this is a personal opinion—Elgar is as fine, forgive me, a finer
composer than Bruckner.'*

He reached Vienna a day and a half late at half past three in the
morning after the most disagreeable journey of his life.

At three o'clock the previous morning, while he was passing
through the Soviet-occupied zone of Austria, two Soviet soldiers
with guns had unceremoniously entered his sleeping compartment.
They examined his papers, then bade him get up, dress and pack his
things. He was without the requisite 'four-zones' pass, they conveyed, and must leave the train at once. He tried to explain who he
was and produced every document he could think of, to no purpose.
He was all but hustled on to the permanent way with others; he
was not the only passenger to be 'rooted out', as he put it. Carrying
two suitcases, one of them heavy with scores and band parts, he
was made to trudge knee-deep through snow, an armed soldier on
either side of him, to the zonal boundary. Ahead lay a railway
bridge. The escort-soldiers gestured at him to cross it. The American
zone lay on the far side. Precariously he picked his way over,
stepping from sleeper to sleeper, for there was nothing to tread on
between. If he had slipped there would have been a considerable
drop. Reaching an American military outpost he slumped down by
the stove and awaited transport for Vienna via Linz, where he spent
the rest of that day, reflecting ruefully upon his services to the
Soviet cause during the war, when he cheerfully arranged reams of
Russian music for bands and choirs to celebrate Soviet victories.

By next morning he was beginning to smile. He pictured what
had happened to him as though looking at a film and found it funny
on the whole. He had three stop-go, stop-go rehearsals, essays in
ruthless perfectionism. A thing that gratified him about the Vienna
Symphony Orchestra was the players' skill at sight-reading; they
were as good at it, he said, as Englishmen—which, he added, was
saying a lot. The crowd in the Grossermusikvereinsaal gave fur-
rowed concentration to Elgar's E flat, a symphony from 'das Land

* Quoted in *The Morning News*, Vienna, organ of the British occupying
Forces, 4th March, 1947.

ohne Musik', and clapped it cordially without, however, giving the impression that they thought more of Elgar than of Bruckner. . . .

In Copenhagen he conducted the Danish Royal Orchestra, at a concert to celebrate their jubilee, in Walton, Haydn and Tchaikovsky (*Francesca da Rimini*) to the delectation of King Frederick, himself a musician, who later on conducted the band of his Royal Danish Guards with a willow baton which Sargent had given him. With crowned heads and heirs-apparent he was at ease and in the swim. He would let it be known discreetly during a Continental tour that he had passed a morning in Brussels playing violin sonatas with the Queen Mother of Belgium. It was she, of course, who took the violin parts. In the open-air theatre beneath the Acropolis he took the State Orchestra of Greece through Handel-Harty, Mendelssohn and Sibelius in the presence of King Paul, Queen Frederica and five thousand other Athenians. While on his foreign rounds, he crowed as disarmingly as a schoolboy over his *Messiah* recording with the Huddersfield Choral Society ('83,000 sets sold in a few weeks!'), and boasted how he had just conducted nine concerts in eight days to 40,000 hearers, about a quarter of them at a curious, reverberating music festival in Harringay sports arena,* where 'bookings totalled 4,000—and 5,000 more turned up!'

When they got down to the aesthetic brass tacks of his complex activities, the illuminati of music were rarely impressed. At a time when others were newly revelling in or rediscovering Schoenberg, Mahler, Bartók, Nielsen and post-1939 Stravinsky, Sargent found few paths, blazed no trails. Yet he always gave the impression that whatever he did had never been done and couldn't have been done by anybody else. That other conductors (even Beecham, up to a point) kept quiet about their doings, as distinct from their opinions, was beside the point. Sargent's rise and glory, the uniqueness that vested him like a tunic, made old-fashioned professional reticence seem fusty. Even mischances served to show what a momentous person he was.

* Certain of these Harringay concerts (June 1947) are among the outstanding flops of musical history. On successive nights Beecham conducted to 2500 and something over 1000 in an auditorium with 10,000 seats and prices as low as 1s 6d.

A sharp attack of dysentery which prevented his conducting Elgar, Holst and Handel-Harty in Ankara at an Anglo-Turkish music festival got up by Turkey's education minister incidentally canvassed the fact that Ankara was to have been a staging post on the way back from India, where he had been staying with the Mountbattens, India's last Viceroy and Vicereine. From glittering guest quarters at New Delhi he wrote to a friend that his illness, 'a complete blessing', had obliged him to take three weeks' complete holiday in surroundings that were an Arabian Nights entertainment. Government House, he noted, had five hundred servants. The Stamford urchin inside him stared wide-eyed. In other cities or quarters, other sights and impressions. These were crucial times of transition. India was in the process of making herself into a sovereign democratic republic. From one flourishing city (unidentified) he brought back an image of hundreds of children 'wandering like stray dogs in the early morning and scavenging a breakfast, if you can call it that, from the dustbins in the streets, too languid to wipe away the flies that have settled on their diseased eyelids'.

He met the Mountbattens next in Wembley Stadium, on the rim of London, at the ceremonial opening of the 1948 Olympic Games. They were in the royal party. He had charge of all the concerted music, that is to say, music of edifying, patriotic and topical sorts sung by a gigantic choir drawn from seven of London's biggest and accompanied by the massed bands of the Brigade of Guards. The stadium held enough people to populate a fair-sized town. It was a broiling day. Sun fell ruthlessly on international committeemen of the Games as they lined up on the turf in top hats and frock coats. It had fallen with equal ruthlessless on instruments the bandsmen left behind them when they went for a drink during the rehearsal break that morning. Sargent put his hand on a tuba. 'Feel that,' he said to one of his singers. 'They'll all be out of tune.' And so they were. But exceedingly few in the Wembley populace that day noticed anything wrong. With the sun for spotlight, he was escorted across the green when the time came by two Guards officers with bared swords and took his place on a high rostrum wearing mortar board and doctoral gown over his morning coat. The day before there had been a discussion with Oliver about which doctoral gown to wear. He had choice among three: Oxford, Durham and Liverpool.

'Everything,' ventured Oliver, 'depends on the weather. You see, sir, the Durham robes, cream silk, black and purple, will look beautiful if it's a fine day. The Oxford ones are scarlet. If it's a dull day, they might be better.'

'Tell you what we'll do,' said Sargent, 'we'll take both gowns and choose our fancy dress according to the weather.'

Naturally the Durham gown won the day.

That afternoon he conducted the National Anthem, Quilter's setting of Kipling's 'Non nobis domine' ('That noise which men call Fame, / That dross which men call Gold, / For these we undergo / Our *hot* and godless days') and the *Hallelujah* Chorus, the crowd joining in the first and last items at discretion. Sargent was not the only one to comment on Kipling's fourth line. Even the godfearing were done to a turn, he laughed.

'What's it like conducting such a crowd in such a place?' somebody inquired.

'Like taking a jellyfish for a walk on an elastic lead,' he said.

CHAPTER TWENTY-SIX

INTERNATIONAL

H E HAD never had a metropolitan orchestra he could call his own except, perhaps, if the term may be extended, the Liverpool Philharmonic. This, although based on the provinces, for a while outshone or, at any rate, won equal prestige with certain national ones, and might, for all practical purposes, have been run from London W.1. The scene was radically changing, however. Star players who had settled in Liverpool during the war were back on London platforms and recording floors, and these were dominated by two new or recently founded orchestras, Beecham's Royal Philharmonic and the impresario Walter Legge's Philharmonia, whose advent lifted playing standards generally and helped eventually to make London 'the musical capital of Europe', in the eyes of certain foreign judges.

There had been a time when the London Philharmonic Orchestra was, or might have been, Sargent's fief. That time had passed. There is testimony that he and the L.P.O. players, a self-governing body, were not merely at cross purposes from time to time but chronically at loggerheads. One incident that rankled was his alleged rescoring of brass parts in the finale of Brahms's Symphony No. 1. After a wartime rehearsal of this, horns and trombones got together mutinously and took the matter to the committee. 'We are going to play what Brahms wrote, as Brahms wrote it,' they said, 'or not at all.' There was a sharp wrangle. Sargent had his way. On the night the finale was played as he wanted it played. The mood of dissent remained, however, and spread from the brass to other sections. 'At length,' it is recalled by one who was closely concerned with L.P.O. administration, 'representative players begged that he should no longer be engaged to conduct, because they feared that one day the whole orchestra might walk out on him. For some years Sargent conducted the L.P.O. only for other managements (e.g. when we were mutually involved with some choral society); he never appeared during this time at concerts promoted by ourselves.'

With foreign promoters bidding ever more urgently for his services, it was realized that a permanent London rostrum in addition to that of the Royal Choral Society, although conducive to international prestige, would inevitably prove an awkward piece to fit into the jigsaw of 'forward commitments' here, there and everywhere. Another consideration, as we have seen in the case of Australia, was that good money could be earned abroad. His fees in the summer of 1950 for nine or ten weeks and twelve public concerts (of which more later) in Latin South America came to over £3,500, a sum not greatly encroached on by hotel bills, since as often as not he was put up and fêted by ambassadors and their wives and staffs. At home, however, a rostrum of great repute and greater potential was soon to be vacated.

Sir Adrian Boult, who formed the B.B.C. Symphony Orchestra in 1930, serving it with sober distinction and, in point of repertory, unquenchable versatility, was to retire in 1950, although professionally in the prime of life, under a B.B.C. age limit of sixty. The choice of his successor—or, as mooted at one stage, successors —began to exercise the Governors of the B.B.C. long before the appointed day. Sargent was approached on their behalf as early as the spring of 1948. When asked whether he would be interested in succeeding Boult he made the point that, although the prospect was most attractive, he could not be expected for the sake of a principal conductorship to drop or seriously curtail his commitments with English choral societies and actual or prospective ones with twenty or so foreign or Commonwealth orchestras. The B.B.C. negotiators appreciated this and suggested a contract which would engage him for part of the year only, leaving him free to spend the rest of his time on other rostrums. The Symphony Orchestra being permanent in the literal sense, playing all the year round except for the annual vacation, a part-time appointment on these lines would inevitably mean his sharing the B.B.C.'s public and studio rostrums with other batons. Which batons? What would be their relative status? These questions were delicately nibbled at. As to other aspects, there was no thought of reimposing the age limit of sixty which, if he took over in 1950, would leave him with a run of but five years. The B.B.C.'s idea now was to contract a conductor for a term of years, renewal to be matter for negotiation. It could not be said that the money was much of a bait. Although B.B.C. publicity was not forthcoming on such matters, it was put about unofficially that in the recent past the Corporation had on occasion paid no more for a whole year's conducting services (not exclusive services, admittedly) than Latin South America was to pay Sargent for ten weeks, namely £3,500; and that hitherto the top year-round salary had been £5,000. The feeling now was that a conductor's pay should vary according to the number of concerts he conducted from season to season.

No sooner were the negotiations well launched than Sargent took off in a flying boat for a second round of concerts in Johannesburg, South Africa, with spillover concerts in Pretoria, under the joint aegis of the British Council and the South African Broadcasting Corporation.

*

His first visit to Johannesburg had been in 1946. This was the first time that city had seen a conductor of international repute. On his first night the approaches to the City Hall were jammed with motorcars, and the demand for seats was such that extra ones had to be put on the organ steps at the back of the platform. The orchestra was a new one, seventy strong, named the Johannesburg City Orchestra. A number of players had been brought in from Capetown and Durban who, if they were typical of those so-called 'starchy' communities, summed up Johannesburg as a place where classical music, on the rare occasions it was performed, had to compete with the crackle of chocolate wrappings, the crunch of ice-cream wafers and monkey nuts, the striking of matches by chain smokers and assorted coughs and groans and snores.

At his first rehearsal Sargent said: 'I want people to go away from this concert feeling they've enjoyed a wonderful spiritual experience'. What his players made of that is matter for speculation. At rehearsal they were undergoing an intensive spiritual experience on their own account. How the man kept *at* them! 'More *vibrato*, more warmth,' he urged the strings during the *Walk to the Paradise Garden*.'This is a beautiful love scene. You cannot get a pianissimo with so much bow. Get the warmth not from the bow but from the left hand. Play only the notes in the part! Touching the A string while you're supposed to be playing your E string isn't what Delius had in mind. You are making your quavers too long. . . . That's better. . . . Now you're making them too short! . . . Making the same mistake twice is enough. I shall hardly be able to tell you what I think of you if you make it a third time. . . .' From Delius he turned to orchestral excerpts from *The Mastersingers*. In a corridor backstage a native cleaner with horn-rimmed glasses paused with scrubbing brush in hand, gripped by the lordliness of the Procession of the Masters; then, realizing he was being watched by a white stranger, mumbled apologetically, 'That is one big music' and started scrubbing again. Sargent kept up his stoppings and adjurings, his rallyings and restartings for three hours. A section leader told his wife that lunchtime: 'Believe it or not, we all had more energy at the finish than when we began.'

The symphony at his first concert was Sibelius's No. 2. Before the end of one of the movements some of the people in the guinea seats started clapping. Without turning round he silenced them with a dismissive flap of the left hand. Audiences the world over love a rebuke. There was a hullabaloo of worship at the end.

During his two visits (1946 and 1948), he conducted ten or more concerts with the Johannesburg orchestra (augmented to ninety on the second occasion), his symphonies being the two Elgars, Sibelius's No. 1, as well as No. 2, the *New World*, Beethoven's No. 4, the *Pathétique* and Prokoviev's *Classical*. Coming as it did after *The Young Person's Guide*, which made audiences in many climes and both hemispheres love Britten and Sargent in equal parts, Elgar's A flat sent many South Africans home nonplussed. On the night Beethoven's Fourth was played a citizen of note entered the hall smoking a cigar after the first item on the programme and went on smoking it. At no concert during either visit was anybody seen actually to light up during the music, but always many stayed in their seats and smoked during the interval. As a result the second half of any programme was performed under a blue haze. Beecham was expected in Johannesburg later that season. 'Sir Malcolm,' wrote a local commentator, 'is tolerant. If this sort of thing happens when Beecham is here he may wash his hands of us and depart.'

The orchestra came in for discreet praise from Sargent, who likened it to an egg laid by local enterprise. His duty had been to hatch the egg. 'It has turned out,' he concluded, 'to be a songbird of no mean proportions.' Some may have reflected that a songbird is usually praised not for its size but for its singing. The singing of this one was not to everybody's complete satisfaction. When the orchestra was only seventy strong a critic in *The Star* of Johannesburg suggested that in parts of *Don Juan* the brass outbalanced the strings, which could have been doubled in number advantageously, the violins particularly. Both then and after the orchestra had been augmented to ninety, a minority complained of overpraise. By producing performances of outstanding value from an untried orchestra, noted one correspondent, Sargent had confounded all who had thought such an achievement impossible. 'Yet,' he continued, 'if all the great conductors now living had brought the combined Vienna Philharmonic, London Philharmonic and Philadelphia orchestras to Johannesburg, the praise in some quarters [whether in print or by word of mouth] could not have been more effusive. . . . Such attitudes are not as flattering to an eminent artist as they are intended to be.' A second correspondent conceded that while some of the concerts had been quite enjoyable, their quality might have been better; it was quite unreasonable to expect any visiting conductor, however famous, to prepare adequately two merged orchestras (i.e. the 'City' orchestra and the radio orchestra) for five concerts in ten days.

In a city which had taken Sargent to its heart—and found, as many cities had done or were to do, that he had gone to its head as well—such notes of doubt or dissent made little impression. The Johannesburgers were conquered. In return he said nice things about them and South Africans generally. Over the air he declared that Johannesburg audiences need not fear comparison with any in the world: 'You probably do not realize,' he went on, 'that you are a charming people. A stranger feels he is welcome and appreci-

ated here and forgiven his differences of behaviour and speech. . . .
That is not always so, even in our Commonwealth of Nations.'

For any informed Australian who chanced to be listening in the
last sentence may have had an invidious ring, Australia being the
one Commonwealth country he knew really well.

*

Back in London talks with the B.B.C. continued intermittently.
Other names as well as his own were passing from mouth to mouth.
The truth was that Sir Malcolm's was not the only name the
Governors had in mind. The case stood roughly thus: Sargent and
other outstanding conductors were, in modern conditions as against
those applying when the Symphony Orchestra had been founded
twenty years earlier, 'bespoke' for so many platforms and so far
ahead that no Chief Conductor could, in fact, conduct anything like
all B.B.C. concerts even if he cut out studio concerts (no celebrated
conductor was keen on these) and confined himself to the Corporation's public ones. It was therefore proposed that the B.B.C.'s
musical year should be divided into 'main seasons' in which two
other conductors should take part as well as Sargent. The two others
whom the B.B.C. approached were Sir John Barbirolli and Rafael
Kubelik, later musical director of the Royal Opera House but at this
time in America, where presently he took charge of the Chicago
Symphony Orchestra. Apparently there was to be no *primus* among
the *pares*. Somebody styled the projected arrangement a 'condominium', presumably on the principle that sonorous names are
best for arrangements not likely to work. After the news had
'leaked', giving rise to misconceptions, it was protested that the
B.B.C. had never entertained the idea of imposing a 'batting order'
on the trio and that notions to the contrary were the fruit 'perhaps of
ignorance, perhaps of natural malignity'.* As things fell out,
Kubelik was unable to leave America for private reasons, and
Barbirolli declined to be deflected from the Hallé Orchestra. The

* Letter by Sir Steuart Wilson, sometime Head of B.B.C. Music, *Truth*, 5th
March, 1954. It should be added that according to Michael Kennedy (*The Hallé
Tradition*) Barbirolli was offered 'the succession' to Boult. On precedent this
would have meant something more than a share of 'condominium'.

field was thus left unimpeded for Sargent. Negotiations were interrupted, however, by his darts to the Continent. One of these has not yet been narrated.

In October 1949 he made his début at La Scala, Milan, where he conducted not opera but the opening symphony concert of the season, the first English conductor, he maintained, ever to conduct the Scala orchestra in the Scala theatre. Inevitably, he opened with *Cockaigne*. Milan had not heard it before and seemed pleased. He ended, almost as inevitably, with Sibelius's No. 1. This, too, he claimed, had not been done in Milan before. Years later he spoke of the occasion with a scorn unusual in him.

'They didn't,' he said, 'understand it in the least, although the great tune of the finale might have been written specially for them. It's almost Puccini. At the end they all started walking out. It looked as if I wasn't going to have a "call". I decided to deal with the situation. Instead of going off through the wings, I halted among the last fiddle desks and came back. This set off clapping among a handful. I walked back to the wings and came back again. More clapping, this time a bit louder and longer. It was heard by people out in the corridors and foyer. "Ah, a success!" they thought. "We must be in on this!" And back they came. At the finish I got something like an ovation. But they didn't understand Sibelius.'

Back to the negotiations with the B.B.C. Early in April 1950 he put out a denial that he had been appointed the B.B.C.'s new conductor. 'That,' commented *amateurs* of musical politics, 'appears to be that.' A surprise was in store for them.

Exactly a month later the B.B.C.'s day press officer 'telexed' an announcement to Fleet Street and all B.B.C. regional press officers that Sir Malcolm Sargent had accepted an offer to succeed Sir Adrian Boult as Conductor of the Symphony Orchestra ('Chief Conductor' in a later version) and that he would assume consultative and administrative functions with the opening of the B.B.C.'s Promenade Concert season on 23rd July. It was added that an assistant would be appointed (the choice fell on the late John Hollingsworth, assistant conductor at the 'Proms' only) and that Sir Malcolm would still be available for 'much of his important work' with the chief choral societies and orchestras both at home and

abroad. A briefing that went out to publicity officers acknowledged
that no single conductor could undertake the B.B.C.'s highly varied
and specialized output of music. 'It is a fact,' it was added, 'that
guest conductors already make a considerable contribution to the
programmes to the extent of more than twenty weeks in the year.
Sir Malcolm will be responsible as Conductor for the general state
of the orchestra and will discuss all the programme plans with the
B.B.C.'s Head of Music without incurring the administrative
responsibility for them. . . . The present arrangement will extend his
concert conducting [he was already committed to a number of
Summer and Winter 'Prom' concerts] to a total of not less than six
months in a year.'

The date of this announcement was 4th May, 1950. At noon on
the 8th he took off from London Airport for his first conducting
tour of South America, landing in Buenos Aires two evenings later.
He had had a distinguished send-off. At the Canning Club a god-
speed luncheon arranged in his honour by friends of Latin South
America had been attended by the ambassadors of Brazil, Chile and
Uruguay; and two days earlier he had been received (as he exul-
tantly announced) 'by the King and Queen in the morning, had
luncheon with Mr. Churchill and tea with Mr. Attlee—all on the
same day'. He was taking a fair amount of British music with him.
At the top of the pile was Ralph Vaughan Williams's latest symphony, the Sixth in E minor, which everybody but its composer
found laden with 'message' and very disturbing indeed.

*

He was away until the third week in July, visited four republics
and conducted State or radio orchestras in Buenos Aires (four
concerts), Montevideo (two concerts), Rio de Janeiro (one concert)
and Santiago de Chile (six concerts with the Chilean Symphony
Orchestra under the auspices of the Faculty of Music, Santiago
University). In most cases he was given six rehearsals per concert,
some of them fantastically timed. Those in Buenos Aires started at
10 p.m. and went on until 1.30 in the morning. One of these sessions
ended a day which had begun with a 9 a.m. rehearsal call and had
taken in a press conference, a luncheon at which he had kept the

whole table in a roar, and an hour's broadcast concert early in the evening. Of any other man it would have been said he was working hard for his £3,500. But again he confounded all comparisons. As well as working all hours and wringing every minute's advantage from nearly sixty rehearsals, each at least three hours long, he took in such tourist sights as were handily accessible, went for a cruise in Guanabara Bay (Rio), paid a call on Heitor Villa-Lobos, the veteran Brazilian composer, and said the right things with the right charm when his host played him bad records of his own music, was recognized and greeted spontaneously by a swarm of young skiers at a Chilean mountain resort, and was received in audience at their respective palaces by two Presidents, one of whom addressed him thus: 'We Uruguayans are fond of all English people, Sir Malcolm—but especially fond of you!'

The former 'organisata de la Catedrale de Meltor [sic] Mowbray', as one print called him, found it all very cordial—and at times capricious. Two days before his Rio concert, advertised for 4 p.m., the time was changed to 3 p.m. by the Prefect of Police, who wanted the Teatro Municipal cleared betimes for an evening function connected with presidential politics. Afternoon concerts in Rio started late as a matter of course. That was well known. Audiences were in the habit of arriving late to balance things up. What would happen, however, if people arrived late for a four o'clock concert which had actually started at three? Sargent had visions of his concluding piece, Vaughan Williams's *A London Symphony*, played to an empty hall and of the audience coming in when he was ready for going out. The night before the concert Rio broadcast programmes were interrupted six times with news of the changed time. Never before had a symphony concert in Brazil enjoyed such publicity. For *Cockaigne* the house was thin. By the interval, however, all seats were taken; people were standing in the pit and second gallery. 'Tremendous success', 'attendance almost unprecedented', said the British Council's man on the spot in his report to London. After the concert Sargent's dressing-room was besieged by orchestral players, people of fashion and persons of diverse ages and temperaments who said they were composers and wanted to show him manuscripts.

His opening at the Teatro Colón, Buenos Aires, with the noted

Colón orchestra involved caprice of a less happy kind. Again there was forceful advance publicity. A press conference two days before the event netted thousands of words and double-column or three-column 'spreads'. Vaughan Williams's Sixth was his main theme. Whether what he said was designed to pull in Latin temperaments or keep them away is hardly a moot point. 'A frightening symphony,' he called it. 'For a symphony to be frightening is perhaps a good thing. Here we have the complete testament of a man who, in his seventies, looks back on the human sufferings of his time. I never conduct the Sixth without feeling that I am walking across bomb sites. . . . Chaos, despair, desolation and the peace that flows from desolation. . . .'

Somebody doubted whether the Buenos Aires public would be able to take in the music's full meaning.

'A city which can't understand the Sixth Symphony of Vaughan Williams,' answered Sargent, '*deserves* to be bombed.' He was sure, he added hastily, that Buenos Aires was far too intelligent to deserve any such fate.

Another questioner doubted whether any public without direct experience of war, which certain movements of the symphony were said to depict, would be able to detect any such meaning in it.

'Intelligent people don't require experience to make them understand,' suggested Sargent. 'Are not the sorrows of other people *our* sorrows?' His interpretation, he stressed, was a purely personal one. (It happened to tally with that of several noted music critics.) Vaughan Williams, he declared, had always refused to give his own interpretation of the symphony's meaning. This was hardly a complete statement of the case. The composer's attitude was that the Sixth didn't need to be interpreted, any more than his other symphonies did. He was angered by people who read 'war' into either the Sixth or the Fourth or 'peace' into the Fifth. To one correspondent he wrote: 'I do NOT BELIEVE IN meanings or mottoes'; to another, 'It never seems to occur to people that a man might just want to write a piece of music.'

When the Colón orchestra first essayed the Scherzo of the Sixth at one of his midnight rehearsals Sargent stuck his fingers in his ears and burst out laughing. But his lean, dominating energy and his Latin good looks, which made him almost seem of common blood with the players, quickly transformed the scene. Directors of the theatre 'crept' into the stalls, according to an English observer's letter, to see how things were going and size him up. Their last 'promotion' had been Wilhelm Furtwängler. Would the Englishman, they wondered, be outmatched, overshadowed? Whatever doubts they had were quickly assuaged. 'After my first rehearsal,' reported Sargent, 'they raised the price of the tickets. After my second rehearsal they raised the prices again'—to the season's top level. The only thing they are alleged to have vacillated about was the time the concert should begin. They talked alternately about three in the afternoon and five. The concert was billed for a Sunday. Not until the Friday morning did they make up their minds. The concert, they announced, was to start at 9.30 p.m. Tickets were on sale for three days only. As a result of this dickering and the inadequate advertising that resulted the theatre was a quarter empty and, at the outset, tepid. Whether or not there was anything in the war-and-desolation thesis, the grand mould, emergent mysticism and general 'Englishness' of Vaughan Williams's Sixth were advantageously set off by the theatre's contrasting interior: six gilded tiers and lordly lamps which someone likened to monster peonies. The Colón was not the only South American house in which Sargent conducted the Sixth that year. It did not sweep the Latins off their feet and had not been expected to. The *Young Person's Guide*, now coming to be known by its sub-title, *Variations and Fugue on a Theme of Purcell*, was a different matter. However far he journeyed from Britain, the 'Purcell Variations' always made people's eyes shine and often brought them to their feet. At the Colón it earned him ten calls. He was grateful to Britten for helping him to such ebullient successes. Around this time he said: 'For Britten's genius—and I say "genius" advisedly—I have the greatest admiration. I derive enormous pleasure from conducting his music; it is always perfectly written. But I am waiting for him to tackle an opera or oratorio on a really profound subject. He hasn't done this yet.' Fifteen years later he spoke warmly of the *War Requiem*, with its text from the Liturgy and Wilfred Owen's poetry. What he had waited for had, perhaps, come to pass.

Apart from Vaughan Williams's Sixth and *London*, the symphonies on this tour were Haydn's No. 88 in G, Beethoven's No. 8, Mozart's *Jupiter*, Schubert's No. 5, Brahms's No. 2 and No. 4 and Sibelius's No. 5, this last reserved for Santiago, the first music by Sibelius ever performed in Chile. Miscellaneous pieces included works by Purcell, Ireland, Bliss, Holst, *Till*, the Handel-Harty *Water Music* and Elgar's Serenade for Strings. There were two concertos: Walton's for viola and Dvořák's for 'cello. With Beethoven's Symphony No. 8, the Dvořák concerto (Fournier in the solo part) crowned the second of two clamorously successful concerts promoted by Amigos de la Música. This concert had been run together in seven days, tickets weren't on sale until twenty-four hours in advance, and people queued for unreserved places from nine in the morning. For want of a concert hall a giant cinema was used; 4,000 packed it to the roof. At half past twelve the following morning, the concert having ended, the street outside was blocked with people mobbing Sargent's car, pelting it with flowers and thrusting programmes through the windows for his signature. Hitherto only *prime donne* and the occasional virtuoso fiddler had been able to touch off fevers of this sort and on this scale. Why not delight in mass genuflections if you have to endure them? Sargent's delight was boundless, as most other men's would have been. Did it strengthen or deflect the artist in him? On this point there would have been no doubt in Hugh Allen's mind.

It is engrossing to follow his fifteen thousand miles of travel and triumph through the eyes of diplomats and British Council officers whom he met on his way and in most cases formed lasting friendships with. At least one British ambassador, trying his hand at music criticism, set down his impressions for The Right Hon. Ernest Bevin, M.P., P.C., His Majesty's Secretary of State for Foreign Affairs.* Classifying his despatch as restricted, he sent it off by air bag.

---

* They were thus addressed as a matter of protocol and for reference to the British Council rather than for the Foreign Secretary's personal attention. At the same time, the despatch suggests that the tag widely applied to Sargent of 'Britain's musical ambassador' was accepted in competent quarters as something more than a figure of speech.

Of one concert H.M. Ambassador wrote that, 'opening with a rather uninspiring tone-poem by [a South American composer], Sargent had quickly warmed his audience into responsiveness by the brilliant tones he was able to extract from it [the orchestra, presumably]. . . . Appreciation was further stirred by his delicate interpretation of Vaughan Williams's Sixth Symphony. . . . Eventually his skilful handling of the exuberant Britten [Purcell Variations] brought the house down. No sooner had he reached the robust climax of this work than the audience rose as one man and cheered him to the echo for many minutes. I am assured that a visiting conductor, particularly one new to this country, has seldom obtained so warm an ovation.' From less august hands but professionally more practised ones as he flew from city to city came other assessments. It is striking to find Elgar's Serenade for Strings written off as 'too sugary' for Montevidean tastes. He played this at one of his two concerts, attended by twelve rehearsals, in the Uruguayan capital with S.O.D.R.E., Montevideo's radio orchestra.

'On being asked his opinion of their playing . . . after the first rehearsal,' ran the report to London, 'Sir Malcolm's reply was "Rough, rough!" and even after two weeks he confessed to a certain dissatisfaction with their performances. The musicians of S.O.D.R.E. are very badly underpaid, and as a result most of them have to work at several jobs to make a living. They have very little time to study and practise, and in the more difficult works this lack becomes very obvious. . . . Sir Malcolm is doubtful about the possibility of popular appeal of Vaughan Williams's Sixth Symphony, and, although the interpretation of it was exceedingly good in view of the short time available for its rehearsal, the audience did not seem to take to the work, which is understandable, I feel, since it is so closely associated with the experience of war.' Elsewhere his Brahms (Symphony No. 2) brought the critics under scrutiny. 'Some of them,' it was found, 'while paying tribute to the English conductor's musicianship and quality of performance, found it difficult to accept his interpretation of certain works, notably those of Brahms. Following the lead of Dr. G——, a critic who has come to the fore through his invariable tendency to attack established reputations, they hold that Brahms was conducted on all too light and superficial a level and missed the turgid depths which previous conductors have generally evoked.'

Before he left any city, local concert promoters, music society chairmen and the like wrung from him either a promise to return soon or give the matter serious thought. He returned in June–July 1952, giving concerts first in Buenos Aires, then hopping much as before from republic to republic and city to city, this time adding Lima (Peru) to his itinerary. He flew 17,000 miles in seven weeks— 'Never an empty seat,' he exclaimed at the end of it. 'Always half the programme made up of British works—Delius, Vaughan Williams, Britten, Walton. . . . Terribly tense excitement in Santiago. . . . In Lima the orchestra played Handel's *Water Music*, then got up and cheered their own performance!'

*

Coming back to 10 a.m. rehearsal calls in London must have been a chilling business in more senses than one after all the sunshine, professional gratulation and flowers. There were flowers at home, true; public gratulation as well. Had he not been given a laurel wreath dotted with white and red carnations on the last night of his first 'Proms' season as the B.B.C.'s chief conductor? Had not this wreath been subscribed for by hard-core 'Prommers', those who queued, and gloried in queueing, for anything up to twenty-four hours on the Albert Hall pavement for standing places? And had not that first season attracted over 280,000 people in eight weeks— the highest aggregate attendance for any concert series in the world? In these externals he rejoiced. There was no other conductor who on such occasions cast anything like the same spell. Here was a satisfaction which nothing could rob him of.

Yet something was wanting. He had not yet learned how to hit it off with orchestral players, how to make himself their venerated comrade. They found him too much the precisian, one who rigidly enforced not only the printed text of classical music but also, from time to time, his own scoring variants. There is no doubt about the animosity which built up. Presumably his 'antennae' warned him of this. But more than once he was told of it to his face.

CHAPTER TWENTY-SEVEN

'OBVIOUSLY, OLD HAYDN. . .'

SHORTLY BEFORE he assumed his B.B.C. post I asked him what music meant most to him. He singled out, as I had expected he would, *Messiah*, the B minor Mass, the Saint Matthew Passion Music, Beethoven's Choral Symphony and *The Dream of Gerontius*, his five 'spiritual peaks'. 'But why stop at five?' he went on. 'To answer your question thoroughly I should finish by reciting the entire classical repertory. In my library there are a thousand selected scores, works I especially love doing. Quite five hundred of these are as familiar to me as the palm of my hand. I could start rehearsing any one of them at a moment's notice.'

'They are not all,' I observed, 'of the *Messiah* or *Gerontius* class.'

'Heavens, no! They include lots of light music. The *Nutcracker* suite, for instance. And the *Poet and Peasant* Overture, a masterpiece in its way.'

Even taking into account musical comfits of this class, a working repertory of five hundred scores drawn from a favoured selection of twice that number seemed so much at variance with the limits and iterations of his typical programmes that I felt and looked surprised. I have no reason to suppose he was overestimating. Yet out of five hundred claimed I found it hard offhand to think of more than ninety or a hundred symphonies or allied pieces which had Sargent connotations. Schooled listeners before whom he appeared as a 'musical ambassador' occasionally found his credentials humdrum. Early in 1955 he took the Philadelphia Orchestra from its home city to Washington and New York where, remarking that 'People are so kind to me', he stayed with the British Ambassador and Britain's representative to the United Nations respectively. For purity and precision of sound his Carnegie Hall concert seems to have been prodigious. This was conceded even by Paul Henry Lang in next morning's *New York Herald Tribune*. About the English works which the Philadelphians had peerlessly played, however, Lang was scathing. Vaughan Williams's *The Wasps* Overture? 'A pleasant trifle that sounds like Rimsky-Korsakov with bowler, mackintosh and umbrella.' Britten's 'Purcell' Variations? 'Full of cute tricks that are hard to take for adult nerves; the piece cannot be taken seriously. . . . This Britten piece is strictly for youth concerts. When Sir Malcolm comes to us as a musical ambassador,' concluded Lang, evoking a new and fashionable Italian conductor in New York at the same time as Sargent, 'he should not emulate Mr. Cantelli and his also-rans. There is plenty of substantial British music that American audiences would like to hear.' His other pieces at the Carnegie Hall were the *Royal Fireworks* music and Sibelius's Symphony No. 2, the Walton Symphony being reserved for Constitution Hall, Washington, where it was cheered. From Olin Downes (*New York Times*) his Sibelius earned one of the warmest encomiums of his career, a notice which, for all its piled-up similes, was fit to compare with Cardus's of his Elgar No. 2 in Sydney. Here, for once, wrote Downes, was a conductor who 'dared to take the symphony as slowly as the composer intended. . . . He played the slow movement like a bard of old . . .; the movement towered . . . it had in it something of the large utterance of the early gods'.

*

It was clear that his duties with the B.B.C., which acknowledged a special duty to contemporary and other unestablished music, would take him from time to time beyond or wide of his familiar beat, i.e. from *Messiah* and Mozart to Walton, the later Vaughan Williams symphonies and the *Firebird* suite.

'Posterity will say,' he prophesied, 'that of composers now living Sibelius is the first and Vaughan Williams the second.' Stravinsky? Too clever by half, it seemed.

Openly during his Brains Trust days and privately at all times, he was cautious, tepid or tart about most music in idioms later than neo-Romantic ones. I have heard him say, 'You see a youngster come on to the Albert Hall platform who has had a wretched symphony performed (don't blame me for choosing it—that's the B.B.C.'s responsibility). When the youngster appears he's applauded for kindness' sake, to give him a bit of encouragement. If he didn't come on there wouldn't be the same applause. . . . There are too many bad symphonies about. Why don't professors of composition encourage youngsters to write sonatas instead? Same form, exactly the same problems—but so much cheaper to put on! After every Promenade season we hold a *post mortem* on box office returns. It's fascinating to see which concerts are booked solid as soon as they're announced; and what a difference a piece by—well, you know the sort of composer I mean—makes to an otherwise popular scheme. *Leonora* No. 3, the *Emperor* Concerto with Solomon as soloist and the Fifth Symphony will pack the place. Add one modern work and hundreds will stay away and there'll be a loss of two hundred pounds or so.' He was disdainful of art which purported to express the spirit of the age, not because of the dubious aesthetics involved but because the 1950s were an age not worth expressing and the contemporary world a 'rotten' one, whence religion and the right sort of art offered escape. When friends gently rebuked him for such ideas he retorted: 'But of course I'm an escapist. Escape is the whole art of living. Religion is the first and most important form of it. Music is the second. If many modern works give one a feeling of restlessness, that is because of this "spirit of the age" which composers are trying to express. I'm afraid they express it very well. The modern composer has certainly done his job. Whether we want him to do it or not is another matter.'

His notion of the ideal 'Proms' season was one which, avoiding new scores (these had airing enough, he considered, at specialist festivals and in other concert series), presented a balanced sequence of 'accepted' works for a special kind of audience. There were certain 'Prom' nights which gave him a comforting glow to look back upon and which offer a clue to his policy. For example: 'The other night we did Verdi's Requiem. Out of a total audience of six thousand, five thousand were young people hearing it in the flesh for the first time. Rather a thought, that. . . .' Generally speaking he regarded concertgoers as under his tutelage. On this point he could be at one and the same time arrogant and non-committal, as emerges from a collating of some of his Brains Trust opinions: 'The trouble is, one never quite knows what the public wants. You can never say the public should be given what it likes, because we can't ever find out what the public is, nor can you find out exactly what it likes. . . . Who wants the opinion of the general public on what is good art? All we want is the general public to come and listen to good music. We don't really ask its opinion of what is best. We want it to have a general appreciation of what is good and be rather eclectic. . . . It is time that has proved to the public, or rather, the public through time has decided what it continues to like. . . . If the public don't like a work I believe to be good, I don't therefore say it's bad. I'd say it's a work the public at present doesn't like. Maybe it will like it in fifty to a hundred years' time. But their opinion of a work of art is of no importance to me. What is of importance is whether they'll come and hear it, whether I dare put it on again, whether it's going to lose money or not. . . .'

The crucial test on repertory and its expansion came not with the Promenade Concerts but with the B.B.C. Symphony Orchestra's public concerts each winter. During Sargent's first three seasons these were still held at the Royal Albert Hall. The transfer to the Royal Festival Hall occurred in 1952. A run through Sargent's own contributions to these series which, of course, he shared with eminent guest conductors, refreshes the eye even more than a look over his Courtauld–Sargent and Liverpool Philharmonic schemes. The attention is caught by some thirty performances between the 1949–50 season and the 1956–57 one, his last as the orchestra's chief, not necessarily because they are of works he had never done before, although a number were first performances in London or anywhere, but rather because they give the impression of a man stepping outside the circle of his predilections; of a man getting away from himself, in short. In his first season, for example, he conducted the Alban Berg violin concerto with Max Rostal (he repeated it in 1956 with André Gertler); returned to the Bartók Concerto for Orchestra, of which, it will be remembered, he had given the first English performance in Liverpool; coupled *Ein Heldenleben* with the same composer's *Metamorphosen*; and proceeded in later seasons to other works of Richard Strauss's sunet—the Four Last Songs and the 1946 revision of the symphonic fantasia on *Die Frau ohne Schatten*. Among new English music, he turned his hand to the *Ritual Dances* of his one-time pupil, Michael Tippett; and, with choral forces and solo singers, took on Carl Orff's *Carmina Burana*, Ernest Bloch's *Avodath Hakdesh* (Sacred Service) and the oratorio *Golgotha* by the Swiss composer Frank Martin. So that the main text may be relieved of a lengthened string of titles, other 'tangential' performances are listed in a footnote.*

*

In the main broadcasting studio at Maida Vale, London, and other places where the B.B.C. Symphony Orchestra rehearsed and performed his coming was likened by old hands to a salt breeze, a newly-switched on electric current and what-not. The same metaphors had been used twenty years earlier or more when he livened up the B.B.C.'s old studio under the Waterloo Bridge. Again his briskness and brightness bred goodwill.

Yet his first disciplinary move did not prosper. He conveyed to the orchestra that he expected everybody to be tuned and ready before he made his entry for rehearsal. Most other celebrated conductors achieved this without difficulty. Sargent himself usually did so when abroad. For some reason, however, the B.B.C. players were recalcitrant. At his first 'Prom' rehearsal in 1950 his appearance was the signal for so much mutual 'shushing' around the orchestra that, in the phrase of an onlooker, the place might have been a station full of steam trains. After other demonstrations of the same sarcastic kind Sargent threw in his hand, insisting no longer, but, owing to an acute allergy, never accustomed or reconciled himself to the

* The order is chronological, i.e., that of the seasons in which these works figured between 1950 and 1957: Alan Rawsthorne, Symphony No. 1; Elizabeth Maconchy, *Coronation* Overture; Prokoviev, Symphony No. 5; Honegger, the *King David* oratorio (in a double-bill with Holst's *Hymn of Jesus*); Racine Fricker, Symphony No. 1; Samuel Barber, Symphony No. 1; Carl Nielsen, Symphony No. 5; Shostakovitch, Symphony No. 5; Respighi, *The Fountains of Rome*; Edmund Rubbra, Piano Concerto in G (first performance); Vaughan Williams, Symphony No. 8; Walton, the Johannesburg Festival Overture (first London performance); and Shostakovitch, Symphony No. 9.

tuning-up process—'which some people enjoy,' he said, 'but which I find extremely painful.' There was an occasion on tour in Leeds when, during a rehearsal pause, he tried to give instructions to the second violins but could not do so because of retuning cacophonies.

'But we've got to tune,' said the leader in reply to his expostulation. There were other string players who judged that, never having been a string player himself, he could not imaginatively realize the technical problems of string intonation. The upshot at Leeds that day was a dispute which ended with a distraught Sargent cancelling the rehearsal. Years later he cited an American practice, said to have been 'agreed' by the musicians' union, whereby a rehearsal did not officially begin or the players start earning their fees until the whole orchestra was seated *and* in tune. A rehearsal ran three hours from then, not a minute before—'and,' he added, 'nobody is ever late!'

When Sargent took it over the B.B.C. Symphony Orchestra had a full strength of ninety-six players. Of this number fifty or sixty were strings, most of whom sat in the usual receding order of desks and pairs, an arrangement which made it hard for the man on the rostrum, however sharp his ear, to judge the form and merit of the remoter players. In the spring of 1952 he called a general audition of strings, the first, it seemed, since the orchestra's founding twenty-two years earlier. One by one players from all desks but the leading ones—first violins and second, violas and 'cellos (the double-basses were excepted because of their different deployment)—came up before a jury comprising Sargent, Paul Beard (the orchestra's principal violin and leader), the principals and sub-principals of the sections involved, an orchestral administrator and an independent assessor. Each player had to go through a piece of his or her choice and sight-read specially devised exercises, new sets of these coming up every day to ensure against 'leaks'. The hearings went on for a fortnight. In the end eight rank-and-file players were given three months' notice and replaced. A letter went on their behalf to the Director-General of the B.B.C., Sir William Haley, complaining that the auditions had been based on solo standards rather than orchestral ones, a distinction hard to follow. Sargent vindicated himself in a broadcast talk. 'Occasions do come,' he said, 'when changes have to be made for the good of an orchestra. It is only occasionally that a contract cannot be renewed, but when that does happen it is a painful business.'

The string choir had been 'weeded', then. It remained to keep it up to the mark. In time for that year's Promenade Concerts he worked out and put into operation a searching game of musical chairs. Taking his string leaders after rehearsal one day to a restaurant in St. John's Wood, he lunched them royally, then outlined a reform which he had already discussed with Paul Beard. Its aim was to do away with the whole concept of back-desk players and back-desk playing. The leading desks, at which principals and sub-principals sat, were to stay unchanged. But throughout a given series of concerts the players at all remaining desks would move back and forth according to a rota system designed to give everybody a bit of limelight. Thus, during the first week, the second desks of violins, violas and 'cellos would retire to the rearmost positions, and the back-desk pairs, moving up, would play second desk. A week later, second desk would move back to third desk, making room for another pair from the end of the line: and so on, until every pair had had their week up front immediately behind their section leaders.

Sargent was as pleased with his innovation as a child with a new toy, and visiting conductors are said to have marvelled at it. He described the change as drastic, but didn't apologize on that account; he trusted that the vitality of the entire orchestra would benefit. He was now able, he explained, to get into closer personal touch with all his string players. He and his section leaders could better acquaint themselves with the former rearguarders' temperaments and desk quality—'and,' he added, 'their less good qualities'. The rota was widely interpreted as a substitute for further general auditions; no more of these were, in fact, held under Sargent. With all string players taking their turns at what he called 'an important frontline job', everybody was almost as much on his mettle as when playing exercises and test pieces before a contract panel. The business of redeploying twenty desks or so every week is said to have worried the managerial side to exasperation point; and there were open grumbles from the string hierarchy. When the idea was first mooted a player at one of the forward desks was heard to say: 'I don't want people playing wrong notes behind me.' Overhearing this, Sargent put in: 'I don't want people playing wrong notes anywhere.' As a supplementary reform he had the rehearsal floor at Maida Vale painted with numbered squares for the precise positioning of players. This, he hoped, would promote sound-balance and control. Scores and specifications vary, however. Uniform placing proved of little use. Soon the markings were ignored. 'Back to Square One', said a wag.

Whether the string rota was worth the planning problems and minor hurts to *amour propre* that it produced has often been questioned. Yet it was widely accepted that Sargent's liveliness and drive soon gave B.B.C. playing a gloss and briskness which had not been conspicuous before. It is time, therefore, to take another look at Sargent in the 'workshop'. Of his pre-war rehearsal methods and holdings-forth we have a lively account in Bernard Shore's book, *The Orchestra Speaks*. The impressions that follow concern his main B.B.C. tenure (1950–57) and to a lesser extent his continued chief-conductorship of the 'Proms'. They derive mainly from notes made by a leading player during rehearsals.

Again there is evidence that, although his beat adhered scrupulously to the musical letter, he sometimes modified the letter according to ideas of his own. Haydn often came in for attention. Thus of the thunderstorm music in *The Seasons*: 'This is one of the things that obviously old Haydn was doubtful about. He didn't know which instrument to put the lightning on. Obviously he wanted whatever percussion instruments he could get. But unfortunately he did not put them in the score. He should have done so. I have written parts in accordingly.' The additions were for timpani and side-drum. Of an orchestral interlude in *The Creation* he said to the strings: 'Play what is written. If it's nice, all right. If it isn't, we'll alter it.' Again, of a Haydn symphony: 'In this movement Haydn put a barline in the wrong place. It should have been [notated as] two 3/8 bars. That would have been musically correct. But of course they didn't do things like that in those days.' In another Haydn context, which had repeat notes for the double-basses, he said: 'Play single notes here. When you play many notes and "scrub" you defeat your own object and make less sound.'

Nor was Mozart sacrosanct. 'This,' he said of scoring in one of the Masses, 'sounds funny. Mozart obviously wrote this work in a hurry. There is no part for violas in the whole work. He should have had violas, I think. No doubt he sat at the organ and filled in all kind of things.' In went a viola line; it reproduced the 'cello line an octave higher. The beauty of a melody or theme could wring a vivid phrase from him. One of the movements of Mozart's fourteenth piano concerto (K.456) must, he said, be 'as warm as an operatic aria'. He added cryptically: 'It's full of hairpins.' In Elgar's *The Kingdom* he said to the strings: 'Make that passage sound like ointment.' Again to the strings, this time in the Larghetto of the E flat Symphony: 'It is so ravishing and beautiful that it's unrehearsable.' Of a single note in the *Enigma* Variations he asserted: 'If you could play that note half as beautifully as Elgar intended it, then you would all be great artists.' A particularly difficult passage in the Elgar A flat symphony went well. He complimented the orchestra thus: 'What a comfort it must be to each one of you to know that [tonight] this passage is going to be *together*'—i.e. played as if by one man (as, in fact, it was).

He could be as high-handed with Beethoven as with Haydn. 'If what Beethoven wrote [in the slow movement of Second Symphony] comes off,' he decreed, 'then the notation is right. If there's any doubt we must adjust.' Calling for a *rubato* effect somewhere in the Eighth, he committed himself to the view that '*rubato* didn't exist in Beethoven's day'. A comment remembered long—and with feeling—concerned the *Pastoral* Symphony: 'We must know where to put the grace notes. Of course, they should have been notated in the preceding bar. You see, as orchestral players you miss the point. Had you been soloists you would have seen it at once.'

He once accused 'old Handel' of not knowing which notes to accent in the *Hallelujah* Chorus; Sullivan of writing so difficult a unison for violins in *Di Ballo* that 'Heifetz himself would no doubt be very pleased if he could play it'; and Dvořák of not altogether knowing his business. Pulling up the orchestra in one of the latter's Slavonic Dances, he said: 'With all respect to Mr. Dvořák, he has made a mistake with the scoring here. He has given both strings and woodwind *forte*. One should be a little less [loud] than the other.'

Some of his generalizations were shrewd or quaint. Others ruffled people. His players were not without scholarship. One thing they jibbed at was his frequent use of 'obvious' and 'obviously' in relation to matters of classical notation and scoring which are in fact contentious. Here are sample *dicta*, with the note-taker's comments in brackets: 'I am not a good enough conductor to conduct a *mezzo-forte* tune in the oboe with the bassoon playing *piano* behind.' 'One of the hardest things in the world is to play a tune when all the notes are of equal length.' (Comment: 'Everybody laughed at that. It's so true.') 'Any mental trick that makes music sound good is worth using.' 'You may find a few misprints in your parts. Compositors are not always as clever as composers.' 'Music is only a matter of concentration. With a bit of technique and concentration you can play anything.' (Comment: 'He loved to lecture the orchestra. He'd say a thing like that and ruin everything.') 'That [some symphony movement or section] went so well, it was so good, that I want to make sure it's all right, so let us play it again.' (Comment: 'This was annoying. If you've done a thing well at rehearsal it's likely you'll do it well at the concert. Doing it a second time at rehearsal just for the sake of the thing means that it won't go as well.') To wind players: 'Music comes before tonguing. Make tonguing your slave, not your master.'

This last generalization was followed not long afterwards by a case in point. In some work which cannot now be identified readily, he said to the woodwind:

'I can't understand you woodwind players. This passage is perfectly easy. Listen.' He sang the theme illustratively while 'tickatickaticking' the notes according to tonguing technique.

A bassoon: 'Thank you, Sir Malcolm. I can do that, too.'

Sargent: 'Why don't you, then?'

Bassoon: 'Because I have a reed in my mouth—and you haven't.'

Sargent: 'All right, all right, I acknowledge the correction.'

For all the brushes and tensions, much jollity entered into his relations with his players. He often took the whole hundred or so, administrative people as well, to the London Zoo for a cocktail party on the Fellows' lawn or, perhaps, more solid entertainment in the Fellows' restaurant where, he would say, one could always get a good meal: 'The Zoo buys the best possible food for the animals—no tinned stuff for them!—and the Fellows get what's left.' The party was usually joined by a few of Sargent's eminent friends—two or three actors, maybe, a portrait painter, a best-selling writer, a fashionable politician. Usually held on one of the orchestra's free nights towards the end of the 'Proms' season, these parties were painstakingly and lavishly organized. Keepers would parade an assortment of safe, exotic beasts and reptiles for anybody to fondle who wished. Having made an initial stir by leading in a cheetah on a chain, Sargent would pass round a python or a chimpanzee for cuddling. Sometimes the proceedings were high spirited. 'It's a bit startling,' remembers a distinguished 'cellist, 'to have a boa constrictor flipped round your neck by a member of the House of Peers when you have a glass of burgundy in your hand and a mouth full of chicken sandwich.'

Although not much of a fraternizer, he would throw open his dressing-room whenever, as occasionally happened on tour, members of the administrative staff could not find a cloakroom for their things. In such a situation, if a girl had a new hat he would try it on before the looking glass. 'How do I look?' he would ask. 'Charming!' would be the reply. 'Good!' he would return in his brisk fashion, handing over his bowler hat, 'I'll keep it, you have mine.' At all times he unerringly scented whip-rounds for players who were sick or in other misfortune. Theoretically the players kept such matters strictly to themselves. But invariably the collector would find himself surreptitiously cornered by Sargent, finger on lips. A five-pound note would be thrust upon him with the words, 'When that's done, come back for another.' Such kindlinesses were so far from being calculated with an eye to esteem that he gave the impression of being unable to help himself; his hand went to his wallet almost by reflex action.

That was one Sargent. As we have seen, there was another Sargent, the restless, insatiable precisian. On a September morning in 1952 he rehearsed the 'Purcell' Variations and Fugue of Britten for the last night of the Proms. Scored for two flutes and piccolo, Variation A is aerial and swiftly moving.

The first flute in those days was a noted section leader and teacher, Geoffrey Gilbert, who had been a Beecham principal. Having a young newcomer in his section, Gilbert had intended going through the variation before the rehearsal began, so that they should be prepared for Sargent up to a point. An unforeseen change in the rehearsal schedule prevented this. Not surprisingly, at the run-through Variation A did not go well. Sargent had the three players do the variation again and again on their own, i.e. without accompaniment from other orchestral 'voices'. Memories differ as to just how many repeats he asked for. In Gilbert's recollection he asked for up to ten. On his asking for an eleventh, or whatever the inordinate total was, Gilbert feared the freshman's nerve might break. Without mentioning the nature of his anxiety, since to have done so would have made the freshman jumpier still, he suggested to Sargent that the variation be shelved for the present. 'If you'll leave it to me,' he added, 'I'll see it's rehearsed and ready for you before the concert.' Sectional arrangements of this kind are often made in emergencies. Sargent would have none of it.

'You must do it here,' he insisted. 'Now! This is the time to do it.'

Gilbert: 'I'm very sorry. I'm not prepared to play it any more.'

Sargent: 'If you feel like that you'd better leave the rehearsal.'

Gilbert dismantled his flute, cleaned and packed it up and withdrew to the rear of the studio. There he sat on a sofa, curious to know what would happen next. 'No,' said Sargent turning round, 'I mean leave the studio.'

As soon as the rehearsal ended Orchestral Management were on the telephone to Sargent, anxious to intervene and help. 'Leave this to me,' answered Sargent. 'The B.B.C. could never get a better flute player than Geoffrey Gilbert. I'm going to ask him round to my flat for a drink. We'll talk it over.'

The talk lasted for an hour, and Gilbert did much of the talking. He unburdened himself of much that other seasoned players might have endorsed. In his relations with professionals, he argued, Sargent did not take the correct psychological line. In difficult passages the player came up against many problems which the conductor was not aware of. Naturally, a conductor wanted everything that was possible. The player's concern was to give everything that was practicable. Beecham had a knack of making a player feel that whatever he did was exactly what Beecham wanted. Whereas Sargent had no confidence in the ability of players to do anything on their own account. He thought *he* was doing it all. . . .

There were no high words. The tone of the discussion was earnest, its outcome nil. In consequence Gilbert left the B.B.C. later and became first flute with the Royal Philharmonic Orchestra, thus rejoining Beecham. Eleven years later, Beecham being dead, Sargent took the R.P.O. to Russia and conducted them in three great cities. Again he did the 'Purcell' Variations and Fugue. Again he had Geoffrey Gilbert as his first flute. At a rehearsal in Moscow on a bitter winter day after an overnight air journey from Kiev, everybody fagged and the orchestra riddled with head colds and influenza, he asked the clarinets and bassoons if they thought it necessary to re-do their variations and, on being told 'No', excused them. He then said: 'We'll do the flute one.'

'But,' objected Gilbert, 'I don't want to do mine, either. It was all right in Kiev last night.'

'It was not very good,' said Sargent.

'What was wrong with it?'

'It was not very good.'

For a moment it looked as though, after eleven years, history was going to repeat itself. This time Gilbert did not persist, however. As soon as the variation was over he packed up and left the hall.

CHAPTER TWENTY-EIGHT

ROYAL (AND OTHER) OCCASIONS

SOME HONOURABLE Member having, out of the blue, asked in the House of Commons who was responsible for 'official music' in the Royal Navy and the Royal Marines, the Parliamentary Secretary to the Admiralty replied that Sargent had been appointed the Royal Marines' honorary adviser in music. Another honourable (and gallant) Member who happened to be a vice-admiral asked waggishly what official music might be, a question which, the House having a sense of humour all its own, raised laughs. He was told the point at issue had no reference to the *kind* of music but the occasions on which it was played. This seemed to satisfy everybody. As has already been mentioned, the honorary advisership, which took effect in the summer of 1949, was specifically devised, on Lord Mountbatten's prompting, for Sargent and ended with Sargent's death. In his official capacity he made but one public appearance at home. This was in 1950. To raise funds for Greek earthquake refugees, he conducted a civilian choir of over two hundred voices and a Royal Marines Symphony Orchestra of ninety players, pick of R.M. light orchestras throughout Portsmouth Command, on two successive nights in the gymnasium of the Portsmouth R.N. Barracks, which had been converted for the occasion into a concert hall seating 3,000. Major Vivian Dunn,* in charge of R.M. music in the Command, rehearsed the orchestra arduously for a month. Then Sargent came down and rehearsed them for a day and a half. His repeat programme included the *Walk to The Paradise Garden*, his own edition of Arne's *Rule Britannia*

---

* Later Lt.-Colonel Dunn, Principal Director of Music, Royal Marines.

and the first movement of Vaughan Williams's *Sea Symphony*, all played brightly and euphoniously by musicians in Number One full dress uniform with scarlet and gold chevrons, scarlet collars with gold lace and shoulder knots in gold or yellow braid according to rank. Before the first of the two concerts he was entertained by Admiral Sir Algernon Willis, Commander in Chief, Portsmouth Command, in H.M.S. *Victory*, and said he could think of no finer inspiration for the *Sea Symphony* than dining aboard Nelson's flagship.

Little more was heard of his interest in the Royal Marines until the summer of 1953. For the Coronation of Queen Elizabeth II in June of that year, Mountbatten, as Commander-in-Chief Mediterranean, brought home some twenty ships, leaving the rest on station, and flew his flag in H.M.S. *Glasgow*. Sargent came aboard off Spithead to confer with him and Fleet musicians about twin Coronation concerts he had been asked to conduct in Malta. Again there was to be a repeat programme. Arrangements for it were planned in detail. First he was asked which he would prefer—the Commander-in-Chief's Maltese Orchestra, a string ensemble which had been based on Admiralty House, Valletta, for over a century, or a military ('brass') band of the sort cultivated afloat as well as ashore. He opted for a military band. Orders were given for a hundred players to be recruited from ships' bands of the Mediterranean Fleet and the Malta-based Third Commando Brigade. These and an inter-services male voice choir were to perform arrangements (for the most part) of fifteen numbers starting with *Pomp and Circumstance* No. 1 and ending with the Arne-Sargent 'Rule Britannia.' On the whole it was a programme to make 'emancipated' music lovers, however loyal, feel thankful that most reigns are long and coronation concerts of the conventional sort rare.* Having organized to the point of rigidity a scheme which might have benefited by variants at the eleventh hour, he made off to the Royal Festival Hall,

---

* The other items were the National Anthem, the Hymn of Malta, a *Water Music* suite, Walton's *Crown Imperial* March, the dances from *Henry VIII*, the *Tannhäuser* Overture, three choruses ('Hearts of Oak', Here's a health unto her Majesty' and 'Jerusalem') Jeremiah Clarke's Trumpet Voluntary, Handel's Largo, *The Yeomen of the Guard* Overture and the prelude to *Lohengrin* Act III.

which was having Coronation concerts* on its own account, and there conducted *A Sea Symphony* in its entirety. In the audience were musicians from the Mediterranean Fleet and its shore establishments. Some of them went backstage to the conductor's room at the end. They congratulated him on his performance of the *Sea Symphony* especially. The air was loud with 'Splendid, sir!' 'Smashing!' 'Terrific!' and so on. 'What did *you* think of it?' asked Sargent, turning to a twenty-four-year-old who had not yet opened his mouth. 'Oh, sir,' came the reply, 'I cried!'

The speaker was Joseph Sammut, who had recently been installed as conductor of the Commander-in-Chief's Maltese Orchestra. Later that year Sammut conducted at a State dinner party during Queen Elizabeth's visit to the island. Afterwards, in accordance with naval custom, he took port with the guest of honour and the Commander-in-Chief. 'You are very young to be a bandmaster,' observed the Queen. 'I am exactly the same age as your Majesty,' bowed Sammut. Impressed by the young man's personality and professional promise, Sargent made him his private pupil and brought him for a while to London. He took him to all his B.B.C. rehearsals and at Albert Hall Mansions gave him lessons in score-reading, matters concerning *tempo*, phrasing, orchestral balance and how to beat time in all metres with both hands. For all this the pupil was not required to pay a penny. At rehearsal once he talked during the music. 'If that happens again,' warned Sargent, playing the bogy man, 'I shall send you back home.' Sammut remembers the rebuke with affection. Like several before him, he took in Sargent's teachings and baton technique so well that on returning to Malta he could be identified almost at a glance when conducting as a Sargent pupil. After his master's death he wrote: 'As a teacher he was wonderful . . . God bless him.'

*

* There were eight of these, Sargent, Beecham, Boult and Barbirolli conducting two each. Sargent was at the rostrum on Coronation night itself, when he conducted Britten's *Spring Symphony* and Elgar's A flat Symphony. At his other concert he did the Walton violin concerto and the *Perfect Fool* ballet music as well as *A Sea Symphony*.

Sargent flew to Malta a few weeks after the Coronation. The first
of the Coronation concerts, billed for the Orpheum cinema at
Gzira, was six days off. Band parts reached the island about the
same time as he. There had been no preliminary rehearsals. Having
nearly a week's grace, he made it his first business to join the
Commander-in-Chief's party off the Island of Gozo, north-west of
Malta, for a day's spear-fishing. These parties were much talked of
in Valletta. People who had been out on them came back with
remarkable accounts of Mountbatten's prowess. He spent much
time under water with an aqualung, diving to an average depth of
fifty or sixty feet. Often he got down to eighty or a hundred feet,
once to a hundred and eighty. He had speared fish bigger than
himself; and two naval divers used to accompany him for alternate
dives, the strain being too much for one man. On this occasion
Sargent, who later on became something of an aqualung adept, did
not go down. Instead, lying on an inflated raft and watching through
an observation hatch, he put in three twenty-minute spells of fish
spotting, his duty being to hail the Commander's craft to come
alongside when he spotted anything of promise. It was blazing
weather. Next day he was laid up with sunburn and, as on a previous
holiday with the Mountbattens, dysentery, though this time of the
virulent type known as 'Malta dog'. He was ill for four days. During
three of those days he should have been rehearsing. The Fleet
Bandmaster rehearsed in his stead. When he did take over, shaky but
indomitable, his touch was transforming. In all he took five rehearsals, recovering stamina as he went along. On the day of the
first concert he was on the rostrum from ten in the morning until
late afternoon, when balance tests were made for the microphones.

The first concert was for an invited audience of the glittering sort.
The second was for everybody lucky enough to get in. Both nights
were sweltering. Sweat dripped from the ends of bandsmen's noses.
At the intervals Sargent changed completely, having brought a
massive wardrobe to Malta. He never wilted or crumpled. At the
end, when the audience had applauded their fill, the musicians stood
up in a body spontaneously and gave him an ovation that started
everybody off again. After his last 'call' on the second night he left
two batons on the stand. There was a rush and jostle to grab these.

A press of excited Maltese who had not been able to get into the cinema blocked the stage door and pavement. As had happened in Buenos Aires the police were unable to get near. Friends elbowed a way out for him. Identifiable by the silver figure of a naval signalman on its bonnet, the Commander-in-Chief's Rolls-Royce was waiting only a few yards away. How he traversed those few yards and got into the motor-car is not clearly remembered by anybody who helped him, such was the hubbub and excitement.

After the concerts came his cruise with the Mediterranean Fleet and his transfer from ship to ship by helicopter and 'high line', matters which, as described in the opening chapter, he reminisced about with Mountbatten the day before he died. A further incident of that holiday must be added here. The Commander-in-Chief took the entire Fleet into Naples and put massed bands ashore to beat Retreat on the jetty, a ceremonial of marching and counter-marching in quick and slow time to music, followed by the singing of the Evening Hymn; the lowering of the White Ensign as Sunset is played by solo bugle; and the singing of 'Rule Britannia' and the National Anthem. All this was followed by parties aboard *Surprise* and *Glasgow*. Watching alongside Sargent in *Glasgow* was an American woman who, after the last note and the last manœuvre, turned to him and said, 'That was very beautifully done.' 'Do you have anything like it in your country?' he asked. 'No.' 'Why not?' 'I'm afraid our people would laugh.' 'Did you laugh?' 'No, I wept.'

Not only did Sargent weep often and unashamedly. Those near him sometimes wept. Theirs, like many of his, were tears of wonder. His emotionalism could be contagious.

*

As his sixtieth birthday approached he overworked as unbendingly as in the 1930s and 1940s, travelled an enormously greater mileage, dashed with little respite from torrid cities to grilling ones and paid less attention to his health than was good for him. Occasionally his body gave warning. With his second Proms season nicely launched he dashed off to sandwich in an orchestral concert at the Dome, Brighton. At the morning rehearsal he went down with a lung infection. He had to drop the concert and was away from the Proms for three weeks, his dates being taken by four substitute conductors. Weak at the knees, he reappeared for a Beethoven night and sat on a high stool to conduct. Horder gave him a medical check at the interval.

Nothing was to cure him of the 'dashing-off' propensity. Many of his dashes were to places remoter than the Dome. Soon after the 1954 Proms he flew to Tokyo, a city aching, it seemed, for his Beethoven (Sixth and Seventh symphonies), *Enigma* Variations and what by this time had become his routine Delius, Walton and Holst pieces. On the journey out he probably had his head in the vocal score (rehearsal edition) of Walton's new opera, *Troilus and Cressida* with supplementary sheets listing some hundred and seventy corrections. Early in December he was to conduct the première of *Troilus* at Covent Garden, the second 'grand season' assignment there of his career, the first having been three not very distinguished performances of Charpentier's *Louise* under Beecham's rule in 1936.

With the capital's three orchestras—the Tokyo Symphony, founded soon after Japan's surrender in 1945, the N.H.K. Orchestra (equivalent to the B.B.C. Symphony Orchestra) and the Kansai Orchestra—he conducted four concerts before audiences who until then had never set eyes on a European baton. As always happened in far-off cities, thousands fell in love with him. At his opening concert, with the Tokyo Symphony Orchestra, the city's biggest auditorium was so packed that in the top gallery young men and women spread paper on gangway steps and sat there, lost to the world. At the end there was an ovation that lasted for ten minutes. A girl in a kimono gave him a bunch of carnations. He gave a carnation from it to the orchestra's leader. Renewed ecstacy. After he had signed 'more miniature scores than I do after a Promenade concert', a clapping crowd at the stage door watched him drive off with the British Ambassador. Afterwards he had much to tell of how well he got on with Japanese players; how intent they had been on bowing as he wished, on taking breaths where he wished, on nuancing as he wished. 'And then,' he went on, 'having got the detail right and the way you want it in performance, this mystic thing happens, a thing one doesn't understand, except that the personal impact of the conductor upon the players is such that they perform as he had hoped. . . . I never want to hear more beautiful performances of Beethoven's Sixth and Seventh than I got from the Tokyo orchestras.'

For the *Enigma* Variations the N.H.K. Orchestra gave him five rehearsals. 'I shall never forget the first one. They had never seen the music before. The moment they sensed the beauty of it, the strings got a new loveliness of tone. Another wonderful thing was the intentness with which players would listen to the others while waiting for their own cues.' This performance, again, was 'one of the greatest thrills I have ever had musically.' There were so many of these in thirty or forty years that one wonders whether the glow of particular occasions may not have tended to disturb his scale of comparison and judgment. The man who more than once said, 'The most important music in the world is that which I happen to be performing at any given moment,' conceivably indulged transient illusions of the same kind about the relative merit of the performances he conducted.

While in Tokyo he came upon one musical phenomenon which he knew could never be emulated in the West. 'In the theatre of the Imperial Palace,' he narrated, 'I was given a special performance by the Emperor's private band, who played music that has existed for a thousand years on instruments most of which were three or four hundred years old. These musicians practised from nine thirty in the morning until five o'clock every day.'

He asked how often they performed. The leader said, 'Well, regularly.' 'What do you mean by regularly?' pursued Sargent. Leader: 'Once.' Sargent: 'Once a week?' Leader: 'Oh, no! Once a year.'

In so far as Western terms and practice are relevant, Sargent's account pointed to hundreds of rehearsals for one performance. At the Proms he was given seven rehearsals for three concerts and considered himself well treated. 'Thirty or forty years ago,' he would say, 'Henry Wood was getting only four for six.'

*

Commissioned by the B.B.C., *Troilus and Cressida*, with text by Christopher Hassall after Chaucer's version of the Trojan tale, was not only a new opera but Walton's first. It was assured of a fashionable first night long before the curtain went up. To the pulling power of Sargent's name were added those of a producer (George Devine) and a designer (Hugh Casson) in vogue outside opera houses as well as within and, more important, a feeling that something was on the way which combined sumptuousness, extrovert approach and romantic appeal, three qualities which had never been linked—and had rarely appeared even one at a time—in typical English opera since the war. As the first night approached there were rumours of difficulties, contentious words and hard feelings at rehearsal. Some of these rumours were not far from the truth. What unnerved some of the singers was that Sargent declined to beat certain of their unaccompanied passages. 'Without the beat it's terribly difficult,' they would say. To which Sargent would reply that a beat wasn't necessary. These bars were silent for the orchestra; he would join the singers at the end. 'But,' came the objection, 'the rhythm goes on for the orchestra as well as for us whether they're silent or not, and sometimes the metre changes on the way. A beat would help us all.' Deadlocks of this kind were not easily resolved.

It was alleged also that he itched to alter Walton's scoring here and there, not in the sense of making it sound better but with the intention of making it 'safer'. In some cases he questioned acoustical implications, offering Walton advice on instrumental or other combinations which he thought would be either ineffective or hazardous in the theatre. Some of his points had to do with gaps between rhythmical stresses in, or entries by, the orchestra, on the one hand, and those for the chorus on the other. His argument was that certain of these 'discrepancies', although deliberately calculated, might give some listeners, at any rate, the impression that the chorus were coming in off beat. On the purely orchestral side there was dispute over a passage no longer in the score, having been deleted in revision, where bass-flute was doubled by clarinet. In performance the effect had always come off. At a refresher rehearsal, however, Sergent pronounced it dangerous.

'The clarinet won't come in on the beat. Let's have it out,' he argued.

Walton insisted on keeping the clarinet in. On the whole he does not seem to have rejoiced in Sargent's technical solicitudes.

Technicalities apart, there was a chronic difficulty. The conducting score, not yet engraved, was in parts hardly legible. To make matters worse, Sargent refused to wear spectacles or, at any rate, had not reconciled himself to doing so. (He usually carried an eye-glass, an elegant one in a tortoise-shell frame, but used it rarely and circumspectly.) This above all other factors is said to have been the one that made the atmosphere at rehearsals acrimonious. How, if he had to be constantly peering for the notes, could he cut a dash on the rostrum? The thought must have perturbed him? The first night was in many ways brilliant. Everybody conceded that. There were more smart people in the Opera House who had never been seen there before than veterans could recall. Hundreds stayed on for what is said to have been the biggest first-night party ever held there.

Was the occasion brilliant in the 'interpretative' sense? By provoking extremists of the *avant-garde* to intemperate scorn, the performance certainly promoted the cause of neo-Romanticism in general and Walton's art in particular. But that has little to do with brilliance. What of Sargent's part? Next morning's *Times* said: 'The performance went well . . . Sir Malcolm Sargent, who has not been at an operatic desk for years, was vigilant, served the singers with tact and elicited from the orchestra that stringency which is one of the marks of Walton's orchestral writing.' To those on the stage his tact and vigilance may have been less in evidence. It was noted that in performance, as at the rehearsals, he habitually counted the bars to himself, mouthing 'One, two, three, four' and so on—not a reassuring sign in a conductor who is supposed to have substantially mastered the text. Geraint Evans, then coming into view as a singer-actor of rare gifts, sang the small part of Antenor, Captain of the Trojan Spears. In the first act Antenor has a brush with the High Priest, who is all for a parley with the Greeks. 'Never! Never!' retorts Antenor *impetuoso*, *ff*. For this entry Sargent flung his left arm out and up with a magnificent display of cuff. Physically it was a splendid cue. Geraint Evans had never had a better. But it was a bar too soon. He stood his ground, knees metaphorically knocking, and, wondering in spite of himself whether he was doing the right thing, came in a bar later—as the composer meant him to.

Not only was the first-night performance 'inaccurate' according to Waltonians. They maintain that in successive revivals *Troilus* has never had an accurate performance in London. 'This unfortunate opera,' they call it.

*

Between 1954 and 1958 he did a certain amount of stately gadding with the B.B.C. Symphony Orchestra, taking them at one time or another to Belgium, Germany and the Scandinavian countries. With him went the familiar parcels of scores and band parts: Vaughan Williams's Sixth and *London* symphonies, that of Walton, the *New World*, four out of Sibelius's seven symphonies, a Haydn pair, Brahms's First and Beethoven's Second. Among tonepoems and miscellaneous pieces the most demanding was *Ein Heldenleben*, which he did in Bergen. This work now meant as much to him as *Till Eulenspiegel* and *Don Juan*, perhaps more. One of his finest performances of it had been to a half-full Free Trade Hall (Manchester). A poor house, whenever it happened to him, brought out the fighter in Sargent, giving added fire to his musicianship. More of this when we come to a certain Ostend occasion. Again his health sometimes wavered; his temperature would persistently hover a little above normal; in the afternoons he would have a grey look. Even at these times his energy crackled on preternaturally. George Willoughby, the B.B.C.'s orchestral and concerts manager, kept a solicitous eye on him and, as a friend may, gave him orders for his own good. On top of travel and rehearsal labours there were social excitements which made a toll on his stamina.

There were two especially effervescent nights at the concert hall in the Tivoli Gardens, Copenhagen (June 1956). His programmes included the *London* and *Pathétique* symphonies, the Britten-Purcell variations, the Rossini-Respighi suite and sprightly or poetic pieces by Berlioz, Mendelssohn and Grieg. Concealed behind a curtain in the royal box, King Frederick followed certain of the performances from score. Speaking as one conductor to another, Sargent had offered him one of the rehearsals if he graciously wished to take it. The King had thanked him and regretfully declined, less from protocol, it was felt, than from shyness. During one of the intervals Sargent was summoned to the suite behind the royal box for august compliments and musical gossip. At home the B.B.C.'s Third Programme was standing by for a relay of the second half of the programme. The chat looked like overrunning the deadline.

Willoughby tactfully broke in on it, saying: 'Excuse me, but we are on the air in two minutes.' Sargent took his leave of the King with a humorous aside: 'This bloody broadcasting ruins everything.'

After the Tivoli concerts there were late parties. He was the soul of both. But again his temperature was playing tricks. From Copenhagen he flew to Bergen. At the airport he was met by Willoughby, who saw at a glance that he was unwell. He admitted to being a bit off colour. He promised to do nothing more that afternoon than a token rehearsal—'They [the orchestra] know it all already.' The promise was not kept. He gave his orchestra a full three-hour stretch, sparing neither himself nor others. The day after the concert was a free day. He solemnly undertook to rest—'In bed, don't forget,' counselled Willoughby. He made a noise that could be taken to mean assent. That night he went to yet another party. Next morning, joining a party of his players, he went sightseeing far and near like any unencumbered holidaymaker and didn't rest for a minute of the day.

When he was wholly fit, his quenchless energy coped goodheartedly with other people's perplexities on the spur of the moment. After a concert in the Apollo Theatre, Düsseldorf (tour of Germany and Holland, 1954), he joked, teased and laughed all the way to Hamburg. There he got off the train to find a press conference lined up for him on the platform. As he acquitted himself zestfully among the microphones and flash-bulbs, something went wrong with some of the party's personal luggage, that of George Willoughby and Clifford Curzon among others. (On this trip Curzon was playing solo in three piano concertos—the *Emperor*, that of Alan Rawsthorne and Mozart's A major (K.488).) Looking in later at the Vierjahreszeiten hotel, he noticed that Willoughby's face was glum.

'What's the matter with you, George?' he asked.

'Our stuff hasn't turned up. They must have taken it to the wrong hotel. I must go find it.'

'No,' bade Sargent, 'you must do nothing of the sort. Go down to the bar and have a drink. Relax. Leave it to me.'

Getting a list of other hotels from the porter, he went off in a car and was back an hour later with a load of reclaimed bags and suitcases, having sorted everything out.

'There,' he said, '— simple!'

*

The Scandinavian tour (1956) took him and the B.B.C. orchestra to a Sibelius festival in Helsinki. They had been chosen to do Symphonies No. 1, No. 3 and No. 7, *Finlandia*, *En Saga*, *Scènes historiques* and *Tapiola*, spread over two concerts. At the end of the second concert he received a laurel wreath and affectionate roars. Afterwards he went out to Järvenpää for a talk with the patriarch himself. With him he took a memento from the orchestra, an album in which he had added his signature, with words of tribute, to those of all the players and staff members, from leader to instrument-porters: over a hundred names. Sibelius was in his eighty-first year, frail and shrunk of face, his great cranium a memorial to fierce musical imaginings which had burnt out decades earlier. He had a warm greeting for the youth of sixty-one. In England Sargent's Sibelius readings had occasionally incurred adverse criticism in a small but influential field, the reason advanced being that his speeds, dynamics and other treatment departed from those of Sibelius's compatriot Robert Kajanus, whose recordings circulated widely in the 1930s and later. About this Sargent felt sore. He said to me during the mid-1950s: 'For some reason the Kajanus recordings used to be widely accepted as authoritative. They are nothing of the kind. Sibelius does not recognize them as such. I have that from Sibelius himself. Every time I conducted one of his works I was slated in certain quarters because I didn't ape these repudiated discs but got my readings direct from the scores.' The 1956 meeting was not their first. He spoke often of the happiness he knew in the old man's presence; how they used to walk in the grounds of Ainola, Sibelius's villa at Järvenpää and in the tall forest beyond 'which', he would say, 'is so essential a part of his music.' Whenever he conducted in Finland there would be a friendly telegram from the composer the following day. In the drawing-room at Albert Hall Mansions was a special table with two framed and signed photographs—one of Sibelius, 'with gratitude and admiration', the other of Ralph Vaughan Williams with a like inscription.

From Helsinki to Stockholm. The first of his two concerts in the Swedish capital was a gleaming royal occasion. In the Konserthuset he conducted Haydn's Symphony in D major No. 104, Sibelius's No. 1, a piece by the Swedish composer Hilding Rosenberg and the Britten-Purcell before an audience that included Queen Elizabeth II and Prince Philip, who were in Sweden on a State visit for the opening of the Olympic Equestrian Games, King Gustav and his Queen, Princess Margaret and many other illustrious people, the Mountbattens among them. Never before had the B.B.C. Symphony Orchestra played to more emeralds, diamonds, orders, decorations, patrician profiles and social consequence. On such occasions Sargent not only conducted but, as an English commentator once put it, played a second rôle, that of the Master of Ceremonies. At the end of the last rehearsal he would instruct his players on how many bars of which national anthem they were to play (sometimes 'the Queen' was cut to six bars in deference to the host country); precisely at what moment to stand up when monarch, president or governor-general entered and withdrew; above all, how important it was that everybody should stand up as one man, without hesitation or raggedness. These are matters with which few conductors bother themselves, although assuredly they are a conductor's business. As a result most orchestral players behave sporadically on gala occasions, looking to each other for cues like outsiders at a funeral service in an unfamiliar rite. There were some in the B.B.C. orchestra who had little private regard for official pomps. But, they reflected, if pomps had to be complied with it was well that the job should be done efficiently. And Sargent's efficiency in this matter was allowed to be prodigious. Nor, on this Stockholm occasion, did pomp and panoply get in the way of the music. The tumult after the Sibelius symphony at the end, with everybody on his feet and clapping, two monarchs and their consorts included, is cited in Lord Mountbatten's words at the beginning of this book as a signal instance of Sargent's 'ambassadorial' sway. Next day it was announced that King Gustav had made him a Commander of the Order of the North Star, first class.

On the way to another royal concert, this time at the Brussels Exposition of 1958, he and his orchestra halted at Ostend to play the *Water Music* suite, Sibelius's No. 2 and Beethoven's fourth piano concerto (soloist Denis Mathews) in the Kursaal. Possibly because so many Belgians were already being siphoned off to the Exposition, bookings were disconcertingly bad. At the end of the afternoon rehearsal he said to the players: 'I understand that it will be a poor hall tonight. We know the music is first class. The only thing that need worry us is if, by any chance, we don't give a first-class performance.'

There were only a hundred and fifty in the hall that night. At the interval he conspired with Paul Beard, his leader, to make the best of what, for anybody else, would have been a demoralizing situation. What he said to Beard was roughly as follows:

'At the end, Paul, I bow. Then I bring you up. Then I go off. You remain standing. I come back for my second bow. Then you sit. I go off. You remain seated. I come back for my third call. I bring you up again. Then I go off leaving you up. I come back for a fourth call. You are still standing. I shake hands with you and the leaders all round. I go off. I come on again for my fifth call. I get hold of you by the hand and draw you off the stage.'

All this worked to perfection. The audience hugely enjoyed a feat not of showmanship but of pluck and high spirits that kept up the orchestra's morale in dismal circumstances and, beyond that, did something for English prestige. After his fifth call, to continued clapping, Sargent did not so much draw Paul Beard off the platform as drag him. He gave the impression of saying or thinking: 'Really, we can't stay here *all* night, even if all these thousands want us to do so.'

*

For his two concerts at the Brussels Exposition that summer he was joined by '*my* choir', as he affectionately called it, that of the

Huddersfield Choral Society,* which for over thirty years, in recording sessions and on public platforms, was as much a pillar of his career as the Royal Choral Society itself. A shuttle service of six planes flew two hundred and fifty singers to Brussels in what was said to be the biggest 'single party' air movement ever mounted from the North of England. Their jubilation at being chosen with the B.B.C. orchestra, the band of H.M. Scots Guards and the Duke of Edinburgh in person to represent Britain officially during the festival's 'English days' was damped a little by their first experience of the concert hall in the exhibition grounds.

Their first business here was a rehearsal of *Belshazzar's Feast*. They found themselves strung out in straight lines instead of in the usual horseshoe formation, on a platform inadequately tiered, behind the orchestra rather than overlooking it and too far away from Sargent for comfort or confidence. Acoustically the hall was so unresponsive that, as one singer put it, 'you felt you were singing in an open field.' This feeling of inhibition persisted on the night: one of those glittering and slightly glacial occasions when the diplomatic corps is much in evidence and nobody can be sure who is there for the music and who enduring it as a matter of duty. In the royal box King Baudouin sat bolt upright in his ceremonial chair and listened to every bar with what looked like painful scrupulosity. Sargent had only two calls. The King and the Duke of Edinburgh then rose to leave, the Duke giving the choir a genial smile and wave. Hundreds hastened out of the hall to see the illustrious pair drive off. It was all too clear that for them the music had been an incidental and minor part of the proceedings. The second concert brought *Gerontius*. By this time the choir were more or less inured to the hall's dry acoustic; the attentiveness of the audience and their cordiality at the end were consoling.

In the ordinary way the Huddersfielders under Sargent did not receive or need consolation; they were givers of it. As well as consoling they chilled spines and made people marvel. Up to the mid-1960s he conducted them on a dozen or more international occasions,

* In much of this section I follow Sidney H. Crowther, joint author of *The Huddersfield Choral Society: 1836–1936, 1936–1961*, Huddersfield Examiner Letter Press Dept.

mostly abroad. Some of the trips called for general stamina on top of good voices and taut musical discipline. At Edinburgh in 1948 they came off an overnight train at five in the morning, plunged into full rehearsals with little respite and, at two festival concerts, sang *Belshazzar*, the Fauré Requiem and the finest B minor Mass which, Sargent told them later, he had ever conducted. Artur Schnabel, who heard all three performances, went further. He said it was the finest choral singing he had heard anywhere in the world. Trips to the Continent were strenuous in a different way. Everybody up at six in the morning. Hours on the road and in the air. Touch-down early afternoon. Quick settling-in at hostel or guest house. Jolly group meals—and no time to loiter over them. Then to a strange hall for early evening rehearsal with an unfamiliar orchestra. Or perhaps the first rehearsal would be for choir only. Everything had to be run through and touched up. Even with so ingrained a piece as *Messiah* Sargent was chary of taking chances.

He and the Huddersfielders took *Messiah* to the Continent six times. They opened the Vienna musical festival with it in 1958, giving two performances as well as an afternoon rehearsal for television when a temperature outside of 85 degrees (F.) was aggravated inside the Grossermusikvereinsaal by blazing camera arcs. The women singers had put on their concert dresses, the men their dinner jackets, to make a better picture. The players of the Vienna Symphony Orchestra, less meticulous, took their coats off, rolled up shirtsleeves, cast off ties. Sargent was displeased but could do nothing about it. As will be seen, this form of indiscipline, as he considered it, irked him literally to the end. After the Vienna *Messiah* he got an ovation of fourteen minutes. A year later he and the Huddersfielders did two *Messiahs* in West Berlin. His ovation after the second one lasted for fifteen minutes. People stamped and bravoed and waved handkerchiefs. . . . In June 1963 he took the Huddersfield *Messiah* to Munich. From there they flew to Portugal for repeat performances in Oporto and Lisbon. On all three occasions Sargent had the audience stand not only for the 'Hallelujah' chorus, according to the English tradition, but also, in memory of Pope John, newly deceased, for the sequence of four brief choruses starting with 'For by man came death'. Everybody stood for a minute in silent homage, orchestral players with the rest. The most impressive spectacle of all was in Lisbon. Here Sargent conducted before an audience of six thousand in an arena which had housed a circus the night before. During the silence and during the performance tears streamed down men's faces as well as women's. In such solemnities Sargent gloried yet was sincere to the core. He handled, timed and, in effect, produced them with fervour, soul and professional certitude.

Again he regarded his *Messiah* production as a vindication of 'anti-purist' doctrine and practice. For these Continental performances he never flew out more than a hundred and fifty voices (on his 1963 tour he had only a hundred and twenty-eight)—puny forces alongside those he habitually used at home. Vienna, Berlin and Munich, however, tended to think of *Messiah* in terms of 'chamber' choirs and orchestras of correspondingly limited size. For many, perhaps most, concertgoers in these places the forces imported by Sargent were grandiose. The success of his two West Berlin performances, referred to above, moved him to something like exultation. The ovation had been unique, he claimed. People were saying that Berlin had not known an audience like it in twenty years. That showed how people wanted their *Messiah* performed. And how Handel wanted it, too—'Handel wanted it done big!'

Other works in his baggage on tour included, as has been mentioned, *Belshazzar's Feast*, which crackled with the original Leeds-1931 voltage and roused listeners to elation wherever he took it except for the unlucky night in Brussels. Typical Sargent readings of *Belshazzar* were the thing which, above all, impressed foreigners with British choral discipline. Here and there admiration was qualified by a note that approached raillery. After a *Belshazzar* which he conducted in Vienna one Austrian critic wrote that the choir's power and discipline reminded him of a demonstration by 'the old British Navy'. According to another they sang with as much enthusiasm and patriotism 'as if winning back colonies for Merry Old England'.

In 1965 he took two 'plane loads of Huddersfielders, one hundred and eighty voices, to Boston, Mass., for the 150th anniversary of that city's Handel and Haydn Society, the oldest singing group in the United States. Here they were pitted as festival guests against fourteen other choirs from twelve countries in two hemispheres: over a thousand singers in all. For Handel's *Israel in Egypt* at their first concert they got a standing ovation of respectable duration. For *Belshazzar* next night there were people in Symphony Hall who had motored for a hundred or two hundred miles and meant to motor back home when the concert was over. Nor was this the only form of accolade. The programme was sponsored by a mammoth insurance company and two other mammoths who dealt in razor blades and electrical appliances. *Belshazzar* 'tore the roof open', in a Bostonian's phrase. At the end everybody was on his feet, roaring and adoring. As they watched Sargent take endless calls in his tranquil, triumphant way, that of a man in the prime of life, women were saying to each other: 'They say he's seventy, would you believe it? Isn't he fan*tast*ic?'

He looked as much at ease, as buoyed up, as at a first or last night of the Proms. He stood for England as much as for music. His patriotism was of the secure sort, never downcast. In the old-fashioned way he considered England worth 'standing' for. It was a task. He had a talent for it. And it was a privilege.

CHAPTER TWENTY NINE

B.B.C. DOWNS AND UPS

EOPLE DID not, generally speaking, talk with Sargent. They
listened to him. On the whole the listening was good. Much
of his talk was about himself and his doings, past and to
come. One of the amiable, perplexing things about Sargent was
that, while exquisitely mindful and considerate for many others, he
could, by fits and starts, be as egocentric as a spinning top. As has
been conveyed earlier in this book, the child factor in him made
egocentricity likeable. It is notorious that egocentrics do not, as a
rule, know much about themselves. During various conversations
over fifteen or twenty years I probed him for self-assessment. How,
in his view, did other people see him? How did he see himself?
Such questions he answered readily, though sometimes with a
touch of wryness. Thus:

'I know people say I'm superficial, that I lack profundity. I
reply, "All right, if I haven't got any profundity, let's have a look
at yours." They aren't forthcoming. And, anyway, who can judge
of profundity? . . . You say you have detected a new note in my
work this last six years [i.e. from 1950 onwards]. I can't say I've
detected anything of the kind myself. Perhaps you didn't know my
work well enough before that. True, a man mustn't stand still. If
he stands still he goes back . . . I simply cannot listen to my gramophone recordings of five years ago. I'd like to have them all destroyed. This has nothing to do with improved recording technique;
only with quality of performance. I invariably feel I can do better.
I'm always discovering something new in the classics. I found
something entirely new in Dvořák's Fourth Symphony this morning.
I've been discussing it with Paul Beard. . . . '

Did he, I ask, listen much to other conductors' recordings?

'When preparing a modern piece I make a point of hearing any recording that may have been made by the conductor who did the first performance. This I compare with other outstanding versions. I usually borrow discs for this purpose from the B.B.C. or other libraries. If I tried to own every record I listen to for professional purposes, I should need a warehouse to stock them in. As it is my private collection is immense.

'My gramophone listening, being professional, differs from that of most people. I never sit back at home and listen to records for pleasure. I usually conduct six hours a day, and that goes on for five, sometimes six days a week. Which is quite enough music for any man. When I get home I don't want to hear any more. . . . When I have to listen I do so with the score on my knee. I do not necessarily hear a piece through. I may listen to eight bars here, twelve bars there, repeating them over and over again to study some detail of balance or interpretation. Used in this way records are a great *technical* aid. But they are no substitute for score-study, which is the old-fashioned way.' He repeated the charge quoted in an earlier chapter that young conductors of the post-war period relied too much on records. 'They *learn* from the gramophone. Thus they give readings that lack individuality and are just imitations.'

By whom and when he was first named 'Flash Harry' it would be hard to establish. My impression is that the nickname was first in circulation among orchestral players before the war and that they used it in no spirit of adulation. Sargent had his own version of its origins, as reported below. By the early 1960s it had been taken up by young Prommers and affectionately shortened to 'Flash'. Their affection he prized. But:

'I have never enjoyed it [being called "Flash"] very much. Curious thing how the nickname was given me. I was on the air in a Brains Trust in London with Joad, Huxley and others. Malcolm Sargent says his piece. Then the announcer introduces Malcolm Sargent conducting the Hallé Orchestra in Manchester. There was a character called "Flash" in a strip cartoon at the time. He could flash from pole to pole. Well, I flashed from London to Manchester in a second. So I became known as "Flash". It built up from that. If the name means meretricious and fake it has nothing to do with me. The fact is that I travel much faster and further than most musicians do. In that sense "Flash" was suitable enough. One day I'm at the Albert Hall. Next day I'm in Tokyo. Beecham said "Flash in Japan". If it means quickness I don't mind in the least. If it means imitation, fake glamour, I don't agree at all.

'There's nothing meretricious in my preparation of music. I rehearse for hours and hours with the greatest care. I am more careful than in my youth. From the start I could read a score brilliantly, spotting mistakes, getting the hang of complicated rhythms. But now I take more time. Where I used to spend fifteen hours in preparation I now spend fifty. I wake up in the small hours and switch the light on. Always I have three or four scores by my bedside. I put in a couple of hours on them, marking all bowing for the strings, all breathing for the wind and working out problems of balance. Then I put the light out and have a little more sleep. For this year's Proms [1961] I have learned twenty-five new scores. That has meant working nineteen hours a day.'

He often reverted to his early years and drew lessons from them:

'There are two things that come not back to Man. One is the spoken word. The other is the lost opportunity. So many young people don't grasp the opportunities that come their way. Once opportunities go they're gone for good. Young Sargent, the local boy, was asked to write a piece for Henry Wood's charity concert at Leicester. I wrote *Windy Day*. I was asked to conduct it. I conducted it. A friend of mine knew Moiseiwitsch and praised my piano playing to him. Moiseiwitsch said he would like to hear me. I played for him. He was impressed. He gave me lessons and never charged for them. Wood and Moiseiwitsch were my two great opportunities as a youngster. I don't believe such things are a matter or luck or chance. They are the working out of a personal pattern and destiny, the sort of thing that gradually becomes clear in a man's life.'

Of inner change, faith and the changing world:

'My illness in 1933–34 was the biggest thing that happened to me. That and the death of Pamela. Two years of enforced leisure and a certain amount of pain led to a general mellowing of one's character. These influences, immensely reinforced by the later sorrow, gave me an understanding for sick people and a sympathy for them which one could not have achieved by imagination alone. People who have not suffered, who have never been ill, are like people in neutral countries when other countries are at war. They don't *know.* . . . Faith? I had Christian faith from my earliest days. I was born with it. No virtue in that. One regrets wasting time, the sharp word that may have given pain to friends and acquaintances—even to enemies. Yes, I have lots of enemies. [On reflection he changed this to: 'Yes, I *may* have enemies.'] But I am not a good hater. I find it hard to dislike people for disliking me—because you see, I don't like myself. . . . Sometimes I regret I haven't given more time to specializing in certain composers. But then I tell myself that *somebody* has to be a general practitioner of music, as Henry Wood was, and it looks as if that is to be my lot. . . .

'There are things I don't believe in. I don't believe that human society is progressing. I do not believe that general progress is inevitable. I don't believe that humanity is making any headway at all. I don't think much of philosophy-without-religion. It gave us Nazism and Communism. Since then science has given us the radio-guided hydrogen bomb and the possibility of worldwide ruin, obliteration. But the rottener the world becomes the more intense is one's love for things that are not of this world. There has to be escape from horror. One escape is music; beauty given by God through the agency of human genius. The other is religion: the approach to God himself.'

*

Old faces went from the B.B.C. Symphony Orchestra and new ones came in, though the changes, as in any orchestra of quality, were so gradual as to be hardly noticed. In due time Paul Beard retired from the leadership and was followed by another artist of individuality and mettle, Hugh Maguire. On big nights at the Proms and elsewhere the routine for conductor's calls went on as before. Everything was timed and calculated with that sixth sense which is proper to showmanship. . . . The last piece ends in a blaze of brass and glory. Applause detonates. The Maestro gives his brisk bow and frank smile. He flings his arms out and up at the audience as if taking every one of us to his bosom; then, in the same movement, swings round and waves the players to their feet. While his back is to the audience he says to the leader: 'Stay up until I come back. As soon as I come back, sit down.' He goes off, listens backstage to the applause, returns precisely when he judges it to be slackening and flings his arms up at the audience as before. The ovation swells like a stoked bonfire. On leaving the rostrum a second time he says: 'It's going very well, Mr. Maguire. Stay seated.' Returning a third time he repeats his first performance, swinging round from the audience to wave up the players. He says: 'I think there's another one in it, Mr. Maguire. Remain standing'. And so the raptures continue until the Maestro judges the time has come to end. His last bow of the evening could not be called dismissive, yet there is something of finality in it. Ecstasy is over. People start moving towards the exits. . . .

His leaders, principals and rank-and-file co-operated loyally in these routines, though with mixed feelings. Some murmured that they were splendid for Sargent but didn't have much to do with music. One way of appeasing an effervescent audience at the end of a concert was to play something more. That had been Beecham's way. After the *Prince Igor* dances or the *Jupiter* Symphony he would shake an orchestral snippet out of his sleeve of the sort he was pleased to call 'lollipops'. The Beecham custom was continued by younger batons. When Sargent took the London Philharmonic Orchestra to the East and Australia in 1962 he was joined in the latter country by John Pritchard as associate conductor. In Adelaide, Melbourne and Brisbane Pritchard conducted Walton's Symphony No. 2 with considerable success and when the audience went on applauding gave them, by way of 'extra', Chabrier's *Marche joyeuse* or the *Perpetuum mobile* of Johann Strauss.

'I must say, John, you carry these things off,' said Sargent after the Brisbane concert. 'I can't do anything at all with encores.*

* Not to be taken literally. During this tour he conducted at least two encores: the Rakoczy March at Perth, W. Australia, and a piece which I have not been able to identify at Colombo, Ceylon.

After Schubert's Ninth [which he had conducted in the same hall the night before] how can you pick up the threads with anything smaller ?'

*

For his internal dealings with the B.B.C. we must turn the calendar back somewhat.

Among the controllers and administrators at Broadcasting House there were some who delighted in Sargent's spell over mass audiences. The spell was great already and had a greater potential. If the B.B.C. had been a body of commercial promoters, reasonably progressive but mindful of box office, Sargent's career as chief of the B.B.C. Symphony Orchestra might have lasted longer and perhaps taken a different shape. There were others in Broadcasting House who resented the Sargent personality cult, as they thought it. Even his feat of moral salvage at Ostend (see the preceding chapter) made them curl their lips; for the life of them they could not see anything more in it than rank showmanship. Sargent, on the other hand, was sometimes made impatient by what he regarded as the B.B.C.'s musical compartmentalism and bureaucracy. Repertory and programme-planning were other matters which had in them the seed of dissension.

'Can conductors . . . perform really well works they don't like ?' he had been asked on the Brains Trust in 1945.

'Oh yes, obviously they can,' he had replied. 'Many conductors can give good performances of works they may feel are not worthy of serious thought. A serious artist hates having to do this and avoids it if he can. But if he has to do it and is an honourable person, he takes care to perform it perfectly. . . . A good conductor performing a bad work which he dislikes will get a better performance than a bad conductor who likes it.'

There were limits to professional compliance, however.

From time to time he took the orchestra into the provinces. The programme planners asked him to open one of his provincial concerts with a five-minute orchestral piece by a contemporary composer whose name has not been divulged. Sargent set up the full score on his piano and invited a knowledgeable B.B.C. friend to

13*

Albert Hall Mansions. First he played the score through, then repeated chords sequences and other bits of it.

'Does that make sense?' he repeatedly asked. 'Has it got any musical meaning?' He told his friend, and his friend told the planners, that he had no intention of conducting the piece; and he was as good as his word.

'That', comments the friend, 'was the turning point in his relations with the B.B.C. He wouldn't do as he was told. Could you imagine anybody making such demands on a Toscanini, or a Furtwängler, or a Beecham?'

Early in August 1956 he mentioned to me casually that he was not on the staff of the B.B.C. Nobody had supposed he was. 'I have a gentlemen's agreement with them,' he went on. 'It is subject to cancellation by either side.' He mentioned that he would be conducting the Proms the following year and showed me the rehearsal and opening dates in his 1957 diary. Although I did not take it in at the time, he was conveying to me that his relations with the B.B.C. had radically changed. Something over a month later the B.B.C. put out this message to their publicity officers and the news agencies: 'In order to give Sir Malcolm Sargent greater freedom for his many engagements it has been mutually agreed by him and the B.B.C. that from the autumn of 1957 he will relinquish his position as conductor-in-chief of the B.B.C. Symphony Orchestra. He will be conductor-in-chief of the Promenade Concerts and chief guest-conductor of the B.B.C. Symphony Orchestra in sound and television and at other times of the year.' Rudolf Schwarz, then in charge of the City of Birmingham Symphony Orchestra, was named at the same time as his successor.

It was certainly the fact that multiplying commitments abroad compelled him to trim his home schedules. It was also true that in retaining his headship of the Promenade Concerts, during which period Schwarz was to stand down, he would be retaining and nursing the professional charge closest to his heart. 'The eight weeks of the Proms,' he used to say, 'are the most important work of my year.' Even so, several professional intimates have the impression that he looked back wistfully to his original tenure and regretted that, in a sense which cannot be used of any chief guest, however much he may be to the fore, he no longer had an orchestral of his own.

Although they knew that, outside the Proms, he would be taking many of their studio and other concerts, the players of the B.B.C. orchestra decided that something should be done to mark the end of his régime. Many of them had been restive under his rule, but that did not seem to weigh any longer. They gave him an elegant and affectionately conceived present: seven crystal goblets designed and engraved by an artist-craftsman to symbolize the seven movements of Holst's *Planets* suite—swan for Venus, flight of birds for Mercury, and so on. With these classical symbols were linked images of some of the beasts and reptiles he had loved to show his players at the Zoo. In the drawing-room at No. 9 the goblets joined, or were later joined by, other mementoes of an equally ingenious and allusive sort. One of the most splendid of these was a glass bowl engraved with portraits of some among his favourite composers, Handel, Sibelius, Elgar and Dvořák; his favourite flowers—carnations, roses and lilies; and likenesses of some of his pets—Hughie the budgerigar and two singing dogs given to him in Australia, which he named Troilus and Cressida: the whole surmounted by crossed 'cello and bassoon by way of crest. The bowl came to him on his seventieth birthday from the National Youth Orchestra of Great Britain, which he often conducted and sometimes helped to train.

A glance, while we are in Sargent's drawing-room, at the signed photographs there of royal personages. So much was heard for so many years about this august gallery in general terms that a more particular account may be of interest. From the fireplace the royal photographs spread to tables and window sills. The sequence began with the present Queen Mother, as Consort, wearing Garter sash and tiara among palatial marble; signed Elizabeth R. Then a group: Queen Elizabeth II with the Duke of Edinburgh, Prince Charles and Princess Anne, all smiling upon a new baby, Prince Andrew, whom the Queen is dandling; signed Elizabeth R and Philip. Nearby Princess Marina ('Christmas 1962, with all best wishes—Marina') smiled upon a frilly cot in which her grandson George Philip Nicholas was having a sound sleep; and posed with her daughter Princess Alexandra and her sons the Princes Edward and Michael, for a group photograph taken in 1948. After these came two more studies of the Queen Mother. One showed her in her sitting-room with a pair of corgis; the other with a perky grand-child on her knee, Prince Charles, Princess Anne and a lone corgi being in attendance. Finally: Lord and Lady Mountbatten, pre-sumably in New Delhi, both in full viceregal fig, she seated on a throne, he standing, with 'Dickie' and 'Edwina' and the year 1948 written beneath.

There were grudging souls who thought it in questionable taste to house this collection in a room where professional business was habitually transacted. The portraits and their inscriptions denoted genuine cordiality. It could have been argued with equal cogency that to keep them out of sight would have been churlish. It has been mentioned that the present Queen and her sister Princess Margaret went to some of his children's concerts when they were small. These were not their only meetings. During the war he was often received at Windsor Castle. He would play the piano, and sometimes, the princesses would dance to his playing.

*

The pace quickened on most of his old conducting routes, Australia to the Americas, South Africa to Israel; and to the old routes was added a new one, Soviet Russia, of which some account will be given in the next chapter. His pace on holiday was little less strenu-ous than the professional one. He busied himself under burning skies, in exotic landscapes and by exotic seas, storing up visual magic and prodigies of sound. Such experiences fortified in him an old truth: that the earth's beauty is something for which to thank and worship God. He came out with this revolutionary and splendid archaism at the annual general meeting of the Incorporated Society of Musicians in 1957.

The Society had made him its president. Most of his presidential address was devoted to music, true. But his exordium, a longish one, was about diving in tropical waters and the unbelievable beauty of the fish that haunt coral reefs; the fairylike chimes and tinklings of myriad tree frogs chirruping their 'miniature evensong' in Bermuda; the cosmic thunder of water hurtling by the ton over the lip of the Victoria Falls. These phenomena were advanced not simply as pretty pictures or nature's tone-poems but as an argument for Deism; as proving that the main purpose of Man's existence is delight and adoration. With a touch that was summary and jaunty he put the evolutionary hypothesis in what he considered to be its proper place (not a very high one) and snapped his fingers at Darwin, Freud, Nietzsche and Schopenhauer. All this must have given mild scandal or raised scoff among those I.S.M. delegates who were agnostics or outright unbelievers. In such situations he knew well what he was about. His intention was to preach a little and, perhaps, tease a little. At other times his touch was not always so sure. Coming back from holiday in a Central African game reserve, where he had watched wild life from tree platforms, he spoke of a herd of elephant coming down to a water hole for their evening drink. He described family parties: papa elephant, mama elephant with brood alongside. It was not a matter of drinking only. The broods must have their bath 'before going to bed'. Sometimes a mother elephant would turn a baby elephant over in the water to make sure its neck was clean. A happy domestic scene was broken by loud trumpetings. Some sentinel elephant, realizing the herd were being watched, was sounding the alarm. Up they all came splodging out of the water and charged for cover. Overturned in the gallop, a particularly small baby, three weeks old, perhaps, trumpeted panickily at baby pitch and brought the entire herd to a halt. A protective ring was formed round the casualty. Mother elephant, deftly using her trunk, set baby on his legs and patted him comfortingly on the bottom. After which the herd moved on again. Stampede was over. They now moved slowly, at the baby's tempo; and that, he concluded, was most considerate of them. He had watched wonderstruck . . .

His word picture was not without charm. Admittedly it occurred in a talk on the B.B.C.'s Children's Hour. As an essay in anthropomorphism, however, it may have struck some young listeners, even, as on the sentimental side.

From such a key he could modulate at a moment's notice to amiable self-deprecation. When the Royal Philharmonic Society gave him its gold medal (1959) he said: 'I have never realized my ideals in any performance I ever directed. I am very young in this profession, but I feel that I am slowly improving. Perhaps one day I shall give a performance worthy of this honour, which I regard as a reward for endeavour rather than achievement.' Or the modulation could be to grief; and the grief might shake him like a tree in a tempest.

One of his happiest concerto partnerships was with Solomon Cutner, the pianist, known professionally throughout his platform career as Solomon *tout court*. Their Beethoven and Brahms performances at the Proms drew prodigies of dedication from an immense young audience, who gave to the music and to the partnership a silence that almost had weight, as if it were a precious substance. One afternoon news came to the Maida Vale studio that Solomon had suffered a stroke and had lost the use of his left hand. Sargent was about to start a rehearsal session. On the instant he was a torn man. Returning to the conductor's room he abandoned himself to the pain of pity and loss, weeping like a child. Cancelling the rehearsal was out of the question. In any case he would not have permitted it. Those near him spoke what words of comfort they could. After twenty minutes they got him out and to the rostrum. His face was swollen and wet with tears.

Another storm ravaged him when Sibelius died in September 1957. At the time Sargent was conducting Sibelius's Fifth at Helsinki University. Sibelius had been more than the greatest living composer. Retrospectively he became 'the direct successor, the only real successor, to Beethoven.'* Something less than a year later the hour struck for music's second greatest, in his assessment. Without presage and pain Ralph Vaughan Williams died suddenly an hour before an August dawn in 1958, eighty-five years old. For himself and others his age had been so light a burden that there seemed little reason why his tale of symphonies should not lengthen. What proved to be his last had been the Ninth in E minor; and he had chosen Sargent for its première, with the Royal Philharmonic

* Quoted by Erkki Savolainen, *Look at Finland*, Winter 1966-7. In December 1965, the Finnish Government made Sargent Commander (1st Class) of the Order of the White Rose of Finland.

Orchestra, Sargent first gave the symphony a run-through with the R.P.O. at St. Pancras Town Hall. This rehearsal, three hours long, cost £250 and was paid for by the composer: a severe judgment on English musical economics. There was only one other rehearsal. It was held on the morning of the concert (2nd April, 1958); and all that can be said is that Sargent did the best he could. The critics made much of two obvious writing points—an important solo for the flügel horn, newcomer to symphonic contexts, and textures for a saxophone group—but were otherwise cool or dubious. The composer listened from the ceremonial box at the Royal Festival Hall. The way from the box backstage to the platform was so long and taxing for an old man that when the performance ended he got up and acknowledged the audience's warm ovation from where he was. Sargent radiantly joined him to share the clapping and the photographers' flash bulbs. That night, the composers widow has written* 'Malcolm . . . appeared to have wings on his shoes.'

There were many other Vaughan Williams nights for him to remember. His conducting, for instance, of the first London performance (January 1955) of the Christmas cantata *Hodie* ('To-Day'), music for mixed chorus and soloists to one of R.V.W.'s textual brantubs: Gospels and Prayer Book to John Milton and Thomas Hardy. His attempts (not altogether successful) to better the wind machine effects in the *Sinfonia Antartica* (Festival Hall, April 1953) by having the horn players whistle into their instruments. His hearing, before it was officially 'born' of the Sixth Symphony: four performances of it in a row on the piano by Michael Mullinar in the company among others of Boult and Barbirolli. His unveilings of three Vaughan Williams operas—*Riders to the Sea* (after J. M. Synge, 1937), *Sir John in Love* (1929) and *Hugh the Drover* (1924), this last almost a quarter of a century earlier—nostalgically linked between the newly emancipated young organist with the dews of Melton Mowbray still upon him and the courted, panegyrized gentleman who spent a good third of his working days in foreign parts or in aeroplanes on his way to them.

It is said that the plain technical directions in Vaughan Williams's

* *R.V.W.*, *A Biography of Ralph Vaughan Williams* by Ursula Vaughan Williams London, Oxford University Press, 1964.

scores as to how he wanted them played had not always been immune from his attempts at 'improvements' and tinkerings. A rehearsal is remembered of *A Pastoral Symphony* at the Queen's Hall. During the third movement, *Moderato pesante*, a voice sounded sharply from the balcony: 'What do you think you are doing, young man? I know what I wrote!' The voice was that of Vaughan Williams, Jove in person. Thunderbolts were in the air. R.V.W.'s death, like Solomon's came to his ears shortly before a rehearsal. Again a broken, tearful figure appeared on the rostrum. As a practising artist Solomon had been silenced while in his fifties, that is to say, while in his prime. Sargent's disarray and distress had been the more acute for that. But the deprivation he felt at Vaughan Williams's passing went as deep and lasted long. He had taken half the symphonies to many parts of the globe. He tenaciously believed in them. They were part of his mission on earth; certain of them were high among the adventures and fervours of his early manhood. The grief he felt was far outside the compass of ordinary concert goers.

*

Before we come to his last foreign tours, which were the grandest and most 'ambassadorial' of his career, it is expedient to take stock of his further dealings with the B.B.C. and its orchestra and of new B.B.C. policies which encroached upon his duties—though not upon his personal sway—at the Promenade Concerts. His dealings with the orchestra included a resounding rehearsal quarrel, the last of a series which had unhappily punctuated his career from the early days. Contemporary accounts of the incident were one-sided for a simple reason. The other party to the quarrel, Hugh Maguire, the leader, found the situation distasteful and for a long time declined to talk about it. After four years it is possible to form some idea of what happened. Again the trouble sprang from orchestral tuning.

The occasion was a full rehearsal at Maida Vale of Holst's *Choral Symphony*, a work which musicians generally did not hold in such high regard as did Sargent. Shortly before the intermission Sargent halted the music to give instruction to some singer or singers. Maguire's impression is that he was speaking to the solo soprano, who was well within earshot. Another account suggests that he was speaking to a section of the choir. Many in the orchestra, the leader among them, took the opportunity to retune. Suddenly Sargent broke off whatever instruction he was giving and, looking down at Maguire, snapped: 'You mustn't tune while I'm talking. It creates a disturbance. You must give me your full attention all the time during a rehearsal.'

'But,' said Maguire, 'you had relaxed your attention from the orchestra. You were having a discussion with a specific artist.' As Maguire remembers it, the exchange continued as follows:

Sargent: 'At all times you must give me your full attention.'

Maguire: 'For Pete's sake! We've been giving you our full attention for three days on this one wretched piece of music. Please don't treat us like children.'

Sargent: 'If you don't wish to give me your full co-operation, why don't you go?'

Maguire: 'Well, it would be a good thing, perhaps, if you would remember that I am host here [a reference to his authority as orchestral leader] and that you are the guest [a reference to the fact that Sargent was no longer permanent chief conductor]. A guest doesn't usually invite his host to leave his house. But on this occasion I shall be delighted.'

After Maguire had withdrawn Sargent announced from the rostrum that he was sorry if he had been rude. This eased a painful situation but did not resolve it. Intermediaries learned that each party expected the other to apologize. After a lot of flurry and telephoning it was arranged that both should meet in the conductor's room before a rehearsal next day. They were in mollified mood. Maguire made the first approach. 'I'm sorry about yesterday,' he said. 'Let's get on with the rehearsal.' To which Sargent: 'That's all right, old chap. It's all forgotten.' They entered the rehearsal arm in arm. The orchestra cheered. Yet their relationship was never cordial in a professional sense. After his fifth Proms season he broke away and devoted himself to solo work and chamber music.*

* The opening concert of the 1968 Proms, in Sargent's memory, being an extra 'date', Maguire was invited to lead the B.B.C. Orchestra as 'stand-in'. In accepting he was glad, incidentally, to be associated with this public tribute to 'a man who was exceptional in many ways.'

Photo: Frederick Bass—by courtesy of E.M.I.

In the control room at Kingsway Hall, London, with Sir William Walton
during a recording of Walton's Symphony No. 1

Photo: Frederick Bass

Among pupils from his old school (Stamford) who came up for his 70th birthday concert, sung by the Royal Choral Society and two other choirs on 29th April 1965, were his two grandsons, Nicholas (left) and Simon

Meantime there had been a change of spirit at the Proms. In 1959 a new Controller of Music was appointed by the B.B.C. William Glock, the newcomer, was widely known as a lecturer and writer on music; he had breadth of taste and was enterprising in his exploration of 'new paths'. His prospectus for the 1960 season spoke of the need for a critical review of the Proms as an institution, craved for 'a bolder purpose', and argued that this purpose should be reinterpreted in the spirit of Henry Wood. Had not Wood, while putting Prommers through their symphonic A.B.C. introduced them half a century earlier to newfangled and sometimes fearsome stuff by Sibelius, Scriabin and Schoenberg? In pursuit of a newly-defined objective, that of representing 'all that is most vital in orchestral music from the eighteenth century to the present day', Glock and his fellow planners studded their programmes as the seasons went on with works by Berg, Stravinsky, Webern, Charles Ives, Pierre Boulez, Searle, Gerhard and others which were not only new to the Proms but had never seemed likely to get a hearing there. At the same time foreign orchestras and foreign conductors (Stokowski, Giulini, Gennadi Rozhdestvensky, for example) began to share the burden and the glory with British orchestras and British guest batons. Because of the new repertory trends the device of split programmes came into more frequent use. Sargent would conduct music after his own heart in one half, and some other conductor—often one of his English juniors—would conduct more problematical fare in the other half. He fell in with these arrangements good-humouredly, even generously.

At the end of January each year Glock would go round to Albert Hall Mansions for the annual programme conference, taking with him a draft scheme for fifty odd concerts set out in detail on huge sheets, four programmes to a sheet. Sargent's interest in the Proms was passionate. On detail he was insatiable. He always wanted to know what the twenty or thirty guest conductors had been 'pencilled' for. He was known to say, when a favourite piece of his had been allocated to somebody else: 'Oh, what a pity's he's got *that*. I would have so much liked to do it myself.' As the programmes, his own included, were read out he contented himself for the most part with such comments as: 'Yes . . . lovely. Yes . . . I'm quite

14

happy.' Proposed programme splits were detailed. For example:
'How about this. We'd like you to do the *Prince Igor* dances and
Shostakovich's Tenth Symphony. Then Colin [Davis] does
[Stravinsky's] *Oedipus Rex*. All right?' A splendid plan, thought
Malcolm. 'Now I wonder what you'll think of this one. The idea is
that you do the *Magic Flute* Overture and Schumann's 'Spring'
Symphony in the first half and Meredith Davies the *War Requiem*
in the second half, first time at the Proms. As you know, Davies
did a lot of work with Britten on this, and we thought it would be
a good thing, you know, if—' Sargent, too, thought it would be a
good thing; a capital thing. Down went another programme tick.
Yet another tick for Norman Del Mar in Mahler's Sixth Symphony
bracketed with Malcolm in *Belshazzar's Feast*. When conducting
Belshazzer he had Prommers of all ages in the palm of his hand.
In this Prommers were as audiences had been everywhere for thirty
years.

During the second year of Glock's régime Sargent spoke to me
of the transmitted characteristics of Prom crowds—'young, keen,
enthusiastic, as if they were going to a football match. In type they're
exactly the same as in my young days. The only differences are
their wider knowledge of music and their greater curiosity about
things they haven't heard before. When Wood conducted Schoenberg's Five Pieces for Orchestra in 1912 everybody booed.' 'Not
everybody, surely?' I demurred. 'Well, there was a hell of a lot of
booing. That wouldn't happen now. The younsters have got used
to hearing serious things and out-of-the-way things. It's fascinating
to see how willing they are to give a fair hearing to experimental
stuff. We saw that last year with the electronic music, although there
was a certain amount of grinning. [The reference is to Luciano
Berio's *Perspective*, a five movement-piece composed of synthe-
sised electronic sound played on a tape-machine and fed into the
auditorium through loudspeakers at the Prom concert of 8th August,
1960—the first occasion, it was claimed, that anything of the kind
had been presented at any orchestral concert anywhere.] They
are less readily shocked than youngsters used to be. They are willing
to accept anything. Of course, we must be careful not to give them
anything that is not worth listening to.'

Reid: 'Do you consider that some of the new stuff which is being given to them at the Proms is not worth listening to?'

Sargent: 'Some things are less worthy than others. Don't think, by the way, that this is any criticism of William Glock. I hold him in the greatest regard, affection and admiration. But he would be the first to admit that not all the pieces put on are of equal importance.'

His language was not always so circumspect. Awaiting his turn at the rostrum on 'split' programme mornings, he sometimes heard young colleagues putting the orchestra through pieces of 'less equal importance'. He usually dismissed them as rubbish.

It was evident that programme splitting could not solve the central repertory problem which the B.B.C. had on its hands. From 1960 onwards the repertory had evolved because the Symphony Orchestra was mastering and playing many new things. It followed from this that Sargent could not, in the technical sense, keep abreast. Up to 1957, as chief conductor, he was conducting the B.B.C. orchestra, Proms apart, perhaps seventy times a year. Afterwards his concerts were cut down to perhaps one fifth that number. The notion was that Proms programmes should derive in part from the music the orchestra played at other times of the year. Thus Sargent was cumulatively handicapped. A time came when it was felt that his Promenade assignments should be corrected to a more realistic proportion. Every year there were forty-nine Prom concerts. It had been no uncommon thing for him to conduct roughly half of them. In 1965 his allocation was twenty-three. Del Mar was his runner-up that year. But Del Mar conducted only five. When the Proms-planning conference began the following January the B.B.C. offered him a minimum of sixteen Prom concerts a season with the B.B.C. Symphony Orchestra on a guarantee that would run for five years. The arrangement would not preclude his taking additional concerts with any of the eight, nine or more other orchestras who served the series.

The negotiations cannot have been agreeable for any of the negotiators involved. At first Sargent resisted. His attitude, as some on the other side sensed it, was that of a man who thinks an attempt is being made to inch him off the throne. 'If that had really been our intention,' somebody at Broadcasting House commented later, 'it's hardly likely that we would have offered him a five-year arrangement. If it hadn't been for contractual complications on the administrative side we would have offered him an even longer run. We wanted to keep him. We wanted the Prommers to see plenty of him.'

He asked how many of his programmes would be split ones, i.e. two-conductor nights? Not more than six a year, he was assured. At length he agreed to the cut-back. He must have done so with a heavy heart. The retraction did not amount to much, but such a thing had never happened before; it was the first time in music that he had voluntarily given up anything. For what turned out to be his last Proms season the B.B.C. put him down for seventeen programmes (four of them split ones) with the B.B.C. orchestra and one with the Royal Philharmonic Orchestra. His runners-up—still a long way behind—were Gennadi Rozhdestvensky, who conducted four times, and Boult, Barbirolli, Colin Davis and Bernard Haitink, who conducted three times each.

*

It is not to be denied that the Prommers included a fairly vehement anti-Sargent minority who were not to be swept under the carpet as musically illiterate. I stumbled upon them during the 1965 season, when handling sample opinions of Prommers for a survey in *The Spectator*.* In general the minority complained that outside his specialities—i.e. the works, especially choral ones, of Elgar, Vaughan Williams, Walton and Holst—he was guilty of some or many performances that sounded under-rehearsed and even suggested overwork; that he was given twice (or thereabouts) too many concerts, thus standing in the way of other conducting talents, some of them rising ones; and that his Beethoven in particular was marred by overslow slow movements ('heavy-footed' was a typical adjective) and quick movements that went to the other extreme. For Beethoven's 'Choral' Symphony that year he had piled up singers from the B.B.C. Chorus, B.B.C. Choral Society and the Croydon Philhar-

* *The Public and the Proms*; *Report on the 'Spectator' Inquiry* by Charles Reid, *Spectator* 8th October, 1965.

monic Society. 'Without doubt,' commented one amateur critic, 'this was the worst performance of the season. I suppose nothing can stop Flash subjecting this complex and enigmatical work to bang-bang Handel Festival treatment, with every choir in London mobilized except the Golder's Green Glee Club?' Yet in a season which marked the Proms débuts of (among others) Rudolf Kempe, Istvan Kertesz, Antal Dorati, Rozhdestvensky and Boulez, each with a big or biggish following, in some cases a fairly youthful one, he was voted the season's best conductor by a substantial lead, a compliment of note bearing in mind three things: his years, which were either marvelled at or simply not noticed by a society in which years weren't much venerated; the vast number of Proms he had conducted (his last one that year was his 499th)—enough, the cynic might have said, to make people tired of him; a sequence of aesthetic revolutions which, in forty years, were supposed to have discredited all the musical styles he conspicuously stood for; and youth's fashionable gallop, then gathering speed, towards iconoclasm and against authority in the arts or anywhere else.

What Prommers liked most among the music he conducted that year was what people had liked from the start. There had been a tingling *Belshazzar. Gerontius* had touched yet another multitude to the quick. When the tenor, came to Gerontius's line 'I can no more; for now it comes again, that sense of ruin which is more than pain', Sargent wept openly. He had done the same at earlier performances, and there were over-confident sceptics in the orchestra then who had muttered, 'Oh God, he's at it again!', as if the tears were 'put on'. This time the mutterers were silent. The fact that he was seventy may have had something to do with this. Sargent's great nights that year had a solemnity and warmth that set them apart and made them immune. One night was a Seventieth Birthday Concert, each item in a sense a Sargent trophy: Elgar's Second Symphony and 'Cello Concerto (the latter with Jacqueline du Pré), *The Hymn of Jesus* and Walton's 'Coronation' Te Deum. The Walton had been one of three Te Deums—the others being those of Verdi and Dvořák—which were sung for him at a massive concert put on for him by the Royal Choral Society, whose choir was joined for the occasion by those of the Huddersfield Choral Society and the

Leeds Philharmonic Society. This choice of Te Deums reverted to the sermon-by-way-of-presidential address which (see the preceding chapter) he had preached to the I.S.M. delegates in 1957.

'The first object of music,' he said on the eve of the R.C.S. celebration, 'is to make people happy. It is a joyous thing, a form of thanksgiving. The reason why I'm having three Te Deums at my birthday concert is because I feel the only thing one can do at seventy is say: *Thank you very much.*'

CHAPTER THIRTY

U.S.S.R. — U.S.A.

ALL THE GREAT London orchestras except that of the B.B.C., whose financial case was different, took it in turns during the post-war decades to languish at death's door. Last rites and warnings of bankruptcy had a magical effect. They put the patient back on his feet. With renewed glow and resiliency, he returned to the business of living and usually made a better job of it.

This, roughly, is what happened in the late 1950s to Sargent's partner of Courtauld and 'blitz' days, the London Philharmonic Orchestra. Faced by a crescendo of debt and overdraft, the management toyed at one time with the idea of selling their only real asset, the seventy-nine-year lease on their offices in the West End. This would have appeased the creditors. But it would also have killed the L.P.O. What ultimately saved them was sacrifice by the players (e.g. of contractual guarantees, including holiday pay and sick pay), backed by forebearing creditors, a private benefaction, grants or guarantees from public funds and a certain livening up of concert policy. One sign of the livening up was Sargent's activity on L.P.O. rostrums.

Demands were thickening upon him from five continents and a dozen or more countries. Like other promoters, the L.P.O. had to take their place in a queue of 'forward commitments'. For a dozen concerts in the early months of 1962 they opened negotiations with him as early as the autumn of 1958. Half of these concerts were at the Royal Festival and Royal Albert halls, the other half in the provinces.

Only one concert irked him. The provincial tour took him among other places to a 'super cinema' in the Midlands on a Sunday afternoon. The occasion illustrated conditions which were apt to face an orchestra engaged in pulling itself up by the bootstraps. The schedule that day admitted of only ninety minutes' rehearsal; not enough, he complained afterwards, considering that a number of new players had been brought in who weren't familiar with the main piece of the day, Sibelius's Symphony No. 2. Then as to sound. The platform sloped the wrong way, the back part being lower than the front, a handicap acoustically. The horns had a special problem; they found themselves blowing into a thick curtain which muffled their tone. He counselled the L.P.O. that if they ever again played in this cinema its manager should be required to instal platform 'rises' and an acoustical screen at the back six feet high.

No conductor had a surer eye for practical detail of this sort. Nor has there ever been a conductor more mindful of old associates. One of the dates was at Hastings. Fifteen miles away along the coast George Karl Russell lived in retirement. The man who, nearly forty years earlier, had helped young Sargent to found the Leicester Symphony Orchestra was past seventy, battered by ill fortune and folly but not forgotten. He had two years to live. Sargent invited him to his Hastings concert. There is reason to believe that he remembered the pathetic old man in other ways.

*

These provincial comings and goings and the London concerts were the prelude to an adventure as imaginative and trenchant in its way as the fabled 'blitz' tour itself. In February 1962, sponsored by the British Council, the Arts Council and the Australian Broadcasting Commission, he and the L.P.O. at full strength (over ninety players) took off from London Airport in two airliners on the first leg of the most extensive tour ever undertaken by a British orchestra. In India, Hong Kong, the Philippines, Australia and Ceylon, countries which had never seen a major British orchestra before, they gave thirty-two concerts in forty-three days, including successive concerts in cities separated by seas or oceans and up to seventeen hours' flying time. Sargent's stint was twenty-four concerts, the other eight being taken by John Pritchard, the L.P.O.'s principal conductor and future artistic director, who joined the orchestra in Australia.

During the first half of the tour, that is to say, from his opening night in Bombay to his vast *Belshazzar's Feast* in Adelaide, he put himself down for only one free day in three weeks, during which time he ceaselessly rehearsed, conducted, journeyed and officially hobnobbed at vast receptions in grilling or humid heat. He travelled in the grand manner; fell into the way of ordering champagne for himself and his table companions as soon as a flight took off; had a Rolls-Royce meet him in on every runway; and, as usual, was put up by governors, high commissioners, magnates and grandees. In Delhi, Prime Minister Nehru greeted him with his most winning smile, for they had been friends since Sargent's visit to the Mountbattens during the last months of the Viceregency, and listened to the music (a Beethoven piano concerto, *On Hearing the First Cuckoo*, *Enigma* Variations) with splendid impassivity. In general, official residences and gubernatorial quarters were run according to time-honoured rules and social usages. Some of the private houses where he stayed had brought themselves up-to-date. Changes of social ambience called for adaptability on the part of a guest. Under the stress of the tour even Sargent's adaptability threatened to give out. In one city he stayed under the roof of a very rich man. The rich man's daughter said to a new-made friend: 'We have Sir Malcolm staying with us. What a strange man he is!'

'Why do you say that?'

'Well, Daddy has a big house. Sir Malcolm has his own rooms, and he is well looked after. I have my own wing. Every Friday night I entertain a crowd of friends. Last night we were dancing to the gramophone in my room. Soon before midnight Sir Malcolm appeared. He was in a silk dressing gown. He came straight in and went over to the gramophone and switched it off. He said: "Never play music of that kind when I'm a guest in this house". Then he stalked out.'

The halls where he played, the atmosphere of his concerts and the audiences who attended them were even more diverse in type than the places where he stayed; but such contrasts were a professional

14*

challenge, and he met most of them with smiling tranquillity, as of old. His two Bombay concerts (Sibelius's Symphony No. 2, Tchaikovsky's No. 5, *L'Après-midi d'un faune*, *The Walk to the Paradise Garden*, *Firebird*, the Britten-Purcell Variations, etc.) were given in an open-air auditorium, the orchestra backed by an acoustical shell which did not serve, for the sound was capricious and woolly. In Calcutta they played in a new and as yet unfinished theatre. Often there were rehearsal calls after early breakfast for late evening concerts to avoid the main heats. The Indian climate and that of other countries on the route imposed new divisions of the working day which, with the varying food, put the players under strains which artists are supposedly not able to take and always do.

Out of Calcutta at ten in the morning. The same evening they touched down in Hong Kong for five concerts in the new City Hall. All five were sold out, the audiences aggregating 8,500. Tickets had sold at up to six times their face value. The most glitteringly dressed, 'see-and-be-seen' audiences in Hong Kong's musical history listened with every appearance of concentration to Debussy, Elgar, Prokoviev, Britten, Sibelius, Vaughan Williams. Everything reached them as sharply defined as under a magnifying glass. After Tchaikovsky's No. 5 and a Mozart concerto with a young Chinese woman playing the solo part on the last night, Sargent said he had never conducted in a hall with better acoustics. 'Never let bad orchestras play here,' he advised. 'The badness of their playing would be shown up so mercilessly that you would all walk out.' After Hong Kong two and a half hours in the air brought them to Manila in the Philippines. Excused their tail coats, although Sargent retained his, the players performed with open shirt necks and matching cummerbunds. Here they gave two concerts in a baseball stadium filled with rattan chairs, the first attended by ambassadors and other celebrities, both by a multitude in beach wear, a host of mosquitos and roaring electric fans. He opened on the first night with the *Mastersingers* Overture. In this the electric fans were often smothered by Wagner. The harp-and-flute introduction to *Brigg Fair* was another matter. No sooner was this well started than he halted and asked the audience concernedly: 'Can you hear us all right? Can you hear well? The electric fans are making so much noise. I hope they are not bothering you.' There were reassuring shouts. That night he conducted four works, all strenuous or otherwise exacting. When taking his bow after each number he was seen to be sweating copiously. At the end he was given a consoling ovation.

Two days after Manila he and his players were welcomed on arrival at Perth Airport (W. Australia), by a horn and a cornet from the State symphony orchestra, who piped them on to the tarmac with the Toreador Song and 'When the saints come marching in'. The size of the orchestra was noted wistfully. In the matter of orchestral strengths Australia, or parts of it, was still at a disadvantage. The L.P.O. were touring thirty violins, twelve violas, ten 'cellos and eight double-basses. The equivalents in the Perth orchestra were 20/5/6/3. In the Capitol Theatre the following night Sargent's Sibelius (Symphony No. 5), especially its string chordings and unisons, was listened to with awe and envy.

On to Adelaide. For *Belshazzar's Feast* and the Dvořák Te Deum he had brought in specially coached singers from as far off as Christchurch, New Zealand. There were four hundred voices on the platform. Adelaide usually made do on important occasions with choirs half that size or less and with orchestras half as big as the L.P.O. Again, however, the conditions and the acoustics were on the raw side. That year Adelaide was treating itself to an arts festival. Sargent conducted three festival concerts and Pritchard two in a cavernous hall on an agricultural showground. The platform was level, which meant that people near the front couldn't see the wind for the strings. To make up for this they had a splendid view on symphonic nights of bare wooden tiers intended on a subsequent night for the choir. Yet nobody who was anybody in Adelaide missed a note. On the first night the centre of the city became a vast traffic jam. Inside the hall camera arcs rigged on scaffolding made a warm night warmer still. A fanfare whipped the audience to its feet when the Governor-General entered. As had happened on uncounted occasions the world over, Sargent's timing, the whiplash of his baton, his tie, his hair, his carnation and the preternatural straightness of his back engraved themselves on every eye which had not seen them before and turned formality into something that quickened pulses. An overloaded programme began after nine o'clock and ended at twenty minutes to midnight. It included what one commentator called a diplomatic gesture to Australian music, namely, a sinfonietta by an Australian composer. There were yawns. Yet the Maestro prevailed. After Schubert's 'Great' C major Symphony at the end of his last concert people stood, shouted and stamped.

For the same symphony he got an ovation on the same scale at his third concert in Melbourne. On the whole, however, Melbourne did not live up to his earlier triumphs. Within nine days there were seven highly-priced concerts at the Town Hall. Two of these had been Menuhin concerto nights with the resident orchestra. The other five were the L.P.O. dates. As a result of this concentration of good things the hall was somewhat underbooked. And on the last night there were latecomers. Over a hundred missed Kodaly's *Theatre Overture*. When they trickled in for the second piece, Elgar's Introduction and Allegro, he took out his watch and showed it to them in rebuke. In Sydney he said publicly that the Melbourne latecomers had been an awful nuisance. His Sydney programme included Sibelius's No. 5, which he conducted three nights in succession. The *Morning Herald* critic reproved him for a fussy beat at the point in the finale where the horns start their great rocking theme. The same writer complained further that Sargent's triplicate programme might have been chosen twenty years before. Why twenty? Of the main pieces one (the Sibelius) had been in the repertory for over forty years, the two others (Vaughan Williams's Tallis Fantasia and the *Firebird* music) for over fifty. If typical Sargent programmes had been innovatory he would not have been able to get through so much work, cover such a lot of ground and perform his 'ambassadorial' function so well. Even so, plodders in his wake cannot avoid the impression of creeping staleness, of a repertory that was becoming claustrophobic.

Rounding off Australia with two nights in Brisbane, where he got five calls and applause that raised the roof (Schubert's 'Great' C major had scored again), he took to the air and descended two days later at Ratmalana airport, Colombo, Ceylon, for the last and most extraordinary engagement of the tour. For want of a ready-made auditorium of the right size, the airport's maintenance hangar had been converted to house the orchestra and seat an audience of between four and five thousand. On the morning of the concert Lady Morley, the wife of the British High Commissioner, went with Sargent to a brief rehearsal. The hangar was thronged by weed-cleaners and ditch diggers from the airport and a neighbouring estate. A family of crows nesting in the roof quarrelled and squawked. One purpose of the rehearsal was to run through the Ceylonese national anthem, which Sargent, always attentive and prompt with such courtesies, had orchestrated for the occasion. The traffic jam that night was worse than anything Adelaide had known. The Governor-General himself got embedded in it despite frantic bell-sounding by police pilot cars. By special dispensation three coaches carrying the orchestra were allowed to leave the specified route and cut across the airfield; otherwise they would have been hopelessly late on the platform. Again the heat was a problem. They played in their shirtsleeves but kept on their white ties. Sargent waited for interminable minutes on the rostrum while droves of latecomers found their seats and settled down. As usually happened in 'gala' situations, the most expensive seats were occupied in the main by smartly dressed people whose social zeal outweighed whatever musicality they had. They cannot have made much of L'Après-midi or Brahms's No. 2. During a pause in the Enigma Variations there was a burst of clapping. Sargent silenced it with the dismissive flap of the hand which he had used to the same end in Johannesburg sixteen years before. But the night ended radiantly. After affectionate tumults and many recalls Sargent spoke from the rostrum.

'Whoever wrote that East is East and West is West and never the twain shall meet was a donkey,' he said. 'One of the bonds between us is Johannes Brahms. Brahms never dreamed that his D major Symphony would be played one day in an airport hangar.'

There were facetious addenda by players: 'If it comes to that, Brahms never dreamed of airport hangars.' 'If he'd dreamed of airport hangars they'd have put him off writing symphonies in any key.'

The following night, after nineteen hours' flying, they were home. Other foreign tours were in prospect. In 1963 he would be taking the Royal Philharmonic Orchestra to Soviet Russia and the United States. These journeys were to mark the last psychological turning point of his career.

*

He was no stranger to Russian audiences. The 1963 visit was his third. He had made his début there in May 1957. In Moscow with the State Symphony Orchestra of the Soviet Union and in Leningrad with the Leningrad Philharmonic he conducted on that occasion some half a dozen concerts in three weeks, commanding big houses and, at times, frenzied applause. In 1957, as in 1963, he went into battle without a buttonhole; carnations were hard to come by in Moscow. (For his first night in 1962, he managed to have one flown out to him by British European Airways.) Not missing what they had never known, Russian audiences, relatively untainted by the society frills and irrelevancies of 'gala' music in the West, responded to the streamlined exactitudes of his beat and to most of the music he conducted like audiences everywhere, even gala ones. His opening programme in 1957 included the Prokoviev 'Cello Concerto, Op. 125, with the great Rostropovich as soloist, and Brahms's Symphony in C minor. Afterwards he talked in English on Moscow radio with running translation. The audience, he said, had given them (not 'me'; he was careful to bring in Rostropovich and the orchestra) a reception such as he had seldom experienced anywhere in the world. 'I am rather overwhelmed,' he added.

Although he took Beethoven symphonies with him as well as the Brahms and ventured further in the Russian repertory than Prokoviev, the main business of his visit was the English foursome of which he never tired: Elgar, Vaughan Williams, Holst and Britten. Again the *Perfect Fool* ballet music. Again *A London Symphony*, which became fairly familiar to regular concertgoers in Moscow. (To it he ultimately added the Tallis Fantasia.) Again the *Young Person's Guide*. It dazzled infallibly. One Elgar performance which he greatly prized was that of the Introduction and Allegro by the Leningraders. He was reported as saying of this that he never wanted to hear better string playing. Did 'never wanted' mean 'never hoped' or 'never expected'? Was 'never better' intended to convey that he had heard strings which were as good? When looked at closely, his compliments often turned out to have loopholes.

He talked eagerly, through interpreters, with Russian composers. Chief among these was Dimitry Shostakovich, the one living foreign composer in whom Sargent expressed an earnest, almost ethical faith. By this time his repertory embraced some of the later Shostakovich symphonies, which now numbered ten; but he retained a particular and quasi-mystical regard for No. 1, Op. 10, whose third (slow) movement spurred him to eloquence. I remember his saying the year before his first Russian meeting with the composer: 'The sadness of this movement is different from any other sadness in music. Sadness in Beethoven has beauty. Here it is the sadness that comes to you as shock, as pain, the pain you feel on seeing starving children with the ribs breaking through their skin and hollow-eyed women in rags.' These words I noted at the time. I reverted to them in a conversation some years later.

'Yes,' he affirmed, 'Shostakovich is in *the line*. He is different from so many of these other fellows [contemporary composers]. "Music is for the greater glory of God and the re-creation of Mankind." So said J. S. Bach. I don't feel these other fellows have the majesty of Bach or that they even strive for it. That is not their approach. They throw away their predecessors. Not so Shostakovich. He has never been a revolutionary. Like all the best composers, he is evolutionary.' On my speculating on what Bach's deistic definition of music's purpose might mean to Shostakovich as an ornament of a supposedly atheistical state, he drew a line between formal belief and the belief which may (he held) be expressed through art. As an illustration he cited Verdi's Requiem, saying: 'It is not surprising to me that Verdi was technically a freethinker. Freethinker or no, he had the Holy Ghost. Laugh at me if you like. That's what I really think.'

When they met in 1957 Shostakovich told him of his Eleventh Symphony, composed in homage to the Russian insurrection of 1905. He had completed two movements, expected to complete the

other two by the autumn, and promised Sargent the first performance outside Russia. Although the '1905' Symphony had its
première (Moscow) that October, the photocopy of the manuscript
did not reach Sargent until the middle of the following January,
eight days before he was to conduct it at the Royal Festival Hall. As
a feat of study and technical mastery against calendar and clock, his
production of the Eleventh and the B.B.C. Symphony Orchestra's
performance of it will not be quickly forgotten; but how many in
the hall that night considered it music to remember? By some it was
judged to be overlong (fifty-five minutes) and as aggressively banal
in parts as Shostakovich's other 'programme' symphony, the
'Leningrad' (No. 7). Music laced with the drum beats, bugle calls,
dirges and bayonet charges of Revolution was conducted with
authority and utter enthusiasm by one who gloried in verse two of
'God Save the Queen' and was smiled upon from every surviving
throne in Europe. Russian apologists took the 'political intensity' of
the Eleventh very seriously indeed and thought it was the most
'democratically acceptable' symphony Shostakovich had written.
Plain people went to hear the tunes. There were plenty of these.
Few of them caught the plain man's fancy.

Sargent went on championing Shostakovich's music, however,
and discreetly espoused Shostakovich's musical ideology which to
some extent accorded with his life-long predilections. From Moscow
he was quoted as praising Shostakovich and other Soviet composers for writing 'honest music', music intended to please the
hearer, not at all a bad thing, he thought, whatever the 'progressives'
might say; a much better thing than 'manufactured' stuff of a kind
the West was getting far too much of. Somebody having misquoted
him, apparently, as declaring himself 'anti-modern, anti-con-
temporary', he adjusted the record by explaining that he was only
against those modern composers whose music was of little value.
Dismissing serial (dodecaphonic) techniques as easily acquired (after
all, he interpolated, children or monkeys could paint 'abstract' after
a fashion), he wrote of composers who, at rehearsal, could not say
whether a note was wrong or right without going back to the score
and working it out 'logically'; and of an occasion when the clarinets
played a whole movement on the wrong instruments, a semitone out

all the way, the composer sitting by blissfully all the while. He ended with a glance at musicians who thought Beethoven over-estimated and who used such phrases as 'If you *must* have Brahms——'.* An interesting aspect of the last sentence is its plural number. From this it would appear that the name of Beethoven had been taken in vain by more than one musician. A letter written by Sargent to an overseas correspondent some three years before his death credits Benjamin Britten—'a most extraordinary fellow!'—with the statement, made in his hearing, that Beethoven was an overrated composer. There is no evidence that he had any other musician in mind.†

*

His 1963 visit to Czechoslovakia, Poland and Soviet Russia with the Royal Philharmonic Orchestra was as grim and inharmonious in its beginnings—and as happy in its sequel—as any enterprise English music has known. Sir Thomas Beecham, the orchestra's founder, had died two years before. There followed an interim of floundering and uncertain management which bred discontent in the players and chronic uncertainty as to the future. Those who planned it hoped that the tour behind the 'Curtain' and a more ambitious one scheduled for the United States and Canada later in the year would restore the R.P.O.'s international rôle and have a tonic effect on box office business wherever they played, home halls included. The orchestra's recently appointed chief conductor, the highly regarded Herr Rudolf Kempe, whose success on English platforms stemmed from his vogue at the Royal Opera House as a conductor of *The Ring*, did what he could to take up the Beecham threads and make a vital new pattern out of them. At the beginning of the year he took the orchestra on a tour of Germany which ended with a rousing

* Gist of letter to *The Daily Telegraph*, 20th February, 1963.
† Britten made no secret of his 'heresies'. In 1959 he said: 'I have no great sympathy for either Brahms or Beethoven, although I admit that both are very great masters . . . I have moved off them. They have failed me. Or I have failed them. . . . Perhaps it is a little oversimplified to say how "bad" they are. It would be truer to say that I am not now sympathetic to certain points of view their music represents.'

performance of Tchaikovsky's *Pathétique* Symphony in Bremen. From Bremen, Kempe having taken his leave of them, the players took an overnight train which reached Marienbad, Czechoslovakia, at lunchtime the following day.

Here Sargent took over, spruce and sprightly, for a programme which repeated the *Pathétique* and took in also the Brahms-Haydn 'St. Antoni' Variations and Beethoven's Symphony No. 8. He rehearsed them the same night. Because of their journeyings and the severe weather the players felt a good deal less resilient and bright than he. The rehearsal was resented as ill-planned. From the start there was a touch of rebellion in the air and a tendency to bicker on technical points. The orchestra were scheduled for over a dozen concerts in eight cities from Marienbad to Moscow. As between city and city there was much programme duplication, identical numbers being spaced out and played all the way along. As the tour trundled on through temperatures below zero, Sargent was felt to be rehearsing needlessly at times. He would be asked: 'But why must we rehearse *this*, Sir Malcolm? We did it last Wednesday.' 'But,' Sargent would reply, 'this is Monday. I haven't conducted it for five days!' It was complained that when there were no working rehearsals he would sometimes call the players for 'seating' rehearsals designed mainly to verify the players' deployment on the platform, a matter which, it was felt, could be safely left to the managerial side. Speaking of their parting with Kempe at Bremen, someone ruefully commented: 'When a new jockey gets on a horse in the middle of the race, the horse doesn't like it. He likes it still less if the new jockey winds him.'

After Prague (Brahms-Haydn, Beethoven's No. 8 and *A London Symphony*, all of which went conspicuously well) the weather became icier and comfort more precarious. A three-night stand in Bratislava (Delius's *Brigg Fair*, Britten-Purcell and *L'Après-midi d'un faune* were added to the repertory here) is remembered by some of the players for roof leaks on an hotel top-floor which had been allotted to them. Water everywhere, it was complained; even bedclothes were wet. Head and chest colds began to take their toll. When Sargent proposed to bring in two Czech principals as replacements his own men stoically preferred to remain on duty.

Shortly before one of the Bratislava concerts it was found that the
Czech radio authorities had made technical arrangements to broad-
cast it 'live' in circumstances which were held to infringe rules of the
Musicians' Union. A sharp dispute ended with an associate of the
R.P.O. administration going into the transmission room and pulling
out the connections with his own hands.

Then came the rail journey from Bratislava towards Cracow: a
nightmare. On the Czech side of the Polish border the train stopped
in a snowbound landscape—with frozen brake mechanism, it was
said—for most of a day. The compartments were heated, but there
was neither food nor drink aboard. At length the crew got the train
moving, and she limped into a station on the Polish side of the
frontier, where everybody got out and waited for motor coaches.
Throughout all this Sargent put on one of the great shows of his
life. His high spirits bubbled. He joked, argued, rallied, teased, told
stories, got mild pranks afoot: all this with a spontaneity which
made misery tolerable for others. On the station platform, wearing
an uncommonly stylish astrakhan hat, he went through fencing
motions with an icicle four feet long. He was working hard, but his
gaiety did not seem forced or overdone. The day's final tribulation
was the motor-coach journey to Cracow, four hungry hours. They
were to have played Cracow that evening but did not get there until
after the concert was timed to be over. At five next morning they
entrained for Warsaw: three concerts with 'rave' audiences.
Moscow they reached during the first week of one of the bitterest
Februaries known.

*

Their first Moscow concert bracketed the Tallis Fantasia, Britten-
Purcell and Beethoven's *Eroica* Symphony. Despite the growing
incidence of illness, the tour machinery had been running smoothly
and peacefully for some days; but the earlier strains still nagged,
and feelings were easily ruffled. Rehearsing the *Eroica* Symphony on
the morning of the concert, Sargent halted at the end of the development section, first movement, and asked the second horn to do
something not required by Beethoven, namely, to mute and 'slur'
(i.e. play *legato*) the famous 'wrong note' horn solo which precedes

MALCOLM SARGENT

the recapitulation.* Feeling that Sargent was casting doubt upon his capability, the second horn objected. Sargent insisted. The second horn, who was a young man, stuck to his point. At length the principal horn, James Brown, stood up and spoke up for his colleague.

'In the R.P.O.', he said, 'we have a tradition of playing this solo. We made a record with you of the *Eroica* with the same players in the horn section. You didn't ask for the second horn to mute and slur then. We don't want it muted and slurred now.'

'You have no tradition in this orchestra,' Sargent is alleged to have whipped back'—only *my* tradition. I have never been so insulted in my life. I refuse to conduct.' With this he walked off, leaving the orchestra in a hubbub. The general feeling is said to have been against the horn section. Whatever resentment most of the players might have felt against him earlier, they were plainly on Sargent's side now.

His refusal to conduct went no further than the rehearsal. He and everybody else turned up for the concert, the hornists feeling like outcasts. In the band room the orchestral librarian brought Brown a message: 'Jim, the old man wants you to go and see him.' At first Brown declined, still feeling rebellious. Finally he decided to take up the entire horn section—five players. Sargent was pacing his room tensely. He greeted his visitors with a smile of relief and said: 'Gentlemen, I never hold a grudge against any person. On this occasion I was very wrong. Can we shake on it?' He went down the line, gripping each player by the hand. Taking Brown aside later he hoped the incident would not be held against him. On this point he was warmly assured: he had won a loyal friend.

That night the Great Hall of the Moscow Conservatoire was packed. People who couldn't get seats stood along the walls or listened from the corridors. The solo for second horn in the *Eroica*, untampered with, went well. Next morning at rehearsal Sargent made an announcement. 'After the concert last night,' he said 'I

---

* The horn sounds four notes, composing the chord of E flat, against B flat and A flat in the violins. On first hearing this Beethoven's friend Ferdinand Ries shouted: 'That damned horn player has come in wrong. It sounds damnably false.'

met Mr. Shostakovich. He said that going to concerts was his hobby but that he had never heard the trio of the *Eroica* [Scherzo] played so magnificently.' Since the trio in question has star parts for three horns, this compliment completely restored the 'outcasts' to favour. A general cheer went up.

Shostakovich was not the only celebrity with whom Sargent had talked in the artists' room. Among others he met Ekaterina Furtseva, who was then the Soviet Minister of Culture. To Madame Furtseva and an attendant group of highly placed Russians he held forth challengingly through an interpreter about Britain's social revolution:

'No heads have been chopped off. There have been no barricades, no bloodshed. But, as compared with my childhood and the almost feudal town where I was brought up, the country has been turned upside down socially, and nobody's the worse off, I suppose.' To illustrate the new interweave of classes and economic groups, he touched upon the antecedents of well-off girls he knew who chose to go out to work. One girl, a confidential secretary, was the daughter of a powerful brewing family with a great country house. Another girl, a former assistant secretary, was a member of the Bowes-Lyon family and thus cousin to the Queen. He spoke of a third girl, the daughter of a marquis with whom he had long been in close friendship. When she went to the Proms the marquis's daughter preferred to queue for a standing place. Whenever he offered her a stall she refused it. Why? Because standing at the Proms was classless and jolly.

Madame Furtseva and the others listened politely to what he was saying but could not take it in. What? A Queen's cousin and a capitalist daughter who did jobs? An aristocrat's daughter who queued like any proletarian? Madame Furtseva looked up at him from beneath an agreeable blonde hairdo in a baffled, almost coquettish way. He told her she was his favourite woman in Moscow. Everybody laughed, and there was no tension. . . .

On to Leningrad. By this time five 'cellists were on the sick list, one of them with pneumonia. They were replaced by magnificent Russian players. From Leningrad the party took off for Kiev in an Ilyushin jet airliner. The take-off struck many on board as fantastically fast; some owned up later to having felt scared. Sargent sat in the forepart of the cabin, reading a score. James Brown who was opposite said in congratulatory tones: 'You seem very calm and cool.'

'I spend half my life spinning round the word in aeroplanes,' returned Sargent. 'I'm not concerned at all.'

'Do you ever get worried?'

'No. Once I get into an aeroplane I am in God's hands. Why should I have anything to worry about?'

Brown was to hear these words from him again in the presence of more immediate danger.

Back from Kiev to Moscow for a final concert, this time before an audience of six thousand in the New Kremlin Palace auditorium. Then home. There were many things to negotiate and mull over: the North American tour for one.

*

The plan was that Sargent should take the R.P.O. out at the end of September and conduct thirty-seven concerts in as many cities. In other cities Georges Prêtre, the French conductor, who had been appointed his assistant for the tour, was to conduct nineteen concerts more, making a total of fifty-six in sixty-four days. Backed by an American recording company, the arrangements were documented and signed in May 1963. But whom did the signatures commit? And to what? With one exception the players were not on contract; to that extent they were free agents. The R.P.O. had been founded by an illustrious baronet, was now being toured by a distinguished knight and had the Queen Mother as their patron. These matters were discreetly stressed in advance publicity along the orchestra's itinerary, which covered 20,000 miles and took in immense populations. Booking opened buoyantly and by midsummer was nearing capacity. It was now that the players began to doubt and to sow doubt in others.

Not long after their return it was painfully borne in upon them that their future as an orchestra was in jeopardy. For sixteen years the R.P.O. had been the preferred orchestra of the Royal Philharmonic Society. That Society let it be known that they would not be using the R.P.O. in 1963-4. The management of the Royal

Festival Hall were planning concerts of their own for the same season. They booked the R.P.O.'s three independent competitors, the London Symphony, London Philharmonic and Philharmonia orchestra, but left the R.P.O. out. At one point the company controlling the R.P.O.'s business affairs thought of merging it with the orchestra of the Royal Opera House. This notion, although nothing came of it, did nothing to alleviate the players' fears and suspicions. They scented a resolve on the part of what some called the Musical Establishment to liquidate the R.P.O. as redundant in a city which had four other symphony orchestras.

One of the leading players puts it thus in retrospect: 'There was no prospect that we should survive into 1964. The only work scheduled for us after the American tour was two children's concerts and the possibility, no more than that, of nine recording sessions. That was how things stood in the summer of 1963. It looked as if we were going to be taken to America by Sargent, brought back and scuttled. We didn't want Sargent, and we didn't want to be scuttled.'

The orchestra's aversion to the trip, which amounted almost to a refusal of it, had been established by one of the leading players, Harry Legge, the violist, who had carefully sounded his colleagues while they were at Glyndebourne that summer for the opera season. When their attitude came to the ears of the R.P.O.'s council of management they deputed Frederick Lloyd, one of their number, to untangle, if he could, a menacing situation. As general manager of the D'Oyly Carte Opera Company, Lloyd knew Sargent well and was a skilled musical negotiator. At Glyndebourne he had repeated consultations with Harry Legge, now the orchestra's spokesman. The main difficulty at this stage was their attitude to Sargent. They still felt sore about the seating and other rehearsals which they considered him to have imposed unnecessarily in Russia and the 'Curtain' countries. If he were to be equally exacting on the American tour, which was on a much bigger and more concentrated scale, the players would not be able to take the strain.

When Lloyd told him of this, Sargent spoke decisively. 'Things have gone much too far,' he said, 'to permit a cancellation of the tour. With fifty-seven halls booked solid a cancellation would make this country's name stink. Please assure them that there's no question of seating rehearsals. The only question is whether we are going to let Britain down.'

Upon this assurance the players agreed to the tour, and a glow of goodwill set in. He took a week's rehearsals at a hall in Bloomsbury. After the last piece had been worked over on the last day he made a short speech. 'I realize,' he said, 'what difficulties the orchestra has been going through. For everybody's sake I want this tour to be a success. I know things weren't always easy between us on the Russian tour. But here we have an opportunity of proving what a great orchestra this is, not only for the orchestra's sake but for the sake of Britain.'

'Difficulties' was an understatement. What Sargent had in mind was the threat of extinction. He was to say later that in America the orchestra was 'fighting for its life'; in other words, that survival depended on the prestige they brought back home with them. The crisis was a stimulant. It brought out the combative crusader in him. He let the players know that their fight was his. That the R.P.O. should cease to exist was out of the question, he told them.

From Ottawa the orchestra worked down through small cities and great, halting in Boston, New York (Carnegie Hall), Washington and Philadelphia among other cities, to New Orleans and other populations in the far South; then swung through New Mexico to the West Coast (San Francisco, Los Angeles), thence striking north for final concerts in Vancouver, Seattle and Anchorage (Alaska). Sargent's dynamic, the unquenchable brightness in his eye, were those of a man under forty. He had one run of eleven concerts in twelve days, another of twelve in thirteen days, many of them in towns far apart. He took seating rehearsals after all. Their purpose was solely or mainly to get the measure of local acoustics. He kept these sessions short and rarely dallied over minutiae. Everything went tranquilly. He found himself at ease and friendly with his players in a way and to a degree which, in the judgment of the widely experienced among them, he had never quite achieved with an orchestra before.

His repertory was a familiar parcel: Sibelius's No. 1 and No. 2; Brahms's No. 4; Vaughan Williams's *London* Symphony, Tallis

Fantasia and *Wasps* Overture; Elgar's Introduction and Allegro, *Enigma* and *Cockaigne*; the *Perfect Fool* ballet music; the *Walk to the Paradise Garden*; the Britten-Purcell variations; Dohnanyi's Orchestral Suite in F sharp minor; and the Handel-Harty *Water Music*. Playing with what he said was 'a fervour and intensity which I have not experienced so consistently before', the orchestra won standing ovations night after night and newspaper notices which for the most part were similar in spirit. An exception was the *Boston Herald*, which complained of over-accentuated brass and bravura treatment that blotted out detail. College and university theatres alternated with great public halls. One of the collegiate promotions was in North Carolina. 'Do not,' pleaded a programme note, 'smoke within the auditorium at any time, enter or change seats during the performance of a number [or] bring in soft drink bottles or paper cups.' The San Francisco concert came under tragic shadow. President Kennedy had been assassinated the day before. Sargent and orchestral spokesmen debated the propriety or otherwise of going ahead with the concert. The British Consul-General was brought into their deliberations. It was decided not to cancel the programme but to modify it. 'Nimrod', from the *Enigma* Variations, played *in memoriam*, swelled nobly and aptly.

Before this there had been an incident of another kind at Jackson (Mississippi), a 'segregationist' town. Before the concert Sargent received two threatening telephone calls and, during the interval, a third from anti-segregationists, one of them a British postgraduate student from Cambridge who was taking a course in sociology at Yale. The effect of both messages, in Sargent's account, was that, since coloured people were not to be allowed in the hall, he must refuse to conduct the concert. His reply was that he had not known of any colour bar imposed by the organization responsible for financing the concert; that he had given concerts in other States where coloured people had been admitted as a matter of course; and that he was himself entirely without colour or racial prejudice, having (he added in a later context*) made music for Chinese, Indians, Sinhalese, Negroes of many tribes and, in case anybody should tax him with 'White segregation', thousands of Communists. The

* Letter to the Editor, *The Guardian*, 6th December, 1963.

second call came through on the afternoon of the concert. Sargent's retort to this, as to the previous one, was that, having signed a contract, he felt obliged to fulfil it. The concert would go on. In that case, said the caller, he would find himself in trouble. (According to another account the caller threatened 'severe action' and said Sargent would be sorry.)

That night he was given police protection inside and outside the hall. Before going on he explained the situation to James Brown, now chairman of the orchestra, who, the point being put to him, agreed that the concert must be given. The hall had been booked solid days ahead. Cancellation was out of the question. A late start was made because of latecomers; there were so many of these that, after conducting 'The Star Spangled Banner' and 'God Save the Queen', Sargent was obliged to step down from the rostrum while they clomped along aisles and up balcony stairs and hunted for their seats. Meantime, at one of the entrances policemen had intercepted the postgraduate student and his companion, a Negro. Both had tickets. They were arrested, charged with disturbing the peace and held for nineteen hours before release on bail. The interval came after the *Water Music* and the Dohnanyi Suite. During it Sargent again sent for James Brown and told him of a further telephone threat, just received. The gist of it was: 'You have gone against our advice and proceeded with the concert. Stop now or face the consequences.' It was agreed that the consequences must be faced, whatever their nature. Brown complimented Sargent on his sangfroid in view of the risk he might be taking individually. Sargent replied, as after the Leningrad take-off: 'Well Mr. Brown, I am in the hands of God.' He went back and conducted a wholly Sargentesque Brahms No. 4 and was judged to be the coolest person on a platform which, judging by what some said after the event, was by no means free from apprehension. As Sargent had suggested, police coverage in and about the hall would probably have been sufficient to nip trouble in the bud if anybody had tried to start any. Nevertheless there was a certain amount of jumpiness. Without disturbance the Brahms went on its majestic way to full-close. It was followed by the twenty-fourth ovation of the tour, a massive one. The student and his Negro friend came to no harm, the charges against them being dropped. When the incident threatened to flare into controversy at home, Sargent let it be known that, with the help of the British Consul-General, he had been partly responsible for securing the student's release.

From Alaska, after the Anchorage concert, they took off for London. The tour had been emphatically successful. It had won the R.P.O. precisely the kind of attention and homage they had set out to win. The need now was to strike while the iron was hot. They had left Alaska early on a December morning. That night they were rushed from London Airport to a candlelit press party on sawdust floors in an ancient Fleet Street tavern. Again Sargent reaffirmed that the R.P.O. must and should live; that its passing was unthinkable. Not only was it unthinkable; thanks to Sargent's help in the background and reorganization from the roots up it seemed exceedingly unlikely. Even before the tour began steps had been taken towards new life. Forming themselves into a limited liability company, each putting in ten pounds as founding capital, R.P.O. players were now governing their own affairs through a board of six members with James Brown its chairman, as has been mentioned.

*

During the phase of doubt and flounder Rudolf Kempe had resigned from the chief conductorship. He now came back as the R.P.O.'s artistic director, an appointment which pleased Sargent. On the flight from Alaska he said to a member of the new board: 'Congratulations, you've got the right man.' There were some who wanted him made patron of the orchestra. When sounded on this possibility he preferred that his name should not go forward; it was against general practice, he felt, for a conductor to become directly and personally associated with any orchestra in such a way. But, he repeated, he would do whatever he could to help the orchestra in other capacities. His help was soon forthcoming. Frozen, as they saw it, out of the Festival Hall, the orchestra tapped a new public. In May they started a series of Sunday concerts week by week at the Odeon Cinema, Swiss Cottage, outside the centre of London. Sargent inaugurated and nursed the series with a zeal which counted much towards their success. As well as appearing on the Odeon rostrum he obtained work for the R.P.O. with the Royal Choral Society, and whenever there was any call for it spoke up forcefully for the orchestra in musical conclaves against those who were not its friends.

Soon after his death the R.P.O. chanced to play twice on the same day in Sargent's old place of training, Peterborough Cathedral. They played for children in the afternoon and for grown-ups at night. At both concerts, after making solemn music, they stood for a long, introspective moment in memory of the man who had fought their fight. They stood for him again at the Royal Choral Society's opening concert that season. On all three occasions they meant what they were about. Sargent was gone. But not before winning them over for good.

CHAPTER THIRTY-ONE

THE NAUGHTIEST, NICEST ...

UP TO HIS seventieth birthday, April 1965, and for eighteen months after it, his quickness and stamina seemed to defy time and nature. Never did a septuagenarian throw off such sparks. They were sparks of the sort that come from a certain kind of firework. They dazzled, they entertained, but never hurt and never burned. In a professional world not given to charitable judgments he was conspicuous for tactful, even kindly reticence. On his own confession he was capable of 'snapping' at rehearsal. As a battling beginner he had been capable of the acid rebuke when crossed or obstructed. But the acid was gone. Men of insight who had seen much of him for thirty years said that Sargent was almost the only person they knew who never, to their knowledge, ran people down behind their backs; and this was my impression. Instead of damning an errant composer by name he would refer to 'a certain type of modern musician'. It is true that imputations of this order, while protecting the individual offender, may spread impartially to those who have not offended at all. To that extent they are unfair. But not as unfair as professional backbiting. Of this Sargent was never guilty, for it was not in his nature.

He was readier than ever for sallies and sorties. Late in 1964 he flew to Turkey and met the homing London Symphony Orchestra on the last stretch of a world tour on which they had been conducted by six other international batons. In an Istanbul cinema, after the Handel-Harty *Water Music* and the Mendelssohn violin concerto, in which a Turkish girl played the solo part, he did Tchaikovsky's Symphony No. 5 with a substantial finale cut which is remembered by a competent witness as 'positively jolting'. On from Turkey to

Israel. In Tel Aviv and Ein Gev he repeated No. 5 and cut the finale again. Somebody mildly asked why. 'Because it's too long!' he cheerfully explained.

Ein Gev is a 'kibbutz' noted for the musical keenness of its people. Getting there involved Sargent and the players in a motor-coach journey of four and a half hours. The day was cold, wet and daunting: and another challenge for Sargent. As lively as a cricket, he kept up the spirits of everybody within range. In a modest way and on a minor scale it was his Polish border performance over again. Ein Gev's concert hall had an austere look, seated three thousand and drew music lovers from a wide radius. At this concert, as at the others in Tel Aviv and Jerusalem, there were emotional reunions with men and women, 'intellectuals' for the most part, who had met him in what was then called Palestine during the late 1930s and who remembered his endeavours then and later for persecuted and displaced Jewish musicians. These acts of intercession are said to have been noted by the Nazis. 'It has been discovered,' he said years afterwards,* 'that many hundreds of civilians were down in Hitler's "[Black] Book" to be shot at sight, absolutely contrary to international law, when they took London, and that I was among them. I'm awfully proud of that.' It seems that he learned this from a friend who had early access to Gestapo papers after the war. The peace which had since come upon the world was of a queasy sort in certain countries. During the concert some heard or thought they heard gunfire. The Syrian border was not far away; racial tensions and skirmishings were as bad as at the time of his armoured car tours a generation earlier, perhaps worse.

He continued to spend half his life 'spinning round the world in aeroplanes', though not with the zest of the 'airminded'. He had long before defined air travel as 'one of the dullest things' and sighed after the days when getting to a far-off country was enjoyable because of other countries and peoples one saw on the way there. 'When you're jumped through the air,' he lamented, 'all that is blocked out. Everything's the same.' Towards the end of his seventieth year, the morning after an Albert Hall concert, he packed characteristic scores—Sibelius's Second Symphony to Dvořák's

* On B.B.C. Woman's Hour, 15th May 1952.

Seventh, the Britten-Purcell variations and the *Paradise Garden* entr'acte to *Don Juan* and the Tallis Fantasia—for his seventh tour of Australia and an excursion to New Zealand. He spent that night, the next day and the following night in the air. He came down the gangway at Sydney soon after seven in the morning, to be annexed after little delay by reporters, microphones and television cameras. Taking off again at ten, he reached Melbourne an hour and a half later. There were more television interviews (he entered such things in his diary with amused relish), followed by a business conference with broadcasting chiefs, greetings to the Governor-General's aide-de-camp, a dinner party with old friends and incidental preoccupations which in themselves would have driven any other man to lock himself in a quiet room and lie down. On this trip he put in dinner parties, luncheons, official receptions, ceremonial suppers and one full blown banquet to the total of twelve in eleven days; he gave one formal speech and talked torrentially the rest of the time. He seems to have done all this without a slip of the tongue and without glazing an eye.

His two concerts with the Victorian (Melbourne) Symphony Orchestra, preceded by fifteen hours of rehearsal, were billed for the Sidney Myer Bowl, a pleasance in ten acres of parkland on the outskirts of the city. Modelled on California's celebrated Hollywood Bowl, this had a stage big enough for several symphony orchestras at a time (those of Melbourne and Sydney had combined for the inaugural concert five or six years earlier), a canopy to shelter an audience of two thousand as well as the players, and, beyond the canopy, upsloping and outlying lawns where anything up to a hundred thousand could sit or sprawl. Sargent went there the day after his arrival for a look at the lighting and orchestral seating. 'Never leave anything to chance or take anything for granted' had been his policy for fifty years. He was told about the forest of microphones, the man in the control pit who attended to sound levels and the spaced-out loudspeakers, each fractionally delayed in a sequence which ensured that, wherever you sat or stood and however far off you were, the sound reached you on the same beat as the live sound coming from the stage. On his first night, conducting two symphonies among other pieces—Sibelius's No. 2 and Haydn's

No. 86 in D—he had an audience of 20,000. The night was warm and still. The brilliant lights of the canopy showed up a pink sea of faces; the glow reached the perimeter of the Bowl where mounted police patrolled on greys. On the following night he did Dvořák's No. 7, *Paradise Garden* and Britten-Purcell before 25,000. The evangelist Billy Graham had drawn 70,000, Australia's leading group of 'pop' singers 100,000. Nobody expected crowds of that size for symphonic music, even with Sargent on the rostrum.

Playing talent still had to be shared out between the Australian cities. Extra strings had been brought in; also a leading flute from Sydney and a leading oboe from Adelaide. In an acoustical setting with which he familiarized himself to some extent as he went along, Sargent seems to have imparted what had come to be recognized as his special mould and touch to Haydn, Sibelius and the rest. Conspicuously beautiful phrasing went along with tight discipline and utter efficiency. Everything had been carefully thought out. This was to be gathered from next morning's papers. Occasional doubts were breathed. Were not the thinking-out and the efficiency a shade overdone, perhaps? Might not some of the performances have benefited by a touch of 'spontaneous rapture'?

These reservations were put by a writer in *The Age*, Felix Werder. 'Here,' he suggested, 'is an Englishman who feels with his head and thinks with his heart.'

This reversal of functions, supposing it to have happened (it probably did), was no bad thing. Sargent was so vulnerable emotionally that if, while on the rostrum, he had felt with his heart, every symphony he conducted would have wept itself to death. On the other hand, he was so intent on total musical control, so intent on an exactitude which extended from rhythmic detail to the highest melodic flights, that if he had thought with his head the results might have been unbearably arid. Certainly the 'reversal mixture', as we may call it, pleased the Myer Bowl multitudes. After Sibelius's No. 2 he had a standing ovation. Twenty thousand were on their feet in noisy gratitude. The sound with which they had been regaled was likened by one commentator to that of high-quality 'canned' music. This mattered little in the presence of Sibelius's finale tune, one of those great seductive tunes which musical puritans (it is suspected)

Backstage at Royal Albert Hall before making his last appearance,
Saturday 16th September 1967, at a Promenade Concert

Last-night greetings—and farewell—to old friends and colleagues, with 'my beloved Promenaders' in background

Photo: Monitor

secretly cherish while affecting to sniff at; and of Malcolm Sargent, whose person and being lived up to that tune and seemed, in a dashing, romantic way, to be on a par with it. It was hard to think of any other conductor in the world of whom the same could be said, even when the fairly young and handsome ones were taken into account. What twenty thousand had felt in the Myer Bowl was felt by tens of thousands in capitals of deeper musical tradition than Melbourne could lay claim to. The spark and command of his presence crossed cultural divides as well as seas and frontiers.

After his second concert in the Bowl there was neither bed nor sleep for him. He boarded an aeroplane at 1.30 a.m. for his concerts in Christchurch, N.Z., and talked through the night with representatives of the Australian Broadcasting Corporation about his next round of concerts under their aegis. He was to return in mid-April 1966 and stay until the beginning of June for twenty concerts, mostly in Melbourne. In 1967 he was to be back for something which he had long treasured in his mind: a Beethoven festival at which all the symphonies and seven concertos would be performed.

Meantime: to business at Christchurch. His three concerts there launched a pan-Pacific arts festival. They were preceded by a State procession to the cathedral in which, wearing white tie and decorations, he walked with the Prime Minister of New Zealand. After the cathedral service there was an inaugural banquet at which, as guest-of-honour, he spoke more or less extempore for half an hour. All this happened on the day of his arrival after the night without sleep. In the afternoon he had put in a two-hour rehearsal with a festival choir of five hundred voices. Earlier he had managed to squeeze in a television interview. At some point along the line he had gone to bed with the intention of preparing his banquet speech but fell asleep, as might have been expected. Two charter 'planes came in with the Melbourne orchestra next day. He rehearsed them before going on to a civic luncheon. For the festival concerts a barracks had been handsomely decorated inside and turned into a concert hall with three or four thousand seats, the cheapest of which cost a pound; and every seat was taken. The choir were there ostensibly for two performances only: the Polovtsian dances from *Prince Igor* and, by way of peroration, 'Blest pair of sirens'. But Sargent had a

surprise up his sleeve. One of the shorter orchestral pieces he
travelled on this tour was the *Academic Festival* Overture, based by
Brahms on four student songs. In the last of the four, 'Gaudeamus
igitur'—'Let us rejoice'—the orchestra was joined by the choir to
unexpected and rollicking effect. The setting they sang was, of
course, Sargent's own: a pleasantly audacious stroke.

Rehearsals and concerts continued to leapfrog with official
luncheons, dinners of honour, suppers of honour, receptions that
went on into the small hours and busy conclaves with television men
and television cameras. Not only did he survive. He flourished. He
flew home via Sydney (one rest day there, with old friends), Hong
Kong and Delhi; and went to bed—not to sleep but to prepare for
his Ash Wednesday *Gerontius* three days later with the Royal Choral
Society—as if he had never set eyes on the score before.

*

In Commonwealth countries he usually gave the impression of being
at home and among his own; and so he was if warmth and fervour of
friendship are the test. His feeling about foreign parts had a different
nuance. He once said that he never went into any foreign country
uninvited; liked to have the red carpet rolled out for him; duly
walked on it; shot some English music at his hosts; and got away as
quickly as he could. To the extent that he aged while looking little
older, so did the pull of home platforms become more imperious and
nostalgic. There were his choral societies in London and up and
down the country. Above all, there were the Promenade Concerts.

These gave him pride, comfort and a purpose of considerable
moment: that of grafting on to English youth certain traditions
(not musical traditions only) which, he held, had sap and salvation
in them. During years increasingly scarred by hostility between
generation and generation and by youth mobs which, although
small and sporadic, struck some observers as of sinister potential, he
asserted great music and great books, love of country and love of
God as the way, the truth and the cure. On last nights at the Proms
he put over doctrines of this kind, sometimes explicitly, more often
in a tacit way, with a gaiety and virtuosity which could not have
been rivalled by any other leader or teacher in the land.

These last nights have always been famously rowdy. Sargent presided over their din and ebullience with a serene and expert touch. The main music would be listened to with the absorbed silence for which the Prommers were much praised; but before the music began and, more emphatically, at—or towards—the end of it, the Royal Albert Hall exploded into amiable saturnalia led by 'standers' on the ground floor and in the top-gallery. Handbells, klaxons, bicycle horns, squeakers, whistles, Cup-Final rattles, at least one cowhorn and the occasional trumpet added their cacophonies to chanted slogans, snatches of community jingle, shrill cross-talk and round upon round of cheers for musical heroes or musical classics or just for cheering's sake. The end pieces were a fixed and loved routine: a group of Henry Wood's *Sea Songs* for the orchestra, then 'Rule Britannia' (Arne-Sargent) and Parry's *Jerusalem* with everybody joining in at top voice. When rehearsing the Parry and 'Rule Britannia' or 'Land of Hope and Glory', another last-night number, Sargent sometimes turned his back on the orchestra and conducted an empty hall from the point where community singing was due to begin. He did this not to make sure of his timing and gestures (he always said that these came naturally to him and had not to be practised) but rather to enter beforehand into the spirit of 'the night'. Throwing paper streamers at the rostrum until it was richly enmeshed, agitating toy balloons (which occasionally burst near the microphones to startling effect) and ancient umbrellas (open as well as furled), the arena crowd had taken latterly to wearing either boaters stamped on the crown with the Union Jack or silly hats and archaic ones, of which a greater assortment was seen at the Proms than at one time in any other place imaginable.

One musical outrage was permitted every year. The last of the *Sea Songs* was the Hornpipe. As soon as solo violin and solo flute had played their statements of the tune, the arena and most other parts of the hall would start clapping and stamping. They began *sotto voce* and to the orchestra's rhythm; then they would accelerate and louden with confusing and deafening results. Good-humouredly condoned by Sargent and the platform, this racing and drowning of the Hornpipe became an established ritual as well as a lark. Weighty pens and grave voices occasionally made it the text

for sermons on the musical 'callowness' of Prommers in general and
young Prommers in particular.

Sargent would have none of this. The younger end worshipped
him; and he reciprocated with all his heart. For him they were 'the
naughtiest, nicest audience in the world'. *And* the most appreciative.
Did not the younger end, I asked him during the 1961 season,
sometimes overdo their applause? Were they not, perhaps, a little
undiscriminating?

'Not at all!' he insisted. 'Clapping is a good convention. It's a way
of being generous. But the Prommers are not uncritical. They are
no fools. They will remain still and silent throughout a symphony—
even a "difficult" symphony. We saw that the other night. During
the long first movement of Shostakovich's Sixth Symphony, which
is so moving and of such serious temper—you have to listen to it
with the greatest concentration—there wasn't a single cough. They
behaved wonderfully. Some of my Russian friends were there. They
remarked that the common cold which afflicts the English in the
concert hall seemed to have cleared up for once! Bear in mind that
many of the Prommers are adolescents or children and therefore
physically restless. Having remained still throughout a symphony
they have to let off their pent-up energy by being noisy. I can, if
I think fit, stop their applause in a moment. I did so, in fact, last
night. After one piece it struck me that the applause was going on
too long. I simply opened the score of the next piece. Instantly the
applause died down.'

There spoke the virtuoso. As is clear from B.B.C. tapes of several
last-night revels, including speeches of his which were their culminating point,* he could play on a mixed though mainly youthful
crowd of six or seven thousand as upon a keyboard, tolerating their
interruptions with fine calculation and humour, making the hall rock
with facetious sallies, imposing quiet and riveting attention by an
intonation or lift of the hand. He usually began his speech with:
'Ladies and gentlemen! Young ladies, young gentlemen!' Sometimes he would add: 'Boys and girls!' If, after this, there was a toot

---

* Several of these are heard on two long-play discs issued on B.B.C. Radio
Enterprise label: *Sir Malcolm Sargent, Music Maker* (RE 10) and 'My beloved
Promenaders' (REC 22 M).

or a honk too many from top gallery or arena he would tack on
'. . . and kindergarten babies with toy trumpets!' Affectionate
twittings of this kind moved the babies and others to jubilation and,
as likely as not, an extra round of cheers. Once or twice, knowing
well what he was about, he set off demonstrations that were mixed
as well as jovial. Dissentient though jolly boos mingled with approving hurras. Something of this kind happened when he quoted an
eight-year-old godchild of his as saying after a typical Prom ovation:
'Isn't it exciting—you might be a Beatle!' This raised a hilarious
storm. It was clear the the Beatles were not without friends in the
house. 'As a matter of fact,' he went on when he could make himself
heard, 'the Beatles haven't had it all their own way. No fewer than
three hundred young ladies have been carried out swooning during
this year's Proms. . . .' Joyous pandemonium followed.

This was in the decade when Promenade programmes were
beginning to be shot through with certain musical idioms which were
newish and others that were none the less revolutionary for being
anything up to half a century old. Instead of pretending in a dig-
nified way to remain aloof from idioms he didn't like, he indulged in
a dig at them from time to time. For instance: 'A little calculation for
my friends who buy season tickets. . . . The cost [of the music you
hear] works out at a seventh of a penny a minute. Those of you who
listened to Webern's Five Orchestral Pieces Op. 10 [29th August
1961, John Carewe conducting the New Music Ensemble], which
last five minutes—less than a penny, that is—cannot say, even if
you didn't like them very much, that your penny was exactly wasted.'
Through the ensuing hullabaloo of laughter and approving yells,
counter-demonstrators could be plainly heard. Like the Beatles,
Webern had friends in the house. They were not angry friends,
however. On these occasions Sargent had the knack of turning even
musical quarrels, which can be as fierce as political ones, into lighthearted diversions.

Again: 'We find ourselves at the Proms performing new works.
I wish those of you who have friends who are composers would tell
. . . some of them [that if they] listened a little more to Bach,
Beethoven and other classics, read their Shakespeare and perhaps
enjoyed their Bible, they would not be content to offer us . . . mental

obscurities. If I had a school for composers I would put up two mottoes: 1, IF MUSIC BE THE FOOD OF LOVE, PLAY ON. 2, IF NOT, SHUT UP, PLEASE!' This was not as strong as his presidential address to the Incorporated Society of Musicians (1957). (He then complained of the awful amount of 'tripe' that was being composed: trivial and banal stuff, nonsense which tried to disguise its emptiness by mental elaboration and ridiculously complicated notation.) Yet it was strong enough to provoke another hullabaloo with dissentient notes—and no ill feeling.

Getting into a last night was no simple matter. The vast Albert Hall became a pint pot, the demand a gallon. The solution was and is, of course, a ballot for last-night seats and standing places. (The same arrangement applies to first nights, which are equally popular.) Last nights are always on Saturday. After listening to Friday night's concert hundreds of youngsters who have drawn 'standing' tickets will bed down on the Albert Hall pavement to be sure of getting the best places, those up front along the rail, just under the conductor's rostrum. 'Late last night,' Sargent would tell them jokingly, 'I walked round the Albert Hall. You didn't see me. You were fast asleep. I am arranging with the B.B.C. that next year there shall be a Promenade dosshouse!' Apart from last nights and first nights there were as many youngsters who, after waiting outside for hours, stood through *Gerontius*, say, or the 'Choral' Symphony or the *Grande messe des morts*. He contrasted their sense of values with those of delinquent youth gangs who made war on each other—and sometimes on unoffending third parties—under the names of Mods and Rockers. He raised a great shout of laughter by getting the names ingeniously wrong. Mads and Rotters, he called them. It seemed unfair, he said, that so much publicity was given to a few hundred silly youngsters smashing windows in a seaside resort and so little to thousands who stood for hours to hear Elgar, Beethoven and Berlioz. 'My young friends,' he concluded in 1964, 'it is in you that we put our faith in the future.' To which he added a year later: 'You are the salt of the earth!'

Under the B.B.C.'s reduced allocation, he conducted eighteen Promenades in 1966. His programmes that year amounted to a head-and-shoulders if not full-length portrait of Sargent the musician at any age from his middle thirties onwards. One hesitates to repeat titles and opuscula which have recurred often in this narrative; but the 1966 season had special significance and must be outlined in some detail. There were *Gerontius*, the 'Choral' Symphony, *Belshazzar*, Delius's *A Mass of Life* and Vaughan Williams's *Serenade to Music*, all with a pile-up from four or five major choirs. Even for his Gilbert and Sullivan night he drew upon three. His G. and S. devotions at the Proms were high spirited and proselytizing. In an age when many elders of rarified taste regarded these texts as aesthetically outdated and even got angry about them, droves of junior Prommers saw the point and rejoiced in it. Forty-six years after his first 'Savoy' opera season (the reader will remember his opening with *Patience* at Melton), Sullivan's music remained an untarnished miracle for him. *Patience* was among six operas from which he took excerpts that night. Another was *The Mikado*. He often said that 'the two Ms'—Mikado and Messiah—had been the twin pillars of his career.

Symphonies which he did that season were Nos. 2, 4, 5 and 8 by Beethoven (as well as the 'Choral'), Mozart's No. 40 in G minor, Schubert's 'Great' C major, Brahms's No. 2, Sibelius's Nos. 5 and 7, Elgar's No. 2 and Vaughan Williams's *London*. For the rest we had the *Enigma* Variations, the Tallis Fantasia, *Firebird*, the *Perfect Fool* ballet, the *Façade* suite, *On Hearing the First Cuckoo*, Holst's *Beni Mora*. . . . As to piano concertos, he started with the Schumann, ended with Prokoviev's No. 3, chose Rachmaninov's 'Paganini' Rhapsody (not No. 2 in C minor) and Tchaikovsky's No. 2 in G (instead of No. 1 in C sharp minor). All this music was listened to, as usual, with concentration and silence, qualities which, as he never tired of saying, distinguished Promenade audiences from most others. This, for example, had been his farewell at the end of the 1962 season: 'To make music is wonderful. To make great music with a fine orchestra is very wonderful. To make great music with a fine orchestra to an audience which is at times so concentrated in its attention that it's almost *frightening*—to express this is beyond my words. But that is how I feel about it.'

Goodbye speeches, symphonies, choral thunder, handbells, ebullient dins: all were dominated from a ledge at the back of the platform by the bronze bust of Sir Henry Wood who, paternal, rather craggy and reasonably lifelike, seemed to be taking everything in. Every year he was crowned with laurel on the last night. Like the white carnations worn by the orchestral players, the laurel wreath was a gift from organized Promenaders, mostly young. (They always sent up a bouquet for Sargent, too.) After the last concert the wreath would be taken away and placed on Wood's tomb in the musicians' chapel at the Church of the Holy Sepulchre, Holborn—not a difficult place for pilgrims to find, Sargent once mentioned—'but anybody who takes the wrong turning is likely to find himself in a very different place indeed. The Old Bailey, London's Central Criminal Court, is just across the road!' Facetiae of this kind were adroitly timed to offset more fervent thoughts. Henry Wood was the theme which, down the seasons, interwove his lighthearted manner and his more reflective one to the most remembered effect. The sentences that follow were not all spoken on one occasion. They are put together from last-night tapes dating back to 1948, four years after Wood's death:

'I am a few months older than the Promenades. I was born in April. The moment Sir Henry Wood heard about it he created the Promenades to give me something to do when I grew up. . . . He was nicknamed "Timber". He laid the foundations and built the structure of these Promenade Concerts with his heart. And his heart was of oak! . . . I am not referring to the "late lamented" but the late *beloved* Sir Henry Wood. Those of you who know your Shakespeare—and I pity those who don't!—may remember that, over the body of Julius Caesar, Mark Antony said: "The evil that men do lives after them; the good is oft interred with their bones". Now that is not always true. I think of no evil when I think of Henry J. Wood; and, my word! I can think of no good that has been interred with him. . . . On the North Door of St. Paul's Cathedral it says . . . *Si monumentum quæris circumspice*, which means, as all you Latinists know, "If you seek a monument, look around you." If we seek a monument to Henry Wood we look around us [here]. *You* are his monument—and a pretty good one, too. . . . The Promenades, like *Charley's Aunt*, are still running. Our great founder, always to be remembered and revered, gave the first Promenade concert seventy-two years ago. He little knew then that he would be . . . immortal, [for] I am quite sure the Promenades will never stop. I call for three cheers for Sir Henry Wood. Hip-hip. . . .' The cheers were a cataract. This happened on a night when squeakers and tooters had interrupted once or twice too often. A moment before the cheers he had asked in mock petulance: 'Would some nannies take those toys away?'—a stroke which silenced the offenders and enchanted seven thousand others.

His custom was to end his speech with what came to be known as the Promenaders' Thanksgiving. The words varied a little from year to year. An early version began: 'Blessed art Thou Who hast revealed Thyself in music.' The last version ran: 'We thank Thee Who hast revealed Thyself in great music and for giving us the understanding of it.' One year there were two in the audience who had learned to love music by watching the players and the singers and the Prommers' faces on telecasts over many years. 'They are here for the first time at a concert,' he announced. 'They tell me their love of music is intense. But they were born deaf and have never heard a note of anything . . . in their lives.' Before reciting the Thanksgiving he said: 'Last year I was brave enough to give you a little prayer. . . . But I think, you know, that now we ought to be pretty grateful for having ears to hear.' At the end he said what a privilege it had been to work for the Promenaders once more. 'We shall meet again', he continued, 'on July the twenty-second, nineteen-sixty-seven, when we shall start our seventy-third season.'

A Prommer: 'It's a date!' (loud laughter).

'Until then', he concluded, 'may I wish you the chance of hearing lots of good music? Have a good time—good night!'

The rendezvous was not kept. He was to make a further last-night speech. But he was to conduct no more Promenade Concerts. That of Saturday, 17th September, 1966, was his last.

CHAPTER THIRTY-TWO

PROLOGUE TO DEATH

FOR THE FIRST time people began to say that Malcolm was looking tired. 'Terribly tired' was William Glock's phrase. Glock's impression was that Sargent was glad, after all, to have been relieved to some extent of the old Promenades burden. There were days when age came upon him like a mask, incongruous and disquieting. The voice remained young, its vibrancy that of a taut string. The mask seemed to have little to do with the voice. Then the mask would go, or almost go, as suddenly as it came. On the rostrum he still looked something of a stripling from the middle distance. The white flecks over the ears were an irrelevancy.

Yet by the autumn of 1966 he was a sick man. He was losing appetite and weight. Late in November, taken with pain, he told the Royal Choral Society and the Royal Philharmonic Society that he would not be able to conduct their joint concert at the end of the month; and went into hospital, ostensibly with an acute disc lesion in the back. The bulletins which followed disclosed much graver matters. The first mention of jaundice came after he had been under observation for something over a week; it was announced that there was to be an exploratory operation on the gall bladder. One peculiarly distressing symptom of his disorder was a violent and uncontrollable shaking and shuddering of the whole body. If he had had a weak heart, this alone, he was given to understand, would have been enough to kill him, given his age.

The operation was carried out on 8th December 1966. Bulletins reporting his recovery and steady progress explained that the jaundice had arisen from abscesses on the liver and inflammation of the gall bladder and pancreas. By the end of December he was putting on weight; not only was he eating well but, I was assured, had begun to take more interest in food than he normally did before he was taken ill. Word was put about that the surgeons had found nothing 'malignant'. From what he told friends who visited him in hospital or after his return home in mid-January, it is clear that he had feared cancer. This fear having been assuaged, he was in a state of some jubilation and took a lively technical interest in the ordeal he had undergone. He had by him a surgeons' diagram of the operation. This he showed and expounded eagerly to at least one visitor. As strength slowly came back, so did his curiosity revive and with it an old pleasure, that of acquainting himself with new technicalities in certain fields outside his own. For a while his operation was his hobby.

When not poring with his doctors over X-ray photographs, he was badgering them about how soon he could get back to the rostrum. He had been through this before. Soon after the grave illness and operation of 1933 he had been obliged to put off his maiden visit to Australia for three years. The 1967 visit was to be his ninth. He had no intention of adjourning this. Everything had been detailed and agreed. Between 1st April and 22nd May he was to conduct eight pairs of concerts in Melbourne Town Hall and a single concert at Geelong, seventeen concerts in all. The eight programmes included three that could be described as miscellaneous Sargentry—Dvořák's *New World* Symphony and the Symphonic Variations Op. 78, the Mendelssohn violin concerto, Vaughan Williams's *A Sea Symphony*, Walton's Symphony No. 1 and *Belshazzar* and the usual English odds and ends. It was from this miscellany that two youth concerts on successive nights were compounded. Beethoven was the backbone of the scheme, accounting for five concerts and ten programmes; three overtures, six concertos and all nine symphonies. As well as the choir (from Christchurch, N.Z.), two solo singers and three concerto players would soon be standing by—among them a noted English violinist, Thomas Matthews (listed for the Mendelssohn and Beethoven's D major), who had broken a solo career in 1939 to lead the London Philharmonic Orchestra (on the 'blitz' tour *inter alia*) and was now resident conductor in Hobart,

Tasmania. At the thought of all this his eyes sparkled with excitment. When Anne Chapman saw him in mid-January he was a greyhound straining at the leash. He spoke of the Melbourne concerts with anticipatory joy.

'But, Maestro,' she ventured, 'if the doctors say you must rest you'll *have* to rest.'

'I'm going to Australia,' he answered with bright obstinacy. 'I'm going to conduct those Beethoven concerts.'

He was haggard and obviously frail. Mrs. Chapman did not persist but felt sure he would not be equal to the schedule.

His planning ran far beyond the Melbourne concerts. A week or two after his return to Albert Hall Mansions he was called on by James Brown, of the Royal Philharmonic Orchestra, and an administrative colleague, Archie Newman. He had asked them round to discuss a projected American tour with the R.P.O. in January 1968. Sitting up in green silk pyjamas with the Bible and other pious books at his bedside (one of them was *The Meaning of Holiness*, by Lavelle), he sketched programmes, went over the proposed transport schedule and scrutinized most other aspects of the tour with concentration. Hughie the budgerigar flew about and perched and sometimes chattered. When Sargent needed secretarial help from the office below he blew a football referee's whistle, and up would come a girl with a notebook. The whistle was of the shrill sort he was accustomed to hear on every last night of the Proms. (He once said to an over-zealous whistler: 'If you do that again I shall think it's half-time and go off.') The conference went on for two hours. At the end the American tour was drawn up and perfected. For Brown and Newman it had been exceedingly hard work. In mental quickness and drive it was Sargent who had made the running. Keeping up with him had left them limp. For all his bodily frailness he was the tranquil master of his faculties and emotions. Or so it seemed until near the end. When his callers rose to take their leave Sargent burst into tears and said how good they were to have come. Neither of them read premonition into this. They put it down to the effect of physical weakness on his nerves.

His recovery accelerated, however. Towards the end of February he was immersed in preparations for Beethoven's Missa Solemnis.

For this he returned to the rostrum on 9th March. The performance was with the Royal Choral Society at the Albert Hall. His back was as straight as a soldier's, his manner calm, his beat clear-cut and, to the cursory eye, as brisk as ever. Yet it was in some ways a melancholy evening. Suffering had left a shadow upon his features which few had seen before. There were many empty seats. And the briskness of his beat was not to be mistaken for the old fire. Next morning's *Times* confessed that the performance had 'left much to be desired. . . . It is possible that Sir Malcolm will need a little while before he attains to his former energy'.

Yet his mainspring presently unclogged; a respite began which, since it gave much hope, was cruel in the end. He set off for Australia with a letter from his doctors which, as he mentioned to Anne Chapman, was couched in hieroglyphics beyond any layman's understanding. It gave an account of his illness, operation and progress thus far. The idea was that if he had a relapse while away he should show the letter to a specialist on the spot, who would thus know what to do. In Australia he continued to mend, or that was how it seemed. He showed the letter to a doctor, nevertheless, and later described the consultation to Mrs. Chapman: 'The doctor said, "Well, in the first place you ought, theoretically, to be dead. It's an extraordinary thing to recover from such an operation at your age." ' Sargent expostulated that he was only seventy-one; he didn't think that much of an age. Everybody who understood what he had been through was astonished merely to see him on his feet; that he should be rehearsing and conducting seventeen festival concerts struck them as uncanny. After his opening concert on 1st April, repeated two nights later, Beethoven's second and fifth symphonies being the burden, *The Age* (Melbourne) testified to his 'keen-edged vitality and rapierlike intellectual thrusts', his 'supple, expressive hand' and his 'tremendous assurance'. Certain of his *tutti* chords were likened to the fall of a guillotine blade. Thus it went on for over a month. In May he was complimented in the same newspaper on the dynamic edge and finely judged proportions of Symphony No. 4 and a pair of piano concertos (Nos. 2 and 4) which, in the old Courtauld–Sargent–Schnabel manner, were bracketed on the same night with the same soloist.

Free days were not necessarily rest days. No power on earth could have kept him away from Melbourne Zoo. Wearing one of his double-breasted suits with stripes, eye-glass a-dangle, triangle of spotted handkerchief matching spotted tie, he looked not at all like a survivor from the Thirties; he was a convincing reassertion of them, time recaptured. A cockatoo, indignant of eye, greeted him with 'Hello, darling!' 'Hello indeed!', he answered. He fed unpeeled bananas to a tortoise that was reputed to be a hundred years old and garlanded himself skilfully with a carpet python. He did not, however, suffer his mystical joy in tame animals and wild ones ('most are not afraid of you if you are not afraid of them') to distort his scale of values. At home, he told a Melbourne columnist, he had appealed over the air on separate occasions for prevention of cruelty to children and cruelty to animals. 'Three times as much', he exclaimed, 'came in for the animals as for the children. This, I was told afterwards, is always so. . . . A most awful thing!' He asked the columnist to read his article back before it went to the printer; which drew this reflection from the columnist* next day: 'As a leader [sic] of numerous orchestras for many years, Sir Malcolm has become something of a schoolmaster.' Gaffes of this kind are known to have been committed by him in his heyday. To all appearances, then, he was almost himself again; which meant that, although benign and gay in the main, he could be a shade less felicitous in some situations than others. In letters to Anne Chapman he said he was happy in his work; the Beethoven festival was going admirably; there had been much successful music-making. Above all, he was well, enjoying himself and '(temporarily!)' pleased with life. . . . Every day he played tennis—'but one hour is enough'. And he was resting a good deal; which meant, he hazarded, that he was getting older '(or wiser!)'. On the rostrum he behaved buoyantly and commanded much affection and loyalty. When a critic dismissed some of the English pieces as tedious and Vaughan Williams's *A Sea Symphony* in particular as 'a puffed-up éclair of inordinate length', ardent readers' letters were printed in defence of Sargent and all his works, especially those works (by others) which he had made peculiarly 'his own'.

By the end of the Beethoven festival, in Melbourne and other

* Martin Collins, *The Australian*, 7th April, 1967.

State capitals, during nine visits or tours from 1936 onwards, he conducted an aggregate of nearly a hundred and sixty concerts and towards seven hundred performances of individual pieces, a huge proportion of which, of course, he did twice or more. His work for Australia was nobly sustained and bespoke an affection on his part which matched that of Australia for him. In 1967 he had no concerts in Sydney but did business there and met old friends. The genial Charles Moses who, thirty years earlier, as manager of the Australian Broadcasting Corporation, had inducted him to the Commonwealth's principal rostrums, orchestras and audiences, was now Sir Charles and secretary-general of the Asian Broadcasting Union. Having no lunch-time free for a meeting tête-à-tête, Sargent took Moses along to a private luncheon arranged by the British Council. The party was jolly, Sargent in high spirits. He had been noticeably insistent on their meeting, possibly realizing (as Moses reflected later) that they would not see each other again.

Whatever doubts or premonitions may have visited him, he was still capable of enjoying life and proposed to go on enjoying it. By June he was basking in Hawaii. He swam every day. In the pool of a 'sea life park' were friendly dolphins. He used to tell how they would tow him while he hung on to their dorsal fins. In Honolulu there was a certain amount of business to be done. He began reading the first part of the original draft of this book, breaking off after a hundred pages of typescript to say in a letter home that he found it *excellent* (his italics). The account of the Stamford of his boyhood pleased him especially. Another holiday was planning for October. As things then stood he was to conduct during the early part of the month in Johannesburg; then he would move to a ranch elsewhere in Africa owned by Commander Harold Grenfell, R.N. (Rtd.). Grenfell, whom he had known from the Melton and Oakham days, was one of his two closest men friends. During the last illness he saw more of Sargent than anyone outside the Secretariat at No. 9 and was appointed one of his three executors. Sargent had a little cottage to himself when he stayed on Grenfell's ranch, and spent absorbed hours in the game reserve which was part of the estate. There were two pet cheetahs. He had had himself photographed playing with them for his 1965 Christmas card.

Early July found him in Chicago for his début at the noted Ravinia Park festival. He was to conduct the Chicago Symphony Orchestra, a concerto violinist and a concerto pianist, both Israelis, at two concerts two days apart. The first concert drew an audience of nearly four thousand, the second the better part of five thousand. There were ovations and multiple recalls. The scene is worth recounting.

In the chapter about the Melbourne festival the Myer Bowl was described as a musical pleasance—one of those places where a lot of people under one roof and many more gathered around under the sky and possibly under trees, certainly on grass, listen to fine music on summer nights. Several such pleasances had cropped up in his career. The sequence went back to the hunger years and the pavilion on the mountain side at Mountain Ash.

An hour and a half's drive from the centre of Chicago, Ravinia Park, too, was a pleasance. Its environs, Chicago's North Shore district, were more opulent than South Wales had ever been, and for those who heard music there the years were never hungry. You entered at the park gates for two dollars and either spread a travelling rug on the grass or paid two dollars or four dollars more for reserved seats in the pavilion, which seats three thousand and is open at the sides so that the sound can reach the 'outsiders'. A typical Ravinia audience is made up of well-to-do, 'solid' people, a third to half of them under forty, attentive and earnest listeners with tastes on the conservative side. At the intervals there are restaurant and picnic meals, with a champagne party here and there. On hot nights the men take off their jackets but are inclined to keep their ties on and their shirt collars buttoned.

The day of Sargent's first concert had been a scorcher. By the time the concert began a hot, humid wind was blowing in from Lake Michigan. A populace which had scorched during the day began to boil. Sargent came to the rostrum fully accoutred; the cut of his suit and everything else about him—carnation, cuffs, tie, smile and mien—were a joy to behold or, in the case of males, matter for hopeless envy. He found the orchestra in their shirtsleeves and, although he did not allow the fact to ruffle his manner, felt displeased. Afterwards he let the players know through one of their number that they

had committed a breach of musical etiquette. That night his programme began with the *Perfect Fool* ballet and ended with *A London
Symphony*. Wieniawsky's second violin concerto occurred between.
To all appearances the respite still ran. In next morning's *Chicago
Tribune* the music critic Thomas Willis wrote that, although Sargent
had logged enough years to be called the Dean of British Directors,
nobody would ever guess it. 'With a white carnation in his lapel and
suave manner to match', the notice continued, 'he sets a pattern for
youthful elegance which many of his juniors cannot rival. Without
turning a hair or making an ungraceful gesture, he gets results.'
Through the courtesy of Thomas Willis I have seen letters written
months later by people who were in the audience at either one concert or both. The writers make the same point as he. Who could
believe that a man with jet black hair and so young-looking a frame
was seventy-two? There is an especially eloquent letter from a
Chicago woman whose regard for Sargent stemmed from his third
and last *Messiah* recording with the Huddersfield Choral Society.
From a midway seat in the pavilion this observer had a clear view of
Sargent. She recalls his 'great resiliency, his freedom and grace of
movement', 'the naturalness and poise of his vigour.' Hence the
surprise with which she and her companion read in the programme
note about his age. Both found it hard to believe the news of his
death, which followed so soon after. It was not only people at a distance who thought him in excellent health. Orchestral players,
administrators, festival officials and high office-holders, the girl
secretary who saw to his hotel arrangements: all these, meeting him
at rehearsals and at close quarters backstage, spoke of him as alert,
courteous, amusing and, on points of detail, cheerfully exigent. In
the festival library before rehearsals he examined band parts for
certain of the pieces he was to conduct. They had not been played in
Chicago for years and were unkempt. 'Leave nothing to chance,
take nothing for granted.' True to the old compulsion, he checked
through every folder with a thoroughness which is remembered by
the library staff with awe.

His second concert began, as scores of his concerts had begun,
with Vaughan Williams's *The Wasps*. Then came Prokoviev's fourth
piano concerto, the one for left hand only. He conducted with the

piano between himself and the orchestra; as a result the piano did not, as usually happened during piano concertos at Ravinia and many other places, obstruct the audience's view of the conductor. The symphony was Sibelius's No. 2. One of the retrospective Chicago letters, written by a knowledgable and seasoned concertgoer, emphasizes the uncommonly slow pace at which he took the symphony's last movement: not so much a performance as a *grand statement* of it. The *Allegretto moderato* of Sibelius's No. 2 was the last music he conducted in public. That night marked the end of a long road. It was the night of Saturday 8th July, 1967.

*

The short road of dolour began. Sylvia Darley was at the airport to meet him in from Chicago. The moment she set eyes on him she realized that all was not well. At first the trouble was defined as gastro-enteritis. Pain recurred and his temperature was up. In mid-July he was to have conducted the B.B.C. Symphony Orchestra in Cheltenham. The doctors told him he must not go, and he acquiesced. The customary advance rehearsals for the Promenade Concerts were due to begin on the 17th. He resolved not to forgo these: and, briefly, he had his way. Again he was down for eighteen programmes of typical span: helpings from *The Sorcerer*, *Princess Ida*, *Iolanthe*, etc., at one extreme; Berlioz's *Grande messe* and the 'Choral' Symphony at the other. He was to do various hallowed, customary things as well: *Gerontius*, *Belshazzar's Feast*, Elgar's E flat Symphony and the *Enigma* Variations, *The Planets* and so on; also a score here and there of somewhat newer note—the 'Cello Concerto of Walton and the Tenth Symphony of Shostakovich, for instance. His sickness was gaining upon him quickly. He had become sallow and sunk of face; he could not eat, and his strength was sapped. Those about him knew in their heart of hearts that the labours of a Promenade season were beyond him. But his will was tenacious.

The advance rehearsals were to spread over a week, as usual. He arranged for a chair to be placed on the rostrum. On the first day he walked to it slowly, saluted the orchestra with wan courtesy, then, having seated himself, set to work on three pieces listed for the opening night—Dvořák's *Carnival* Overture, Walton's *Façade* and Haydn's Symphony No. 88 in G major. Occasionally he halted to make routine technical points in a fatigued voice. His gestures and spoken directions, everything he did that day, amounted to no more than a shadow of the old Sargent. There was an intuition among the players that the old Sargent would not be seen again. During pauses he did not find it necessary to call for silence. Silence imposed itself. There was none of the customary stir and chatter. Everybody was grave and most felt compassion; the atmosphere almost that of a sickroom. Observers from Orchestral Management came and went discreetly. There were many anxious telephone calls backstage that day from B.B.C. music-control—'How is it going now?', 'Is he all right?'. The answers did not give much comfort.

Meantime, spurred by hope or illusion, he looked to the future. After the first rehearsal he sent for Harry Danks, the B.B.C.'s principal viola, an artist of long experience and highly regarded in the orchestral world. 'My dear old friend', he said, 'the Royal Choral Society are in a fix. We have slipped up badly. We are doing *Messiah* on 4th January and find that no orchestra in London is free on that date—except, perhaps, the B.B.C. orchestra. I'm told that I could have the B.B.C. orchestra if it didn't play under its own name. Will you be so kind as to speak to some of the players about it?' Danks told him not to worry; he was confident that an orchestra could be fixed. The January date was five and a half months ahead. Reflecting upon the haggard features and his air of debility and doom, Danks reflected that if Sargent lived as long as that it was not likely that he would be fit for any rostrum.

He came down to the second day's rehearsal but finished early. The third day's rehearsal and all the others he missed because of encroaching fever and weakness. Every year on the Thursday before the Promenades there is a private send-off luncheon at Broadcasting House for the people most prominently concerned with running them and performing there. Looking yellow and stricken he took his place at the table as if all were well or soon would be. He quoted his doctors as saying they thought he would be able to conduct Saturday's opening concert; and everybody hoped that this would be the case. It was necessary, none the less, to prepare for the worst. Colin

Davis, then the chief-conductor designate of the B.B.C. Symphony Orchestra, was among the guests. William Glock took him aside and put two questions. Would he take over on Saturday night in case of need? Would he be prepared to stand by for some of the later concerts? Davis said Yes. Contingent arrangements of the same kind were made with other conductors, Boult among them, until all Sargent's programmes had been provisionally reallocated.

For another day Sargent went on hoping and clinging. On the morning of the last day, Saturday 22nd July, he gave in, sending word to Glock that he would not be able to conduct that night. At the opening the Albert Hall platform was bathed in bright gold from camera arcs, not for 'live' viewing but for a film recording telecast at a later date. To the sick man's delight the B.B.C. ran a cable from the dome of the hall to the bedroom at Albert Hall Mansions so that he could follow the filmed part of the concert from his bed on closed-circuit television. He was the only person outside the hall who could see what was going on. In a land where most of the population were viewers he was having a television programme all to himself. The idea that he had put up another record, that again something unique had been done for him, was amusing and flattering; through the fever he felt schoolboyish glee of a sort that age, pain and the nearness of death never quelled.

On the following Monday his doctors, headed by Lord Cohen of Birkenhead, held a consultation. It was decided that he must go into hospital at once and be operated on for acute biliary obstruction. Four days later the operation was performed. It involved the removal of the gall bladder. The hospital where this happened was not named in any bulletin lest the telephone switchboard should be jammed, as it certainly would have been otherwise, by inquiries from all over the country. A bulletin early in August claimed satisfactory progress and said that he could be considered as out of danger, although five days later a letter written by one often at his bedside conveyed that he was not yet free from pain and that he had not begun to receive visitors. With his thoughts on death, whenever it might come, he had chosen and timed orchestral and choral music for any memorial service there might be. He named the slow movement from Elgar's *Serenade for Strings*, Holst's setting of Whitman's *Ode to Death*, Parry's of

Blake's 'And did those feet . . .' *Jerusalem* and his own arrangement of the Dead March in *Saul*. 'If there is to be a memorial service', he said in August, 'I should like Colin Davis to conduct it.' In a crowded Westminster Abbey three weeks after his death, everything was sung and played that he had asked for under Davis's baton.

A man who arranges his memorial service does not necessarily accept that his work is done and death at hand. On the eve of the operation a hope had been expressed by the B.B.C. that he would be sufficiently recovered in time to conduct some final Proms programmes. He had struggled hard against renouncing at a stroke all his remaining dates. He preferred that cancellations and names of substitute conductors should be released by instalments, so that the rostrum should be clear for his return sooner or later. By the end of August, the season then having seventeen more nights to run, he had come to realize, however, that his return as conductor was out of the question. It was announced that he would be conducting no more Promenades that year. He was now home from hospital and talked of going into the country for a few weeks' convalescence. Even so, he hoped and dreamed and went on preparing professionally. Less than a month before the end he was poring with marker pencil over a Dvořák choral work as absorbedly as if committed to doing it with the Royal Choral Society within days.

*

His main preoccupation now, however, concerned the Proms 'finale'. Soon after cancelling his first night he had urged his doctors to do what they could to get him on his feet for the last one. The need was imperious; if the thing were clinically feasible he must bask once more in the tumultuous, teeming affection of his Promenaders. Affection would be no cure; but the buoyant happiness it had given him so often before could sweeten incomparably what days remained to him. He was woefully weak for want of nourishment which he could no longer assimilate normally. How to get him on to the platform and fit him to stand there unaided and make a speech? His doctors thought the thing might be managed. Late on Friday 15th September they arranged for stocks of glucose and salines to be laid in overnight. At eleven the following morning injections began

and continued over a period of seven and a half hours. In that time
he imbibed energy equivalent to that given by a fortnight's eating.
As he phrased it later, quoting a petrol advertisement then much in
view, they had put a tiger in his tank. He invited Colin Davis to his
bedside. During the afternoon they went over the night's arrangements on the assumption that Sargent would be equal to taking
part in them, which could not at that stage be taken for granted.
More than thirty years Sargent's junior, Davis had not often met
him personally up to this time; nor were his musical predilections of
a kind which would naturally bring them together. On the sickbed
he met a man who belied his earlier impressions, such as they were.
It was not the outward change that impressed him so much as the
sense of deepened insight, new wisdom and scales fallen from the
eyes.*

The television cameras were in the hall. In the flat Sargent
watched avidly. Everybody in the orchestra wore the ritual white
carnation—'his' carnation, it might be said. As they 'tracked' the
chockablock arena the cameras showed teenagers in their splendid
silly hats, with slogan-banners, gamps and Union Jacks ready to
unfurl. For the time being they were as avid and quiet as Sargent
himself. Davis reached a number which had not been listed in the
prospectus, the *Soirées musicales*, a suite of Rossini tunes arranged
and orchestrated by Britten. Then came the Henry Wood *Sea Songs*,
leading to the statutory 'Hornpipe' uproar. A motor-car and driver
were waiting outside the Albert Hall Mansions. It was time to go
across. Few apart from Glock and Davis were in the secret. Looking
out from an upper window at the Albert Hall a girl in Concert
Management saw Sargent and Sylvia Darley get into the car and the
car move towards the artists' entrance. She sped down flights of
steps in time to see him in the entry. He was leaning on a stick and
saying 'Hello' and asking how they were to doorkeepers, orchestral
porters, the 'artists' assistant' and everybody in sight. He made his
way slowly downstairs with Sylvia Darley's help to the passage
alongside the artists' room. A television set and a chair had been put
there for him. He watched Monica Sinclair as, with lustre and a

* Colin Davis's considered assessment of Sargent and that of a Carmelite nun
will be found in Appendix 5.

certain admirable truculence, she sang the stanzas of 'Rule Britannia' (his own arrangement of Arne) and the Prommers as they gave patriotic tongue in the refrain. Then it was *Jerusalem*, sung by the multitude, Davis, with his back to the orchestra, beating time to the hall, as Sargent had always done. To Davis also fell the traditional last-night speech. It occasioned jollity and showed him to be on comradely terms with the Prommers. When he spoke of William Glock as the brain whence all the Promenade programmes emanated, Sargent raised his hands and clapped for Glock's delectation, knowing him to be standing behind his chair.

The surprise of the night, the surprise of the year, indeed, was Davis's announcement that Sir Malcolm was in the hall and that he would go and fetch him.

*

As purposed in its opening sentence, this book ends with life's last heady shout in Malcolm Sargent's ear. It was not one shout but many, the same shout over and over, each louder than the last, each followed by cheering and spiced with bells, rattles, buglings. The first shout came when he emerged from the 'bull run' on to the platform. He had set aside his stick and walked without any sign of frailness to the rostrum. He was spruce. He was straight of back. Even now, for all the new contour and compression of the mouth, hinting at pain, he looked younger than seventy-two. As thousands went on roaring in tribute a girl came on to the platform in the name of the young Prommers and gave him a bouquet; then a kiss, with a look on her face that mingled affection and marvel. As he stepped up on to the rostrum Davis cupped his elbow in case he needed support; but his energy was enough for the night. The continuing ovation as he flung his arms out and up in the familiar, all-embracing gesture completed, in a sense, what the doctors and their injections had begun. This was what he had longed for: a last affirmation that multitudes loved him for the music he gave and for the man he was.

He spoke; and his voice had the old ring. Here and there his articulation was slightly slurred. Rehearing it, the listener surmises strain and latent weariness. But the essential pitch and vibrancy were those of Sargent twenty years earlier. So were his moments of drollery—'I feel tonight I am an intruder. [Genial clamour.] I will tell you why. I didn't win a seat in the ballot, and I haven't bought a ticket. [General ecstasy.] . . . I have been told I am not to make a long speech. Hear, hear! I said that. [Joyous din.] I got in first there!' [Din *da capo*.] The speech was not too short for warm-heartedness. He did not deny—'I would be a hypocrite if I pretended otherwise'—that he had sometimes felt sad while listening to broadcast from what, in other circumstances, would have been his twenty-first Promenade season. But what a joy it had been to hear so much magnificent music so magnificently performed by the various orchestras [there had been fourteen] and their conductors! A compliment to 'my old friends and colleagues of the B.B.C. Symphony orchestra' brought the players to their feet for another general tumult. A graceful wave of the arm towards Colin Davis, the orchestra's 'new and very gifted conductor', set everybody off again.

At last the awaited promise: 'I am going to say one more thing. Next year the Promenade Concerts begin on July the twentieth. I have been invited to be here on that night.' Jubilation broke out at this point which seemed likely to go on indefinitely. A lift of the hand brought quiet. 'I have accepted the invitation', he added. (Jubilation as before—but more of it.) 'God willing we all meet again then.' A shout followed which was the most exultant of the night; perhaps of his career.

He stepped down from the rostrum and stood a little to the rear while the orchestra, organ and thousands of voices burst into 'God save the Queen'. There were to be no more rostrums or nostrums. This he probably knew. But he smiled. His eyes were wet and he was content. This was an end. In other words, the threshold.

Appendix One

A short survey of programmes conducted by Sargent at the Robert Mayer concerts for Children, Central Hall, Westminster, between 1924 and 1929

BEETHOVEN 'SELECTIVE'—Symphony No. 1, first movement and last; Symphony No. 2, Larghetto only; *Eroica* Symphony, Marcia funèbre only; Symphony No. 4, Menuetto only; Symphony No. 5, first movement only at one concert, Scherzo and finale only at another; *Pastoral* Symphony, first movement and second ('Scene by the brook') only; Symphony No. 7, Scherzo only; Symphony No. 8, first movement only; Symphony No. 9, Scherzo only.

Beethoven, complete—Symphonies No. 1, 4, 8 and *Eroica*, Violin Concerto (soloist Albert Sammons) and Piano Concerto No. 1 (soloist Schnabel).

Mozart, 'selective'—Allegro from G minor Symphony K. 550; two movements from the Clarinet Concerto (soloist Frederick Thurston).

Mozart, complete—*Jupiter* Symphony (thrice), G minor Symphony (K. 550); A major Piano Concerto (soloist Fanny Davies) and the Sinfonia Concertante for solo violin, solo viola and orchestra (soloists Sammons and Lionel Tertis).

Other 'selectives'—Schubert's 'Great' C major Symphony, first movement only at one concert, last movement only at another; Brahms's Symphony No. 2, first movement only.

Of music in post-classical or 'modern' idioms—more than a smattering of this invaded Central Hall—Sargent once said: 'There's a lot of it we shall probably never learn to enjoy—and perhaps rightly so. . . . If you don't like *all* modern music, don't worry. I don't like all of it myself! Other modern music may seem complicated at first but will become clearer if heard often enough. I've never found *good* modern music difficult for children to hear. I've played Debussy, Stravinsky, Walton and similar composers to children as I have even done in music-halls to unsophisticated audiences, and there's been no trouble at all.'

Contemporary or out-of-the-way composers introduced by him at Central Hall included: Holst (Fugal Overture, movements from the *St. Paul's* Suite, *Jupiter* (a movement from *The Planets* Suite), and ballet music from *The Perfect Fool*, Delius (*On Hearing the First Cuckoo in Spring*), Hugo Wolf (Italian Serenade), Jacques Ibert (Concertino da Camera), Falla (dances from *The Three Cornered Hat*), Arthur Bliss (*Rout*, for soprano and orchestra, with Dorothy Mayer singing the solo part under her professional name, Dorothy Moulton), Stravinsky (two movements at one concert, four at another, from *The Firebird*) and Walton (Viola Concerto, second and third movements with Sammons and Tertis as soloists).

Appendix Two

Courtauld—Sargent concerts, Queen's Hall, 1939 to 1940

IN THIS SERIES he conducted the following works either from the standard repertory or a little wide of it: Elgar's *Falstaff*, A flat Symphony, E flat Symphony and Introduction and Allegro for Strings; Schubert's 'Great' C major Symphony, Dvořák's No. 4, Berlioz's *Fantastic*; four Beethoven symphonies and several of Sibelius's, including No. 3, played at a concert for which No. 4 had been advertised, drawing many to the Queen's Hall with the wrong score under their arms. Occasionally he would bring in a choir. His choral nights included the Verdi Requiem, Beethoven's Missa Solemnis, Berlioz's *Childhood of Christ* (this latter at Samuel Courtauld's behest, it seems) and, for three consecutive nights in January 1933 *Belshazzar's Feast* by William Walton, whose première he had triumphally conducted at Leeds Musical Festival fifteen months earlier.

He conducted also thirteen 'first performances in England'. Arthur Bliss's Serenade for Orchestra and Voice (soloist Roy Henderson) and Szymanowski's Violin Concerto No. 2 (soloist Jelly d'Aranyi) were the first (March 1930). A symphonic suite by Prokoviev, *Nuits d'Egypte* (March 1940), was the last, The concert at which he conducted this was the final one of the Courtauld—Sargent series. During the intervening seasons he introduced new works (apart from those which have already been named) by Delius (*Songs of Farewell*, with Philharmonic Choir); Jean Françaix (Piano Concerto and an orchestral suite, *Le Jugement du fou*); Honegger (*Nocturne* for orchestra); Kodaly (*A Theatre Overture*), Vaughan Williams (Suite for Viola, soloist Lionel Tertis) and Martinu (Music for String Quartet and Orchestra, with Pro Arte Quartet).

Appendix Three

DURING HIS Australian tours of 1936, 1938 and 1939 he conducted either single performances or (as indicated in brackets) more of the following symphonies:
Mozart, the 'Prague' and the G minor K. 455 (2); Haydn, No. 86 in D and No. 88 in G major (2); Clementi in C major; Beethoven, Nos. 1, 5, 7 (2) and 8 (3); Berlioz, *Fantastic*; Brahms, Nos. 1 (2), 3 and 4 (2); Borodin, No. 2 (3); Tchaikovsky Nos. 4 (2), 5 and 6 (2); Elgar, No. 1 (2) and 2 (2); Sibelius, No. 1.

He conducted also tone-poems and miscellaneous works as follow: Elgar, *Enigma* Variations (2), *Cockaigne* Overture (3) and Serenade for Strings (3); R. Strauss, *Don Juan* (3) and *Till*; Delius, *On Hearing the First Cuckoo* (2), *Song before Sunrise* (2); Berlioz, *Rakoczy* March (4), *Trojan* March, *Carnaval Romain* and *Beatrice and Benedict* overtures; Stravinsky, *Firebird* Suite; Debussy, *L'Après midi d'un faune*; Rossini-Respighi, *Boutique Fantasque* Suite (2); Holst, *Jupiter* and ballet music from *The Perfect Fool*; Rimsky-Korsakov, *Capriccio espagnole*, *Scheherazade* and Suite from *The Golden Cockerel*; Sargent, *An Impression on a Windy Day*; Handel-Harty, *Music for the Royal Fireworks*; Grieg, Lyric Suite; Wagner, orchestral excerpts from *The Mastersingers*; and, among overtures the following, many of them more than once: *Coriolanus*, *Rosamunde*, *Semiramide*, *Di Ballo*, *Ruy Blas*, *Fingal's Cave*, *Merry Wives of Windsor*, *Freischütz*, *Tannhäuser* and *The Mastersingers*.

Concertos, etc. (soloists' names within brackets):
Liszt E flat, piano (Beatrice Tange), Hungarian Fantasia (Vina Barnden, piano); Chausson, *Poème* (Ernest Llewellyn, violin); Brahms in D, violin (2: Lionel Lawson and Haydn Beck); Franck, Symphonic Variations (Marshall Sumner, piano); Rachmaninov No. 2, piano (Valda Aveling); Jacques Ibert, Concertino da camera, saxophone

(Sigurd Rascher); Haydn, in F, cembalo (Mancell Kirby); Boëllman, Fantasia and Dialogue for organ and orch. (Renée Nizan); Miriam Hyde, piano (Miriam Hyde); Schumann A minor, piano (Hilda Woollmer); Mozart, A major K. 488, piano (Merle Robertson) and D major, K. 218, violin (Vaughan Hanly); Beethoven, D major, violin (Giulia Bustabo); Mendelssohn, E minor, violin (Giulia Bustabo); Poulenc, D minor, two pianos (Frank Hutchens and Lindley Evans); Glazounov, F minor, piano (Louise Gargurevich); Bach, E major, violin (2: Lyndall Hendrickson and Jeanne Gautier) and A minor, organ (Marcel Dupré); Handel, A major, organ (Marcel Dupré).

Appendix Four

DETAILS FOLLOW of one three-session day during the 'Blitz' Tour. It was the second such undertaken by the orchestra during a week's return visit to Glasgow and is dated Saturday 16th November, 1940. The three programmes are as follows: 1 p.m.: *Lohengrin* prelude, *Valse Triste* (Sibelius), *Romeo and Juliet* (Tchaikovsky), *Carmen* suite, pianoforte solos by Eileen Joyce, *Shepherd Fennell's Dance* (Gardiner), an arrangement of the *Barcarolle* (Offenbach) and the *William Tell* overture; 3.30 p.m.: *Poet and Peasant* overture, 'Unfinished' Symphony (Schubert), *l'Arlésienne* suite (Bizet), pianoforte solos, Eileen Joyce, *The Ride of the Valkyries*, Three Dances from *Henry VIII* (German) and the *Tannhäuser* overture, 5.45 p.m.: Waltz from *The Sleeping Beauty* (Tchaikovsky), *The Londonderry Air* (arr. Grainger), Symphony No. 5 (Tchaikovsky), pianoforte solos, Eileen Joyce, *Peer Gynt* suite (Grieg) and *Pomp and Circumstance* No. 1 (Elgar).

Appendix Five

The following was written by Colin Davis after I asked him about his last meetings with Sargent and the impressions they left:

'WHEN I FIRST went to see him in hospital during his illness I got the impression that he was either not quite aware of what was in store for him or had not come to terms with the harshness of his condition. I was with him again before the last night of the Proms. It seemed to me then that his external personality—the barricade which he had erected over the years to defend himself—had very largely fallen away, and one had the impression of being much closer to the man as he really was. This was especially so on the afternoon before the last night, when we discussed the effects upon himself of his desire to appear on the platform at the end of the concert. I think that by this time he certainly knew that he would not live very long. He had obviously come closer to himself and did not seem to have any emotional reaction to the possibility of his death.

'On the other hand, he seemed unable to relinquish the idea that he should make one more public appearance. These had meant so much to him for so long that I do not particularly blame him. Some of us sense that they had in fact been the greater part of his life and that the affection granted him by the public made up for that which was denied him by professional colleagues.

'I cannot say that I ever had what I would describe as a "real" conversation with him or that I ever really sensed what was at the back of his mind, but then, our acquaintance was very brief and under rather trying circumstances. If, in what I have said, you sense ingratitude on my part, this is not intended at all. Malcolm Sargent was always very nice to me and full of encouragement.'

The regard which, as Davis mentions, he enjoyed outside professional circles expressed itself in private letters as well as in public ovations. An unusual and moving letter came to him from a nun in a Carmelite convent, one of a group who, when Pope Pius X was canonized in May 1954, listened to the rite, as relayed from Rome, on a radio receiver specially brought into the convent. The receiver remained in the house for an extra day, 'and,' continued the writer, 'we were allowed to listen to your concert. . . . To hear a full symphony orchestra was a sudden, overwhelming, breathtaking pleasure. . . . Some of us had heard no [symphonic] music since we entered the convent nearly thirty years earlier. We felt we must say, Thank you—to you very specially and to each in the orchestra. You can probably take Schubert's "Unfinished" Symphony in your daily round without being awestruck and [possibly] without being aware of the magic and loveliness of an exquisite phrase of music that you are letting escape into the air. But we were left just praising God for His goodness in giving such gifts to man. We cannot show our gratitude by applause or coming to another concert, but we have our own job to do for God, and we can include you and all the orchestra in that. So please be sure that you will always be in the prayers of the Carmelite nuns, together with all your families and intentions. And one day we hope that the loveliness of the things of God that we are occupied with will fall on your ears as strikingly and compellingly as your music came to us.'

The letter was quoted by Sargent in a talk about the Promenade concerts for the B.B.C.'s Home Service on 29th August, 1954.

Acknowledgements

OF THE RESEARCH MATERIAL that went to make this book, quite half, i.e., about a quarter of a million words, was either noted down from friends, associates and colleagues of Sir Malcolm or transcribed in archives, the richest of these latter being those of the B.B.C. For thirty or forty years he spoke often and copiously over the air. As a conspectus of his opinions and a biographical fringe-source, the transcripts of his broadcasts have been of great value. So: my thanks to the Governors of the British Broadcasting Corporation and to Mr. R. L. W. Collison, formerly their Librarian, and now of the University Research Library of Los Angeles.

As to Sargent's Stamford years and his first musical ventures there and in Melton Mowbray, I am especially indebted to his sister, Miss Dorothy Sargent; Mrs. D. B. Tillson, a singer in his first amateur operatic seasons; Mrs. Ernest Huxley, née Kathleen Tinkler, daughter of Mrs. Frances Tinkler, his first piano teacher; and Mrs. Jean M. Furness who, as well as drawing upon memory, let me see letters which he wrote over the years to herself and her late husband, Dr. Harold Furness.

Warm thanks equally:

To Mrs. Anne Chapman, his former secretary, for help whose value is, I trust, clear from the text; Admiral of the Fleet the Earl Mountbatten of Burma, for his moving account of a lively friendship; His Eminence Cardinal John Heenan, Cardinal Archbishop of Westminster; Sir Thomas Armstrong, Principal of the Royal Academy of Music, whose conversations brought Sargent's pupilage in Peterborough Cathedral's organ loft to vivid life; Sir William Walton; Sir Michael Tippett; Sir Adrian Boult; Sir William McKie, former Master of Music, Westminster Abbey; Mr. Keith Falkner, Principal of the Royal College of Music; Dr. Herbert Howells, academic colleague and intimate friend; and to Sir Gerald Kelly, P.P.R.A., for permission to reproduce his portrait of Sargent.

To Mr. Wilfred Aris, of Coalville; and to Mrs. Horace Lee (née Grace Burrows), Mr. Arthur Thornley, Mr. Simeon Iliffe, and Mr. Reginald Rudd for their accounts respectively of Pte. Sargent, D.L.I., and his first symphonic seasons in Leicester. To Miss Phyllis Dabbs (Secretary); Mr. Arnold Greir, organist and some-time Hon. Secretary; and Mr. and Mrs. Montagu H. Spicer, veteran singing members, of the Royal Choral Society; also to Mr. Thomas Charles Fairburn, producer of the Society's famous *Hiawatha* pageants;

To Miss Bridget D'Oyly Carte, controller of the D'Oyly Carte Opera Company for many years; Mr. Frederick Lloyd, the com-pany's general manager; and seven former principal singers, for their memories of the company's London seasons, 1926 and 1929–30. To Sir Robert and Lady Mayer, founders of the Robert Mayer Concerts for Children; Mr. Samuel Kutcher, their orchestral leader for several seasons; and to Mr. M. W. Pitts-Tucker, of Courtaulds Ltd., for access to archives of the Courtauld-Sargent Concerts;

To Mr. William Glock, B.B.C. Controller of Music; Mr. Colin Davis, Chief Conductor, B.B.C. Symphony Orchestra; Mr George Willoughby, former Concerts and Orchestral Manager, B.B.C.; Mr. Harry Danks and Mr. Alex Nifosi, members of the orchestra; and Miss Freda Grove, the present Concerts Manager. To Sir Charles Moses, former general manager; Mr. William G. James, former Federal music controller; and Miss Pat Kelly, present archi-vist, of the Australian Broadcasting Commission;

To Sir David Webster, sometime chairman, Royal Liverpool Philharmonic Society; and to Miss Jessie Brown, Mr. W. R. Fell, Mr. Robert A. Brown and Mr. Sydney Lunt, former accountant to the society, manager of the Philharmonic Hall, orchestral player and orchestral manager respectively. To Lieut.-Col. F. Vivian Dunn, former Principal Director of Music, Royal Marines; Mr. Joseph Sammut, conductor, of Malta, and Capt. Ernest S. Ough, R.N. (Retd.), sometime Fleet Bandmaster, Mediterranean Fleet; To Mr. Anthony Pini, Mr. Geoffrey Gilbert and Mr. Hugh Maguire for throwing particular light on something which had to be faced: the uneasy and sometimes unhappy relations that long prevailed between Sargent and orchestral players generally.

To Mr. David Bicknell, head of International Artists Department, E.M.I.; Mr. Eric Bravington, managing director, London Philharmonic Orchestra and Mr. Thomas Russell, his predecessor; Mr. James Brown, former chairman of the Royal Philharmonic Orchestra and his colleague Mr. Archie Newman. To Mr. Gwyn Prosser, managing director of the *Aberdare Leader*, Glam., and an authority on the history of the Three Valleys Festival; Mr. R. A. Pugsley, music critic of the *Leicester Mercury*; Mr. Thomas Willis, music critic of the *Chicago Tribune*—

And to many other singers, players, writers, musical contrivers and musical administrators who helped in lesser degree.

INDEX